CIMA
STUDY TEXT

Intermediate Paper 9

Management Accounting: Decision Making

BPP's NEW STUDY TEXTS FOR CIMA's NEW SYLLABUS

- Targeted to the **syllabus** and **learning outcomes**

- Quizzes and questions to check your understanding

- Incorporates CIMA's new Official Terminology

- Clear layout and style designed to save you time

- Plenty of exam-style questions

- Chapter Roundups and summaries to help revision

- Mind Maps to integrate the key points

BPP Publishing
July 2000

First edition July 2000

ISBN 0 7517 3137 4

British Library Cataloguing-in-Publication Data
A catalogue record for this book
is available from the British Library

Published by

BPP Publishing Ltd
Aldine House, Aldine Place
London W12 8AW

www.bpp.com

Printed in England by DA COSTA PRINT
35 - 37 Queensland Road, London N7 7AH
(0207 700 1000)

We are grateful to the Chartered Institute of Management Accountants for permission to reproduce past examination questions and questions from the pilot paper. The suggested solutions to the illustrative questions have been prepared by BPP Publishing Limited.

Contents

REVIEW FORM & FREE PRIZE DRAW

ORDER FORM

> Multiple choice questions form a large part of the exam. To go with the Study Text, we have produced a bank of **multiple choice question cards**, covering the syllabus. This bank contains exam style questions in a format to help you revise on the move.

THE BPP STUDY TEXT

Aims of this Study Text

To provide you with the knowledge and understanding, skills and application techniques that you need if you are to be successful in your exams

This Study Text has been written around the **Management Accounting: Decision Making** syllabus.

- It is **comprehensive**. It covers the syllabus content. No more, no less.

- It is written at the **right level**. Each chapter is written with CIMA's precise learning outcomes in mind.

- It is targeted to the **exam**. We have taken account of the pilot paper, questions put to the examiners at the recent CIMA conference and the assessment methodology.

To allow you to study in the way that best suits your learning style and the time you have available, by following your personal Study Plan (see page (ix))

You may be studying at home on your own until the date of the exam, or you may be attending a full-time course. You may like to (and have time to) read every word, or you may prefer to (or only have time to) skim-read and devote the remainder of your time to question practice. Wherever you fall in the spectrum, you will find the BPP Study Text meets your needs in designing and following your personal Study Plan.

To tie in with the other components of the BPP Effective Study Package to ensure you have the best possible chance of passing the exam (see page (vi))

Recommended period of use	Elements of the BPP Effective Study Package
Three to twelve months before the exam	**Study Text** Use the Study Text to acquire knowledge, understanding, skills and the ability to use application techniques.
One to six months before the exam	**Practice & Revision Kit** Attempt the tutorial questions and complete the interactive checklists which are provided for each topic area in the Kit. Then try the numerous examination questions, for which there are realistic suggested solutions prepared by BPP's own authors.
From three months before the exam until the last minute	**Passcards** Work through these short, memorable notes which are focused on what is most likely to come up in the exam you will be sitting.
One to six months before the exam	**Success Tapes** These audio tapes cover the vital elements of your syllabus in less than 90 minutes per subject. Each tape also contains exam hints to help you fine tune your strategy.
Three to twelve months before the exam	**Breakthrough Videos** Use a Breakthrough Video to supplement your Study Text. They give you clear tuition on key exam subjects and allow you the luxury of being able to pause or repeat sections until you have fully grasped the topic.

BPP PUBLISHING

HELP YOURSELF STUDY FOR YOUR CIMA EXAMS

Exams for professional bodies such as CIMA are very different from those you have taken at college or university. You will be under **greater time pressure before** the exam - as you may be combining your study with work. There are many different ways of learning and so the BPP Study Text offers you a number of different tools to help you through. Here are some hints and tips: they are not plucked out of the air, but **based on research and experience**. (You don't need to know that long-term memory is in the same part of the brain as emotions and feelings - but it's a fact anyway.)

The right approach

1   **The right attitude**

Believe in yourself	Yes, there is a lot to learn. Yes, it is a challenge. But thousands have succeeded before and you can too.
Remember why you're doing it	Studying might seem a grind at times, but you are doing it for a reason: to advance your career.

2   **The right focus**

Read through the Syllabus and learning outcomes	These tell you what you are expected to know and are supplemented by Exam Focus Points in the text.
Study the Exam Paper section	The pilot paper is likely to be a reasonable guide of what you should expect in the exam.

3   **The right method**

The big picture	You need to grasp the detail - but keeping in mind how everything fits into the big picture will help you understand better. <ul><li>The **Introduction** of each chapter puts the material in context.</li><li>The **Syllabus content, learning outcomes** and **Exam focus points** show you what you need to **grasp**.</li><li>**Mind Maps** show the links and key issues in key topics.</li></ul>
In your own words	To absorb the information (and to practise your written communication skills), it helps to **put it into your own words.** <ul><li>**Take notes.**</li><li>Answer the **questions** in each chapter. As well as helping you absorb the information you will practise your written communication skills, which become increasingly important as you progress through your CIMA exams.</li><li>Draw **mind maps**. We have some examples.</li><li>Try 'teaching' a subject to a colleague or friend.</li></ul>

Give yourself cues to jog your memory	The BPP Study Text uses **bold** to **highlight key points** and **icons** to identify key features, such as **Exam focus points** and **Key terms.** • Try **colour coding** with a highlighter pen. • Write **key points** on cards.

4   The right review

Review, review, review	It is a **fact** that regularly reviewing a topic in summary form can **fix it in your memory**. Because **review** is so important, the BPP Study Text helps you to do so in many ways. • **Chapter roundups** summarise the key points in each chapter. Use them to recap each study session. • The **Quick quiz** is another review technique to ensure that you have grasped the essentials. • Use the **Key term** index as a quiz. • Go through the **Examples** in each chapter a second or third time.

Suggested study sequence

Tackle the chapters in the order you find them in the Study Text. Taking into account your individual learning style, you could follow this sequence.

Key study steps	Activity
Step 1 **Topic list**	Each numbered topic is a numbered section in the chapter.
Step 2 **Introduction**	This gives you the **big picture** in terms of the **context** of the chapter, the **content** you will cover, and the **learning outcomes** the chapter assesses - in other words, it sets your **objectives for study.**
Step 3 **Knowledge brought forward boxes**	In these we highlight information and techniques that it is assumed you have 'brought forward' with you from your earlier studies. If there are topics which have changed recently due to legislation for example, these topics are explained in more detail.
Step 4 **Explanations**	Proceed methodically through the chapter, reading each section thoroughly and making sure you understand.
Step 5 **Key terms and Exam focus points**	• **Key terms** can often earn you *easy marks* if you state them clearly and correctly in an appropriate exam answer (and they are indexed at the back of the text). • **Exam focus points** give you a good idea of how we think the examiner intends to examine certain topics.
Step 6 **Note taking**	Take brief notes if you wish, avoiding the temptation to copy out too much.

BPP
PUBLISHING

Key study steps	Activity
Step 7 **Examples**	Follow each through to its solution very carefully.
Step 8 **Case examples**	Study each one, and try to add flesh to them from your own experience - they are designed to show how the topics you are studying come alive (and often come unstuck) in the real world.
Step 9 **Questions**	Make a very good attempt at each one.
Step 10 **Answers**	Check yours against ours, and make sure you understand any discrepancies.
Step 11 **Chapter roundup**	Work through it very carefully, to make sure you have grasped the major points it is highlighting.
Step 12 **Quick quiz**	When you are happy that you have covered the chapter, use the **Quick quiz** to check how much you have remembered of the topics covered.
Step 13 **Question(s) in the Question bank**	Either at this point, or later when you are thinking about revising, make a full attempt at the **Question(s)** suggested at the very end of the chapter. You can find these at the end of the Study Text, along with the **Answers** so you can see how you did. We highlight those that are introductory, and those which are of the standard you would expect to find in an exam.

Developing your personal Study Plan

Preparing a Study Plan (and sticking closely to it) is one of the key elements in learning success.

Step 1. How do you learn?

First you need to be aware of your style of learning. There are four typical learning styles. Consider yourself in the light of the following descriptions and work out which you fit most closely. You can then plan to follow the key study steps in the sequence suggested.

Learning styles	Characteristics	Sequence of key study steps in the BPP Study Text
Theorist	Seeks to understand principles before applying them in practice	1, 2, 3, 4, 7, 8, 5, 9/10, 11, 12, 13 (6 continuous)
Reflector	Seeks to observe phenomena, thinks about them and then chooses to act	
Activist	Prefers to deal with practical, active problems; does not have much patience with theory	1, 2, 9/10 (read through), 7, 8, 5, 11, 3, 4, 9/10 (full attempt), 12, 13 (6 continuous)
Pragmatist	Prefers to study only if a direct link to practical problems can be seen; not interested in theory for its own sake	9/10 (read through), 2, 5, 7, 8, 11, 1, 3, 4, 9/10 (full attempt), 12, 13 (6 continuous)

Step 2. How much time do you have?

Work out the time you have available per week, given the following.

- The standard you have set yourself
- The time you need to set aside later for work on the Practice & Revision Kit and Passcards
- The other exam(s) you are sitting
- Very importantly, practical matters such as work, travel, exercise, sleep and social life

Note your time available in box A.

A ☐ Hours

Step 3. Allocate your time

- Take the time you have available per week for this Study Text shown in box A, multiply it by the number of weeks available and insert the result in box B.

  B ☐

- Divide the figure in Box B by the number of chapters in this text and insert the result in box C.

  C ☐

Step 4. Implement

Set about studying each chapter in the time shown in box C, following the key study steps in the order suggested by your particular learning style.

This is your personal **Study Plan**.

Short of time: *Skim study technique?*

You may find you simply do not have the time available to follow all the key study steps for each chapter, however you adapt them for your particular learning style. If this is the case, follow the **skim study** technique below (the icons in the Study Text will help you to do this).

- Study the chapters in the order you find them in the Study Text.

- For each chapter, follow the key study steps 1-3, and then skim-read through step 4. Jump to step 11, and then go back to step 5. Follow through steps 7 and 8, and prepare outline answers to questions (steps 9/10). Try the Quick quiz (step 12), following up any items you

can't answer, then do a plan for the Question (step 13), comparing it against our answers. You should probably still follow step 6 (note-taking), although you may decide simply to rely on the BPP Passcards for this.

Moving on...

However you study, when you are ready to embark on the practice and revision phase of the BPP Effective Study Package, you should still refer back to this Study Text, both as a source of **reference** (you should find the list of key terms and the index particularly helpful for this) and as a **refresher** (the Chapter roundups and Quick quizzes help you here).

And remember to keep careful hold of this Study Text - you will find it invaluable in your work.

SYLLABUS AND LEARNING OUTCOMES

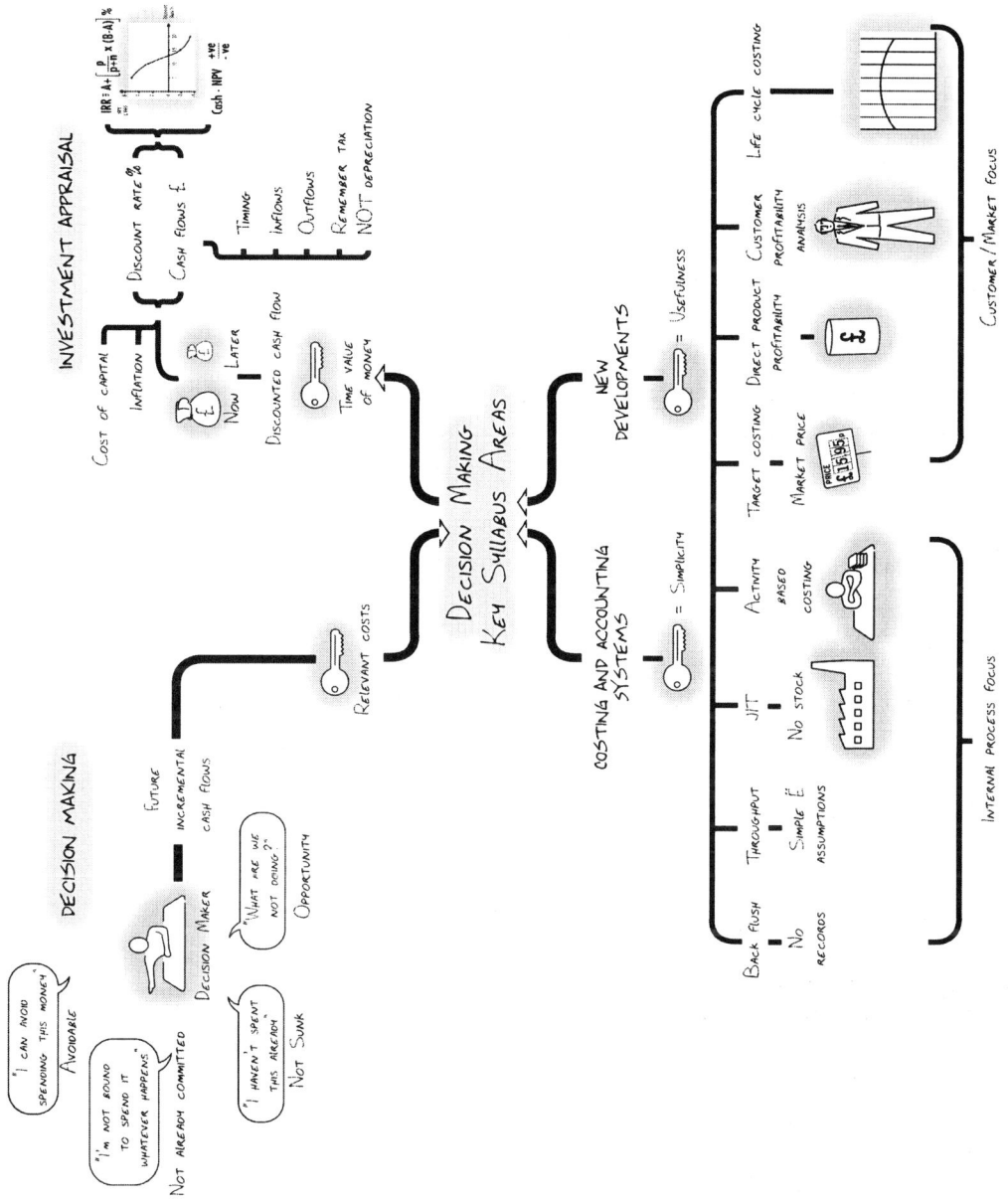

BPP
PUBLISHING

SYLLABUS AND LEARNING OUTCOMES

Syllabus overview

Decision Making builds on the introduction to costing and accounting systems and decision making provided by Management Accounting Fundamentals and Performance Measurement, and covers investment appraisal, international business and management accounting issues and developments.

While this paper will develop students' ability to apply a range of management accounting techniques and decision-making tools to the modern business environment, students will also have to demonstrate an understanding of these tools and the issues that surround their use.

Students require knowledge of the history of management accounting since they have to understand why management accounting needs to evolve to remain relevant.

Students must also appreciate the contribution made by information technology to management accounting.

Aims

This syllabus aims to test the student's ability to:

- Evaluate costing and accounting systems
- Apply and evaluate techniques used in management decision making
- Apply and evaluate alternative methods of investment appraisal
- Discuss new developments in business and management accounting

for a wide range of sectors, including manufacturing, retail and service.

Assessment

There will be a written paper of 3 hours. Section A will use objective testing for 20% of the marks. Section B will be a compulsory question for 30% of the marks. Section C will offer a choice of one question from two for 25% of the marks and Section D will offer a choice of one question from two for 25% of the marks.

Learning outcomes and syllabus content

9(i) Decision making – 40%

Learning outcomes

On completion of their studies students should be able to:

- Identify and discuss relevant costs and benefits

- Identify and discuss qualitative factors

- Identify and discuss external pricing strategies

- Evaluate external pricing strategies using sales variance analysis

- Explain and demonstrate transfer pricing in an international context

- Apply and evaluate profit maximisation

- Prepare and interpret reports using Pareto analysis

- Apply and discuss the experience and learning curve

- Discuss risk and uncertainty

- Apply and discuss decision trees

- Evaluate the value of information

- Evaluate costing systems for decision making

Syllabus content

	Covered in chapter
• Relevant costs and benefits	1
• Joint cost allocations, common costs	2
• Qualitative factors	1
• Sales mix, quantity, market size and market share variances (Note: these variances will be calculated on a units basis using sales revenue, contribution or gross profit)	4
• Transfer pricing: no market/imperfect market for intermediates, negotiated prices, dual pricing, two-part tariff and supplementing full cost with subsidies to spread risk	5
• External pricing strategies: premium pricing, penetration pricing, market skimming, optional extras, loss leaders, product differentiation, product bundling	4
• International transfer pricing: taxation, currency, remittance of funds	5
• Profit maximisation (Note: the use of calculus is not required)	2
• Pareto analysis	3
• Risk and uncertainty	3
• Decision trees	3
• Learning curve (Note: derivation of the learning index and the learning rate is required)	3
• Alternative costing systems	2

9(ii) Costing and accounting systems – 25%

Learning outcomes

On completion of their studies students should be able to:

- Apply and evaluate activity-based costing and activity-based management

- Apply and evaluate direct product profitability

- Apply and evaluate alternative costing and accounting systems: backflush accounting, throughput accounting, overhead allocation (Japanese), absorption costing, marginal costing, activity based costing, integrated/interlocking accounting (Note: detailed accounting entries are not required)

- Apply and evaluate target costing

- Apply and evaluate life cycle costing

Syllabus content

	Covered in chapter
• Activity-based costing and activity-based management	6
• Customer profitability analysis	6
• Direct product profitability	6
• Just-in-time and backflush accounting	7
• Theory of constraints and throughput accounting	7
• Behavioural aspects of alternative costing systems	6
• Target costing	7
• Life cycle costing	7, 9

9(iii) Investment appraisal – 25%

Learning outcomes

On completion of their studies students should be able to:

- Explain the capital budgeting process
- Evaluate projects using investment appraisal techniques
- Evaluate alternative investment appraisal techniques
- Discuss the relevance of qualitative factors
- Prepare project cashflows that take account of taxation and inflation
- Evaluate mutually exclusive projects with unequal lives
- Apply sensitivity analysis to cashflows
- Calculate abandonment values
- Discuss post-completion appraisal
- Discuss investment centres
- Calculate return on investment and residual income
- Evaluate return on investment and residual income
- Discuss the behavioural implications of return on investment and residual income

Syllabus content

	Covered in chapter
• Capital budgeting process	8
• Investment appraisal techniques: payback, discounted payback, accounting rate of return, net present value, internal rate of return	8
• Taxation	9
• Inflation	9
• Unequal lives	9
• Project abandonment	9
• Sensitivity analysis	9

	Covered in chapter
• Post-completion appraisal	8
• Return on investment	10
• Residual income	10

9(iv) New developments – 10%

Learning outcomes

On completion of their studies students should be able to:

- Discuss the history of management accounting
- Compare and contrast management accounting and financial accounting
- Evaluate management accounting for the modern business environment
- Discuss international business developments
- Discuss international management accounting issues and developments

Syllabus content

	Covered in chapter
• Management accounting	11
• Principles of financial accounting: rules, concepts, reporting framework	11
• History of management accounting	11
• International business developments	11
• International management accounting issues and developments	11

BPP PUBLISHING

THE EXAM PAPER

Format of the paper

		Number of marks
Section A:	objective test questions	20
Section B:	one compulsory question	30
Section C:	one question from two	25
Section D:	one question from two	25
		100

Time allowed: 3 hours

Analysis of pilot paper

Section A

1.1 Backflush accounting
1.2 Expected values
1.3 Market size and market share variances
1.4 Divisional profit maximisation
1.5 Operational gearing
1.6 Sensitivity analysis
1.7 Real cost of capital
1.8 NPV with inflation

Section B

2   Contracts: accept or reject

Section C

3   Direct product profitability
4   Investment appraisal

Section D

5   ABC. Customer profitability. Pareto analysis
6   Cost management in the modern business environment

WHAT THE EXAMINER MEANS

The table below has been prepared by CIMA to help you interpret exam questions.

Learning objective	Verbs used	Definition
1 Knowledge What you are expected to know	• List • State • Define	• Make a list of • Express, fully or clearly, the details of/facts of • Give the exact meaning of
2 Comprehension What you are expected to understand	• Describe • Distinguish • Explain • Identify • Illustrate	• Communicate the key features of • Highlight the differences between • Make clear or intelligible/state the meaning of • Recognise, establish or select after consideration • Use an example to describe or explain something
3 Application Can you apply your knowledge?	• Apply • Calculate/compute • Demonstrate • Prepare • Reconcile • Solve • Tabulate	• To put to practical use • To ascertain or reckon mathematically • To prove with certainty or to exhibit by practical means • To make or get ready for use • To make or prove consistent/compatible • Find an answer to • Arrange in a table
4 Analysis Can you analyse the detail of what you have learned?	• Analyse • Categorise • Compare and contrast • Construct • Discuss • Interpret • Produce	• Examine in detail the structure of • Place into a defined class or division • Show the similarities and/or differences between • To build up or compile • To examine in detail by argument • To translate into intelligible or familiar terms • To create or bring into existence
5 Evaluation Can you use your learning to evaluate, make decisions or recommendations?	• Advise • Evaluate • Recommend	• To counsel, inform or notify • To appraise or assess the value of • To advise on a course of action

BPP PUBLISHING

TACKLING OBJECTIVE TEST QUESTIONS

Of the total marks available for this paper, objective test questions comprise:

A	10%
B	20%
C	30%
D	40%
E	50%

The objective test questions (OTs) in your exam contain five possible answers. You have to **choose the option that best answers the question**. The four incorrect options are called distracters. There is a skill in answering OTs quickly and correctly. By practising OTs you can develop this skill, giving you a better chance of passing the exam.

You may wish to follow the approach outlined below, or you may prefer to adapt it.

Step 1. Skim read all the OTs and identify what appear to be the easier questions.

Step 2. Attempt each question - **starting with the easier questions** identified in Step 1. Read the question thoroughly. You may prefer to work out the answer before looking at the options, or you may prefer to look at the options at the beginning. Adopt the method that works best for you.

Step 3. Read the five options and see if one matches your own answer. Be careful with numerical questions, as the distracters are designed to match answers that incorporate common errors. Check that your calculation is correct. Have you followed the requirement exactly? Have you included every stage of the calculation?

Step 4. You may find that none of the options matches your answer.

- Re-read the question to ensure that you understand it and are answering the requirement

- Eliminate any obviously wrong answers

- Consider which of the remaining answers is the most likely to be correct and select the option

Step 5. If you are still unsure make a note and continue to the next question.

Step 6. Revisit unanswered questions. When you come back to a question after a break you often find you are able to answer it correctly straight away. If you are still unsure have a guess. You are not penalised for incorrect answers, so **never leave a question unanswered!**

Exam focus. After extensive practice and revision of OT, you may find that you recognise a question when you sit the exam. Be aware that the detail and/or requirement may be different. If the question seems familiar read the requirement and options carefully - do not assume that it is identical.

Part A
Decision making

Chapter 1

INFORMATION FOR DECISION MAKING I

Topic list		Syllabus reference	Ability required
1	Relevant and non-relevant costs	(i)	Identify and discuss
2	Some rules for identifying relevant costs	(i)	Identify and discuss
3	The relevant cost of scarce resources	(i)	Identify and discuss
4	Relevant costs and minimum pricing	(i)	Identify and discuss
5	The assumptions in relevant costing	(i)	Identify and discuss
6	Qualitative factors in decision making	(i)	Identify and discuss

Introduction

Welcome to **Management Accounting - Decision Making**. This chapter begins with the most obvious starting point for this subject: the provision of cost information for **decision making**.

As a management accountant you may make decisions, but your principal role will be in **providing management information**. Your job is to present that information to the decision makers to help them to reach their decision, and to make recommendations and give advice and suggestions to the decision makers.

In this chapter you will learn how to identify the **relevant costs and benefits** in each decision, so that management time is not wasted in considering information that is not relevant to the decision. You will also learn about the importance of considering the **qualitative factors** in every decision.

Learning outcomes covered in this chapter

- **Identify** and **discuss** relevant costs and benefits
- **Identify** and **discuss** qualitative factors

Syllabus content covered in this chapter

- Relevant costs and benefits
- Qualitative factors

1   RELEVANT AND NON-RELEVANT COSTS   Pilot paper

Relevant costs

1.1   The costs which should be used for decision making are often referred to as **relevant costs**. In its *Official Terminology,* the CIMA defines relevant costs as 'Costs appropriate to a specific management decision. These are represented by future cash flows whose magnitude will vary depending upon the outcome of the management decision made'.

BPP PUBLISHING

1.2 A relevant cost is a future, incremental cash flow.

(a) Relevant costs are **future costs**.

    (i) A decision is about the future; it cannot alter what has been done already. A cost that has been incurred in the past is totally irrelevant to any decision that is being made 'now'. Such costs are **past costs** or **sunk costs.**

    (ii) Costs that have been incurred include not only costs that have already been paid, but also costs that are the subject of legally binding contracts, even if payments due under the contract have not yet been made. (These are known as **committed costs.**)

(b) Relevant costs are **cash flows**. This means that costs or charges such as the following, which do not reflect additional cash spending, should be ignored for the purpose of decision making.

- **Depreciation**, as a fixed overhead incurred.

- **Notional rent or interest**, as a fixed overhead incurred.

- **All overheads absorbed. Fixed** overhead absorption is always irrelevant since it is overheads **to be incurred** which affect decisions.

(c) Relevant costs are **incremental costs**. For example, if an employee is expected to have no other work to do during the next week, but will be paid his basic wage (of, say, £100 per week) for attending work and doing nothing, his manager might decide to give him a job which earns only £40. The **net relevant benefit** is £40 and the £100 is irrelevant to the decision because although it is a future cash flow, it will be incurred anyway whether the employee is given work or not.

Differential costs, avoidable costs and opportunity costs

1.3 Other terms are used to describe relevant costs.

KEY TERM

The CIMA *Official Terminology* defines **incremental** or **differential** costs as 'The difference in total cost between alternatives; calculated to assist decision-making'.

(a) **Differential costs** are relevant costs which are simply the additional costs incurred as a consequence of a decision.

KEY TERM

Avoidable costs are defined as 'The specific costs of an activity or sector of a business which would be avoided if that activity or sector did not exist' (CIMA *Official Terminology*).

(b) **Avoidable costs** is a term usually associated with shutdown or disinvestment decisions, but it can be applied to control decisions too.

KEY TERM

Opportunity cost is 'The value of a benefit sacrificed when one course of action is chosen, in preference to an alternative. The opportunity cost is represented by the forgone potential benefit from the best rejected course of action'.

(CIMA *Official Terminology*).

(c) Opportunity cost is a useful concept when there are a number of possible uses for a scarce resource.

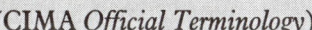

Question 1

An information technology consultancy firm has been asked to do an urgent job by a client, for which a price of £2,500 has been offered. The job would require the following.

(a) 30 hours' work from one member of staff, who is paid on an hourly basis, at a rate of £20 per hour, but who would normally be employed on work for clients where the charge-out rate is £45 per hour. No other member of staff is able to do the member of staff in question's work. *opp cost.*

(b) The use of 5 hours of mainframe computer time, which the firm normally charges out to external users at a rate of £50 per hour. Mainframe computer time is currently used 24 hours a day, 7 days a week.

(c) Supplies and incidental expenses of £200.

Required

Calculate the relevant cost or opportunity cost of the job.

Answer

The relevant cost or opportunity cost of the job would be calculated as follows.

	£
Labour (30 hours × £45)	1,350
Computer time opportunity cost (5 hours × £50)	250
Supplies and expenses	200
	1,800

Non-relevant costs

1.4 A number of terms are used to describe costs that are **irrelevant** for decision making because they are either not future cash flows or they are costs which will be incurred anyway, regardless of the decision that is taken.

Sunk costs

KEY TERM

A **sunk cost** is 'A past cost not directly relevant in decision-making' (CIMA *Official Terminology*).

1.5 Examples of sunk costs include the following.

(a) **Dedicated fixed assets**. Suppose a company purchased an item of computer equipment two years ago for £20,000. It has been depreciated to a net book value of £7,000 already,

but in fact it already has no resale value because of developments in computer technology. The equipment can be used for its existing purpose for at least another year, but the company is considering whether or not to purchase more modern equipment with additional facilities and so scrap the existing equipment now.

In terms of decision making and relevant costs the existing equipment, which initially cost £20,000 but now has a net book value of £7,000, is a sunk cost. The money has been spent and the asset has no alternative use. 'Writing off' the asset and incurring a 'paper' loss on disposal of £7,000 would be irrelevant to the decision under consideration.

(b) **Development costs already incurred**. Suppose that a company has spent £250,000 in developing a new service for customers, but the marketing department's most recent findings are that the service might not gain customer acceptance and could be a commercial failure. The decision whether or not to abandon the development of the new service would have to be taken, but the £250,000 spent so far should be ignored by the decision makers because it is a sunk cost.

Committed costs

1.6 A **committed cost** is a future cash outflow that will be incurred anyway, whatever decision is taken now about alternative opportunities. Committed costs may exist because of contracts already entered into by the organisation, which it cannot now avoid.

Notional costs

> **KEY TERM**
>
> The CIMA *Official Terminology* definition of a **notional cost** is 'A cost used in product evaluation, decision-making and performance measurement to represent the cost of using resources which have no conventional 'actual cost'.

1.7 **Examples of notional costs in cost accounting systems**

(a) Notional rent, such as that charged to a subsidiary, cost centre or profit centre of an organisation for the use of accommodation which the organisation owns.

(b) Notional interest charges on capital employed, sometimes made against a profit centre or cost centre.

Historical costs

1.8 Although **historical costs** are irrelevant for decision making, historical cost data will often provide the best available basis for predicting **future** costs.

Fixed and variable costs

Non-relevant variable costs

1.9   There might be occasions when a variable cost is in fact a sunk cost. For example, suppose that a company has some units of raw material in stock. They have been paid for already, and originally cost £2,000. They are now obsolete and are no longer used in regular production, and they have no scrap value. However, they could be used in a special job which the company is trying to decide whether to undertake. The special job is a 'one-off ' customer order, and would use up all these materials in stock.

In deciding whether the job should be undertaken, the relevant cost of the materials to the special job is nil. Their original cost of £2,000 is a **sunk cost,** and should be ignored in the decision.

However, if the materials did have a scrap value of, say, £300, then their relevant cost to the job would be the **opportunity cost** of being unable to sell them for scrap, ie £300.

Attributable fixed costs

1.10   There might be occasions when a fixed cost is a relevant cost, and you must be aware of the distinction between 'specific' or 'directly attributable' fixed costs, and general overheads.

(a)   **Directly attributable fixed costs** are those costs which, although fixed within a relevant range of activity level are relevant to a decision for either of the following reasons.

(i)   They would increase if certain extra activities were undertaken. For example, it may be necessary to employ an extra supervisor if a particular order is accepted. The extra salary would be an attributable fixed cost.

(ii)   They would decrease or be eliminated entirely if a decision were taken either to reduce the scale of operations or shut down entirely.

(b)   **General fixed overheads** are those fixed overheads which will be unaffected by decisions to increase or decrease the scale of operations, perhaps because they are an apportioned share of the fixed costs of items which would be completely unaffected by the decisions. An apportioned share of head office charges is an example of general fixed overheads for a local office or department. General fixed overheads are not relevant in decision making.

BPP
PUBLISHING

2 SOME RULES FOR IDENTIFYING RELEVANT COSTS   Pilot paper

The relevant cost of materials

2.1 The **relevant** cost of raw materials is generally their **current replacement cost** unless the **materials have already been purchased but will not be replaced.** The relevant cost of using them will then be the **higher** of the following.

- Their current resale value
- The value they would obtain if they were put to an alternative use

If the materials have no resale value and no other possible use, then the relevant cost of using them for the opportunity under consideration would be nil.

You should test your knowledge of the relevant cost of materials by attempting the following question.

Question 2

Darwin Ltd has been approached by a customer who would like a special job to be done for him, and who is willing to pay £22,000 for it. The job would require the following materials.

Material	Total units required	Units already in stock	Book value of units in stock £/unit	Realisable value £/unit	Replacement cost £/unit
A	1,000	0	-	-	6.00
B	1,000	600	2.00	2.50	5.00
C	1,000	700	3.00	2.50	4.00
D	200	200	4.00	6.00	9.00

Material B is used regularly by Darwin Ltd, and if units of B are required for this job, they would need to be replaced to meet other production demand.

Materials C and D are in stock as the result of previous over buying, and they have a restricted use. No other use could be found for material C, but the units of material D could be used in another job as substitute for 300 units of material E, which currently costs £5 per unit (and of which the company has no units in stock at the moment).

Required

Calculate the relevant costs of material for deciding whether or not to accept the contract.

Answer

(a) **Material A** is not yet owned. It would have to be bought in full at the replacement cost of £6 per unit.

(b) **Material B** is used regularly by the company. There are existing stocks (600 units) but if these are used on the contract under review a further 600 units would be bought to replace them. Relevant costs are therefore 1,000 units at the replacement cost of £5 per unit.

(c) 1,000 units of **material C** are needed and 700 are already in stock. If used for the contract, a further 300 units must be bought at £4 each. The existing stocks of 700 will not be replaced. If they are used for the contract, they could not be sold at £2.50 each. The realisable value of these 700 units is an opportunity cost of sales revenue forgone.

(d) The required units of **material D** are already in stock and will not be replaced. There is an opportunity cost of using D in the contract because there are alternative opportunities either to sell the existing stocks for £6 per unit (£1,200 in total) or avoid other purchases (of material E), which would cost 300 x £5 = £1,500. Since substitution for E is more beneficial, £1,500 is the opportunity cost.

(e)   **Summary of relevant costs**

	£
Material A (1,000 × £6)	6,000
Material B (1,000 × £5)	5,000
Material C (300 × £4) plus (700 × £2.50)	2,950
Material D	1,500
Total	15,450

The relevant cost of using machines

2.2   Using machinery will involve some incremental costs

- Repair costs arising from use
- Hire charges
- Any fall in resale value of owned assets which results from their use

2.3   Depreciation is **not** a relevant cost.

2.4   EXAMPLE: THE RELEVANT COST OF USING MACHINES

Sydney Ltd is considering whether to undertake some contract work for a customer. The machinery required for the contract would be as follows.

(a)   A special cutting machine will have to be hired for three months for the work (the length of the contract). Hire charges for this machine are £75 per month, with a minimum hire charge of £300.

(b)   All other machinery required in the production for the contract has already been purchased by the organisation on hire purchase terms. The monthly hire purchase payments for this machinery are £500. This consists of £450 for capital repayment and £50 as an interest charge. The last hire purchase payment is to be made in two months' time. The cash price of this machinery was £9,000 two years ago. It is being depreciated on a straight line basis at the rate of £200 per month. However, it still has a useful life which will enable it to be operated for another 36 months.

The machinery is highly specialised and is unlikely to be required for other, more profitable jobs over the period during which the contract work would be carried out. Although there is no immediate market for selling this machine, it is expected that a customer might be found in the future. It is further estimated that the machine would lose £200 in its eventual sale value if it is used for the contract work.

Required

Calculate the relevant cost of machinery for the contract.

2.5   SOLUTION

(a)   The cutting machine will incur an incremental cost of £300, the minimum hire charge.

(b)   The historical cost of the other machinery is irrelevant as a past cost; depreciation is irrelevant as a non-cash cost; and future hire purchase repayments are irrelevant because they are committed costs. The only relevant cost is the loss of resale value of the machinery, estimated at £200 through use. This user cost will not arise until the machinery is eventually resold and the £200 should be discounted to allow for the time value of money. However, discounting is ignored here.

BPP
PUBLISHING

(c) **Summary of relevant costs**

	£
Incremental hire costs	300
User cost of other machinery	200
	500

Question 3

A machine which originally cost £12,000 has an estimated life of ten years and is depreciated at the rate of £1,200 a year. It has been unused for some time, however, as expected production orders did not materialise.

A special order has now been received which would require the use of the machine for two months.

The current net realisable value of the machine is £8,000. If it is used for the job, its value is expected to fall to £7,500. The net book value of the machine is £8,400.

Routine maintenance of the machine currently costs £40 a month. With use, the cost of maintenance and repairs would increase to £60 a month.

Ignore the time value of money.

What is the relevant cost of using the machine for the order?

A £240   B £520   C £540   D £620   E £940

Answer

The correct option is **C** as follows.

	£
Loss in net realisable value of the machine through using it on the order £(8,000 – 7,500)	500
Costs in excess of existing routine maintenance costs £(120 – 80)	40
Total marginal user cost	540

If you selected option A you incorrectly included the depreciation cost. **Depreciation is not relevant** because it is not a future cash flow.

Option B is incorrect because it allows for only one month's increased maintenance cost. The special order will take two months.

Option D is incorrect because it includes all of the maintenance cost to be incurred. £40 per month **would be incurred anyway** so it is only the **incremental** £20 that is relevant.

Option E is incorrect because it considers the net book value of the machine. This is not relevant to the decision because it does not affect **future cash flows**. Book value is simply the result of a bookkeeping accounting exercise.

---

3   THE RELEVANT COST OF SCARCE RESOURCES   Pilot paper

3.1   When a decision maker is faced with an opportunity which would call for the use of a scarce resource, the total **incremental cost** of using the resource will be higher than the direct cash cost of purchasing it. This is because the resource could be used for other purposes, and so by using it in one way, the benefits obtainable from using it another way must be forgone.

3.2   A numerical example may help to clarify this point. Suppose that your company is considering a contract. The work would involve the use of certain equipment for five hours and its running costs would be £2 per hour. However, your company faces heavy demand for usage of the equipment which earns a contribution of £7 per hour from this other work. If the contract is undertaken, some of this work would have to be forgone.

3.3 The contribution obtainable from putting the scarce resource to its alternative use is its **opportunity cost**. Since the equipment can earn £7 per hour in an alternative use, the contract under consideration should also be expected to earn at least the same amount. This can be accounted for by charging the £7 per hour as an opportunity cost to the contract and the total relevant cost of 5 hours of equipment time would be as follows.

	£
Running costs (5 × £2)	10
Internal opportunity cost (5 × £7)	35
Relevant cost	45

It is important to notice that the variable running costs of the equipment are included in the total relevant cost.

3.4 A rule for identifying the relevant cost of a scarce resource is that the **total relevant cost** of the resource consists of the sum of the following.

- The **contribution/incremental profit forgone** from the next-best opportunity for using the scarce resource **and**

- The **variable cost** of the scarce resource.

3.5 EXAMPLE: RELEVANT COSTS OF LABOUR AND VARIABLE OVERHEADS

Gloria Ltd has been offered £21,000 by a prospective customer to make some purpose-built equipment. The extra costs of the machine would be £3,000 for materials. There would also be a requirement for 2,000 labour hours. Labour wages are £4 per hour, variable overhead is £2 per hour and fixed overhead is absorbed at the rate of £4 per hour.

Labour, however, is in limited supply, and if the job is accepted, men would have to be diverted from other work which is expected to earn a contribution of £5 per hour towards fixed overheads and profit.

Required

Assess whether the contract should be undertaken.

3.6 SOLUTION

The relevant costs of the scarce resource, labour, are the sum of the following.

- The variable costs of the labour and associated variable overheads
- The contribution forgone from not being able to put it to its alternative use

Fixed costs are ignored because there is no incremental fixed cost expenditure.

	£
Materials	3,000
Labour (2,000 hours at £4 per hour)	8,000
Variable overhead (2,000 hours at £2 per hour)	4,000
	15,000
Opportunity cost:	
Contribution forgone from other work (2,000 hours × £5 per hour)	10,000
Total costs	25,000
Revenue	21,000
Net loss on contract	(4,000)

The contract should not be undertaken.

BPP PUBLISHING

3.7 It is worth thinking carefully about labour costs. The labour force will be paid £8,000 for 2,000 hours work, and variable overheads of £4,000 will be incurred no matter whether the men are employed on the new job or on other work. Relevant costs are future cash flows arising as a direct consequence of a decision, and the decision here will not affect the total wages paid. If this money is going to be spent anyway, should it not therefore be ignored as an irrelevant cost?

3.8 The answer to this crucial question is 'no'. The labour wages and variable overheads are relevant costs even though they will be incurred whatever happens. The reason for this is that the other work earns a contribution of £5 per hour **after having covered** labour and variable overhead costs. Work on the purpose-built equipment ought therefore to do at least the same.

4 RELEVANT COSTS AND MINIMUM PRICING

4.1 The **minimum price** for a one-off product or service contract is its total relevant costs: this is the price at which the company would make no incremental profit and no incremental loss from undertaking the work, but would just achieve an incremental cost breakeven point. The following example will illustrate the technique.

4.2 EXAMPLE: MINIMUM PRICE USING AN OPPORTUNITY COST APPROACH

Minimax Ltd has just completed production of an item of special equipment for a customer, only to be notified that this customer has now gone into liquidation.

After much effort, the sales manager has been able to interest a potential buyer who might buy the machine if certain conversion work could first be carried out.

(a) The sales price of the machine to the original buyer had been fixed at £138,600 and had included an estimated normal profit mark-up of 10% on total costs. The costs incurred in the manufacture of the machine were as follows.

	£
Direct materials	49,000
Direct labour	36,000
Variable overhead	9,000
Fixed production overhead	24,000
Fixed sales and distribution overhead	8,000
	126,000

(b) If the machine is converted, the production manager estimates that the cost of the extra work required would be as follows.

Direct materials (at cost) £9,600
Direct labour
  Department X: 6 workers for 4 weeks at £210 per worker per week   5040
  Department Y: 2 workers for 4 weeks at £160 per worker per week   1280

(c) Variable overhead would be 20% of direct labour cost, and fixed production overhead would be absorbed as follows.

Department X: 83.33% of direct labour cost
Department Y: 25% of direct labour cost

(d) Additional information is available as follows.

   (i) In the original machine, there are three types of material.

      (1) Type A could be sold for scrap for £8,000.

(2) Type B could be sold for scrap for £2,400 but it would take 120 hours of casual labour paid at £3.50 per hour to put it into a condition in which it would be suitable for sale.

(3) Type C would need to be scrapped, at a cost to Minimax Ltd of £1,100.

(ii) The direct materials required for the conversion are already in stock. If not needed for the conversion they would be used in the production of another machine in place of materials that would otherwise need to be purchased, and that would currently cost £8,800.

(iii) The conversion work would be carried out in two departments, X and Y. Department X is currently extremely busy and working at full capacity; it is estimated that its contribution to fixed overhead and profits is £2.50 per £1 of labour.

Department Y, on the other hand, is short of work but for organisational reasons its labour force, which at the moment has a workload of only 40% of its standard capacity, cannot be reduced below its current level of eight employees, all of whom are paid a wage of £160 per week.

(iv) The designs and specifications of the original machine could be sold to an overseas customer for £4,500 if the machine is scrapped.

(v) If conversion work is undertaken, a temporary supervisor would need to be employed for four weeks at a total cost of £1,500. It is normal company practice to charge supervision costs to fixed overhead.

(vi) The original customer has already paid a non-returnable deposit to Minimax Ltd of 12.5% of the selling price.

Required

Calculate the minimum price that Minimax Ltd should accept from the new customer for the converted machine. Explain clearly how you have reached this figure.

4.3 SOLUTION

The minimum price is the price which reflects the relevant costs (opportunity costs) of the work. These are established as follows.

(a) Past costs are not relevant, and the £126,000 of cost incurred should be excluded from the minimum price calculation. It is necessary, however, to consider the alternative use of the direct materials which would be forgone if the conversion work is carried out.

	£
Type A	
Revenue from sales as scrap (note (i))	8,000
Type B	
Revenue from sales as scrap,	
minus the additional cash costs necessary to	
prepare it for sale (£2,400 – (120 × £3.50)) (note (i))	1,980
Type C	
Cost of disposal if the machine is not converted	
(a negative opportunity cost) (note (ii))	(1,100)
Total opportunity cost of materials types A, B and C	8,880

By agreeing to the conversion of the machine, Minimax Ltd would therefore lose a net revenue of £8,880 from the alternative use of these materials.

Notes

(i) Scrap sales would be lost if the conversion work goes ahead.

(ii) These costs would be incurred unless the work goes ahead.

(b) The cost of additional direct materials for conversion is £9,600, but this is an historical cost. The relevant cost of these materials is the £8,800 which would be spent on new purchases if the conversion is carried out. If the conversion work goes ahead, the materials in stock would be unavailable for production of the other machine mentioned in item (d)(ii) of the question and so the extra purchases of £8,800 would then be needed.

(c) Direct labour in departments X and Y is a fixed cost and the labour force will be paid regardless of the work they do or do not do. The cost of labour for conversion in department Y is not a relevant cost because the work could be done without any extra cost to the company.

In department X, however, acceptance of the conversion work would oblige the company to divert production from other profitable jobs. The minimum contribution required from using department X labour must be sufficient to cover the cost of the labour and variable overheads and then make an additional £2.50 in contribution per direct labour hour.

Department X: costs for direct labour hours spent on conversion

6 workers × 4 weeks × £210 =	£5,040
Variable overhead cost £5,040 × 20% =	£1,008
Contribution forgone by diverting labour from other work £2.50 per £1 of labour cost = £5,040 × 250% =	£12,600

(d) Variable overheads in department Y are relevant costs because they will only be incurred if production work is carried out. (It is assumed that if the workforce is idle, no variable overheads would be incurred.)

Department Y 20% of (2 workers × 4 weeks × £160) = £256

(e) If the machine is converted, the company cannot sell the designs and specifications to the overseas company. £4,500 is a relevant (opportunity) cost of accepting the conversion order.

(f) Fixed overheads, being mainly unchanged regardless of what the company decides to do, should be ignored because they are not relevant (incremental) costs. The additional cost of supervision should, however, be included as a relevant cost of the order because the £1,500 will not be spent unless the conversion work is done.

(g) The non-refundable deposit received should be ignored and should not be deducted in the calculation of the minimum price. Just as costs incurred in the past are not relevant to a current decision about what to do in the future, revenues collected in the past are also irrelevant.

4.4 Estimate of minimum price for the converted machine

	£	£
Opportunity cost of using the direct materials types A, B and C		8,880
Opportunity cost of additional materials for conversion		8,800
Opportunity cost of work in department X		
Labour	5,040	
Variable overhead	1,008	
Contribution forgone	12,600	
		18,648
Opportunity cost: sale of designs and specifications		4,500
Incremental costs:		
Variable production overheads in department Y		256
Fixed production overheads (additional supervision)		1,500
Minimum price		42,584

5 THE ASSUMPTIONS IN RELEVANT COSTING

5.1 Relevant costs are future costs. Whenever anyone tries to predict what will happen in the future, the predictions could well be wrong. Cost accountants have to make the best forecasts of relevant income and costs that they can, and at the same time recognise the assumptions on which their estimates are based. A variety of assumptions will be made, and you ought to be aware of them.

> **Exam focus point**
>
> In particular, if you make an assumption in answering an examination question and you are not sure that the examiner or marker will appreciate or recognise the assumption you are making, you should explain it in narrative in your solution.

5.2 Some of the assumptions that are typically made in relevant costing are as follows.

(a) **Cost behaviour patterns are known;** if a department closes down, for example, the attributable fixed cost savings would be known.

This is not necessarily so, and it is always important to question assumptions of this nature. For example, if you are told in an examination question that a factory intends to increase production by 50%, and you are invited to assume in your number work that fixed costs and unit variable costs would be unaffected, it is important to challenge this assumption as a footnote to your solution, making the following points.

- Is it clear that the factory could handle such a large increase in output?

- If so, fixed costs would probably change dramatically, and there might also be a shift in unit variable costs.

(b) **The amount of fixed costs, unit variable costs, sales price and sales demand are known with certainty**. However, it is possible to apply risk and uncertainty analysis to decisions and so recognise that what will happen in the future is not certain. You will cover such techniques in chapter 3 of this text.

(c) **The objective of decision making in the short run is to maximise 'satisfaction',** which is often regarded as 'short-term profit'. However, there are many qualitative factors or financial considerations, other than those of profit, which may influence a final decision: again a footnote may be called for.

(d) **The information on which a decision is based is complete and reliable.** This is obviously unrealistic and decision makers must be made aware of any inadequacies of the information that they are using for their decisions.

6 QUALITATIVE FACTORS IN DECISION MAKING

6.1 Qualitative factors in decision making are factors which might influence the eventual decisions but which have not been quantified in terms of relevant costs or benefits. They may stem from two sources.

- Non-financial objectives

- Factors which might be quantifiable in money terms, but which have not been quantified, perhaps because there is insufficient information to make reliable estimates

Exam focus point

Decision making questions in the exam often ask you to detail 'other factors that should be considered' after you have completed the figurework for the decision. However, even if the question does not invite you to do so, it is a good idea to get into the habit of adding a few notes concerning 'other factors'. This applies especially if you feel that you have made any assumptions that could be challenged.

Examples of qualitative factors

6.2 Qualitative factors in decision making will vary with the circumstances and nature of the opportunity being considered. Here are some examples.

(a) The **availability of cash**. An opportunity may be profitable, but there must be sufficient cash to finance any purchases of equipment and build-up of working capital.

(b) **Inflation**. The effect of inflation on the prices of various items may need to be considered, especially where a fixed price contract is involved in the decision: if the income from an opportunity is fixed by contract, but the costs might increase with inflation, the contract's profitability would be over-stated unless inflation is taken into account.

(c) **Employees**. Any decision involving the shutdown of a plant, creation of a new work shift, or changes in work procedures or location will require acceptance by employees, and ought to have regard to employee welfare.

(d) **Customers.** Decisions about new products or product closures, the quality of output or after-sales service will inevitably affect customer loyalty and customer demand. It is also important to remember that a decision involving one product may have repercussions on customer attitudes towards a range of products. For example, a company which sells a range of garden tools and equipment under a single brand name should consider the effects on demand for the entire brand range if one product (for example a garden rake) is deleted, or a new product of poor quality is added.

(e) **Competitors**. In a competitive market, some decisions may stimulate a response from rival companies. For example, the decision to reduce selling prices in order to raise demand may not be successful if all competitors take similar action.

(f) **Timing factors**

    (i)   There might be a choice in deciding when to take up an opportunity. The choice would not be 'accept or reject'; there would be three choices.

- Accept an opportunity now
- Do not accept the opportunity now, but wait before doing so
- Reject the opportunity

(ii) **Other choices which may need to be made**

- If a department is shut down, will the closure be permanent, or temporary? Temporary closure may be a viable proposition during a period of slack demand.

- If a decision is taken to sell goods at a low price where the contribution earned will be relatively small, it is important to consider the duration of the low price promotion. If it is a long-term feature of selling, and if demand for the product increases, the company's total contribution may sink to a level where it fails even to cover fixed costs.

(g) **Suppliers**. Some decisions will affect suppliers, whose long-term goodwill may be damaged by a decision to close a product line temporarily. Decisions to change the specifications for purchased components, or change stockholding policies so as to create patchy, uneven demand might also put a strain on suppliers. In some cases, where a company is the supplier's main customer, a decision to reduce demand or delay payments for goods received might drive the supplier out of business.

(h) **Feasibility**. A proposal may look good in financial terms, but technical experts or departmental managers may have some reservations about their ability to carry it out. For example, a decision may be required to buy some computer equipment, but the departmental manager might have reservations about the willingness of his staff to accept the proposal, the possibility of implementing the scheme by the planned date, and even whether the proposed scheme will actually do the job intended.

(i) **Flexibility and internal control**. Decisions to subcontract work, or to enter into a long-term contract have the disadvantages of inflexibility and lack of controllability. Where requirements may be changeable, it would be preferable to build flexibility into the organisation of operations.

(j) **Unquantified opportunity costs**. Even where no opportunity costs are specified, it is probable that other opportunities would be available for using the resources to earn profit. It may be useful to qualify a recommendation by stating that a given project would appear to be viable on the assumption that there are no other more profitable opportunities available.

(k) **Political pressures**. Some large companies may suffer political pressures applied by the government to influence their investment or disinvestment decisions.

(l) **Legal constraints**. A decision might occasionally be rejected because of doubts about the legality of the proposed action.

BPP PUBLISHING

Chapter roundup

- Relevant costs are **future, incremental cash flows**.

- An **opportunity cost** is the benefit forgone by choosing one opportunity instead of the next best alternative.

- Non-relevant costs include **sunk costs, committed costs, notional costs** and **historical costs.**

- The relevant cost of raw materials is their **current replacement cost** unless the materials have been purchased and will not be replaced, in which case their relevant cost is the higher of their current resale value and the value they would obtain if they were put to an alternative use.

- The relevant cost of a scarce resource is the **sum of the contribution/incremental profit forgone from the next best opportunity for using the scarce resource and the variable cost of the scarce resource.**

- The **minimum price** for a one-off product or service contract is its **total relevant costs.**

- There are a number of **assumptions** typically made in relevant costing

    ° Cost behaviour patterns are known

    ° The amount of fixed costs, unit variable costs, sales price and sales demand are known with certainty

    ° The objective is to maximise satisfaction (short-term profit)

    ° The information on which a decision is based is complete and reliable

- Qualitative factors should always be considered alongside the quantitative data in a decision.

Quick quiz

1   **Tick the correct box** for each of these types of cost.

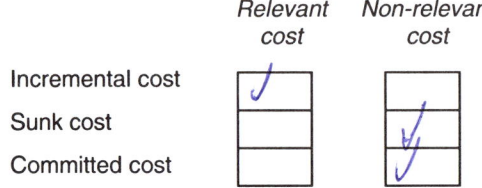

	Relevant cost	Non-relevant cost
Incremental cost	✓	
Sunk cost		✓
Committed cost		✓

2   What is an attributable fixed cost?

3   The **total relevant cost** of a scarce resource is equal to the sum of the **variable cost** of the scarce resource and

   A   the price that the resource would sell for in the open market
   B   the fixed cost absorbed by a unit of the scarce resource
   C   the contribution forgone from the next-best opportunity for using the scarce resource
   D   the price that would have to be paid to replace the scarce resource
   E   Zero. No other costs need to be added

4   Name three qualitative factors which may be relevant to decisions.

Answers to quick quiz

1   Relevant; non-relevant; non-relevant

2   A fixed cost which is relevant to a decision because it would be affected by the decision being taken

3   C

4   Availability of cash, employee morale, competitors' reactions

Now try the questions below from the Exam Question Bank

Number	Level	Marks	Time
Q1	Examination	25	45 mins
Q2	Examination (Pilot)	30	54 mins

BPP
PUBLISHING

Chapter 2

INFORMATION FOR DECISION MAKING II

Topic list		Syllabus Reference	Ability required
1	Joint cost allocations	(i)	Apply and evaluate
2	Profit maximisation	(i)	Apply and evaluate
3	Alternative costing systems	(i)	Evaluate

Introduction

In this chapter we will be continuing our study of the usefulness of management information for decision making. We begin by returning to a subject which you learned about in your **Management Accounting Fundamentals** syllabus: process costing. You will be learning how to allocate **joint product** costs and considering the usefulness of the resulting information.

You will also be studying further analysis of decision data and reviewing the various costing systems which may be used as the basis for decision making.

Learning outcomes covered in this chapter

- **Apply** and **evaluate** profit maximisation

- **Evaluate** costing systems for decision making

Syllabus content covered in this chapter

- Joint cost allocations, common costs

- Profit maximisation

- Alternative costing systems

1 JOINT COST ALLOCATIONS

1.1 In your studies of *Management Accounting Fundamentals* you learned the techniques of process costing, which is the costing method which applies when goods or services are produced in a sequence of continuous processes. Now we are going to turn our attention to the methods of accounting for **joint products** and **by-products** which arise as a result of a continuous process.

KEY TERM

Joint products are defined in CIMA *Official Terminology* as 'Two or more products produced by the same process and separated in processing, each having a sufficiently high saleable value to merit recognition as a main product'.

1.2 Features of joint products

- They are produced in the **same process**.
- They are **indistinguishable** from each other until the **separation point**.
- They each have a **substantial sales value** (after further processing, if necessary).
- They **may require further processing** after the separation point.

1.3 For example in the oil refining industry the following joint products all arise from the same process.

- Diesel fuel
- Petrol
- Paraffin
- Lubricants

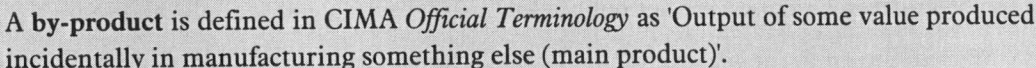

KEY TERM

A **by-product** is defined in CIMA *Official Terminology* as 'Output of some value produced incidentally in manufacturing something else (main product)'.

1.4 A by-product is a product which is similarly produced at the same time and from the same common process as the 'main product' or joint products. The distinguishing feature of a by-product is its **relatively low sales value** in comparison to the main product. In the timber industry, for example, by-products include sawdust, small offcuts and bark.

1.5 What exactly distinguishes a joint product from a by-product?

The answer lies in management attitudes to their products, which in turn is reflected in the cost accounting system.

(a) A **joint product** is regarded as an important saleable item, and so it should be **separately costed**. The profitability of each joint product should be assessed in the cost accounts.

(b) A **by-product** is not important as a saleable item, and whatever revenue it earns is a 'bonus' for the organisation. It is not worth costing by-products separately, because of their relative insignificance. It is therefore equally irrelevant to consider a by-product's profitability. The only question is how to account for the 'bonus' net revenue that a by-product earns.

Problems in accounting for joint products

1.6 Joint products are not separately identifiable until a certain stage is reached in the processing operations. This stage is the **'split-off point'**, sometimes referred to as the **separation point**. Costs incurred prior to this point of separation are **common or joint costs**, and these need to be allocated (apportioned) in some manner to each of the joint products. In the following sketched example, there are two different split-off points.

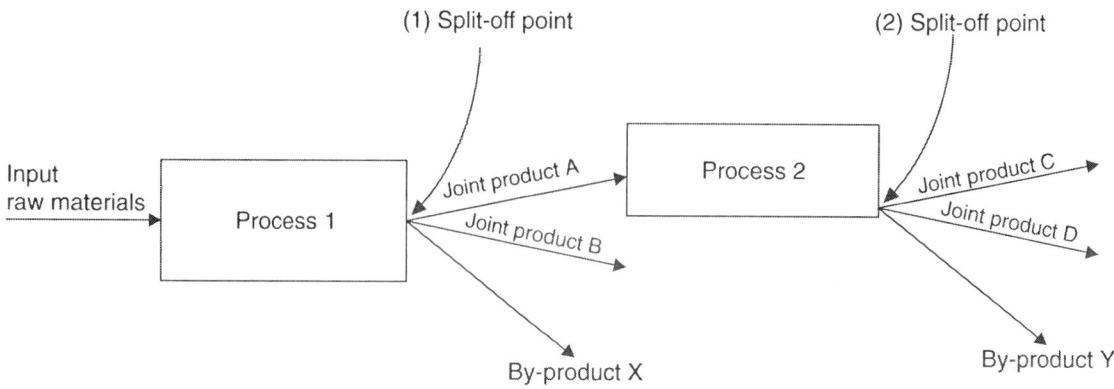

1.7 The special problems in accounting for joint products are basically of two different sorts.

(a) **How common costs should be apportioned** between products.

(b) Whether it is more profitable to **sell a joint product at one stage of processing, or to process the product further** and sell it at a later stage. In the above diagram, product A has been processed further but product B has been sold at the split-off point.

We will return to the second problem later in this section. Let us for now consider the first problem.

Apportioning common costs to joint products

1.8 The problem of costing for joint products concerns **common costs,** that is those common processing costs shared between the units of eventual output up to their 'split-off point'. Some method needs to be devised for sharing the common costs between the individual joint products for the following reasons.

(a) **To put a value to closing stocks** of each joint product.

(b) **To record the costs and therefore the profit from each joint product.** This is of **limited value** however, because the costs and therefore profit from one joint product are influenced by the share of costs assigned to the other joint products. Management decisions would be based on the apparent relative profitability of the products which has arisen due to the arbitrary apportionment of the joint costs.

(c) Perhaps to assist in **pricing decisions**.

1.9 **Some examples of the common costs problem**

(a) How to spread the common costs of oil refining between the joint products made (petrol, naphtha, kerosene and so on).

(b) How to spread the common costs of running the telephone network between telephone calls in peak rate times and cheap rate times, or between local calls and long-distance calls.

1.10 **Methods used to apportion common costs to joint products**

- Physical measurement

- Relative sales value apportionment method 1; sales value at split-off point

- Relative sales value apportionment method 2; sales value of end product less further processing costs after split-off point

- A weighted average method

Dealing with common costs: physical measurement

1.11 With physical measurement, the common cost is apportioned to the joint products on the basis of the proportion that the output of each product bears by weight or volume to the total output. An example of this would be the case where two products, product 1 and product 2, incur common costs to the point of separation of £3,000 and the output of each product is 600 tons and 1,200 tons respectively.

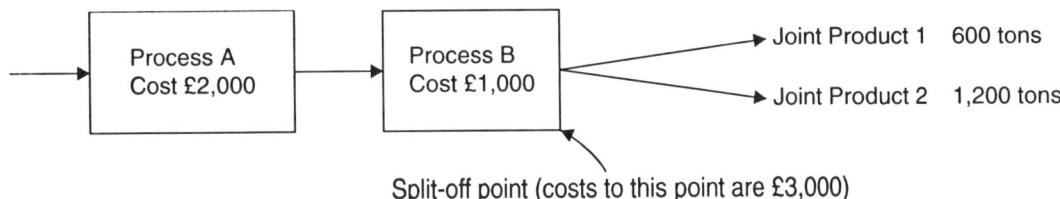

Product 1 sells for £4 per ton and product 2 for £2 per ton.

The division of the common costs (£3,000) between product 1 and product 2 could be based on the tonnage of output.

	Product 1		*Product 2*	*Total*
Output	600 tons	+	1,200 tons	1,800 tons
Proportion of common cost	$\dfrac{600}{1,800}$		$\dfrac{1,200}{1,800}$	
	£		£	£
Apportioned cost	1,000		2,000	3,000
Sales	2,400		2,400	4,800
Profit	1,400		400	1,800
Profit/sales ratio	58.3%		16.7%	37.5%

1.12 This method is unsuitable where the products separate during the processes into **different states,** for example where one product is a gas and another is a liquid. Furthermore, this method does not take into account the **relative income-earning potentials of the individual products,** with the result that one product might appear very profitable and another appear to be incurring losses.

Dealing with common costs: sales value at split-off point

1.13 With relative sales value apportionment of common cost, the cost is **apportioned according to the product's ability to produce income.** This method is most widely used because the assumption that some profit margin should be attained for all products under normal marketing conditions is satisfied. The common cost is apportioned to each product in the proportion that the sales value of that product bears to the sales value of the total output from the particular processes concerned. Using the previous example where the sales price per unit is £4 for product 1 and £2 for product 2.

- Common costs of processes to split-off point   £3,000
- Sales value of product 1 at £4 per ton   £2,400
- Sales value of product 2 at £2 per ton   £2,400

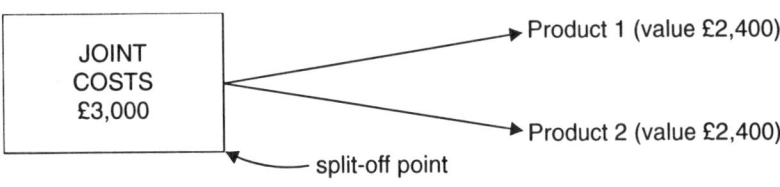

	Product 1	Product 2	Total
Sales	£2,400	£2,400	£4,800
Proportion of common cost apportioned	$\left(\dfrac{2,400}{4,800}\right)$	$\left(\dfrac{2,400}{4,800}\right)$	
Apportioned cost	1,500	1,500	3,000
Sales	2,400	2,400	4,800
Profit	900	900	1,800
Profit/sales ratio	37.5%	37.5%	37.5%

1.14 A comparison of the different gross profit margins resulting from the application of the above methods for allocating common costs will illustrate the greater acceptability of the relative sales value apportionment method. Physical measurement gives a higher profit margin to product 1, not necessarily because product 1 is highly profitable, but because it has been given a smaller share of common costs.

Dealing with common costs: sales value minus further processing costs

1.15 Joint products may have no known market value at the point of separation, because they need further separate processing to make them ready for sale. The allocation of common product costs should be accomplished as follows.

(a) Ideally, by determining a **relative sales value at the split off point** for each product.

(b) If a relative sales value cannot be found, a residual sales value at the split-off point can be determined.

  • Take the final sales value of each joint product
  • Deduct the further processing costs for each product

  This residual sales value is sometimes referred to as the **notional** or **proxy sales value** of a joint product.

1.16 EXAMPLE: SALES VALUE MINUS FURTHER PROCESSING COSTS

JT Ltd has a factory where four products are originated in a common process.

During period 4, the costs of the common process were £16,000. Output was as follows.

	Units made	Units sold	Sales value per unit
Product P1	600		
Product Q1	400		
Product R	500	400	£7
Product S	600	450	£10

Products P1 and Q1 are further processed, separately, to make end-products P2 and Q2.

	Units processed	Units sold	Cost of further processing	Sales value per unit
Product P1/P2	600	600	£1,000	£10 (P2)
Product Q1/Q2	400	300	£2,500	£20 (Q2)

Required

Calculate the costs of each joint product and the profit from each of them in period 4. There were no opening stocks.

1.17 SOLUTION

(a) It is helpful to begin a solution to joint product problems with a diagram of the process.

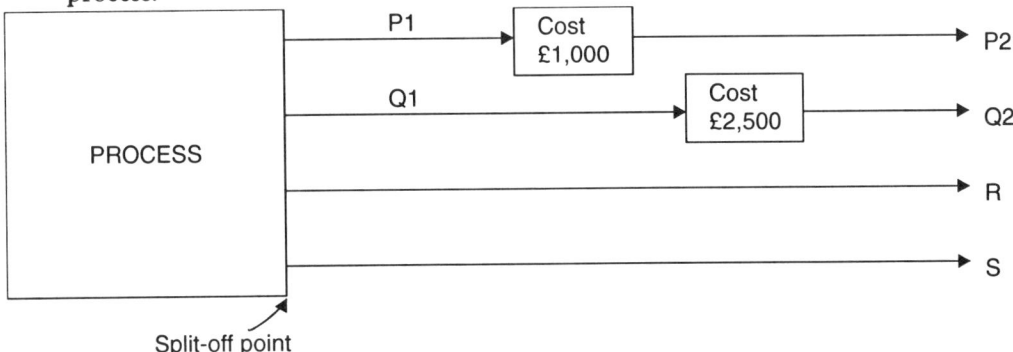

Split-off point

(b) Next we calculate the notional sales values of P1 and Q1 at the split-off point.

	P2 £	Q2 £
Sales value of production	6,000	8,000
Less further processing costs	1,000	2,500
Notional sales value, P1, Q1	5,000 (P1)	5,500 (Q1)

(c) Now we can apply sales values to apportion common costs.

Joint product	Sales value of production £	%	Apportionment of common costs £
P1	5,000	25	4,000
Q1	5,500	27 ½	4,400
R	3,500	17 ½	2,800
S	6,000	30	4,800
	20,000	100	16,000

(d) We can now draw up the profit statement.

	P1/2 £	Q1/2 £	R £	S £	Total £
Common costs	4,000	4,400	2,800	4,800	16,000
Further processing	1,000	2,500	-	-	3,500
Cost of production	5,000	6,900	2,800	4,800	19,500
Less closing stock	0	1,725	560	1,200	3,485
Cost of sales	5,000	5,175	2,240	3,600	16,015
Sales	6,000	6,000	2,800	4,500	19,300
Profit	1,000	825	560	900	3,285
Profit/sales ratio	17%	14%	20%	20%	17%

Question 1

Calculate the profit for the period and the value of closing stocks if common costs are apportioned using the units method.

Answer

Joint product	Units produced	%	Apportionment of common costs £
P1	600	28.6	4,576
Q1	400	19.0	3,040
R	500	23.8	3,808
S	600	28.6	4,576
	2,100	100.0	16,000

Profit statement

	P1/2	Q1/2	R	S	Total
	£	£	£	£	£
Common costs of production	4,576	3,040	3,808	4,576	16,000
Further processing	1,000	2,500	-	-	3,500
Cost of production	5,576	5,540	3,808	4,576	19,500
Less closing stock	0	1,385	762	1,144	3,291
Cost of sales	5,576	4,155	3,046	3,432	16,209
Sales	6,000	6,000	2,800	4,500	19,300
Profit/(loss)	424	1,845	(246)	1,068	3,091
Profit/sales ratio	7%	31%	-	24%	16%

Dealing with common costs: weighted average method

1.18 The weighted average method of common cost apportionment is a development of the units method of apportionment. Since units of joint product may not be comparable in physical resemblance or physical weight (they may be gases, liquids or solids) units of each joint product may be multiplied by a weighting factor, and '**weighted units**' would provide a basis for apportioning the common costs.

1.19 EXAMPLE: WEIGHTED AVERAGE METHOD

MG Ltd manufactures four products which emerge from a joint processing operation. In April, the costs of the joint production process were as follows.

	£
Direct materials	24,000
Direct labour	2,000
	26,000

Production overheads are added using an absorption rate of 400% of direct labour costs. Output from the process during April was as follows.

Joint product	*Output*
D	600 litres
W	400 litres
F	400 kilograms
G	500 kilograms

Units of output of D, W, F and G and to be given weightings of 3, 5, 8 and 3 respectively for apportioning common costs.

Required

Apportion the joint costs.

1.20 SOLUTION

Total costs are £26,000 for direct cost plus £8,000 overhead. The costs would be £34,000, apportioned as follows.

Joint product	*Output* Units	*Weighting*	*Weighted units*
D	600	3	1,800
E	400	5	2,000
F	400	8	3,200
G	500	3	1,500
			8,500

The costs are therefore apportioned at a rate of £34,000/8,500 = £4 per weighted unit.

Joint product	*Apportionment of common cost* £
D	7,200
E	8,000
F	12,800
G	6,000
	34,000

1.21 Now that you have learned all of the methods of allocating joint costs to products you should be able to appreciate the arbitrary nature of such cost allocation. The resulting product costs should never be used as a basis for decision making because the apparent relative profitability of the products has arisen due to the arbitrary apportionment of the joint costs.

The further processing decision

1.22 A different type of decision making problem with joint products occurs when there is a **choice between selling part-finished output or processing it further**. This decision problem is best explained by a simple example.

1.23 EXAMPLE: FURTHER PROCESSING

Alice Ltd manufactures two joint products, A and B. The costs of common processing are £15,000 per batch, and output per batch is 100 units of A and 150 units of B. The sales value of A at split-off point is £90 per unit, and the sales value of B is £60 per unit. An opportunity exists to process product A further, at an extra cost of £2,000 per batch, to produce product C. One unit of joint product A is sufficient to make one unit of C which has a sales value of £120 per unit.

Should the company sell product A, or should it process A and sell product C?

1.24 SOLUTION

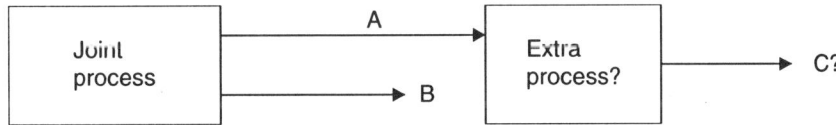

The problem is resolved on the basis that product C should be sold if the sales value of C minus its further processing costs exceeds the sales value of A.

	£
Sales value of C, per batch (100 × £120)	12,000
Sales value of A, per batch (100 × £90)	9,000
Incremental revenue from further processing	3,000
Further processing cost	2,000
Benefit from further processing in order to sell C	1,000 per batch

1.25 If the further processing cost had exceeded the incremental revenue from further processing, it would have been unprofitable to make and sell C. It is worth noting that the **apportionment of joint processing costs between A and B is irrelevant to the decision**, because the total extra profit from making C will be £1,000 per batch whichever method of apportionment is used.

BPP PUBLISHING

Question 2

PCC Ltd produces two joint products, Pee and Cee, from the same process. Joint processing costs of £150,000 are incurred up to split-off point, when 100,000 units of Pee and 50,000 units of Cee are produced. The selling prices at split-off point are £1.25 per unit for Pee and £2.00 per unit for Cee.

The units of Pee could be processed further to produce 60,000 units of a new chemical, Peeplus, but at an extra fixed cost of £20,000 and variable cost of 30p per unit of input. The selling price of Peeplus would be £3.25 per unit.

Required

Ascertain whether the company should sell Pee or Peeplus.

Answer

The only relevant costs/incomes are those which compare selling Pee against selling Peeplus. Every other cost is irrelevant: they will be incurred regardless of what the decision is.

	Pee			*Peeplus*
Selling price per unit	£1.25			£3.25
	£		£	£
Total sales	125,000			195,000
Post-separation processing costs	-	Fixed	20,000	
	-	Variable	30,000	50,000
Sales minus post-separation (further processing) costs	125,000			145,000

It is £20,000 more profitable to convert Pee into Peeplus.

Costing by-products

1.26 A by-product is a supplementary or secondary product (arising as the result of a process) whose **value is small relative to that of the principal product**. Nevertheless the by-product has some commercial value and its accounting treatment usually consists of one of the following.

(a) **Income** (minus any post-separation further processing or selling costs) from the sale of the by-product **may be added to sales of the main product,** thereby increasing sales turnover for the period.

(b) The sales of the by-product may be treated as a **separate, incidental source of income** against which are set only post-separation costs (if any) of the by-product. The revenue would be recorded in the profit and loss account as '**other income**'.

(c) The **sales income of the by-product may be deducted from the cost of production** or cost of sales of the main product.

(d) The **net realisable value of the by-product may be deducted from the cost of production of the main product.** The net realisable value is the final saleable value of the by-product minus any post-separation costs.

The choice of method will be influenced by the circumstances of production and ease of calculation, as much as by conceptual correctness. The method you are most likely to come across in examinations is method (d). An example will help to clarify the distinction between the different methods.

1.27 EXAMPLE: METHODS OF ACCOUNTING FOR BY-PRODUCTS

During November, Splatter Ltd recorded the following results.

Opening stock	main product P, nil	
	by-product Z, nil	
Cost of production	£120,000	

Sales of the main product amounted to 90% of output during the period, and 10% of production was held as closing stock at 30 November.

Sales revenue from the main product during November was £150,000.

A by-product Z is produced, and output had a net sales value of £1,000. Of this output, £700 was sold during the month, and £300 was still in stock at 30 November.

Required

Calculate the profit for November using the four methods of accounting for by-products.

1.28 SOLUTION

The four methods of accounting for by-products are shown below.

(a) **Income from by-product added to sales of the main product**

	£	£
Sales of main product (£150,000 + £700)		150,700
Opening stock	0	
Cost of production	120,000	
	120,000	
Less closing stock (10%)	12,000	
Cost of sales		108,000
Profit, main product		42,700

(b) **By-product income treated as a separate source of income**

	£	£
Sales, main product		150,000
Opening stock	0	
Cost of production	120,000	
	120,000	
Closing stock (10%)	12,000	
Cost of sales, main product		108,000
Profit, main product		42,000
Other income		700
Total profit		42,700

(c) **Sales income of the by-product deducted from the cost of production in the period**

	£	£
Sales, main product		150,000
Opening stock	0	
Cost of production (120,000 – 700)	119,300	
	119,300	
Less closing stock (10%)	11,930	
Cost of sales		107,370
Profit, main product		42,630

(d) **Net realisable value of the by-product deducted from the cost of production in the period**

	£	£
Sales, main product		150,000
Opening stock	0	
Cost of production (120,000 – 1,000)	119,000	
	119,000	
Less closing stock (10%)	11,900	
Cost of sales		107,100
Profit, main product		42,900

1.29 You should note that whatever method is selected, the by-product closing stock has no value.

Question 3

Randolph Ltd manufactures two joint products, J and K, in a common process. A by-product X is also produced. Data for the month of December 20X2 were as follows.

Opening stocks	nil	
Costs of processing	direct materials	£25,500
	direct labour	£10,000

Production overheads are absorbed at the rate of 300% of direct labour costs.   *30,000*

		Production Units	Sales Units
Output and sales consisted of:	product J	8,000	7,000
	product K	8,000	6,000
	by-product X	1,000	1,000

The sales value per unit of J, K and X is £4, £6 and £0.50 respectively. The saleable value of the by-product is deducted from process costs before apportioning costs to each joint product. Costs of the common processing are apportioned between product J and product K on the basis of sales value of production.

Required

Calculate the profit for December 20X2. Analyse this profit by individual products.

Answer

The sales value of production was £80,000.

	£	
Product J (8,000 × £4)	32,000	(40%)
Product K (8,000 × £6)	48,000	(60%)
	80,000	

The costs of production were as follows.	£
Direct materials	25,500
Direct labour	10,000
Overhead (300% of £10,000)	30,000
	65,500
Less sales value of by-product (1,000 × 50p)	500
Net production costs	65,000

The profit statement would appear as follows (nil opening stocks).

	Product J		£	Product K		£	Total	£
Production costs	(40%)		26,000	(60%)		39,000		65,000
Less closing stock	(1,000 units)		3,250	(2,000 units)		9,750		13,000
Cost of sales			22,750			29,250		52,000
Sales	(7,000 units)		28,000	(6,000 units)		36,000		64,000
Profit			5,250			6,750		12,000

2   PROFIT MAXIMISATION

2.1 In many examination questions on decision making, the objective will be to maximise the profit of the organisation in question. You will need to be completely confident in the manipulation of decision making data to provide appropriate advice to management. In this section of the chapter we will look at a number of different types of decision to give you an idea of the sort of decision that you may be required to tackle.

Shutdown problems

2.2 **Decisions to be made in shutdown or discontinuance problems**

- Whether or not to close down a product line, department or other activity.
- If the decision is to shut down, whether the closure should be permanent or temporary.
- If there is a choice about the timing of the closure, when should it take place.

2.3 EXAMPLE: ADDING OR DELETING PRODUCTS

A company manufactures three products, Pawns, Rooks and Bishops. The present net annual income from these is:

	Pawns	Rooks	Bishops	Total
	£	£	£	£
Sales	50,000	40,000	60,000	150,000
Variable costs	30,000	25,000	35,000	90,000
Contribution	20,000	15,000	25,000	60,000
Fixed costs	17,000	18,000	20,000	55,000
Profit/loss	3,000	(3,000)	5,000	5,000

The company is concerned about its poor profit performance, and is considering whether or not to cease selling Rooks. It is felt that selling prices cannot be raised or reduced without adversely affecting net income. £5,000 of the fixed costs of Rooks are direct fixed costs which would be saved if production ceased. All other fixed costs, it is considered, would remain the same.

2.4 SOLUTION

By stopping production of Rooks, the consequences would be a £10,000 fall in profits:

	£
Loss of contribution	(15,000)
Savings in fixed costs	5,000
Incremental loss	(10,000)

2.5 Suppose, however, it were possible to use the resources realised by stopping production of Rooks and switch to producing a new item, Crowners, which would sell for £50,000 and incur variable costs of £30,000 and extra direct fixed costs of £6,000. A new decision is now required:

	Rooks	Crowners
	£	£
Sales	40,000	50,000
Less variable costs	25,000	30,000
	15,000	20,000
Less direct fixed costs	5,000	6,000
Contribution to shared fixed costs and profit	10,000	14,000

It would be more profitable to shut down production of Rooks and switch resources to making Crowners, in order to boost profits by £4,000 to £9,000.

Qualitative factors

2.6 As usual the decision is not merely a matter of choosing the best financial option. Qualitative factors related to the impact on employees, customers, competitors and suppliers must once more be considered.

Question 4

A company's product range includes product F, on which the following data (relating to a year's production) are available.

	£
Revenue	200,000
Materials cost	157,000
Machine power cost	14,000
Overheads: type A	28,000
type B	56,000

Type A overheads would be avoided if production of product F ceased, but type B overheads would not be. Both types of overheads are absorbed in direct proportion to machine power cost, and that cost is a purely variable cost.

Required

Determine whether production of product F should be ended.

Answer

	£	£
Revenue		200,000
Less: materials cost	157,000	
machine power cost	14,000	
type A overheads	28,000	
		199,000
Contribution		1,000

Production of product F should be continued, because it makes a contribution of £1,000 a year.

2.7 You may consider by now that you understand the basic principles of selecting relevant costs for decision making and profit maximisation and it may therefore be useful at this stage to test your understanding with a more advanced example. Attempt your own solution before reading on.

2.8 EXAMPLE: SHUTDOWN DECISIONS

Ayeco Ltd, with a head office in Ayetown, has three manufacturing units. One is in Beetown, the second in Ceetown and the third in Deetown. The company manufactures and sells an air-conditioner under the brand-name of Ayecool at a price of £200. It is unable to utilise fully its manufacturing capacity.

Summarised profit and loss statements for the year are shown below.

	Beetown £'000	Ceetown £'000	Deetown £'000	Total £'000
Costs				
Direct materials	200	800	400	1,400
Direct wages	200	900	350	1,450
Production overhead:				
variable	50	300	150	500
fixed	200	600	300	1,100
Sub-total	650	2,600	1,200	4,450
Selling overhead:				
variable	25	200	100	325
fixed	75	250	150	475
Administration overhead	100	450	200	750
Sub-total	850	3,500	1,650	6,000
Head office costs	50	200	100	350
Total	900	3,700	1,750	6,350
Profit	100	300	250	650
Sales	1,000	4,000	2,000	7,000

The management of the company has to decide whether or not to renew the lease of the property at Beetown, which expires next year. The company has been offered an extension to the lease at an additional cost of £50,000 per annum. This situation concerning the lease has been known for some time, so the accountant has collected relevant information to aid the decision. It is estimated that the cost of closing down Beetown would be offset by the surplus obtained by the sale of plant, machinery and stocks.

If Ayeco Ltd does not renew the lease of the Beetown property it has two alternatives.

(a) Accept an offer from Zeeco Ltd, a competitor, to take over the manufacture and sales in Beetown area and pay to Ayeco Ltd a commission of £3 for each unit sold.

(b) Transfer the output at present made in Beetown to either Ceetown or Deetown. Each of these units has sufficient plant capacity to undertake the Beetown output but additional costs in supervision, salaries, storage and maintenance would be incurred. These additional costs are estimated as amounting yearly to £250,000 at Ceetown and to £200,000 at Deetown.

If the Beetown sales are transferred to either Ceetown or Deetown, it is estimated that additional transport costs would be incurred in delivering to customers in the region of Beetown, and that these would amount to £15 per unit and £20 per unit respectively.

Required

Present a statement to the board of directors of Ayeco Ltd to show the estimated annual profit which would arise from the following alternative courses of action.

(a) Continuing production at all three sites
(b) Closing down production at Beetown and accepting the offer from Zeeco Ltd
(c) Transferring Beetown sales to Ceetown
(d) Transferring Beetown sales to Deetown

Comment on your statement, indicating any problems which may arise from the various decisions which the board may decide to take.

2.9 SOLUTION

The main difficulty in answering this question is to decide what happens to fixed cost expenditure if the Beetown factory is closed, and what would be the variable costs of production and sales at Ceetown or Deetown if work was transferred from Beetown.

2.10 It should be assumed that the direct fixed costs of the Beetown factory will be saved when shutdown occurs. These costs will include rent, depreciation of machinery, salaries of administrative staff and so on and it is therefore probably correct to assume that savings on shutdown will include all fixed costs charged to Beetown with the exception of the apportioned head office costs.

2.11 The variable cost of production at Ceetown or Deetown is more tricky, because the variable cost/sales ratio and the contribution/sales ratio differs at each factory.

	Beetown	Ceetown	Deetown
	%	%	%
Direct materials/sales	20.0	20.0	20.0
Direct wages/sales	20.0	22.5	17.5
Variable production overhead/sales	5.0	7.5	7.5
Variable selling overhead/sales	2.5	5.0	5.0
Total variable costs/sales	47.5	55.0	50.0
Contribution/sales	52.5	45.0	50.0

2.12 Labour appears to be less efficient at Ceetown and more efficient at Deetown, but variable overheads are more costly at both Ceetown and Deetown than at Beetown. It is probably reasonably accurate to assume that the variable cost/sales ratio of work transferred from Beetown will change to the ratio which is current at the factory to which the work is transferred. Transport costs would then be added as an additional cost item.

2.13 **Statement of estimated annual profit**

Option 1. Continuing production at all three sites

	£
Profit before rent increase on lease	650,000
Increase in annual cost of lease	50,000
Revised estimate of annual profit	600,000

Option 2. Accepting the offer from Zeeco Ltd

	£	£
Current estimate of total profit		650,000
Less revenue lost from closing Beetown	(1,000,000)	
Direct costs saved at Beetown	850,000	
	(150,000)	
Commission from Zeeco Ltd* (5,000 × £3)	15,000	
Net loss from closure		(135,000)
Revised estimate of total profit		515,000

     * Number of units = £1,000,000 ÷ £200 per unit = 5,000 units.

Option 3. Transfer work to Ceetown

	£	£	£
Current estimate of total profit			650,000
Direct costs saved by closing Beetown		850,000	
Extra costs at Ceetown			
Variable costs (55% of £1,000,000)	(550,000)		
Extra costs of supervision etc	(250,000)		
Extra costs of transport (5,000 units × £15)	(75,000)		
		(875,000)	
Net extra costs of transfer			(25,000)
Revised estimate of total profit			625,000

Option 4. Transfer work to Deetown

	£	£	£
Current estimate of total profit			650,000
Direct costs saved by closing Beetown		850,000	
Extra costs at Deetown			
Variable costs (50% of £1,000,000)	(500,000)		
Extra costs of supervision etc	(200,000)		
Extra costs of transport (5,000 units × £20)	(100,000)		
		(800,000)	
Net savings from transfer			50,000
Revised estimate of total profit			700,000

Conclusion

The preferred option should be to transfer production from Beetown to Deetown, since profits would rise to £700,000, and would be £75,000 higher than profits obtainable from the next most profitable option (option 3).

Comments on the example

2.14 The previous example illustrates how accounting information for decision making can often be presented in a concise form, without the need to reproduce a complete table of revenues, costs and profits for each option. You should study the presentation of the figures above, and note how they show only the relevant costs or benefits arising as a direct consequence of each decision option.

2.15 The eventual management decision may not be to transfer to Deetown, because other qualitative factors might influence the final decision.

(a) Concern for employees at Beetown and the wish to avoid redundancies.

(b) Problems in recruiting additional staff at Deetown.

(c) The possibility that the extra workload at Deetown might reduce labour efficiency there, making costs of production higher than those estimated in the statement.

(d) Difficulties in assembling and organising a transport fleet might persuade management to reject options 3 and 4.

When to close

2.16 As well as being able to deal with 'whether to close' situations you may also be required to handle 'when to close' situations.

2.17 EXAMPLE: WHEN TO CLOSE

Daisy Ltd currently publish, print and distribute a range of catalogues and instruction manuals. The management have now decided to discontinue printing and distribution and concentrate solely on publishing. Stem Ltd will print and distribute the range of catalogues and instruction manuals on behalf of Daisy Ltd commencing either at 30 June 20X0 or 30 November 20X0. Stem Ltd will receive £65,000 per month for a contract which will commence either at 30 June 20X0 or 30 November 20X0.

The results of Daisy Ltd for a typical month are as follows.

	Publishing £'000	Printing £'000	Distribution £'000
Salaries and wages	28.0	18.0	4.0
Materials and supplies	5.5	31.0	1.1
Occupancy costs	7.0	8.5	1.2
Depreciation	0.8	4.2	0.7

Other information has been gathered relating to the possible closure proposals.

(a) Two specialist staff from printing will be retained at their present salary of £1,500 each per month in order to fulfil a link function with Stem Ltd. One further staff member will be transferred to publishing to fill a staff vacancy through staff turnover, anticipated in July. This staff member will be paid at his present salary of £1,400 per month which is £100 more than that of the staff member who is expected to leave. On closure all other printing and distribution staff will be made redundant and paid an average of two months redundancy pay.

(b) The printing department has a supply of materials (already paid for) which cost £18,000 and which will be sold to Stem Ltd for £10,000 if closure takes place on 30 June 20X0. Otherwise the material will be used as part of the July 20X0 printing requirements. The distribution department has a contract to purchase pallets at a cost of £500 per month for July and August 20X0. A cancellation clause allows for non-delivery of the pallets for July and August for a one-off payment of £300. Non-delivery for August only will require a payment of £100. If the pallets are taken from the supplier, Stem Ltd has agreed to purchase them at a price of £380 for each month's supply which is available. Pallet costs are included in the distribution material and supplies cost stated for a typical month.

(c) Company expenditure on apportioned occupancy costs to printing and distribution will be reduced by 15% per month if printing and distribution departments are closed. At present, 30% of printing and 25% of distribution occupancy costs are directly attributable costs which are avoidable on closure, whilst the remainder are apportioned costs.

(d) Closure of the printing and distribution departments will make it possible to sub-let part of the building for a monthly fee of £2,500 when space is available.

(e) Printing plant and machinery has an estimated net book value of £48,000 at 30 June 20X0. It is anticipated that it will be sold at a loss of £21,000 on 30 June 20X0. If sold on 30 November 20X0 the prospective buyer will pay £25,000.

(f) The net book value of distribution vehicles at 30 June 20X0 is estimated as £80,000. They could be sold to the original supplier at £48,000 on 30 June 20X0. The original supplier would purchase the vehicles on 30 November 20X0 for a price of £44,000.

Required

Using the above information, prepare a summary to show whether Daisy Ltd should close the printing and distribution departments on financial grounds on 30 June 20X0 or on 30 November 20X0. Explanatory notes and calculations should be shown.

2.18 SOLUTION

		Handover 30.6.X0 £	Handover 30.11.X0 £	Difference £
Relevant inflows				
Stocks (W2)		10,000		10,000
Pallet sale (W3)		380		380
Rent	(5 × £2,500)	12,500		12,500
Fixed asset sales				
Printing		27,000	25,000	2,000
Distribution		48,000	44,000	4,000
Total inflows		97,880	69,000	28,880
Relevant outflows				
Salaries and wages (W1)		15,500	110,000	(94,500)
Materials and supplies (W2)			142,500	(142,500)
Pallets (W3)		600		600
Occupancy costs (W4)				
Apportioned		29,112	34,250	(5,138)
Direct			14,250	(14,250)
Stem fee	(5 × £65,000)	325,000		325,000
Total outflows		370,212	301,000	69,212
Net inflow/(outflow)		(272,332)	(232,000)	(40,332)

The operation should be kept open until 30.11.20X0.

Workings

1 Salaries and wages

	Printing £	Distribution £	Total £
Costs if 30.6.X0 handover			
2 × £1,500 × 5 months	15,000	-	15,000
£100 × 5 months		500	500
			15,500
Costs if 30.11.X0 handover			
5 months usual costs	90,000	20,000	110,000

2 Stocks

The £18,000 cost of production is a sunk cost from previous periods. Therefore only the income is recorded. Also, the £10,000 income could be seen as one of the opportunity costs of continuing production.

			£
Therefore materials costs are	printing:	(£31,000 × 5 − £18,000) =	137,000
	distribution:	(£1,100 × 5) =	5,500
			142,500

3 Pallets

The alternative flows can be estimated as follows.

Take both deliveries	£
Payment (2 × £500) =	1,000
Resale (2 × £380) =	760
Net flow	240

Take one delivery (ie July)	
Payment	500
Cancellation fee (August)	100
	600
Sale to Stem	380
Net flow	220

Take no deliveries

Cancellation fee   £300

Only the July delivery should be taken.

4   **Site costs**

	Printing £	Distribution £	Total £
Total occupancy costs (5 months)	42,500	6,000	48,500
of which directly attributable (30%/25%)	(12,750)	(1,500)	(14,250)
∴ Apportioned costs	29,750	4,500	34,250
Reduction in apportioned costs (15%)	(4,463)	(675)	(5,138)
Apportioned costs after closure	25,287	3,825	29,112

Operational gearing

> **KEY TERM**
>
> **Operational gearing** is defined in CIMA's *Official Terminology* as 'the relationship of the fixed cost to the total cost of an operating unit.'

2.19   Operational gearing is a term which relates to the make-up of an organisation's cost structure. The greater the proportion of total costs that are fixed, the higher the operational gearing. The significance of operational gearing can best be demonstrated with a numerical example.

2.20   **EXAMPLE: OPERATIONAL GEARING**

Two competing companies had the following results last period

	High Gear Limited £	Low Gear Limited £
Sales revenue	800,000	800,000
Variable costs	100,000	600,000
Contribution	700,000	200,000
Fixed costs	600,000	100,000
Profit	100,000	100,000

Both companies achieved the same profit from the same sales revenue, but you can see that their cost structures are quite different. High Gear Limited has a much higher proportion of fixed costs, or a higher **operational gearing**. This will have an impact when there are any changes in activity. Suppose that sales volumes for next period are forecast to double and that the selling prices and cost behaviour patterns will remain unaltered by this change in activity, ie the make-up of fixed and variable costs remains the same. What will be the budgeted profit for each company for next period?

2.21 SOLUTION

Budgeted profit for next period

	High Gear Limited £	Low Gear Limited £
Sales revenue	1,600,000	1,600,000
Variable costs	200,000	1,200,000
Contribution	1,400,000	400,000
Fixed costs	600,000	100,000
Profit	800,000	300,000

This rather extreme example demonstrates the effect of operational gearing. When sales doubled, the profit for both companies more than doubled, because they both benefit from the gearing effect of the fixed costs. However the advantage to High Gear Limited was far greater because the fixed costs do not increase in line with sales volume.

2.22 You can probably appreciate that, should sales volume fall, the profits of High Gear Limited would fall at a much faster rate than those of Low Gear Limited.

Question 5

Using the data from the example above, and assuming that selling prices and cost structures remain unaltered, the profit/(loss) for the two companies with a sales value of £560,000 will be

	High Gear Limited £	Low Gear Limited £
A	£70,000	£40,000
B	£(110,000)	£70,000
C	£(110,000)	£40,000
D	£(140,000)	£70,000
E	£(140,000)	£(140,000)

Answer

The correct option is C.

	High Gear Limited £	Low Gear Limited £
Sales revenue	560,000	560,000
Variable costs	70,000	420,000
Contribution	490,000	140,000
Fixed costs	600,000	100,000
Profit	(110,000)	40,000

The higher proportion of fixed costs was a disadvantage to High Gear Limited when sales volumes reduced.

The operational gearing ratio

2.23 The operational gearing ratio can be calculated to provide a numerical indication of the level of gearing, as well as a short cut to determine the change in profit for a given change in activity.

> **FORMULA TO LEARN**
>
> $$\text{Operating gearing ratio} = \frac{\text{Contribution}}{\text{Profit}}$$

The operational gearing ratio for High Gear Limited can be calculated from the original data as follows.

$$\text{Operational gearing ratio} = \frac{\pounds 700,000}{\pounds 100,000} = 7:1$$

2.24 This ratio provides a short cut to calculating the revised profit as follows.

Change in profit = original profit × change in sales × operational gearing ratio

This relationship will only apply when cost and selling price structures remain unaltered.

Thus, when sales doubled, change in profit
= £100,000 × 100% increase × 7
= £700,000 increase in profit,
resulting in a new profit of £800,000

When sales reduced from £800,000 to £560,000, a 30% reduction, change in profit
= £100,000 × 30% decrease × 7
= £210,000 decrease in profit,
resulting in a loss of £110,000

2.25 Operational gearing may be an important consideration if, for example, an organisation is considering changing its method of operation. Moving towards a more mechanised approach may increase fixed costs relative to variable costs and thus increase the operational gearing. This would be advantageous if sales volumes are expected to increase in the future, but management would need to be aware that profits would fall more rapidly if activity levels began to decrease.

3 ALTERNATIVE COSTING SYSTEMS

Marginal costing

3.1 In all of the decision making examples that we have seen in these two chapters, marginal costing rather than absorption costing was used to prepare the information on which to base the decision. It is generally accepted that **marginal costing is a better system than absorption costing for providing information for planning, control and decision making.** It allows decision makers much greater flexibility and they can see more easily the consequences of, for example, changing volumes of production or regulating sales demand through pricing.

3.2 Many UK companies still use absorption costing for cost accounting but this provides totally misleading decision making information. For example, suppose that a sales manager has an item of product which is proving difficult to sell. Its historical full cost is £80, made up of variable costs of £50 and fixed costs of £30. A customer offers £60 for it.

(a) If there is no other customer for the product, £60 would be better than nothing and the product should be sold to improve income and profit by this amount.

(b) If the company has spare production capacity which would otherwise not be used, it would be profitable to continue making more of the same product, if customers are willing to pay £60 for each extra unit made. This is because the additional costs are only £50 so that the profit would be increased marginally by £10 per unit produced.

(c) In absorption costing terms, the product makes a loss of £20, which would discourage the sales manager from accepting a price of £60 from the customer. This decision would be a bad one.

(i)   If the product is not sold for £60, it will presumably be scrapped eventually, so the choice is really between making a loss in absorption costing terms of £20, or a loss of £80 when the stock is written off, whenever this happens.

(ii)   If there is demand for some extra units at £60 each, the absorption costing loss would be £20 per unit, but at the end of the year there would be an additional contribution to overheads and profit of £10 per unit. In terms of absorption costing the under-absorbed overhead would be reduced by £30 (the fixed cost part of the product's full cost) for each extra unit made and sold.

3.3   Absorption costing information about unit profits is therefore irrelevant in short-run decisions in which fixed costs do not change (such as short-run tactical decisions seeking to make the best use of existing facilities). In such circumstances the decision rule is to choose the alternative which **maximises contribution**.

Activity based costing (ABC)

3.4   You will have learned about ABC in your studies for Paper 8 and you will return to study and evaluate it as a costing system in more depth later in this text. In the context of ABC's usefulness as a basis for management decisions, many of ABC's supporters claim that it can assist with decision making in a number of ways. It provides accurate and reliable cost information, establishes a long-run product cost and provides data which can be used to evaluate different possibilities of delivering business. It is therefore particularly suited for the following types of decision.

- Pricing
- Promoting or discontinuing products or parts of the business
- Developing and designing changed products, new products or new ways to do business

3.5   The traditional cost behaviour patterns of fixed cost and variable cost are felt by advocates of ABC to be unsuitable for longer-term decisions, when resources are not fixed and changes in the volume or mix of business can be expected to have an impact on the cost of all resources used, not just short-term variable costs.

3.6   Note, however, that an ABC cost is not a true cost, it is simply an average cost because some costs such as depreciation are still arbitrarily allocated to products. An ABC cost is therefore **not a relevant cost for all decisions**.

Chapter roundup

- This chapter began by distinguishing between **joint products** and **by-products**. Joint products are produced simultaneously, and each has a significant sales value compared with the others. A by-product is produced incidentally in manufacturing the main product and has a relatively low sales value in comparison to the main product.

- The problem with costing joint products is apportioning the **common costs** between the products. Common costs or **joint costs** are those incurred before the **split-off** or **separation point**.

- We looked at four different methods of apportioning common costs

    ° Physical measurement

    ° Relative sales value apportionment, using sales value at the split-off point

    ° Relative sales value apportionment, using sales value of the end product less further processing costs after the split-off point

    ° A weighted average method

- We learned that the product costs resulting from joint cost allocations are not useful for decision making purposes.

- When there is a choice between processing part-finished output further or selling it, the further processing is worthwhile **if the further processing cost is lower than the incremental revenue gained from further processing.**

- The usual method of accounting for a by-product is to **deduct its net realisable value from the cost of production of the main product.**

- The relationship between contribution and fixed costs in an organisation is described as **operational gearing**. If fixed costs are high relative to variable costs then the organisation is said to have high operational gearing.

- The higher the operational gearing, the greater will be the increase in profit for a given increase in sales volume.

- **Marginal costing** is generally accepted to be the most useful costing system for the purposes of short term tactical decision making.

- Proponents of **activity based costing** argue that it provides more useful information for longer-term decisions.

Quick quiz

1   Joint cost allocations are essential for the purposes of determining relative product profitability. True or false?

2   When deciding, purely on financial grounds, whether or not to process a joint product further, the information required is:

    (i)   the value of the common process costs;
    (ii)   the method of apportioning the common costs between the joint products;
    (iii)   the sales value of the joint product at the separation point;
    (iv)   the final sales value of the joint product;
    (v)   the further processing cost of the joint product.

    Which of the above statements are correct?

    A   (i), (ii) and (iii) only
    B   (iii), (iv) and (v) only
    C   (iv) and (v) only
    D   (i), (ii), (iv) and (v) only
    E   All of them

3   Which of the following companies has the highest operational gearing?

	Company A £	Company B £
Sales revenue	300,000	1,800,000
Variable cost	180,000	700,000
Contribution	120,000	1,100,000
Fixed costs	30,000	100,000
Profit	90,000	1,000,000

4   Company X has an operational gearing ratio of 3:1 and a profit of £100,000. What profit will be achieved if sales volume increases by 10% and cost and selling price structures remain unaltered?   130,000

Answers to quick quiz

1   False

2   B

3   Company A

4   £130,000

Now try the questions below from the Exam Question Bank

Number	Level	Marks	Time
Q3	Examination	25	45 mins
Q4	Examination	30	54 mins

BPP PUBLISHING

Chapter 3

QUANTITATIVE TECHNIQUES IN DECISION MAKING

Topic list	Syllabus Reference	Ability required
1 Risk and uncertainty in decision making	(i)	Discuss
2 Decisions involving probabilities	(i)	Apply and discuss
3 Decision trees	(i)	Apply and discuss
4 The value of information	(i)	Evaluate
5 The learning curve	(i)	Apply and discuss
6 Pareto analysis	(i)	Apply and interpret

Introduction

In this chapter we will be looking at a number of quantitative techniques that the management accountant can use when preparing information for management decisions.

Decision making involves making decisions now about what will happen in the future. Obviously, decisions can turn out badly, or actual results can prove to be very different from the estimates on which the original decision was based. Ideally the decision maker would know with certainty what the future consequences would be for each choice facing him. But the real world is not normally so helpful, and decisions must be made in the knowledge that their consequences, although perhaps probable, are rarely 100% certain.

Various methods of bringing **uncertainty and risk analysis** into the evaluation of decisions will be described in Sections 1 to 3 of this chapter. You may well think that some methods are more sensible or practical than others, but you should judge each method on its merits, and be able to apply and discuss it in an examination.

The uncertainty about the future outcome from taking a decision can sometimes be reduced by obtaining more information first about what is likely to happen. We can categorise information depending upon how reliable it is likely to be for predicting what will happen in the future and hence for helping managers to make better decisions. **Perfect information** is information that is guaranteed to predict the future with 100% accuracy. **Imperfect information** is information which, although it might be quite good and certainly better than having no information at all, could be wrong in its prediction of the future.

A decision has to be made whether the information (either perfect or imperfect) is worth the cost of obtaining it. A value therefore has to be put on the information and it is the value of information, both perfect and imperfect, that we will be looking at in Section 4 of this chapter.

In section 5 we will be moving on to study **learning curve theory**. You will have learned the basic principles of the theory in your studies for Paper 8 but we will be looking in greater depth at the derivation of the **learning index**.

The chapter will end with a section on **Pareto analysis**, or the 80/20 rule.

Learning outcomes covered in this chapter

- **Discuss** risk and uncertainty
- **Apply** and **discuss** decision trees
- **Evaluate** the value of information
- **Apply** and **discuss** the experience and learning curve
- **Prepare** and **interpret** reports using Pareto analysis

Syllabus content covered in this chapter

- Risk and uncertainty
- Decision trees
- Learning curve
- Pareto analysis

1   RISK AND UNCERTAINTY IN DECISION MAKING

What are risk and uncertainty?

KEY TERMS

Risk involves situations or events which may or may not occur, but whose probability of occurrence can be calculated statistically and the frequency of their occurrence predicted from past records. Thus insurance deals with risk.

Uncertain events are those whose outcome **cannot** be predicted with statistical confidence.

1.1   In everyday usage the terms risk and uncertainty are not clearly distinguished. If you are asked for a definition, do not make the **mistake of believing that the latter** is a more **extreme version of the former.** It is not a question of degree, it is a question of whether or **not sufficient information is available to allow the lack of certainty to be quantified.** As a rule, however, the terms are used interchangeably.

Risk preference

KEY TERMS

- A **risk seeker** is a decision maker who is interested in the best outcomes no matter how small the chance that they may occur.

- A decision maker is **risk neutral** if he is concerned with what will be the most likely outcome.

- A **risk averse** decision maker acts on the assumption that the worst outcome might occur.

1.2   This has clear implications for managers and organisations. A **risk seeking manager** working for an **organisation** that is characteristically **risk averse** is likely to make decisions that are **not congruent with the goals of the organisation**. There may be a role for the management accountant here, who could be instructed to present decision-making information in such a way as to ensure that the manager considers *all* the possibilities, including the worst.

Case example

What is an acceptable amount of risk will of course vary from organisation to organisation. For large public companies it is largely a question of what is acceptable to the shareholders. A 'safe' investment will attract investors who are to some extent risk averse, and the company will thus be obliged to follow relatively 'safe' policies. A company that is recognised as being an innovator or a 'growth' stock in a relatively new market, like *Netscape* or *Yahoo!*, will attract investors who are looking for high performance and are prepared to accept some risk in return. Such companies will be expected to make 'bolder' (more risky) decisions.

1.3   The risk of an individual strategy should also be considered in the context of the overall 'portfolio' of investment strategies adopted by the company.

     (a)   If a **strategy is risky,** but its outcome is **not related to the outcome of other strategies,** then adopting that strategy will help the company to **spread its risks**.

     (b)   If a **strategy is risky,** but is **inversely related** to other adopted strategies, so that if strategy A does well, other adopted strategies will do badly and vice versa, then adopting strategy A would actually **reduce the overall risk of the company's investment portfolio.**

Allowing for uncertainty

Conservatism

1.4   This approach simply involves **estimating outcomes in a conservative manner in order to provide a built-in safety factor.** However, the method **fails to consider explicitly a range** of outcomes and, by concentrating only on conservative figures, may also fail to consider **the expected or most likely outcomes.**

1.5   Conservatism is **associated with risk aversion** and prudence (in the general sense of the word). In spite of its shortcomings it is probably the most widely used method in practice.

Worst possible, most likely and best possible outcomes

1.6   A more scientific version of conservatism is to measure the most likely outcome (or profit) from a decision, the worst possible outcome, and the best that can happen. This will show the **full range of possible outcomes** from a decision, and might help managers to reject certain alternatives because the worst possible outcome might involve an unacceptable amount of loss.

1.7   EXAMPLE: WORST/BEST POSSIBLE OUTCOMES

Omelette Ltd is trying to set the sales price for one of its products. Three prices are under consideration, and expected sales volumes and costs are as follows.

	£4.00	£4.30	£4.40
Price per unit	£4.00	£4.30	£4.40
Expected sales volume (units)			
Best possible	16,000	14,000	12,500
Most likely	14,000	12,500	12,000
Worst possible	10,000	8,000	6,000

Fixed costs are £20,000 and variable costs of sales are £2 per unit.

Required

Determine which price should be chosen.

1.8   SOLUTION

	£4	£4.30	£4.40
Price per unit	£4	£4.30	£4.40
Contribution per unit	£2	£2.30	£2.40
Total contribution:	£	£	£
Best possible	32,000	32,200	30,000
Most likely	28,000	28,750	28,800
Worst possible	20,000	18,400	14,400

The **highest contribution**, based on **most likely sales volume**, would be at a price of **£4.40** but arguably a price of **£4.30 would be much better** than £4.40, since the most likely profit is almost as good, the worst possible profit is not as bad, and the best possible profit is better.

However, **only a price of £4** guarantees that the company would **not make a loss,** even if the worst possible outcome occurs. (Fixed costs of £20,000 would just be covered.) A **risk averse management** might therefore prefer a price of £4 to either of the other two prices.

Sensitivity analysis

> **KEY TERM**
>
> **Sensitivity analysis** is 'A modelling and risk assessment procedure in which changes are made to significant variables in order to determine the effect of these changes on the planned outcome. Particular attention is thereafter paid to variables identified as being of special significance.'   (CIMA *Official Terminology*)

1.9   Sensitivity analysis can provide a basis for analysing the risk in short-term decision opportunities.

1.10   Two useful approaches to sensitivity analysis are:

   (a)   to **estimate by how much costs and revenues would need to differ from their estimated values before the decision would change;**

   (b)   to **estimate whether a decision would change if estimated costs were x% higher than estimated, or estimated revenues y% lower than estimated.**

1.11   The essence of the approach therefore, is to **carry out the calculations with one set of values for the variables** and then **substitute other possible values** for the variables to see **how this affects the overall outcome.**

1.12 EXAMPLE: SENSITIVITY ANALYSIS

Sensivite Ltd has estimated the following sales and profits for a new product which it may launch on to the market.

		£	£
Sales	(2,000 units)		4,000
Variable costs:	materials	2,000	
	labour	1,000	
			3,000
Contribution			1,000
Less incremental fixed costs			800
Profit			200

Required

Analyse the sensitivity of the project.

1.13 SOLUTION

The **margin of safety**, given a breakeven point of 1,600 units, is $(400/2,000) \times 100\% = 20\%$.

Changes in variables which would result in a loss

- More than 25% increase in incremental **fixed costs**
- More than 10% increase in unit cost of **materials**
- More than 20% increase in **unit labour costs**
- More than 5% drop in **unit selling price**

Management would now be able to judge more clearly whether the product is likely to be profitable. The **items to which profitability is most sensitive** in this example are the **selling price** (5%) and **material costs** (10%). Sensitivity analysis can help to **concentrate management attention on the most important forecasts**.

2   DECISIONS INVOLVING PROBABILITIES   Pilot paper

2.1   Although the outcome of a decision may not be certain, there is some likelihood that probabilities could be assigned to the various possible outcomes from an analysis of previous experience.

Expected values

2.2   Where probabilities are assigned to different outcomes, it is common to evaluate the worth of a decision as the expected value, or weighted average, of these outcomes.

> **KEY TERM**
>
> **Expected value** is 'The financial forecast of the outcome of a course of action multiplied by the probability of achieving that outcome. The probability is expressed as a value ranging from 0 to 1.'   (CIMA *Official Terminology*)

If a decision maker is faced with a number of alternative decisions, each with a range of possible outcomes, the **optimum decision** will therefore be the **one which gives the highest expected value**.

KEY TERM

The choice of the option with the highest EV is known as **Bayes' strategy.**

2.3 EXAMPLE: BAYES' STRATEGY

Suppose a manager has to choose between mutually exclusive options A and B, and the probable outcomes of each option are as follows.

Option A		Option B	
Probability	*Profit* £	*Probability*	*Profit* £
0.8	5,000	0.1	(2,000)
0.2	6,000	0.2	5,000
		0.6	7,000
		0.1	8,000

The expected value (EV) of profit of each option would be measured as follows

Probability		*Option A Profit* £		*EV of Profit* £	*Probability*		*Option B Profit* £		*EV of Profit* £
0.8	×	5,000	=	4,000	0.1	×	(2,000)	=	(200)
0.2	×	6,000	=	1,200	0.2	×	5,000	=	1,000
		EV	=	5,200	0.6	×	7,000	=	4,200
					0.1	×	8,000	=	800
							EV	=	5,800

FORMULA TO LEARN

The **expected value** of an opportunity is equal to the sum of the probabilities of an outcome occurring multiplied by the return expected if it does occur:

$$EV = \sum px$$

where p is the probability of an outcome occurring and x is the value (profit or cost) of that outcome.

In this example, since it offers a higher EV of expected profit, option B would be selected in preference to A, unless further risk analysis is carried out.

Question 1

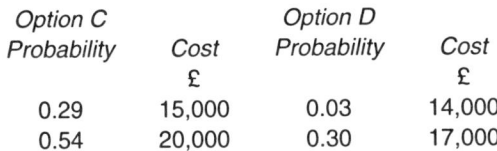

A manager has to choose between mutually exclusive options C and D and the probable outcomes of each option are as follows.

Option C		Option D	
Probability	Cost £	Probability	Cost £
0.29	15,000	0.03	14,000
0.54	20,000	0.30	17,000
0.17	30,000	0.35	21,000
		0.32	24,000

Both options will produce an income of £30,000.

Required

Determine which should be chosen.

Answer

Option C. Do the workings yourself in the way illustrated above. Note that the probabilities are for *costs* not profits.

Limitations of expected values

2.4 The preference for B over A on the basis of expected value is marred by the fact that A's **worst possible outcome is a profit of £5,000**, whereas **B might incur a loss of £2,000** (although there is a 70% chance that profits would be £7,000 or more, which would be more than the best profits from option A).

Since the **decision must be made once only** between A and B, the expected value of profit (which is merely a weighted average of all possible outcomes) has severe limitations as a decision rule by which to judge preference.

2.5 Expected values are more **valuable** as a guide to decision making where they refer to **outcomes which will occur many times over**, for example:

- The probability that so many customers per day will buy a tin of peaches
- The probability that a call centre will receive so many phone calls per hour

Exam focus point

The pilot paper contained a relatively straightforward multiple choice question which required the calculation of an expected value.

EVs and elementary risk analysis

2.6 Where some analysis of risk is required when probabilities have been assigned to various outcomes, an elementary, but extremely useful, form of risk analysis is an extension to the worst possible/most likely/best possible technique we looked at earlier.

2.7 EXAMPLE: ELEMENTARY RISK ANALYSIS

Skiver Ltd has budgeted the following results for the coming year.

Sales Units	Probability	EV of Sales Units
30,000	0.3	9,000
40,000	0.4	16,000
50,000	0.3	15,000
		40,000

The budgeted sales price is £10 per unit, and the expected cost of materials is as follows.

Cost per unit of output £	Probability	EV £
4	0.2	0.8
6	0.6	3.6
8	0.2	1.6
		6.0

Materials are the only variable cost. All other costs are fixed and are budgeted at £100,000.

The **expected value of profit** is £60,000.

	£
Sales (EV 40,000 units) at £10 each	400,000
Variable costs (40,000 × £6)	240,000
Contribution	160,000
Fixed costs	100,000
Profit	60,000

The worst possible outcome would be sales of 30,000 units and material costs of £8 per unit.

If sales are only 30,000 units, the total contribution would be:

(a) £180,000 at a material cost of £4(contribution £6 per unit);
(b) £120,000 at a material cost of £6 (contribution £4 per unit);
(c) £60,000 at a material cost of £8 (contribution £2 per unit).

Since there is a 20% chance that materials will cost £8, there is a **20% chance of making a loss,** given fixed costs of £100,000. This applies only if **sales are 30,000 units**.

If materials cost £8 per unit, there would be a **loss** at sales volumes of both 30,000 and 40,000 units. The **chance** that one or other of these events will occur is **14%**, as calculated below.

Sales	*Probability*	*Material cost*	*Probability*	*Joint probabilities*
30,000 units	0.3	£8	0.2	0.06
40,000 units	0.4	£8	0.2	0.08
		Combined probabilities		0.14

However there is also a chance that sales will be 50,000 units and material will cost £4, so that contribution would be £300,000 in total and profits £200,000. This is the **best possible outcome** and it has a $0.3 \times 0.2 = 0.06$ or 6% probability of occurring.

EVs and more complex risk analysis

2.8 As we have seen, EVs can be used to compare two or more mutually exclusive alternatives: the alternative with the most favourable EV of profit or cost would normally be preferred. However, **alternatives can also be compared** by looking at the **spread of possible outcomes**, and the **probabilities** that they will occur. The technique of drawing up **cumulative probability tables** might be helpful, as the following example shows.

2.9 EXAMPLE: MUTUALLY EXCLUSIVE OPTIONS AND CUMULATIVE PROBABILITY

QRS Ltd is reviewing the price that it charges for a major product line. Over the past three years the product has had sales averaging 48,000 units per year at a standard selling price of £5.25. Costs have been rising steadily over the past year and the company is considering raising this price to £5.75 or £6.25. The sales manager has produced the following schedule to assist with the decision.

Price	£5.75	£6.25
Estimates of demand		
Pessimistic estimate (probability 0.25)	35,000	10,000
Most likely estimate (probability 0.60)	40,000	20,000
Optimistic estimate (probability 0.15)	50,000	40,000

Currently the unit cost is estimated at £5.00, analysed as follows.

BPP PUBLISHING

	£
Direct material	2.50
Direct labour	1.00
Variable overhead	1.00
Fixed overhead	0.50
	5.00

The cost accountant considers that the most likely value for unit variable cost over the next year is £4.90 (probability 0.75) but that it could be as high as £5.20 (probability 0.15) and it might even be as low as £4.75 (probability 0.10). Total fixed costs are currently £24,000 p.a. but it is estimated that the corresponding total for the ensuing year will be £25,000 with a probability of 0.2, £27,000 with a probability of 0.6, £30,000 with a probability of 0.2. (Demand quantities, unit costs and fixed costs can be assumed to be statistically independent.)

Required

Analyse the foregoing information in a way which you consider will assist management with the problem, give your views on the situation and advise on the new selling price. Calculate the expected level of profit that would follow from the selling price that you recommend.

2.10 DISCUSSION AND SOLUTION

In this example, there are two mutually exclusive options, a price of £5.75 and a price of £6.25. Sales demand is uncertain, but would vary with price. Unit contribution and total contribution depend on sales price and sales volume, but total fixed costs are common to both options. Clearly, it makes sense to begin looking at EVs of contribution and then to think about fixed costs and profits later.

(a) A table of probabilities can be set out for each alternative, and an EV calculated, as follows.

Price £5.75

Sales Demand Units	Probability (a)	Variable cost per unit £	Probability (b)	Unit cont'n £	Total cont'n £'000	Joint proba-bility* (a × b)	EV of cont'n £'000
35,000	0.25	5.20	0.15	0.55	19.25	0.0375	0.722
		4.90	0.75	0.85	29.75	0.1875	5.578
		4.75	0.10	1.00	35.00	0.0250	0.875
40,000	0.60	5.20	0.15	0.55	22.00	0.0900	1.980
		4.90	0.75	0.85	34.00	0.4500	15.300
		4.75	0.10	1.00	40.00	0.0600	2.400
50,000	0.15	5.20	0.15	0.55	27.50	0.0225	0.619
		4.90	0.75	0.85	42.50	0.1125	4.781
		4.75	0.10	1.00	50.00	0.0150	0.750
		EV of Contribution					33.005

The EV of contribution at a price of £5.75 is £33,005.

* Remember to check that the joint probabilities sum to 1.

Alternative approach

An alternative method of calculating the EV of contribution is as follows.

EV of contribution   = EV of sales revenue – EV of variable costs

EV of sales revenue = EV of sales units × selling price
= ((35,000 × 0.25) + (40,000 × 0.60) + (50,000 × 0.15)) × £5.75
= 40,250 × £5.75 = £231,437.50

EV of variable costs = EV of sales units × EV of unit variable costs
= 40,250 × ((£5.20 × 0.15) + (£4.90 × 0.75) + (£4.75 × 0.10)) =
40,250 × £4.93 = £198,432.50

∴ EV of contribution = £(231,437.50 – 198,432.50) = £33,005

This method is quicker and simpler, but an extended table of probabilities will help the risk analysis when the two alternative selling prices are compared.

Price £6.25

Sales demand	Probability	Variable cost per unit	Probability	Unit cont'n	Total cont'n	Joint probability	EV of cont'n
Units	(a)	£	(b)	£	£000	(a × b)	£000
10,000	0.25	5.20	0.15	1.05	10.50	0.0375	0.394
		4.90	0.75	1.35	13.50	0.1875	2.531
		4.75	0.10	1.50	15.00	0.0250	0.375
20,000	0.60	5.20	0.15	1.05	21.00	0.0900	1.890
		4.90	0.75	1.35	27.00	0.4500	12.150
		4.75	0.10	1.50	30.00	0.0600	1.800
40,000	0.15	5.20	0.15	1.05	42.00	0.0225	0.945
		4.90	0.75	1.35	54.00	0.1125	6.075
		4.75	0.10	1.50	60.00	0.0150	0.900
			EV of Contribution				27.060

The EV of contribution at a price of £6.25 is £27,060.

Question 2

Calculate the EV of contribution at a selling price of £6.25 using the alternative approach set out above.

(b) The EV of **fixed costs** is £27,200.

Fixed costs	Probability	EV
£		£
25,000	0.2	5,000
27,000	0.6	16,200
30,000	0.2	6,000
		27,200

(c) **Conclusion**

On the basis of EVs alone, a price of £5.75 is preferable to a price of £6.25, since it offers an EV of contribution of £33,005 and so an EV of profit of £5,805; whereas a price of £6.25 offers an EV of contribution of only £27,060 and so an EV of loss of £140.

Additional information

A comparison of cumulative probabilities would add to the information for risk analysis. The cumulative probabilities can be used to compare the **likelihood of earning a total contribution of a certain size with each selling price**.

The table below shows that no matter whether fixed costs are £25,000, £27,000 or £30,000, the **probability of at least breaking even** is much higher with a price of £5.75 than with a price of £6.25. The only reason for favouring a price of £6.25 is that there is a better **probability of earning bigger profits** (a contribution of £50,000 or more), and so although a

risk-averse decision maker would choose a price of £5.75, a risk-seeking decision maker might gamble on a price of £6.25.

Probability of total contri- bution of at least £		*Price £5.75 Probability*		*Price £6.25 Probability*
15,000		1.0000	(1 – 0.0375 – 0.1875)	0.7750
20,000	(1 – 0.0375)	0.9625	(0.775 – 0.025)	0.7500
25,000	(0.9625 – 0.09)	0.8725	etc	0.6600
27,000		0.8725		0.6600
30,000	(0.8725 – 0.1875 – 0.0225)	0.6625		0.2100
35,000	etc	0.2125		0.1500
40,000		0.1875		0.1500
50,000		0.0150		0.1275
60,000		0.0000		0.0150

The disadvantages of point estimate probabilities

2.11   A **point estimate probability** means an estimate of the **probability of particular outcomes occurring**. In the previous example, there were point estimate probabilities for **variable costs** (£5.20 or £4.90 or £4.75) but in **reality**, the **actual** variable cost per unit **might be any amount**, from below £4.75 to above £5.20. Similarly, point estimate probabilities were given for period fixed costs (£25,000 or £27,000 or £30,000) but in reality, actual fixed costs might be any amount between about £25,000 and £30,000.

This is a disadvantage of using point estimate probabilities: they can be **unrealistic**, and can only be an **approximation** of the risk and uncertainty in estimates of costs or sales demand.

The advantages of point estimate probabilities

2.12   In spite of their possible disadvantages, point estimate probabilities can be very helpful for a decision maker.

(a)   They provide some estimate of risk, which is probably **better than nothing**.

(b)   **If there are enough point estimates** they are likely to be a **reasonably good approximation of** a continuous probability distribution.

(c)   Alternatively, it can be **assumed** that point estimate probabilities **represent a range** of values, so that if we had the probabilities for variable cost per unit, say, of £5.20, £4.90, and £4.75 we could assume that those actually represent probabilities for the ranges, say, £5.05 to £5.30, and £4.82 to £5.04 and £4.70 to £4.81.

3   DECISION TREES

KEY TERM

A **decision tree** is 'A pictorial method of showing a sequence of interrelated decisions and their expected outcomes. Decision trees can incorporate both the probabilities of, and values of, expected outcomes, and are used in decision-making.'

(CIMA *Official Terminology*)

3.1   A probability problem such as 'what is the probability of throwing a six with one throw of a die?' is fairly straightforward and can be solved using the basic principles of probability.

       More complex probability questions, although solvable using the basic principles, require a clear logical approach to ensure that all possible choices and outcomes of a decision are taken into consideration. **Decision trees** are a useful means of interpreting such probability problems.

3.2   Exactly how does the use of a decision tree permit a clear and logical approach?

       •   All the possible **choices** that can be made are shown as **branches** on the tree.
       •   All the possible **outcomes** of each choice are shown as **subsidiary branches** on the tree.

Constructing a decision tree

3.3   There are two stages in preparing a decision tree.

       •   Drawing the tree itself to show all the choices and outcomes
       •   Putting in the numbers (the probabilities, outcome values and EVs)

3.4   Every **decision tree starts** from a **decision point** with the **decision options** that are currently being considered.

       (a)   It helps to identify the **decision point**, and any subsequent decision points in the tree, with a symbol. Here, we shall use a **square shape**.

       (b)   There should be a **line**, or **branch**, for each **option** or **alternative**.

3.5   **It is conventional to draw decision trees from left to right**, and so a decision tree will start as follows.

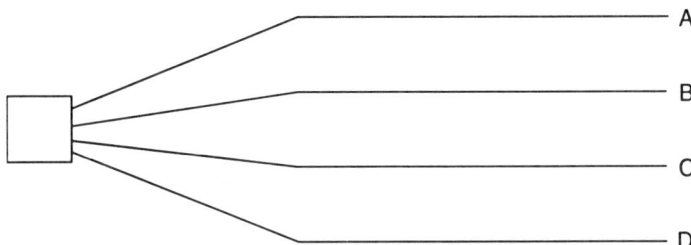

       The **square** is the **decision point**, and A, B, C and D represent **four alternatives** from which a choice must be made (such as buy a new machine with cash, hire a machine, continue to use existing machine, raise a loan to buy a machine).

3.6   •   **If the outcome from any choice is certain, the branch of the decision tree for that alternative is complete.**

       •   If the outcome of a particular choice is uncertain, the various possible outcomes must be shown.

3.7   We show the various possible outcomes on a decision tree by inserting an **outcome point** on the **branch** of the tree. Each possible outcome is then shown as a **subsidiary branch**, coming out from the outcome point. The probability of each outcome occurring should be written on to the branch of the tree which represents that outcome.

3.8   To distinguish decision points from outcome points, **a circle will be used as the symbol for an outcome point.**

In the example above, there are two choices facing the decision-maker, A and B. The outcome if A is chosen is known with certainty, but if B is chosen, there are two possible outcomes, high sales (0.6 probability) or low sales (0.4 probability).

3.9   **When several outcomes are possible, it is usually simpler to show two or more stages of outcome points on the decision tree.**

3.10 EXAMPLE: SEVERAL POSSIBLE OUTCOMES

A company can choose to launch a new product XYZ or not. If the product is launched, expected sales and expected unit costs might be as follows.

Sales		Unit costs	
Units	Probability	£	Probability
10,000	0.8	6	0.7
15,000	0.2	8	0.3

(a)   The decision tree could be drawn as follows.

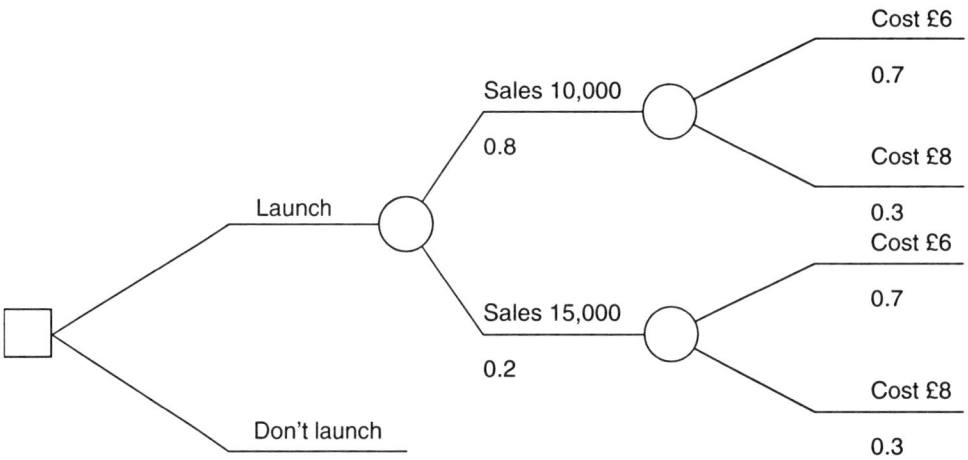

(b) The layout shown above will usually be easier to use than the alternative way of drawing the tree, which is as follows.

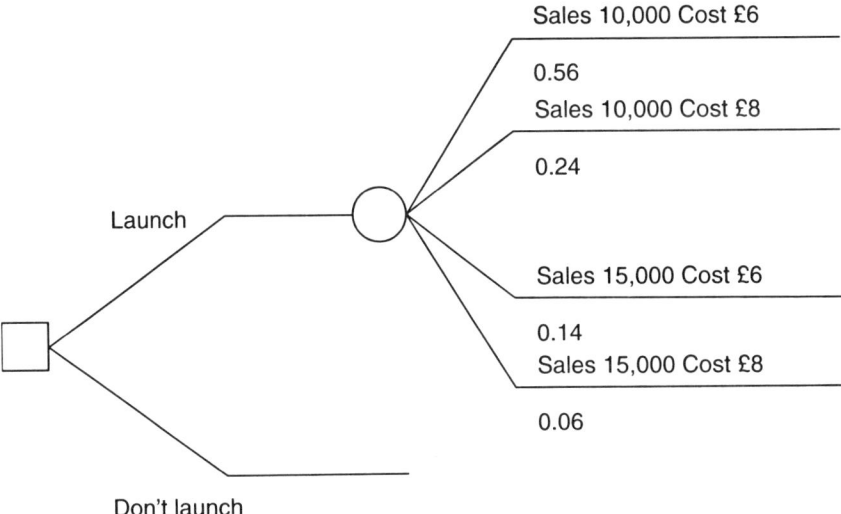

3.11 Sometimes, a **decision taken now** will lead to **other decisions to be taken in the future**. When this situation arises, the decision tree can be drawn as a **two-stage tree**, as follows.

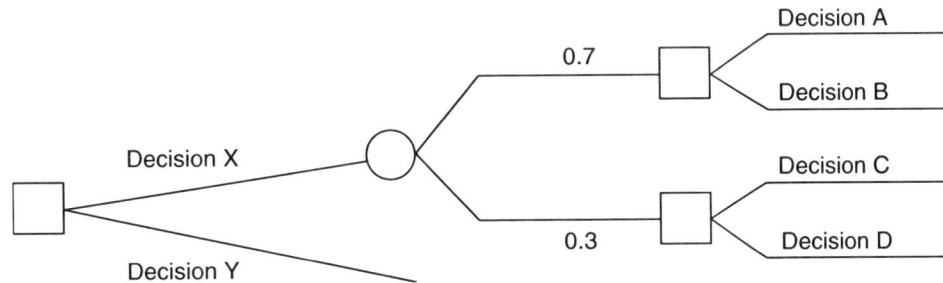

In this tree, either a choice between A and B or else a choice between C and D will be made, depending on the outcome which occurs after choosing X.

3.12 The decision tree should be in **chronological order** from **left to right**. When there are two-stage decision trees, the first decision in time should be drawn on the left.

3.13 EXAMPLE: A DECISION TREE

Beethoven Ltd has a new wonder product, the vylin, of which it expects great things. At the moment the company has two courses of action open to it, to test market the product or abandon it.

If the company test markets it, the cost will be £100,000 and the market response could be positive or negative with probabilities of 0.60 and 0.40.

If the response is positive the company could either abandon the product or market it full scale.

If it markets the vylin full scale, the outcome might be low, medium or high demand, and the respective net gains/(losses) would be (200), 200 or 1,000 in units of £1,000 (the result could range from a net loss of £200,000 to a gain of £1,000,000). These outcomes have probabilities of 0.20, 0.50 and 0.30 respectively.

If the result of the test marketing is negative and the company goes ahead and markets the product, estimated losses would be £600,000.

If, at any point, the company abandons the product, there would be a net gain of £50,000 from the sale of scrap. All the financial values have been discounted to the present.

(a) Draw a decision tree.
(b) Include figures for cost, loss or profit on the appropriate branches of the tree.

3.14 SOLUTION

The starting point for the tree is to **establish what decision has to be made now**. What are the options?

(a) To test market
(b) To abandon

The outcome of the 'abandon' option is known with certainty. There are two possible outcomes of the option to test market, positive response and negative response.

Depending on the outcome of the test marketing, another decision will then be made, to abandon the product or to go ahead.

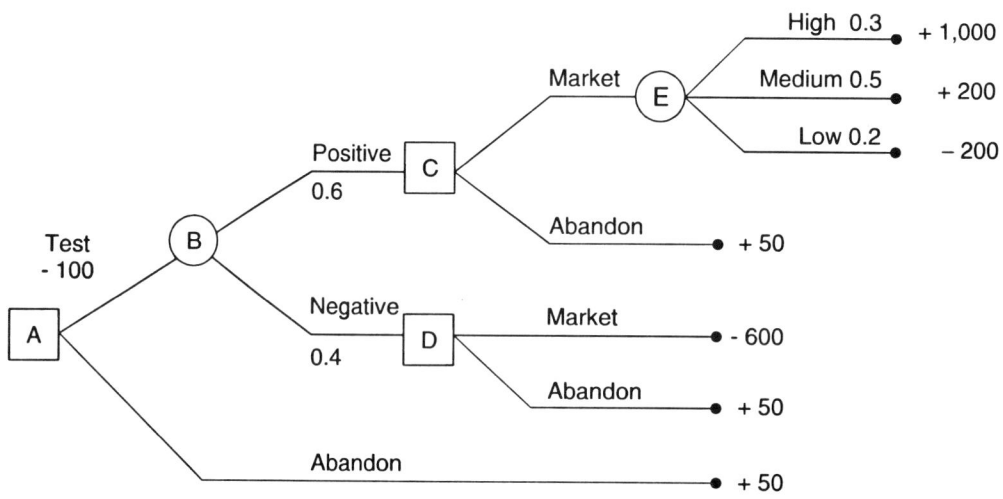

Exam focus point

In an examination, remember to draw decision trees (and *all* diagrams) neatly, using a sharp pencil and ruler. Remember also to label decision points and branches as clearly as possible.

Evaluating the decision with a decision tree

3.15 The EV of each decision option can be evaluated, using the decision tree to help with keeping the logic properly sorted out. The basic rules are as follows.

(a) We start on the **right hand side** of the tree and **work back** towards the left hand side and the current decision under consideration. This is sometimes known as the **'rollback' technique**.

(b) Working from **right to left**, we calculate the **EV of revenue, cost, contribution or profit** at each outcome point on the tree.

3.16 In the above example, the right-hand-most outcome point is point E, and the EV is as follows.

	Profit	*Probability*	
	x	*p*	*px*
	£'000		£'000
High	1,000	0.3	300
Medium	200	0.5	100
Low	(200)	0.2	(40)
		EV	360

This is the EV of the decision to market the product if the test shows positive response. It may help you to write the EV on the decision tree itself, at the appropriate outcome point (point E).

3.17 (a) At decision point C, the choice is as follows.

      (i)   Market, EV = + 360 (the EV at point E)
      (ii)   Abandon, value = + 50

     The choice would be to market the product, and so the EV at decision point C is +360.

  (b) At decision point D, the choice is as follows.

      (i)   Market, value = - 600
      (ii)   Abandon, value = +50

     The choice would be to abandon, and so the EV at decision point D is +50.

The second stage decisions have therefore been made. If the original decision is to test market, the company will market the product if the test shows positive customer response, and will abandon the product if the test results are negative.

3.18 The evaluation of the decision tree is completed as follows.

  (a) Calculate the EV at outcome point B.

$$0.6 \times 360 \quad \text{(EV at C)}$$
$$+ \quad 0.4 \times 50 \quad \text{(EV at D)}$$
$$= \quad 216 + 20 = 236.$$

  (b) Compare the options at point A, which are as follows.

      (i)   Test: EV = EV at B minus test marketing cost = 236 - 100 = 136
      (ii)   Abandon: Value = 50

The choice would be to test market the product, because it has a **higher EV of profit**.

Question 3

Interpret the following diagram in words and figures.

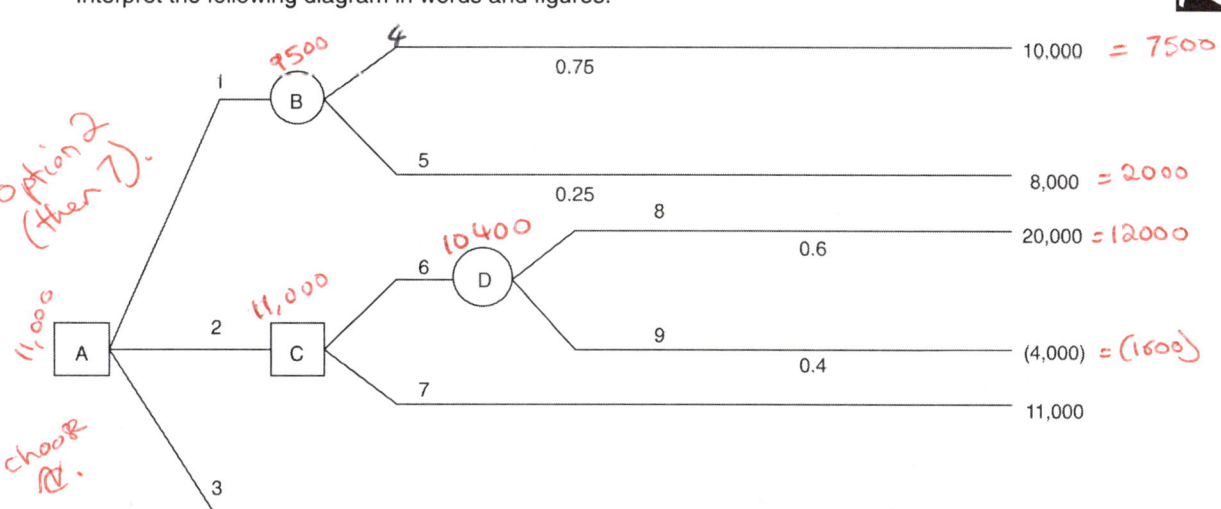

Answer

The square is a point at which a decision has to be made - here a choice between options 1, 2 and 3. A circle represents an event whose outcome is uncertain. Doubtful outcomes (4, 5, 8, 9) have

probabilities assigned to them. To reach the decisions the various outcomes must be evaluated using expected values.

Point B: $(0.75 \times 10,000) + (0.25 \times 8,000) = 9,500$

Point D: $(0.6 \times 20,000) + (0.4 \times (4,000)) = 10,400$

Point C: Choice between 10,400 and 11,000

Point A: Choice between B (9,500), C (10,400 or 11,000) and choice 3 (9,000).

If we are trying to maximise the figure, option 2 and then option 7 are chosen to give 11,000.

If we are trying to minimise it, choice 3 is the one to go for.

3.19 Evaluating decisions by using **decision trees has a number of limitations**.

- The time value of money may not be taken into account.

- Decision trees are not very suitable for use in complex situations.

- The outcome with the highest EV may have the greatest risks attached to it. Managers may be reluctant to take risks which may lead to losses.

- The probabilities associated with different branches of the 'tree' are likely to be estimates, and possibly unreliable or inaccurate.

Exam focus point

A typical examination question on decision trees might require candidates to do the following.

- Draw a decision tree for a problem given in the examination scenario
- Analyse the tree
- Comment on any limitations on evaluating decisions using decision trees

Alternatively, a decision tree may be provided and candidates could be required to explain (with calculations and logic) which decisions should be taken at various points and why.

Question 4

A software company has just won a contract worth £80,000 if it delivers a successful product on time, but only £40,000 if it is late. It faces the problem now of whether to produce the work in-house or to sub-contract it. To sub-contract the work would cost £50,000, but the local sub-contractor is so fast and reliable as to make it certain that successful software is produced on time.

If the work is produced in-house the cost would be only £20,000 but, based on past experience, would have only a 90% chance of being successful. In the event of the software *not* being successful, there would be insufficient time to rewrite the whole package internally, but there would still be the options of either a 'late rejection' of the contract (at a further cost of £10,000) or of 'late sub-contracting' the work on the same terms as before. With this late start the local sub-contractor is estimated to have only a 50/50 chance of producing the work on time or of producing it late. In this case the sub-contractor still has to be paid £50,000, regardless of whether he meets the deadline or not.

Required

(a) Draw a decision tree for the software company, using squares for decision points and circles for outcome (chance) points, including all relevant data on the diagram.

(b) Calculate expected values as appropriate and recommend a course of action to the software company with reasons.

Answer

(a) All values in £'000

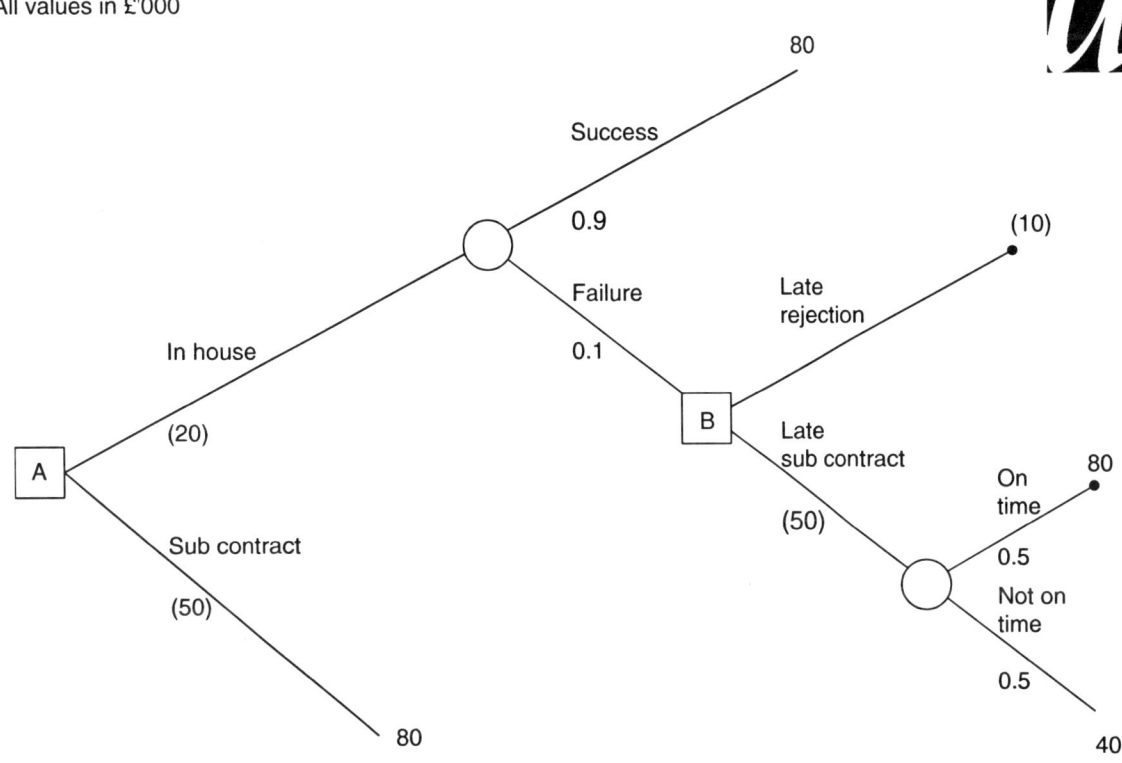

(b) *At decision point B*

EV of late rejection = −10
EV of late sub-contract = (80 × 0.5) + (40 × 0.5) − 50 = 10
The optimum strategy at B is therefore to subcontract with EV = 10.

At decision point A

EV of sub-contract = 80 − 50 = 30
EV of in-house = (80 × 0.9) + (10* × 0.1) − 20 = 53
The optimum strategy at A is therefore to produce in-house with EV = 53.

*This is the optimum EV at decision point B.

Conclusions

The decisions which will maximise expected profits are to attempt initially to produce in-house and if this fails to sub-contract. The expected profit is £53,000.

Assuming that the probabilities have been correctly estimated, the company has a 90% chance of making a profit of £60,000, a 5% chance of making £10,000 and a 5% chance of making a £30,000 loss. If the company is not willing to risk making a loss, the initial option of subcontracting should be taken since this offers a guaranteed profit of £30,000.

Sensitivity analysis and decision trees

3.20 Look again at Question 4. By how much can the probability of success fall before the optimal EV decision changes?

3.21 Suppose the probability of success = p (and so the probability of failure = 1 − p). At decision **point A** we want to find the point where **EV (sub-contract) = EV (in-house)**.

$$30 = (80 \times p) + (10 \times (1 - p)) - 20$$
$$30 = 80p + 10 - 10p - 20$$
$$40 = 70p$$

p   =   0.57

3.22 Since the probability of success can drop to 57% from 90% before we change our decision, we would probably consider the decision insensitive to this factor.

4   THE VALUE OF INFORMATION

> **KEY TERM**
>
> **Perfect information** removes all doubt and uncertainty from a decision, and enables managers to make decisions with complete confidence that they have selected the optimum course of action.

The value of perfect information

4.1   **Estimating a value of perfect information, based on expected values (EVs)**

Step 1.   If we **do not have perfect information** and we must choose between two or more decision options, we would **select** the decision option which offers the **highest EV** of profit. This option will not be the best decision under all circumstances. There will be some probability that what was really the best option will not have been selected, given the way actual events turn out.

Step 2.   With **perfect information**, the **best decision option will always be selected**. Just what the profits from the decision will be must depend on the future circumstances which are predicted by the information; nevertheless, the EV of profit with perfect information should be higher than the EV of profit without the information.

Step 3.   The **value of perfect information** is **the difference between these two EVs**.

4.2   EXAMPLE: THE VALUE OF PERFECT INFORMATION

The management of Ivor Ore Ltd must choose whether to go ahead with either of two mutually exclusive projects, A and B. The expected profits are as follows.

	Profit if there is strong demand	*Profit/(loss) if there is weak demand*
Option A	£4,000	£(1,000)
Option B	£1,500	£500
Probability of demand	0.3	0.7

Required

(a)   Ascertain what the decision would be, based on expected values, if no information about demand were available.

(b)   Calculate the value of perfect information about demand.

4.3   SOLUTION

Step 1.   If there were **no information** to help with the decision, the project with the higher EV of profit would be selected.

Probability	Project A		Project B	
	Profit	*EV*	*Profit*	*EV*
	£	£	£	£
0.3	4,000	1,200	1,500	450
0.7	(1,000)	(700)	500	350
		500		800

Project B would be selected.

This is clearly the better option if demand turns out to be weak. However, if demand were to turn out to be strong, project A would be more profitable. There is a 30% chance that this could happen.

Step 2. **Perfect information** will indicate for certain whether demand will be weak or strong. If demand is forecast 'weak' project B would be selected. If demand is forecast as 'strong', project A would be selected, and perfect information would improve the profit from £1,500, which would have been earned by selecting B, to £4,000.

Forecast demand	*Probability*	*Project chosen*	*Profit*	*EV of profit*
			£	£
Weak	0.7	B	500	350
Strong	0.3	A	4,000	1,200
EV of profit with perfect information				1,550

Step 3.

	£
EV of profit without perfect information (that is, if project B is always chosen)	800
EV of profit with perfect information	1,550
Value of perfect information	750

Provided that the information does not cost more than £750 to collect, it would be worth having.

Question 5

Watt Lovell Ltd must decide at what level to market a new product, the urk. The urk can be sold nationally, within a single sales region (where demand is likely to be relatively strong) or within a single area. The decision is complicated by uncertainty about the general strength of consumer demand for the product, and the following conditional profit table has been constructed.

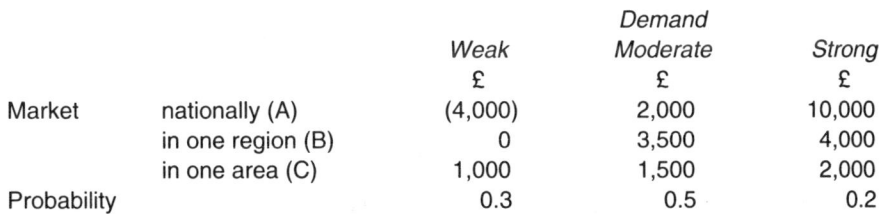

		Demand		
		Weak	*Moderate*	*Strong*
		£	£	£
Market	nationally (A)	(4,000)	2,000	10,000
	in one region (B)	0	3,500	4,000
	in one area (C)	1,000	1,500	2,000
Probability		0.3	0.5	0.2

Required

(a) Ascertain what the decision should be, based on EVs of profit.
(b) Calculate the value of perfect information about the state of demand.

Answer

(a) Without perfect information, the option with the highest EV of profit will be chosen.

	Option A (National)		Option B (Regional)		Option C (Area)	
Probability	Profit	EV	Profit	EV	Profit	EV
	£	£	£	£	£	£
0.3	(4,000)	(1,200)	0	0	1,000	300
0.5	2,000	1,000	3,500	1,750	1,500	750
0.2	10,000	2,000	4,000	800	2,000	400
		1,800		2,550		1,450

Marketing regionally (option B) has the highest EV of profit, and would be selected.

(b) However, if perfect information about the state of consumer demand were available, option A would be preferred if the forecast demand is strong and option C would be preferred if the forecast demand is weak.

Demand	Probability	Choice	Profit	EV of profit
			£	£
Weak	0.3	C	1,000	300
Moderate	0.5	B	3,500	1,750
Strong	0.2	A	10,000	2,000
EV of profit with perfect information				4,050
EV of profit, selecting option B				2,550
Value of perfect information				1,500

Perfect information and decision trees

4.4 When the option exists to obtain information, the decision can be shown, like any other decision, in the form of a decision tree, as follows. We will suppose, for illustration, that the cost of obtaining perfect information is £400.

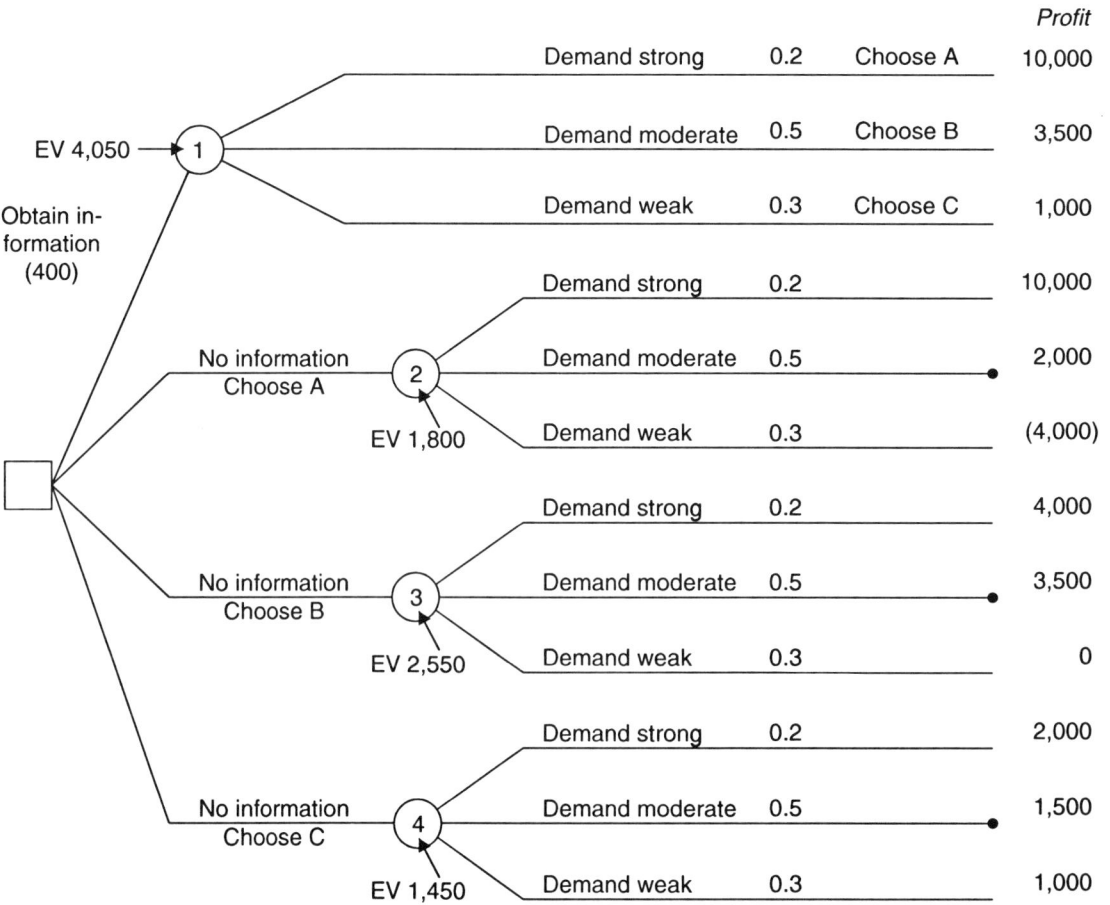

The decision would be to obtain perfect information, since the EV of profit is £4,050 – £400 = £3,650.

4.5 You should check carefully that you understand the logic of this decision tree and that you can identify how the EVs at outcome boxes 1, 2, 3 and 4 have been calculated.

The value of imperfect information

4.6 There is one serious drawback to the technique we have just looked at: in practice **useful information is never perfect** unless the person providing it is the sole source of the uncertainty. Market research findings or information from pilot tests and so on are likely to be reasonably accurate, but they can still be wrong: they provide imperfect information. It is possible, however, to arrive at an assessment of **how much it would be worth paying for such imperfect information, given that we have a rough indication of how right or wrong it is likely to be.**

4.7 The problem is related to what are known as posterior probabilities. Since this causes difficulties for students we shall spend a little more time on the basics.

Prior and posterior probabilities

4.8 Suppose we are considering the sex and hair colour of people in a given group or population consisting of 70% men and 30% women. We have established the probabilities of hair colourings as follows.

	Men	*Women*
Brown	0.60	0.35
Blonde	0.35	0.55
Red	0.05	0.10

This shows, for example, that 5% of men in such a sample have red hair. These probabilities of sex and hair colouring might be referred to as **prior probabilities**.

4.9 **Posterior probabilities consider the situation in reverse or retrospect,** so that we can ask the question: 'Given that a person taken at random from the population is brown-haired what is the probability that the person is male (or female)?' We will look at two ways of producing the answer to such a question.

Method 1: probability tree

4.10 Posterior probabilities can be established by drawing a probability tree as follows.

The probability of a person being a man, given that that person is brown haired is

$$\frac{\text{Probability of being a man and brown haired}}{\text{Probability of being a man or woman and brown haired}} = \frac{0.42}{0.42 + 0.105} = \frac{0.42}{0.525} = 0.80$$

BPP PUBLISHING

Method 2: table

4.11 The information can be presented in a table. Let's suppose that the population consists of 1,000 people.

	Male	Female	Total
Brown	420 (W3)	105 (W4)	525 (W5)
Blond	245	165	410
Red	35	30	65
	700 (W1)	300 (W2)	1,000

Workings

1   $1,000 \times 70\%$
2   $1,000 - 700$
3   $700 \times 60\%$ (the other two values in the column being calculated in a similar way)
4   $300 \times 35\%$ (the other two values in the column being calculated in a similar way)
5   $420 + 105$ (the other two values in the column being calculated in a similar way)

4.12 EXAMPLE: THE VALUE OF IMPERFECT INFORMATION

Suppose that the Small Oil Company (SOC) is trying to decide whether or not to drill on a particular site. The chief engineer has assessed the probability that there will be oil, based on past experience, as 20%, and the probability that there won't be oil as 80%.

It is possible for SOC to hire a firm of international consultants to carry out a complete survey of the site. SOC has used the firm many times before and has estimated that if there really is oil, there is a 95% chance that the report will be favourable, but if there is no oil, there is only a 10% chance that the report will indicate that there is oil.

Required

Determine whether drilling should occur.

4.13 SOLUTION

Read the information given carefully. We are given *three* sets of probabilities.

(a)   The probability that there will be oil (0.2) or there will not be (0.8). These outcomes are mutually exclusive.

(b)   The probability that, if there is oil, the report will say there is oil (0.95) or say there is no oil (0.05).

(c)   The probability that, if there is no oil, the report will say there *is* oil (0.1) or say there is no oil (0.9).

Both (b) and (c) describe conditional events, since the existence of oil or otherwise influences the chances of the survey report being correct.

SOC, meanwhile faces a number of choices which we can show as a decision tree.

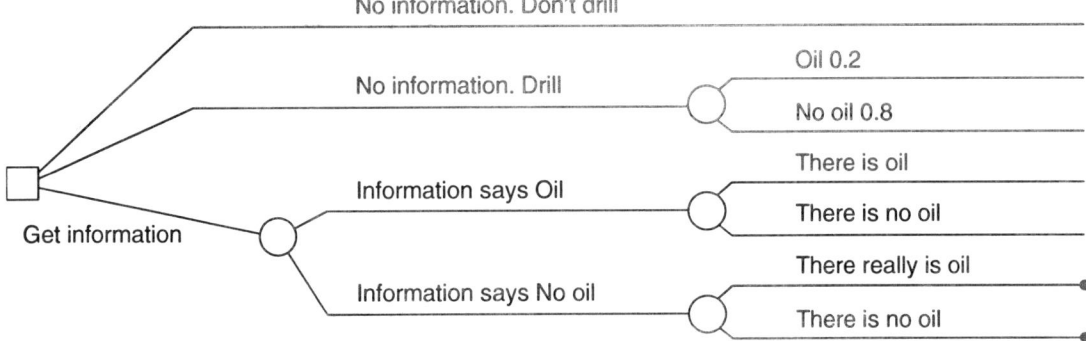

We must now calculate the probabilities of the following outcomes.

- The information will say 'oil' or 'no oil'
- The information will be right or wrong if it says 'oil'
- The information will be right or wrong if it says 'no oil'

If you check the information given in the problem, you will find that these probabilities are not given.

(a) We are told that the engineer has assessed that there is a 20% chance of oil and an 80% chance of no oil (ignoring information entirely). These are the **prior probabilities** of future possible outcomes.

(b) The **probabilities that there will be oil or no oil once the information has been obtained are posterior probabilities**.

Let's adopt the tabular approach as it is the one that students find easiest.

Step 1. We can tabulate the various probabilities as percentages.

		Actual outcome					
		Oil		*No oil*		*Total*	
Survey	oil	19	(W2)	8	(W3)	27	(W4)
result:	no oil	1		72		73	
Total		20	(W1)	80		100	

Workings

1 The engineer estimates 20% probability of oil and 80% of no oil.

2 If there is oil, ie in 20 cases out of 100, the survey will say so in 95% of these cases, ie in 20 × 0.95 = 19 cases. The 1 below the 19 is obtained by subtraction.

3 In the 80 per 100 cases where there is in fact no oil, the survey will wrongly say that there is oil 10% of the time; ie 80 × 0.10 = 8 cases. The 72 below the 8 is obtained by subtraction.

4 The horizontal totals are given by addition.

Step 2. We can now provide all the probabilities needed to complete the tree.

P (survey will say there is oil)   = 27/100   = 0.27
P (survey will say there is no oil)   = 73/100   = 0.73

If survey says oil   P (there is oil)   = 19/27 = 0.704
                          P (there is no oil) = 8/27 = 0.296 (or 1−0.704)
If survey says no oil   P (there is oil)   = 1/73 = 0.014
                          P (there is no oil) = 72/73 = 0.986 (or 1−0.014)

BPP
PUBLISHING

Step 3. We can now go on to complete the decision tree. Let us make the following assumptions. (In an exam question such information would have been given to you from the start.)

- The cost of drilling is £10m.
- The value of the benefits if oil is found is £70m, giving a net 'profit' of £60m.
- The cost of obtaining information from the consultants would be £3m.

An assumption is made that the decision maker will take whichever decision the information indicates is the best. If the information says 'oil', the company will drill, and if the information says 'no oil' it will not drill.

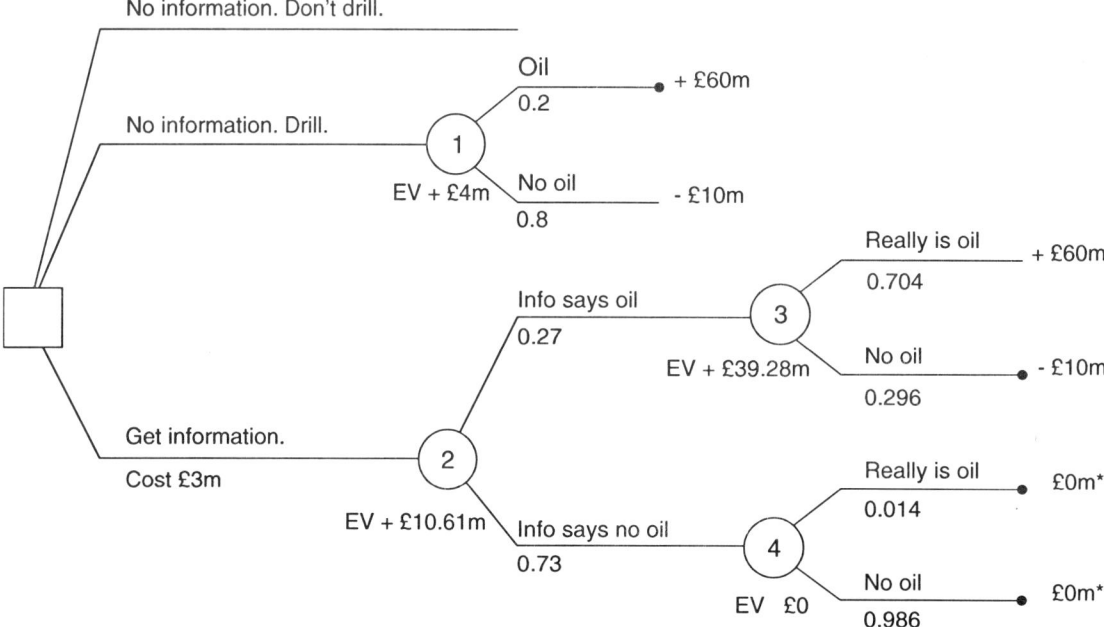

* The information is 'no oil', so the company won't drill, regardless of whether there really is oil or not.

Step 4. We can now perform rollback analysis.

		£m
EV at point 3 =	0.704 × £60m	42.24
	0.296 × (£10m)	(2.96)
		+ 39.28

		£m
EV at point 2 =	0.27 × £39.28m	10.61
	0.73 × £0	0.00
		+ 10.61

Step 5. There are three choices.   EV

(a) Do not obtain information and do not drill   £0
(b) Do not obtain information and drill   +£4 million
(c) Obtain information first, decide about drilling later (£(10.61m − 3m))
                                                                                            +£7.61 million

The decision should be to obtain the information from a test drilling first.

Step 6. The value of the imperfect information is the difference between (b) and (c), £3.61 million.

Exam focus point

If the examiner asks you to calculate the maximum amount that should be paid for a forecast, you need to calculate 'the value of imperfect information' using one of the two methods we have explained.

5   THE LEARNING CURVE

5.1   You will have already learned the basic principles of **learning curve theory** in your studies for Paper 8. In this section of the chapter you will be taking your knowledge a stage further to consider the derivation of the learning index. We will begin our discussion from scratch, to remind you of the basic principles.

5.2   Whenever an individual starts a job which is **fairly repetitive** in nature, and provided that the speed of working is not dictated by the speed of machinery (for example a production line), the worker is likely to become **more confident and knowledgeable** about the work as experience is gained, to become **more efficient**, and **to do the work more quickly**. **Eventually**, however, when the worker has acquired enough experience, there will be nothing more to learn, and so the **learning process will stop**.

When does learning curve theory apply?

5.3   Labour time should be expected to get shorter, with experience, in the production of items which exhibit any or all of the following features.

- **Made largely by labour effort** rather than by a highly mechanised process

- **Brand new** or relatively **short-lived** product (the learning process does not continue indefinitely)

- **Complex** and **made in small quantities for special orders**

The learning curve theory

KEY TERM

The **learning curve** is 'The mathematical expression of the phenomenon that when complex and labour-intensive procedures are repeated, unit labour times tend to decrease at a constant rate. The learning curve models mathematically this reduction in unit production time.'   (CIMA *Official Terminology*)

5.4   More specifically, the learning curve theory states that the **cumulative average time per unit** produced is assumed to **decrease by a constant percentage every time total output of the product doubles**.

5.5   For instance, where an **80% learning effect** occurs, the **cumulative average time required per unit of output is reduced to 80% of the previous cumulative average time when output is doubled**.

- By **cumulative average time**, we mean the **average time per unit for all units produced so far**, back to and including the first unit made.

BPP PUBLISHING

- The **doubling of output** is an **important feature** of the learning curve measurement. With a 70% learning curve, the cumulative average time per unit of output will fall to 70% of what it was before, every time output is doubled.

5.6 EXAMPLE: AN 80% LEARNING CURVE

If the first unit of output requires 100 hours and an 80% learning curve applies, the production times would be as follows.

Cumulative number of units produced		Cumulative average time per unit Hours		Total time required Hours	Incremental time taken Total hours		Hours per unit
1		100.0	(× 1)	100.0			
2*	(80%)	80.0	(× 2)	160.0	60.0	÷ 1	60.0
4*	(80%)	64.0	(× 4)	256.0	96.0	÷ 2	48.0
8*	(80%)	51.2	(× 8)	409.6	153.6	÷ 4	38.4

* Output is being doubled each time.

Notice that the incremental time per unit is reducing at a much faster rate than the average time per unit.

Graph of the learning curve

5.7 This learning effect can be shown on a **graph** as a learning curve, either for **unit times (graph (a))** or for **cumulative total times or costs (graph (b))**.

(a) (b)

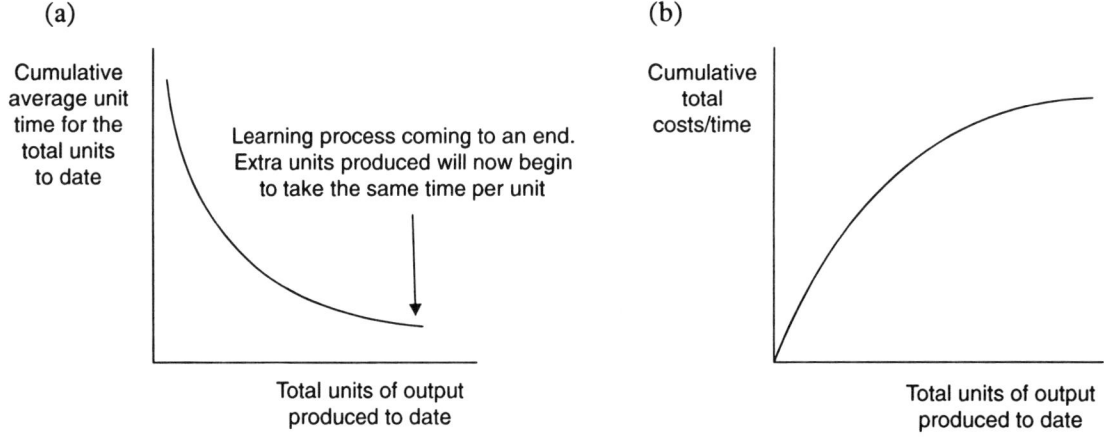

5.8 The curve on graph (a) becomes horizontal once a sufficient number of units have been produced. At this point the learning effect is lost and production time should become a constant standard, to which a standard efficiency rate may be applied.

5.9 EXAMPLE: THE LEARNING CURVE EFFECT

Captain Kitts Ltd has designed a new type of sailing boat, for which the cost and sales price of the first boat to be produced has been estimated as follows.

	£
Materials	5,000
Labour (800 hrs × £5 per hr)	4,000
Overhead (150% of labour cost)	6,000
	15,000
Profit mark-up (20%)	3,000
Sales price	18,000

It is planned to sell all the yachts at full cost plus 20%. An 80% learning curve is expected to apply to the production work. Only one customer has expressed interest in buying the yacht so far, but he thinks £18,000 is too high a price to pay. He might want to buy two, or even four of the yachts during the next six months.

He has asked the following questions.

(a) If he paid £18,000 for the first yacht, what price would he have to pay later for a second yacht?

(b) Could Captain Kitts Ltd quote the same unit price for two yachts, if the customer ordered two at the same time?

(c) If the customer bought two yachts now at one price, what would be the price per unit for a third and fourth yacht, if he ordered them both together later on?

(d) Could Captain Kitts Ltd quote a single unit price for

    (i)   four yachts;
    (ii)   eight yachts;

    if they were all ordered now?

Assuming there are no other prospective customers for the yacht, how would the questions be answered?

5.10 SOLUTION

Number of yachts		Cumulative average time per yacht		Total time for all yachts to date	Incremental time for additional yachts	
		Hours		Hours		Hours
1		800.0		800.0		
2	(× 80%)	640.0	(× 2)	1,280.0	(1,280 – 800)	480.0
4	(× 80%)	512.0	(× 4)	2,048.0	(2,048 – 1,280)	768.0
8	(× 80%)	409.6	(× 8)	3,276.8	(3,276.8 – 2,048)	1,228.8

(a) *Separate price for a second yacht*

	£
Materials	5,000
Labour (480 hrs × £5)	2,400
Overhead (150% of labour cost)	3,600
Total cost	11,000
Profit (20%)	2,200
Sales price	13,200

(b) *A single price for the first two yachts*

	£
Materials cost for two yachts	10,000
Labour (1,280 hrs × £5)	6,400
Overhead (150% of labour cost)	9,600
Total cost for two yachts	26,000
Profit (20%)	5,200
Total sales price for two yachts	31,200
Price per yacht (÷ 2)	15,600

BPP PUBLISHING

(c) *A price for the third and fourth yachts*

	£
Materials cost for two yachts	10,000
Labour (768 hours × £5)	3,840
Overhead (150% of labour cost)	5,760
Total cost	19,600
Profit	3,920
Total sales price for two yachts	23,520
Price per yacht (÷ 2)	11,760

(d) *A price for the first four yachts together and for the first eight yachts together*

	First four yachts		*First eight yachts*	
		£		£
Materials		20,000		40,000
Labour	(2,048 hrs)	10,240	(3,276.8 hrs)	16,384
Overhead	(150% of labour cost)	15,360	(150% of labour cost)	24,576
Total cost		45,600		80,960
Profit (20%)		9,120		16,192
Total sales price		54,720		97,152
Price per yacht	(÷ 4)	13,680	(÷ 8)	12,144

A formula for the learning curve

5.11 The formula for the learning curve shown in Paragraph 5.7(a) is $y = ax^n$

where y = cumulative average time per unit   a = time for the first unit
       x = number of units made so far   n = the learning coefficient or the
                                                index of learning

By calculating the value of n, using logarithms or a calculator, you can calculate expected labour times for certain work.

Exam focus point

You will be provided with the formula in the exam if it is needed.

Logarithms

KEY TERM

The **logarithm** of a number is the power to which ten has to be raised to produce that number.

5.12 If you have never learnt how to use logarithms, the following paragraphs give a brief explanation.

5.13 The **logarithm of a number, x, is the value of x expressed in terms of '10 to the power of'.**

$10 = 10^1$	The logarithm of 10 is 1.0
$100 = 10^2$	The logarithm of $100 = 2.0$
$1,000 = 10^3$	The logarithm of $1,000 = 3.0$

5.14 Your **calculator** will provide you with the logarithm of any number, probably using the button marked log 10^x. For example, the log of 566 is, using a calculator, 2.7528, which means that $10^{2.7528} = 566$.

5.15 When $y = ax^n$ in learning curve theory, the value of **n = log of the learning rate/log of 2**. The learning rate is expressed as a proportion, so that for an 80% learning curve, the learning rate is 0.8, and for a 90% learning curve it is 0.9, and so on.

5.16 For an 80% learning curve, n = log 0.8/log 2.

Using the button on your calculator marked log 10^x

$$n = \frac{-0.0969}{0.3010} = -0.322$$

Question 6

What is the value of n when a 90% learning curve applies?

Answer

n = log 0.9/log 2 = –0.0458/0.3010 = –0.152

5.17 You might also be expected to use the formula to calculate expected labour times for some work.

5.18 EXAMPLE: USING THE FORMULA

Suppose, for example, that an 80% learning curve applies to production of item ABC. To date, (the end of June) 230 units of ABC have been produced. Budgeted production for July is 55 units.

The time taken to produce the very first unit of ABC, in January, was 120 hours.

Required

Calculate the budgeted total labour time for July.

5.19 SOLUTION

To solve this problem, we need to calculate three things.

(a) The cumulative total labour time needed so far to produce 230 units of ABC

(b) The cumulative total labour time needed to produce 285 units of ABC, that is adding on the extra 55 units for July

(c) The extra time needed to produce 55 units of ABC in July, as the difference between (b) and (a)

Calculation (a)

$y = ax^n$ and we know that for 230 cumulative units, a = 120 hours (time for first unit), x = 230 (cumulative units) and n = –0.322 (80% learning curve) and so y = (120) × $(230^{-0.322})$ = 20.83.

So when x = 230 units, the cumulative average time per unit is 20.83 hours.

BPP
PUBLISHING

Calculation (b)

Now we do the same sort of calculation for x = 285.

If x = 285, y = $120 \times (285^{-0.322})$ = 19.44

So when x = 285 units, the cumulative average time per unit is 19.44 hours.

Calculation (c)

Cumulative units	Average time per unit	Total time
	Hours	Hours
230	20.83	4,791
285	19.44	5,540
Incremental time for 55 units		749

Average time per unit, between 230 and 285 units = 749/55 = 13.6 hours per unit approx

5.20 Instead of the formula you can use the graphical methodology (Paragraph 5.7) to determine cumulative average time per unit but you will need considerable drawing skill to obtain an accurate result.

Question 7

X Ltd is aware that there is a learning effect for the production of one of its new products, but is unsure about the degree of learning. The following data relate to this product.

Time taken to produce the first unit	28 direct labour hours
Production to date	15 units
Cumulative time taken to date	104 direct labour hours

The percentage learning effect is

A 70%   B 75%   C 80%   D 90%   E 95%

Answer

The correct answer is **A**.

You could answer this by hit and miss, trying all the learning rates given. But it is quicker to use the learning curve formula in reverse.

Average time taken per unit to date = (104 ÷ 15) = 6.933 hours

Since $y = ax^n$

6.933 = $28(15)^n$

15^n = 6.933 ÷ 28 = 0.2476

Taking logs   n log15 = log 0.2476

Since   log15 = 1.1761 (using log 10^x on your calculator)

and   log 0.2476 = −0.6062

$$n = \frac{\log 0.2476}{\log 15} = \frac{-0.6062}{1.1761} = -0.515$$

$$n = \frac{\log \text{ of learning rate}}{\log 2}$$

$$-0.515 = \frac{\log \text{ of learning rate}}{0.3010}$$

Log of learning rate = $-0.515 \times 0.3010 = -0.155$

Using the button on your calculator probably marked 10^x, −0.155 converts back to a 'normal' figure of 0.70. Thus the learning rate is 70%.

The practical application of learning curve theory

5.21 **What costs are affected by the learning curve?**

(a) Direct labour time and costs

(b) Variable overhead costs, if they vary with direct labour hours worked.

(c) **Materials costs** are usually **unaffected** by learning among the workforce, although it is conceivable that materials handling might improve, and so wastage costs be reduced.

(d) **Fixed overhead expenditure** should be **unaffected** by the learning curve (although in an organisation that uses absorption costing, if fewer hours are worked in producing a unit of output, and the factory operates at full capacity, the **fixed overheads recovered or absorbed per unit** in the cost of the output **will decline** as more and more units are made).

The relevance of learning curve effects in management accounting

5.22 **Situations in which learning curve theory can be used**

• To **calculate the marginal (incremental) cost of making extra units** of a product.

• To **quote selling prices for a contract**, where prices are calculated at cost plus a percentage mark-up for profit. An awareness of the learning curve can make all the difference between winning contracts and losing them, or between making profits and selling at a loss-making price.

• To **prepare realistic production budgets** and more **efficient production schedules**.

• To **prepare realistic standard costs** for cost control purposes.

5.23 **Further considerations that should be borne in mind**

(a) **Sales projections, advertising expenditure and delivery date commitments.** Identifying a learning curve effect should allow an organisation to plan its advertising and delivery schedules to coincide with expected production schedules. Production capacity obviously affects sales capacity and sales projections.

(b) **Budgeting with standard costs.** Companies that use standard costing for much of their production output cannot apply standard times to output where a learning effect is taking place. This problem can be overcome in practice by **establishing standard times for output once the learning effect has worn off** or become insignificant and **introducing a 'launch cost' budget** for the product for the duration of the learning period. Alternatively, a **standard average time per unit** can be estimated for a budgeted volume of output, which makes allowance for the expected learning rate.

(c) **Cash budgets.** Since the learning effect reduces unit variable costs as more units are produced, it should be allowed for in cash flow projections.

(d) **Work scheduling and overtime decisions.** To take full advantage of the learning effect, **idle production time should be avoided** and work scheduling/overtime decisions should take account of the expected learning effect.

(e) **Pay.** Where the workforce is paid a productivity bonus, the time needed to learn a new production process should be allowed for in calculating the bonus for a period.

(f) **Recruiting new labour.** When a company plans to take on new labour to help with increasing production, the learning curve assumption will have to be reviewed.

(g) **Market share**. The significance of the learning curve is that by increasing its share of the market, a company can benefit from shop-floor, managerial and technological 'learning' to achieve economies of scale.

Cost experience curves

5.24 A 'learning curve' is a term usually applied to the time taken by skilled labour element in shop floor production.

KEY TERM

A **cost experience curve** is a term applied to the 'corporate embodiment' of the shop floor, managerial and technological learning effects within an organisation and it expresses the way in which the average cost per unit of production changes over time due to technological and organisational changes as well as changes to factory size, product design, materials used and so on, not just 'learning' by skilled workers.

The experience curve is best exploited by growth and achieving a sizeable market share, so that an organisation can benefit from mass production techniques.

Limitations of learning curve theory

5.25 The limited use of learning curve theory is due to several factors.

(a) The learning curve phenomenon is **not always present**.

(b) It **assumes stable conditions at work** which will enable learning to take place. This is not always practicable (for example because of labour turnover).

(c) It must also **assume a certain degree of motivation** amongst employees.

(d) **Breaks** between repeating production of an item must not be too long, or **workers will 'forget'** and the learning process would have to begin all over again.

(e) It might be difficult to **obtain enough accurate data** to determine the learning rate.

(f) **Workers might not agree** to a gradual reduction in production times per unit.

(g) **Production techniques might change**, or product design alterations might be made, so that it **takes a long time for a 'standard' production method to emerge**, to which a learning effect will apply.

6   PARETO ANALYSIS   Pilot paper

KEY TERM

Pareto analysis is based on the observations of the economist Vilfredo Pareto, who suggested that 80% of a nation's wealth is held by 20% of its population (and so the remaining 80% of the population holds only 20% of the nation's wealth).

6.1 Pareto analysis is the 80/20 rule and it has been applied to many other situations.

• In stock control, where 20% of stock items might represent 80% of the value
• In product analysis, where 80% of company profit is earned by 20% of the products

6.2 EXAMPLE: PARETO ANALYSIS AND PRODUCTS

(a) A company produces ten products which it sells in various markets. The revenue from each product is as follows.

Product	Revenue
	£'000
A	231
B	593
C	150
D	32
E	74
F	17
G	1,440
H	12
I	2
J	19
	2,570

(b) Rearranging revenue in descending order and calculating cumulative figures and percentages gives us the following analysis.

Product	Revenue	Cumulative revenue (W1)	% (W2)
	£'000	£'000	
G	1,440	1,440	56.0
B	593	2,033	79.1
A	231	2,264	88.1
C	150	2,414	93.9
E	74	2,488	96.8
D	32	2,520	98.1
J	19	2,539	98.8
F	17	2,556	99.5
H	12	2,568	99.9
I	2	2,570	100.0
	2,570		

Workings

1   This is calculated as follows:

$1,440 + 593 = 2,033$
$2,033 + 231 = 2,264$ and so on.

2   $(1/2,570 \times 1,440 \times 100)\% = 56.0\%$
$(1/2,570 \times 2,033 \times 100)\% = 79.1\%$ and so on.

(Enter 1/2,570 into your calculator as a constant - do the calculation and then tap the multiplication button twice until 'k' appears on the screen - and then simply enter each cumulative revenue figure and press the 'equals' button to get the percentage as a decimal.)

(c) In this case the **Pareto rule applies** - almost 80% of revenue is brought in by just two products, G and B. **The point of Pareto analysis is to highlight the fact that the effort that is put into a company's products is often barely worth the trouble in terms of the sales revenue generated.**

6.3   You should not expect that the 80/20 rule will always apply as precisely as in the above example. It may be, that, say, 25% of products will account for 90% of revenue. **The basic principle is that a small number of products often yields a high proportion of income.**

6.4 Also, it does not necessarily follow that the products generating the highest income are the most profitable. The costs of producing the products needs to be taken into account. It may be, for example, that products G and B both cost more to produce than the income they bring in, whereas products A, C and E cost virtually nothing. In other words **Pareto analysis can be carried out for costs and contribution as well as for sales.**

Exam focus point

The pilot paper contained a part-question, worth 11 marks, which showed a graph of an organisation's total profit against the percentage of customers serviced. The graph portrayed a clear Pareto distribution and candidates were required to explain the concept encapsulated by the graph and advise on actions to improve profitability (eg take action concerning the less profitable customers).

Further analysis

6.5 Suppose the figures you are given provide some additional information, and you are asked to analyse them and comment on them in a way that will be useful to management.

Product	Revenue £'000	Profit £'000
A	231	46
B	593	108
C	150	52
D	32	7
E	74	16
F	17	4
G	1,440	202
H	12	8
I	2	1
J	19	8
	2,570	452

6.6 An analysis might take the following form.

(a) The revenue figures can be **ranked** and **expressed as percentages** and in **cumulative terms** (as before), and profit can be ranked and analysed in the same way.

The figures are pretty self-explanatory, but make sure that you understand how all of them are calculated, because you may well have to do this yourself in an exam.

Product	Revenue £'000	Rev. %	Cum. revenue £'000	Cum. %	Product	Profit £'000	Profit %	Cum. profit £'000	Cum. %
G	1,440	56.0	1,440	56.0	G	202	44.7	202	44.7
B	593	23.1	2,033	79.1	B	108	23.9	310	68.6
A	231	9.0	2,264	88.1	C	52	11.5	362	80.1
C	150	5.8	2,414	93.9	A	46	10.2	408	90.3
E	74	2.9	2,488	96.8	E	16	3.5	424	93.8
D	32	1.2	2,520	98.1	H	8	1.8	432	95.6
J	19	0.7	2,539	98.8	J	8	1.8	440	97.4
F	17	0.7	2,556	99.5	D	7	1.5	447	98.9
H	12	0.5	2,568	99.9	F	4	0.9	451	99.8
I	2	0.1	2,570	100.0	I	1	0.2	452	100.0
	2,570					452			

This shows us that, whereas the top ranking products are G, B and A in revenue terms, G, B and C are the top three in terms of profit. In **revenue terms** product C produces under 6% of the overall total but in **profit terms** it produces over 10%. Four products each produce 10% or more of the overall **profit**, but only three products individually produce more than 9% of **revenue**.

(b) We can also calculate the **profit margin** (the profit divided by the revenue expressed as a percentage) for individual products and overall. The figures shown below indicate that while most of the products vary slightly around the overall profit margin of 17.6%, some have much higher margins, notably products H, I and J, although these are relatively insignificant in overall revenue terms. The product that provides the greatest amount of revenue and profit, product G, actually has the lowest profit margin of all.

Product	Revenue	Profit	Profit margin
	£'000	£'000	%
A	231	46	19.9
B	593	108	18.2
C	150	52	34.7
D	32	7	21.9
E	74	16	21.6
F	17	4	23.5
G	1,440	202	14.0
H	12	8	66.7
I	2	1	50.0
J	19	8	42.1
	2,570	452	17.6

6.7 Your overall recommendations to management might be to make efforts to **save costs** to **improve the profit margin** of product G, and to put **extra marketing effort** into products C, H, I and J where the potential returns are greatest. Obviously what can be done depends on the nature of the products themselves: the smaller revenue items may be specialist add-ons that are only ever likely to be purchased by a few people.

Diagrammatic representations

6.8 Pareto analysis can be presented in a variety of forms.

(a) On the next page the revenue information is presented as a Pareto curve.

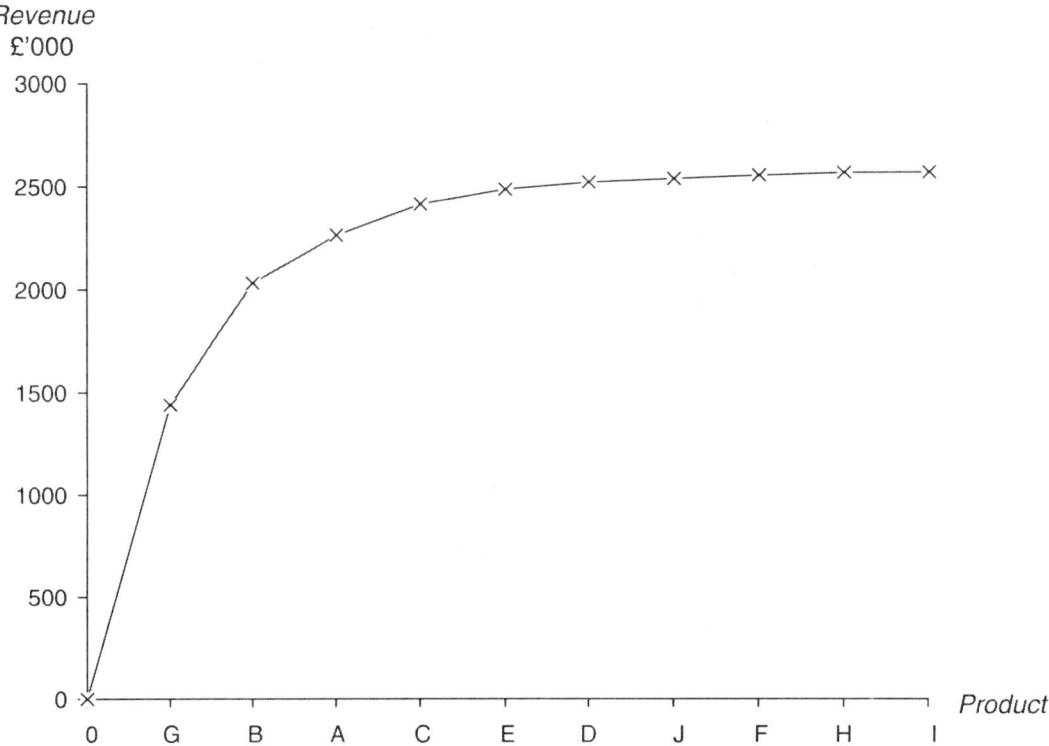

(b) On the next page we show both the revenue and profit figures as percentages in bar charts side by side.

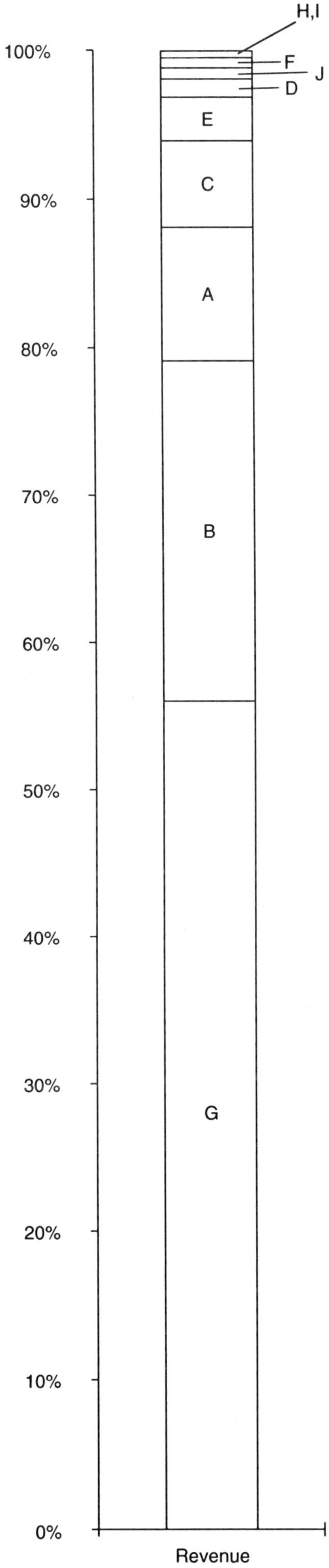

H,I
F
J
D
E
C
A
B
G
100%
90%
80%
70%
60%
50%
40%
30%
20%
10%
0%
Revenue

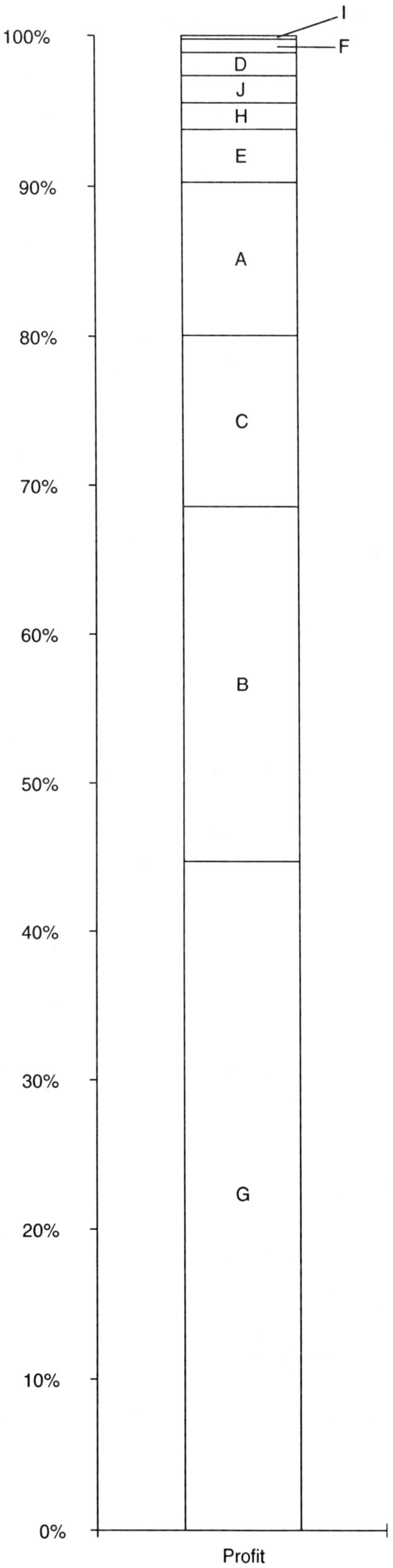

I
F
D
J
H
E
A
C
B
G
100%
90%
80%
70%
60%
50%
40%
30%
20%
10%
0%
Profit

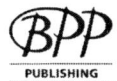

Chapter roundup

- People may be **risk seekers**, **risk neutral** or **risk averse**.

- **Conservatism** involves estimating outcomes in a conservative manner in order to provide a built-in safety factor.

- **Worst/most likely/best outcome** estimates show the full range of possible outcomes from a decision.

- **Two useful approaches to sensitivity analysis**.

  ° Estimate by how much costs and revenues would need to differ from their estimated values before the decision would change.

  ° Estimate whether a decision would change if estimated costs/revenues were x%/y% higher/lower than estimated.

- **Bayes' strategy** is that if a manager is faced with a number of alternative decisions, each with a range of possible outcomes, the optimum decision will be the one which gives the highest expected value (of profit/contribution).

- A **point estimate probability** means an estimate of the probability of particular outcomes occurring. Point estimates do have drawbacks but these can be overcome to some extent and they are the most practical way of analysing risk.

- **Decision trees** are diagrams which illustrate the choices and possible outcomes of a decision. **Rollback analysis** evaluates the EV of each decision option. You have to work from right to left and calculate EVs at each outcome point.

- **Perfect information** is guaranteed to predict the future with 100% accuracy. **Imperfect information** is better than no information at all but could be wrong in its prediction of the future.

- The **value of perfect information** is the difference between the EV of profit with perfect information and the EV of profit without perfect information. We looked at how the **value of imperfect information** can be determined using a probability tree or table.

- **Learning curve theory** is used to measure how, in some industries and some situations, the incremental cost per unit of output continues to fall for each extra unit produced.

- The theory is that the **cumulative average time per unit produced is assumed to fall by a constant percentage every time total output of the product doubles**. Cumulative average time is the average time per unit for all units produced so far, back to and including the first unit made.

- The formula for the learning curve is $y = ax^n$ where n, the learning coefficient or learning index, is defined as (log of the learning rate/log of 2).

- **Pareto analysis** is a simple attention-directing technique highlighting the fact that the real value in anything may be concentrated in just a few areas.

Quick quiz

1 A particular decision maker is concerned with what will be the most likely outcome of a decision. He would be described as

    A   a risk seeker
    B   risk averse
    C   risk neutral
    D   a risk reducer
    E   a risk analyser

2 A probability can be expressed as any value from −1 to +1. True or false?

3   In which of the following decisions would expected values be useful as a guide to decision making.

                                                                                    Most useful   Not as useful

   (a)   Whether to change the logo painted on the window of 700 retail
          outlets

   (b)   Whether to purchase machine X or machine Y

   (c)   Whether to launch product A

   (d)   Deciding on the optimum daily purchases of a perishable item

4   In a particular class of CIMA students, 65% are female and 80% have brown eyes. Given that a student selected at random from this class has brown eyes, to determine the probability that the student is male would require a consideration of

   Prior probabilities

   Posterior probabilities

5   In the formula for the learning curve, $y = ax^n$, what is n and how is its value calculated?

6   Sketch a Pareto curve to demonstrate a situation where 75% of an organisation's profit is derived from 25% of its retail outlets.

Answers to quick quiz

1   C

2   False. Should be 0 to 1.

3   Expected values would be useful for decisions (a) and (d) because they are repeated several times.

4   Posterior probabilities

5   The learning index, calculated as log of the learning rate/log of 2.

6

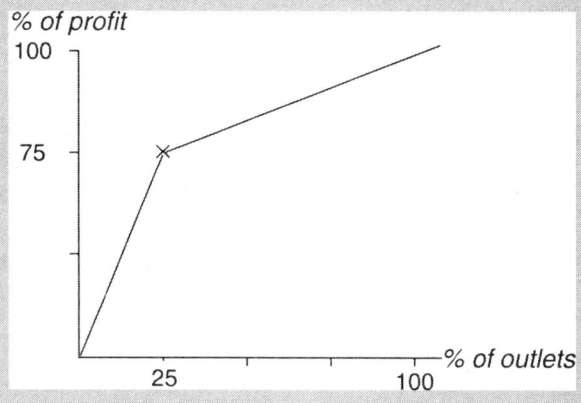

Now try the question below from the Exam Question Bank

Number	Level	Marks	Time
Q5	Examination	13	23 mins

BPP PUBLISHING

Chapter 4

PRICING

Topic list		Syllabus Reference	Ability required
1	Factors influencing the pricing decision	(i)	Evaluate and discuss
2	Cost based approaches to pricing	(i)	Evaluate and discuss
3	Other external pricing strategies	(i)	Identify and discuss
4	Using sales variances to evaluate pricing strategies	(i)	Evaluate

Introduction

Historically price was the single most important decision made by the sales department, but in **modern marketing philosophy** price, while important, is not necessarily the predominant factor. Modern businesses seek to interpret and satisfy consumer wants and needs by modifying existing products or introducing new products to the range. This contrasts with earlier production-oriented times when the typical reaction was to cut prices in order to sell more of an organisation's product.

Notwithstanding this change in emphasis, pricing is very important. Proper pricing of an organisation's products or services is essential to its profitability and hence its survival, and price has an important role to play as a **competitive tool** which can be used to differentiate a product and an organisation and thus exploit market opportunities.

In this chapter we will begin by looking at the factors which influence the pricing decision. Perhaps the most important of these is the level of **demand** for an organisation's product and how that demand changes as the price of the product changes (its **elasticity of demand**). We will then turn our attention to specific approaches to pricing with a look at **cost-based approaches**. The next section of the chapter will discuss the **pricing strategies** to adopt in particular circumstances, such as when a new product is launched.

We will end the chapter by considering how sales variance analysis can help to evaluate the success of pricing strategies.

Learning outcomes covered in this chapter

- **Identify** and **discuss** external pricing strategies
- **Evaluate** external pricing strategies using sales variance analysis

Syllabus content covered in this chapter

- External pricing strategies
- Sales mix, quantity, market size and market share variances

1   FACTORS INFLUENCING THE PRICING DECISION

1.1   In this first section of the chapter you will be learning about the many factors which influence the price which can be charged for a product or service. We will begin by looking at the basic economic analysis of demand.

The economic analysis of demand

1.2 There are two extremes in the relationship between price and demand. A supplier can either **sell a certain quantity, Q, at any price** (as in graph (a)). Demand is totally unresponsive to changes in price and is said to be **completely inelastic**. Alternatively, **demand might be limitless at a certain price** P (as in graph (b)), but there would be no demand above price P and there would be little point in dropping the price below P. In such circumstances demand is said to be **completely elastic**.

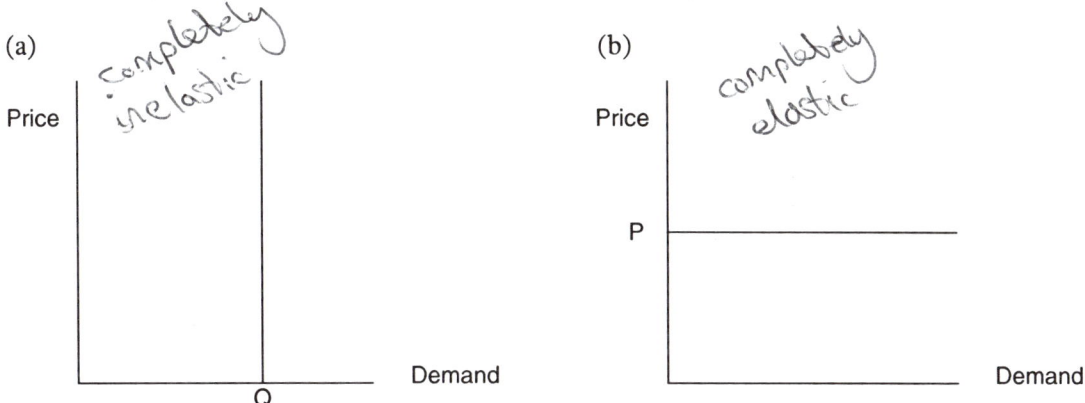

(a) *completely inelastic*

Price

Q — Demand

(b) *completely elastic*

Price

P

Demand

1.3 A more **normal situation** is shown below. The **downward-sloping** demand curve shows that demand will increase as prices are lowered. Demand is therefore **elastic**.

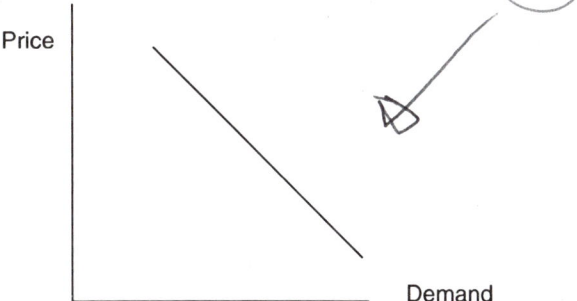

Price

Demand

Price elasticity of demand (η)

KEY TERM

Price elasticity of demand (η) is a measure of the extent of change in market demand for a good in response to a change in its price. It is measured as:

$$\frac{\text{The change in quantity demanded, as a \% of demand}}{\text{The change in price, as a \% of the price}}$$

1.4 Since the demand goes up when the price falls, and goes down when the price rises, the elasticity has a negative value, but it is usual to ignore the minus sign.

1.5 EXAMPLE: PRICE ELASTICITY OF DEMAND

The price of a good is £1.20 per unit and annual demand is 800,000 units. Market research indicates that an increase in price of 10 pence per unit will result in a fall in annual demand of 75,000 units. What is the price elasticity of demand?

BPP PUBLISHING

1.6 SOLUTION

Annual demand at £1.20 per unit is 800,000 units.
Annual demand at £1.30 per unit is 725,000 units.

% change in demand = $(75{,}000/800{,}000) \times 100\% = 9.375\%$
% change in price = $(10p/120p) \times 100\% = 8.333\%$
Price elasticity of demand = $(-9.375/8.333) = -1.125$
Ignoring the minus sign, price elasticity is 1.125.

The demand for this good, at a price of £1.20 per unit, would be referred to as **elastic** because the **price elasticity of demand is greater than 1**.

Elastic and inelastic demand

1.7   The value of demand elasticity may be anything from zero to infinity.

> **KEY TERM**
>
> Demand is referred to as **inelastic** if the absolute value is less than 1 and **elastic** if the absolute value is greater than 1.

1.8   Think about what this means.

- Where demand is **inelastic**, the **quantity demanded falls by a smaller percentage than the percentage increase in price**.

- Where demand is **elastic, demand falls** by a **larger percentage than the percentage rise in price**.

Elasticity and the pricing decision

1.9   In practice, organisations will have only a rough idea of the shape of their demand curve: there will only be a limited amount of data about quantities sold at certain prices over a period of time *and*, of course, factors other than price might affect demand. Because any conclusions drawn from such data can only give an indication of likely future behaviour, management skill and expertise are also needed. Despite this limitation, an **awareness of the concept of elasticity can assist management with pricing decisions**.

(a) (i)   In circumstances of **inelastic demand, prices should be increased** because revenues will increase and total costs will reduce (because quantities sold will reduce).

(ii)   In circumstances of **elastic demand**, increases in prices will bring decreases in revenue and decreases in price will bring increases in revenue. Management therefore have to **decide** whether the **increase/decrease in costs will be less than/greater than the increases/decreases in revenue**.

(b) In situations of **very elastic demand**, overpricing can lead to a massive drop in quantity sold and hence a massive drop in profits whereas underpricing can lead to costly stock outs and, again, a significant drop in profits. **Elasticity must therefore be reduced by creating a customer preference which is unrelated to price** (through advertising and promotional activities).

(c) In situations of **very inelastic demand**, customers are **not sensitive to price. Quality, service, product mix and location** are therefore **more important** to a firm's pricing strategy.

Determining factors

1.10 **Factors that determine the degree of elasticity**

(a) **The price of the good.**

(b) **The price of other goods.** For some goods the market demand is interconnected. Such goods are of two types.

    (i) **Substitutes,** so that an increase in demand for one version of a good is likely to cause a decrease in demand for others. Common examples are rival brands of the same commodity (like *Coca-Cola* and *Pepsi-Cola*), bus journeys versus car journeys.

    (ii) **Complements,** so that an increase in demand for one is likely to cause an increase in demand for the other. Examples are cups and saucers, cars and components.

(c) **Income.** A rise in income gives households more to spend and they will want to buy more goods. However this phenomenon does not affect all goods in the same way.

    (i) **Normal goods** are those for which a **rise in income increases the demand.**

    (ii) **Inferior goods** are those for which **demand falls as income rises,** such as cheap wine.

    (iii) For some goods **demand rises up to a certain point and then remains unchanged,** because there is a limit to which consumers can or want to consume. Examples are basic foodstuffs such as salt and bread.

(d) **Tastes and fashions.** A change in fashion will alter the demand for a good, or a particular variety of a good. Changes in taste may stem from psychological, social or economic causes. There is an argument that tastes and fashions are created by the producers of products and services. There is undeniably some truth in this, but the modern focus on responding to customers' needs and wants suggests otherwise.

(e) **Expectations.** Where consumers believe that prices will rise or that shortages will occur they will attempt to stock up on the product, thereby creating excess demand in the short term.

(f) **Obsolescence.** Many products and services have to be replaced periodically.

    (i) Physical goods are literally 'consumed'. Carpets become threadbare, glasses get broken, foodstuffs get eaten, children grow out of clothes.

    (ii) Technological developments render some goods obsolete. Manual office equipment has been largely replaced by electronic equipment, because it does a better job, more quickly, quietly, efficiently and effectively.

Demand and the market

1.11 Economic theory suggests that the volume of **demand** for a good in **the market as a whole** is influenced by a variety of variables.

- The price of the good
- The price of other goods
- The size and distribution of household income
- Expectations
- Obsolescence
- The perceived quality of the product
- Tastes and fashion

Demand and the individual firm

1.12 The **volume of demand for one organisation's goods rather than another's** is influenced by three principal factors: product life cycle, quality and marketing.

Product life cycle

> ### KEY TERM
>
> **Product life cycle** is 'The period which begins with the initial product specification, and ends with the withdrawal from the market of both the product and its support. It is characterised by defined stages including research, development, introduction, maturity, decline and abandonment.' (CIMA *Official Terminology*)

1.13 Most products pass through the following phases.

Phase	Description
Introduction	The product is introduced to the market. Heavy capital expenditure will be incurred on product development and perhaps also on the purchase of new fixed assets and building up stocks for sale. On its introduction to the market, the product will begin to earn some revenue, but initially demand is likely to be small. Potential customers will be unaware of the product or service, and the organisation may have to spend further on advertising to bring the product or service to the attention of the market.
Growth	The product gains a bigger market as demand builds up. Sales revenues increase and the product begins to make a profit. The initial costs of the investment in the new product are gradually recovered.
Maturity	Eventually, the growth in demand for the product will slow down and it will enter a period of relative maturity. It will continue to be profitable. The product may be modified or improved, as a means of sustaining its demand.
Saturation and decline	At some stage, the market will have bought enough of the product and it will therefore reach 'saturation point'. Demand will start to fall. For a while, the product will still be profitable in spite of declining sales, but eventually it will become a loss-maker and this is the time when the organisation should decide to stop selling the product or service, and so the product's life cycle should reach its end.

1.14 The life expectancy of a product will influence the pricing decision. **Short-life products** must be quite **highly priced** so as to give the manufacturer a chance to **recover his investment** and **make a worthwhile** return. This is why fashion goods and new high technology goods, for example, tend to have high prices.

1.15 We have already mentioned that the current tendency is towards shorter product life cycles. Notwithstanding this observation, the **life cycles** of different products may **vary in terms of length of phases, overall length and shape**.

- Fashion products have a very short life and so do high technology products because they become rapidly out-dated by new technological developments.

- **Different versions of the same product may have different life cycles,** and consumers are often aware of this. For example, the prospective buyer of a new car is more likely to purchase a recently introduced Ford than a Vauxhall that has been on the market for several years, even if there is nothing to choose in terms of quality and price.

Quality

1.16 One firm's product may be perceived to be better quality than another's, and may in some cases actually be so, if it uses sturdier materials, goes faster or does whatever it is meant to do in a 'better' way. Other things being equal, **the better quality good will be more in demand** than other versions.

Marketing

1.17 You may be familiar with the 'four Ps' of the marketing mix, all of which influence demand for a firm's goods.

   (a) **Price**

   (b) **Product**

   (c) **Place** refers to the place where a good can be, or is likely to be, purchased.

   - If a good is difficult to obtain, potential buyers will turn to substitutes.
   - Some goods have no more than local appeal.

   (d) **Promotion** refers to the various means by which firms draw attention to their products and services.

   - A good brand name is a strong influence on demand.
   - Demand can be stimulated by a variety of promotional tools, such as free gifts, money off, shop displays, direct mail and media advertising.

1.18 In recent years, **emphasis** has been placed, especially in marketing, on the importance of **non-price factors in demand**. Thus the roles of product quality, promotion, personal selling and distribution and, in overall terms, brands, have grown. While it can be relatively easy for a competitor to copy a price cut, at least in the short term, it is much **more difficult to copy a successful brand image.**

1.19 Some larger organisations go to considerable effort to estimate the demand for their products or services at differing price levels; in other words, they produce estimated demand curves. A **knowledge of demand curves can be very useful**: for example, a large transport company such as *Stagecoach* might be considering an increase in bus fares or underground fares. The effect on total revenues and profit of the fares increase could be estimated from a knowledge of the demand for transport services at different price levels. If an increase in the price per ticket caused a large fall in demand (that is, if demand were price-elastic) total revenues and profits would fall; whereas a fares increase when demand is price-inelastic would boost total revenue and since a transport authority's costs are largely fixed, would probably boost total profits too.

Markets

1.20 The price that an organisation can charge for its products will be determined to a greater or lesser degree by the market in which it operates. Here are some familiar terms that might feature as background for a question or that you might want to use in a written answer.

> ### KEY TERMS
>
> - **Perfect competition**: many buyers and many sellers all dealing in an identical product. Neither producer nor user has any market power and both must accept the prevailing market price.
>
> - **Monopoly**: one seller who dominates many buyers. The monopolist can use his market power to set a profit-maximising price.
>
> - **Monopolistic competition**: a large number of suppliers offer similar, but not identical, products. The similarities ensure elastic demand whereas the slight differences give some monopolistic power to the supplier.
>
> - **Oligopoly**: where relatively few competitive companies dominate the market. Whilst each large firm has the ability to influence market prices the unpredictable reaction from the other giants makes the final industry price indeterminate. Cartels are often formed.

Other factors

1.21

Influence	Explanation/example
Price sensitivity	This will vary amongst purchasers. Those that can pass on the cost of purchases will be the least sensitive and will therefore respond more to other elements of perceived value. For example, the business traveller will be more concerned about the level of service and quality of food in looking for an hotel than price, provided that it fits the corporate budget. In contrast, the family on holiday are likely to be very price sensitive when choosing an overnight stay.
Price perception	This is the way customers react to prices. For example, customers may react to a price increase by buying more. This could be because they expect further price increases to follow (they are 'stocking up').
Compatibility with other products	A typical example is operating systems on computers, for which a user would like to have a wide range of compatible software available. For these types of product there is usually a **cumulative effect on demand**. The more people who buy one of the formats, the more choice there is likely to be of software for that format. This in turn is likely to influence future purchasers. The owner of the rights to the preferred format will eventually find little competition and will be able to charge a premium price for the product.
Competitors	An organisation, in setting prices, sends out signals. Competitors are likely to react to these signals in some way. In some industries (such as petrol retailing) pricing moves in unison; in others, price changes by one supplier may initiate a price war, with each supplier undercutting the others. Competition is discussed in more detail below.

Influence	Explanation/example
Competition from substitute products	These are products which could be transformed for the same use or which might become desirable to customers at particular price levels. For example, train travel comes under competition as the quality, speed and comfort of coach travel rises. Similarly, if the price of train travel rises it comes under competition from cheaper coach travel and more expensive air travel.
Suppliers	If an organisation's suppliers notice a price rise for the organisation's products, they may seek a rise in the price for their supplies to the organisation on the grounds that it is now able to pay a higher price.
Inflation	In periods of inflation the organisation may need to change prices to reflect increases in the prices of supplies and so on. Such changes may be needed to keep relative (real) prices unchanged.
Quality	In the absence of other information, customers tend to judge quality by price. Thus a price change may send signals to customers concerning the quality of the product. A price rise may indicate improvements in quality, a price reduction may signal reduced quality, for example through the use of inferior components.
Incomes	In times of rising incomes, price may become a less important marketing variable compared with product quality and convenience of access (distribution). When income levels are falling and/or unemployment levels rising, price will become a much more important marketing variable.
Ethics	Ethical considerations are a further factor, for example whether or not to exploit short-term shortages through higher prices.

Competition

1.22 In established industries dominated by a few major firms, it is generally accepted that a price initiative by one firm will be countered by a price reaction by competitors. In these circumstances, prices tend to be fairly **stable**, unless pushed upwards by inflation or strong growth in demand.

If a rival cuts its prices in the expectation of increasing its market share, a firm has several options.

- It will **maintain its existing prices** if the expectation is that only a small market share would be lost, so that it is more profitable to keep prices at their existing level. Eventually, the rival firm may drop out of the market or be forced to raise its prices.

- It may **maintain its prices but respond with a non-price counter-attack**. This is a more positive response, because the firm will be securing or justifying its current prices with a product change, advertising, or better back-up services.

- It may **reduce its prices**. This should protect the firm's market share so that the main beneficiary from the price reduction will be the consumer.

- It may **raise its prices and respond with a non-price counter-attack**. The extra revenue from the higher prices might be used to finance an advertising campaign or product design changes. A price increase would be based on a campaign to emphasise the quality difference between the firm's own product and the rival's product.

2 COST BASED APPROACHES TO PRICING

Full cost-plus pricing

2.1 **In practice cost is one of the most important influences on price**. Many firms base price on simple **cost-plus rules** (costs are estimated and then a profit margin is added in order to set the price). A study by *Lanzilotti* gave a number of **reasons** for the **predominance of this method**.

- Planning and use of scarce capital resources are easier.

- Assessment of divisional performance is easier.

- It emulates the practice of successful large companies.

- Organisations fear government action against 'excessive' profits.

- There is a tradition of production rather than of marketing in many organisations.

- There is sometimes tacit collusion in industry to avoid competition.

- Adequate profits for shareholders are already made, giving no incentive to maximise profits by seeking an 'optimum' selling price.

- Cost-based pricing strategies based on internal data are easier to administer.

- Over time, cost-based pricing produces stability of pricing, production and employment.

KEY TERM

Full cost-plus pricing is a method of determining the sales price by calculating the full cost of the product and adding a percentage mark-up for profit.

2.2 The 'full cost' may be a fully absorbed production cost only, or it may include some absorbed administration, selling and distribution overhead.

2.3 A business might have an idea of the percentage profit margin it would like to earn, and so might **decide on an average profit mark-up** as a general guideline for pricing decisions. This would be particularly **useful for** businesses that carry out a large amount of **contract work or jobbing work**, for which individual job or contract prices must be quoted regularly to prospective customers. However, the percentage profit **mark-up does not have to be rigid and fixed**, but can be varied to suit the circumstances. In particular, the percentage mark-up can be varied to suit demand conditions in the market.

Question 1

A product's full cost is £4.75 and is sold at full cost-plus 70%. A competitor has just launched a similar product selling for £7.99. How will this affect the first product's mark up?

Answer

The cost-plus percentage will need to be reduced by 2%.

2.4 EXAMPLE: FULL COST-PLUS PRICING

Markup Ltd has begun to produce a new product, Product X, for which the following cost estimates have been made.

	£
Direct materials	27
Direct labour: 4 hrs at £5 per hour	20
Variable production overheads: machining, ½ hr at £6 per hour	3
	50

Production fixed overheads are budgeted at £300,000 per month and because of the shortage of available machining capacity, the company will be restricted to 10,000 hours of machine time per month. The absorption rate will be a direct labour rate, however, and budgeted direct labour hours are 25,000 per month. It is estimated that the company could obtain a minimum contribution of £10 per machine hour on producing items other than product X.

The direct cost estimates are not certain as to material usage rates and direct labour productivity, and it is recognised that the estimates of direct materials and direct labour costs may be subject to an error of ± 15%. Machine time estimates are similarly subject to an error of ± 10%.

The company wishes to make a profit of 20% on full production cost from product X.

Required

Ascertain the full cost-plus based price.

2.5 SOLUTION

Even for a relatively 'simple' cost-plus pricing estimate, some problems can arise, and certain assumptions must be made and stated. In this example, we can identify two problems.

- Should the opportunity cost of machine time be included in cost or not?
- What allowance, if any, should be made for the possible errors in cost estimates?

Different assumptions could be made.

(a) **Exclude machine time opportunity costs: ignore possible costing errors**

	£
Direct materials	27.00
Direct labour (4 hours)	20.00
Variable production overheads	3.00
Fixed production overheads	
(at $\dfrac{£300,000}{25,000}$ = £12 per direct labour hour)	48.00
Full production cost	98.00
Profit mark-up (20%)	19.60
Selling price per unit of product X	117.60

(b) **Include machine time opportunity costs: ignore possible costing errors**

	£
Full production cost as in (a)	98.00
Opportunity cost of machine time:	
contribution forgone (½ hr × £10)	5.00
Adjusted full cost	103.00
Profit mark-up (20%)	20.60
Selling price per unit of product X	123.60

(c) **Exclude machine time opportunity costs but make full allowance for possible under-estimates of cost**

	£	£
Direct materials	27.00	
Direct labour	20.00	
	47.00	
Possible error (15%)	7.05	
		54.05
Variable production overheads	3.00	
Possible error (10%)	0.30	
		3.30
Fixed production overheads (4 hrs × £12)	48.00	
Possible error (labour time) (15%)	7.20	
		55.20
Potential full production cost		112.55
Profit mark-up (20%)		22.51
Selling price per unit of product X		135.06

(d) **Include machine time opportunity costs and make a full allowance for possible under-estimates of cost**

	£
Potential full production cost as in (c)	112.55
Opportunity cost of machine time:	
potential contribution forgone (½ hr × £10 × 110%)	5.50
Adjusted potential full cost	118.05
Profit mark-up (20%)	23.61
Selling price per unit of product X	141.66

Using different assumptions, we could arrive at any of four different unit prices in the range £117.60 to £141.66.

Problems with and advantages of full cost-plus pricing

2.6 There are several serious **problems** with relying on a full cost approach to pricing.

- It **fails to recognise** that since demand may be determining price, **there will be a profit-maximising combination of price and demand**.

- There may be a need to **adjust prices to market and demand conditions**.

- **Budgeted output volume** needs to be established. Output volume is a key factor in the overhead absorption rate.

- A **suitable basis for overhead absorption** must be selected, especially where a business produces more than one product.

2.7 However, it is a **quick, simple and cheap** method of pricing which can be delegated to junior managers (which is particularly important with jobbing work where many prices must be decided and quoted each day) and, since the size of the profit margin can be varied, a decision based on a price in excess of full cost should ensure that a company working at normal capacity will **cover all of its fixed costs and make a profit**.

2.8 EXAMPLE: FULL COST-PLUS VERSUS PROFIT-MAXIMISING PRICES

Tiger Ltd has budgeted to make 50,000 units of its product, timm. The variable cost of a timm is £5 and annual fixed costs are expected to be £150,000.

The financial director of Tiger Ltd has suggested that a profit margin of 25% on full cost should be charged for every product sold. The marketing director has challenged the

wisdom of this suggestion, and has produced the following estimates of sales demand for timms.

Price per unit (£)	9	10	11	12	13
Demand (units)	42,000	38,000	35,000	32,000	27,000

Required

(a) Calculate the profit for the year if a full cost-plus price is charged.
(b) Calculate the profit for the year if a profit-maximising price is charged.

Assume in both (a) and (b) that 50,000 units of timm are produced regardless of sales volume.

2.9 SOLUTION

The full cost per unit comprises £5 of variable costs plus £3 of fixed costs (£8 in total). A 25% mark-up on this cost gives a selling price of £10 per unit so that sales demand would be 38,000 units. (Production is given as 50,000 units.) **Profit using absorption costing** would be as follows.

	£	£
Sales		380,000
Costs of production (50,000 units)		
Variable (50,000 × £5)	250,000	
Fixed (50,000 × £3)	150,000	
	400,000	
Less increase in stocks (12,000 units × 8)	(96,000)	
Cost of sales		304,000
Profit		76,000

Profit using marginal costing instead of absorption costing, so that fixed overhead costs are written off in the period they occur, would be as follows. (The 38,000 unit demand level is chosen for comparison.)

	£
Contribution (38,000 × £(10 – 5))	190,000
Fixed costs	150,000
Profit	40,000

Since the company cannot go on indefinitely producing an output volume in excess of sales volume, this profit figure is more indicative of the profitability of timms in the longer term.

A **profit-maximising price** is one which gives the greatest net (relevant) cash flow, which in this case is the **contribution-maximising price**.

Price	Unit contribution	Demand	Total contribution
£	£	Units	£
9	4	42,000	168,000
10	5	38,000	190,000
11	6	35,000	210,000
12	7	32,000	224,000
13	8	27,000	216,000

The profit maximising price is £12, with annual sales demand of 32,000 units.

This example shows that a **cost-plus based price is unlikely to be the profit-maximising price,** and that a **marginal costing approach,** calculating the total contribution at a variety of different selling prices, will be **more helpful** for establishing what the profit-maximising price ought to be.

Marginal cost-plus pricing

> ## KEY TERM
>
> **Marginal cost plus pricing/mark-up pricing** is a method of determining the sales price by adding a profit margin on to either marginal cost of production or marginal cost of sales.

2.10 Whereas a full cost-plus approach to pricing draws attention to net profit and the net profit margin, a variable cost-plus approach to pricing **draws attention to gross profit** and the **gross profit margin,** or **contribution**.

Question 2

A product has the following costs.

	£
Direct materials	5
Direct labour	3
Variable overheads	7

Fixed overheads are £10,000 per month. Budgeted sales per month are 400 units to allow the product to break even.

Required

Determine the profit margin which needs to be added to *marginal* cost to allow the product to break even.

Answer

Breakeven point is when total contribution equals fixed costs.

At breakeven point, £10,000 = 400 (price – £15)
∴ £25 = price – £15
∴ £40 = price
∴ Profit margin = 40 – 15/15 × 100% = $166\frac{2}{3}\%$

2.11 **The advantages of a marginal cost-plus approach to pricing**

(a) It is a **simple and easy** method to use.

(b) The **mark-up percentage can be varied,** and so mark-up pricing can be adjusted to reflect demand conditions.

(c) It **draws management attention to contribution,** and the effects of higher or lower sales volumes on profit. In this way, it helps to create a better awareness of the concepts and implications of marginal costing and cost-volume-profit analysis. For example, if a product costs £10 per unit and a mark-up of 150% is added to reach a price of £25 per unit, management should be clearly aware that every additional £1 of sales revenue would add 60 pence to contribution and profit.

(d) In practice, mark-up pricing is **used** in businesses **where there is a readily-identifiable basic variable cost**. Retail industries are the most obvious example, and it is quite common for the prices of goods in shops to be fixed by adding a mark-up (20% or 33.3%, say) to the purchase cost.

2.12 There are, of course, **drawbacks** to marginal cost-plus pricing.

(a)   Although the **size** of the mark-up can be varied in accordance with demand conditions, it **does not ensure that sufficient attention is paid to demand conditions, competitors' prices and profit maximisation.**

(b)   It **ignores fixed overheads** in the pricing decision, but the sales price must be sufficiently high to ensure that a profit is made after covering fixed costs.

Approach to pricing based on mark-up per unit of limiting factor

2.13   Another approach to pricing might be taken when a **business is working at full capacity, and is restricted by a shortage of resources** from expanding its output further. By deciding what target profit it would like to earn, it could **establish a mark-up per unit of limiting factor.**

2.14   EXAMPLE: MARK-UP PER UNIT OF LIMITING FACTOR

Suppose that a company provides a window cleaning service to offices and factories. Business is brisk, but the company is restricted from expanding its activities further by a shortage of window cleaners. The workforce consists of 12 window cleaners, each of whom works a 35 hour week. They are paid £4 per hour. Variable expenses are £0.50 per hour. Fixed costs are £5,000 per week. The company wishes to make a contribution of at least £15 per hour.

The minimum charge per hour for window cleaning would then be as follows.

	£ per hour
Direct wages	4.00
Variable expenses	0.50
Contribution	15.00
Charge per hour	19.50

The company has a total workforce capacity of (12 × 35) 420 hours per week, and so total contribution would be £8,190 per week, leaving a profit after fixed costs of £3,190 per week.

3   OTHER EXTERNAL PRICING STRATEGIES

Special orders

3.1   A special order is a **one-off** revenue earning opportunity. These may arise in the following situations.

(a)   When a business has a regular source of income but also has some **spare capacity** allowing it to take on extra work if demanded. For example a brewery might have a capacity of 500,000 barrels per month but only be producing and selling 300,000 barrels per month. It could therefore consider special orders to use up some of its spare capacity.

(b)   When a business has **no regular source of income** and relies exclusively on its ability to respond to demand. A building firm is a typical example as are many types of sub-contractors. In the service sector consultants often work on this basis.

The reason for making the distinction is that in the case of (**a**), a firm would normally attempt to cover its longer-term running costs in its prices for its regular product. Pricing for special orders need therefore **take no account of unavoidable fixed costs.** This is clearly not the case for a firm in (b)'s position, where special orders are the only source of income for the foreseeable future.

3.2 The **basic approach** in both situations is to determine the **price at which the firm would break even** if it undertook the work, that is, the **minimum price** that it could afford to charge. It would have to cover the incremental costs of producing and selling the item and the opportunity costs of the resources consumed.

Question 3

DDD Ltd has decided to price its jobs as follows.

- It calculates the minimum price for the job using relevant costs.
- It adds £5,000 to cover fixed costs.
- It adds a 10% profit margin to the total cost.

A customer who has work to be performed in May says he will award the contract to DDD Ltd if its bid is reduced by £5,000.

Required

Assess whether the contract should be accepted.

Answer

Yes or no. Yes, if there is no other work available, because DDD will at least earn a contribution towards fixed costs of 10% of the minimum cost. But no, if by accepting this reduced price it would send a signal to other prospective customers that they too could negotiate such a large reduction.

3.3 The exercise above illustrates the difficulties faced by firms with high overheads. Ideally some means should be found of identifying the causes of such costs. Activity based analysis might reveal ways of attributing overheads to specific jobs or perhaps of avoiding them altogether.

3.4 In today's competitive markets it is very much the **modern trend to tailor products or services to customer demand** rather than producing for stock. This suggests that **'special' orders may become the norm** for most businesses.

New products

3.5 Suppose that Novo plc is about to launch a new product with a variable cost of £10 per unit. The company has carried out market research (at a cost of £15,000) to determine the potential demand for the product at various selling prices.

Selling price £	Demand Units
30	20,000
25	30,000
20	40,000

Its current capacity is for 20,000 units but additional capacity can be made available by using the resources of another product line. If this is done the lost contribution from the other product will be £35,000 for each additional 10,000 units of capacity.

How could we **analyse this information** for senior management in a way that helps them to **decide on the product's launch price?**

3.6 **Tabulation** is the approach to use with a problem of this type.

Selling price £	Demand Units ('000)	Variable costs £'000	Opportunity costs £'000	Total costs £'000	Sales revenue £ '000	Contribution £'000
30	20	200	-	200	600	400
25	30	300	35	335	750	415
20	40	400	70	470	800	330

3.7 The **optimum price to maximise short-term profits is £25.** However, it is quite possible that the aim will **not** be to maximise short-term profits, and a number of other strategies may be adopted, as discussed below.

3.8 The main **objections** to the approach described above are that it only **considers a limited range of prices** (what about charging £27.50?) and it **takes no account of the uncertainty of forecast demand**. However, allowance could be made for both situations by collecting more information.

3.9 A new product pricing strategy will depend largely on whether a company's product or service is the first of its kind on the market.

(a) If the **product is the first of its kind**, there will be **no competition** yet, and the company, for a time at least, will be a **monopolist**. Monopolists have more influence over price and are able to set a price at which they think they can maximise their profits. A monopolist's price is likely to be higher, and his profits bigger, than those of a company operating in a competitive market.

(b) If the new product being launched by a company is **following a competitor's product** onto the market, the pricing strategy will be **constrained by what the competitor** is already doing. The new product could be given a higher price if its quality is better, or it could be given a price which matches the competition. Undercutting the competitor's price might result in a price war and a fall of the general price level in the market.

Market penetration pricing

> **KEY TERM**
>
> **Market penetration pricing** is a policy of low prices when the product is first launched in order to obtain sufficient penetration into the market.

3.10 **Circumstances in which a penetration policy may be appropriate**

- If the firm wishes to **discourage new entrants** into the market

- If the firm wishes to **shorten the initial period of the product's life cycle** in order to enter the growth and maturity stages as quickly as possible

- If there are **significant economies of scale** to be achieved **from a high volume of output,** so that quick penetration into the market is desirable in order to gain unit cost reductions

- If **demand is highly elastic** and so would respond well to low prices.

3.11 Penetration prices are prices which aim to **secure a substantial share in a substantial total market.** A firm might therefore **deliberately build excess production capacity** and set its prices very low. As demand builds up the spare capacity will be used up gradually and unit

costs will fall; the firm might even reduce prices further as unit costs fall. In this way, early losses will enable the firm to dominate the market and have the lowest costs.

Market skimming pricing

> **KEY TERM**
>
> **Market skimming pricing** involves charging high prices when a product is first launched and spending heavily on advertising and sales promotion to obtain sales.

3.12   As the product moves into the later stages of its life cycle, **progressively lower prices will be charged** and so the profitable 'cream' is skimmed off in stages until sales can only be sustained at lower prices.

3.13   The aim of market skimming is to **gain high unit profits early in the product's life**. High unit prices make it **more likely that competitors will enter the market** than if lower prices were to be charged.

3.14   **Circumstances in which such a policy may be appropriate**

(a)   Where the product is **new and different**, so that customers are prepared to pay high prices so as to be one up on other people who do not own it.

(b)   Where the **strength** of demand and the **sensitivity of demand** to price are **unknown**. It is better from the point of view of marketing to start by charging high prices and then reduce them if the demand for the product turns out to be price elastic than to start by charging low prices and then attempt to raise them substantially if demand appears to be insensitive to higher prices.

(c)   Where **high prices** in the early stages of a product's life might **generate high initial cash flows**. A firm with liquidity problems may prefer market-skimming for this reason.

(d)   Where the firm **can identify different market segments** for the product, each prepared to pay progressively lower prices. If **product differentiation** can be introduced, it may be possible to continue to sell at higher prices to some market segments when lower prices are charged in others. This is discussed further below.

(e)   Where products may have a **short life cycle**, and so need to recover their development costs and make a profit relatively quickly.

Premium pricing

3.15   This involves making a product **appear 'different'** through **product differentiation** so as **to justify a premium price**. The product may be different in terms of, for example, quality, reliability, durability, after sales service or extended warranties. Heavy advertising can establish brand loyalty which can help to sustain a premium and premium prices will always be paid by those customers who blindly equate high price with high quality.

Pricing to recover an investment

3.16   An alternative pricing objective that is worth mentioning is to recover the investment in a new product or service as quickly as possible, that is to **achieve a minimum payback**

period. The price is set so as to facilitate this. Such an objective would tend to be used in the following conditions.

- The business is high risk
- Rapid changes in fashion or technology are expected
- The innovator is short of cash

Differential pricing and price discrimination

KEY TERM

Price discrimination is the practice of charging different prices for the same product to different groups of buyers when these prices are not reflective of cost differences.

3.17 In certain circumstances the **same product** can be sold at different prices to **different customers**. There are a number of bases on which such discriminating prices can be set.

Basis	Detail
By market segment	A cross-channel ferry company would market its services at different prices in England and France, for example. Services such as cinemas and hairdressers are often available at lower prices to old age pensioners and/or juveniles.
By product version	Many car models have **optional extras** which enable one brand to appeal to a wider cross-section of customers. The final price need not reflect the cost price of the optional extras directly: usually the top of the range model would carry a price much in excess of the cost of provision of the extras, as a prestige appeal.
By place	Theatre seats are usually sold according to their location so that patrons pay different prices for the same performance according to the seat type they occupy.
By time	This is perhaps the most popular type of price discrimination. Off-peak travel bargains, hotel prices and telephone charges are all attempts to increase sales revenue by covering variable but not necessarily average cost of provision. Railway companies are successful price discriminators, charging more to rush hour rail commuters whose demand is inelastic at certain times of the day.

3.18 Price discrimination can only be effective if a number of **conditions** hold.

(a) The market must be **segmentable** in price terms, and different sectors must show different intensities of demand. Each of the sectors must be identifiable, distinct and separate from the others, and be accessible to the firm's marketing communications.

(b) There must be little or **no** chance of a **black market** developing (this would allow those in the lower priced segment to resell to those in the higher priced segment).

(c) There must be little or **no** chance that **competitors** can and will undercut the firm's prices in the higher priced (and/or most profitable) market segments.

(d) The cost of segmenting and **administering** the arrangements should not exceed the extra revenue derived from the price discrimination strategy.

'Own label' pricing: a form of price discrimination

3.19 Many supermarkets and multiple retail stores sell their 'own label' products, often at a lower price than established branded products. The supermarkets or multiple retailers do this by entering into arrangements with manufacturers, to supply their goods under the 'own brand' label.

Product bundling

3.20 Product bundling is a variation on price discrimination which involves **selling a number of products or services as a package at a price lower than the aggregate of their individual prices**. For example a hotel might offer a package that includes the room, meals, use of leisure facilities and entertainment at a combined price that is lower than the total price of the individual components. This might encourage customers to buy services that they might otherwise not have purchased.

Psychological pricing

3.21 Psychological pricing strategies include **pricing a product at £19.99 instead of £20** and withdrawing an unsuccessful product from the market and then relaunching it at a higher price, the customer having equated the lower price with lower quality (which was not the seller's intention).

Multiple products and loss leaders

3.22 Most organisations sell a range of products. The management of the pricing function is likely to focus on the profit from the whole range rather than the profit on each single product. Take, for example, the use of **loss leaders:** a very low price for one product is intended to make consumers buy additional products in the range which carry higher profit margins.

Case examples

Razor handles are sold at very low prices while razor blades are sold at a higher profit margin. People will buy many of the high profit items but only one of the low profit items - yet they are 'locked in' to the former by the latter.

---

4 USING SALES VARIANCES TO EVALUATE PRICING STRATEGIES

4.1 One way of evaluating the effectiveness of pricing strategies is to use variance analysis. The organisation's pricing strategy will have been determined with a view to achieving a desired sales volume for a period, taking into account the organisation's objectives, the market conditions and so on. The desired sales volume would have been included in the organisation's overall budget for the period. Variances measured against the budget can help to indicate the success or otherwise of a pricing strategy.

Sales volume variance

4.2 You learned how to calculate the sales volume variance in your Paper 8 studies. It measures the increase or decrease in the standard profit or contribution as a result of the sales volume being higher or lower than budgeted. It is calculated as follows.

(actual sales units – budgeted sales units) × standard profit per unit

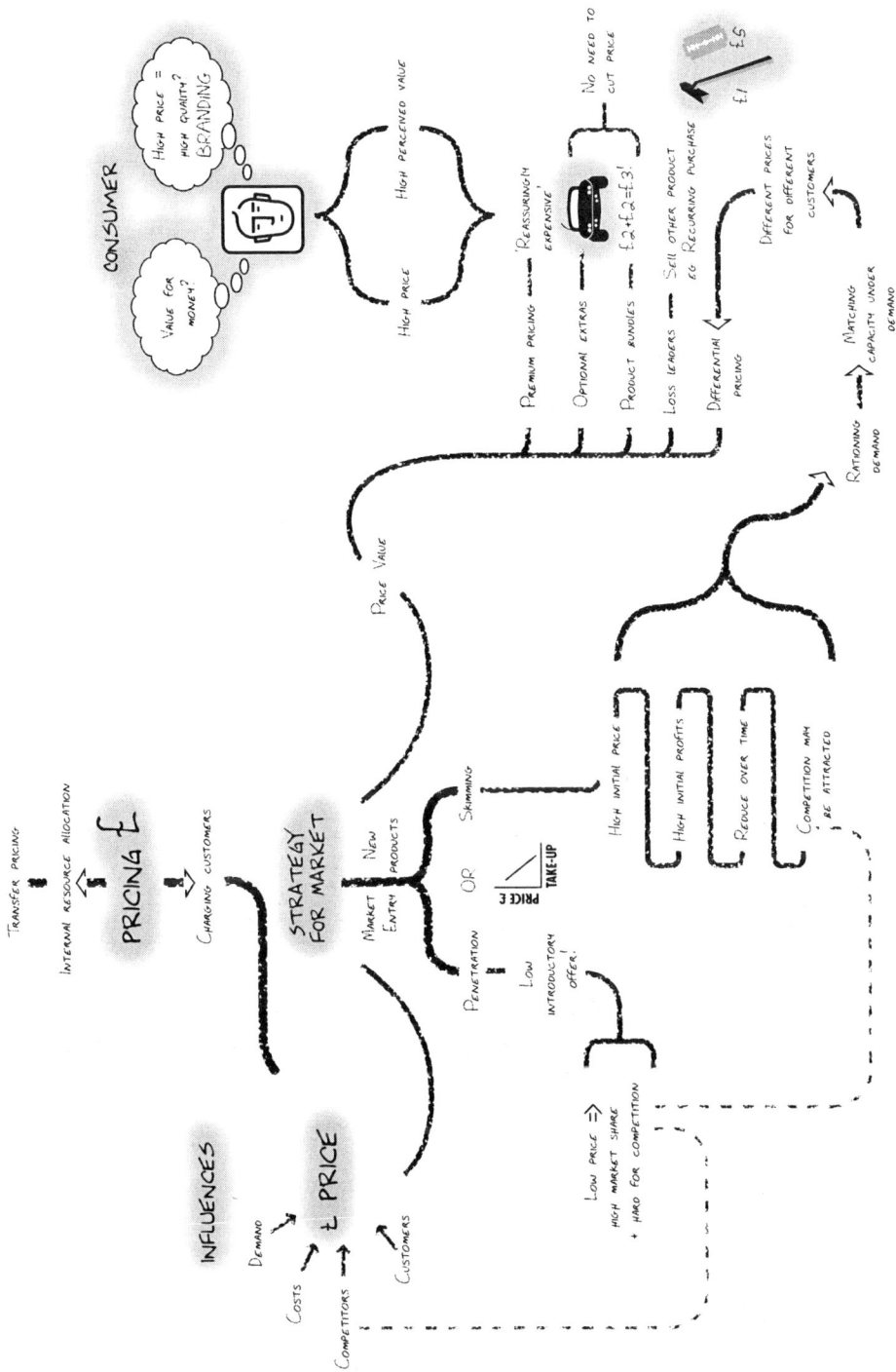

Sales mix and quantity variances

4.3   If a company sells more than one product, it is possible to **analyse the overall sales volume variance** into a **sales mix variance** and a **sales quantity variance**.

KEY TERMS

The **sales mix variance** occurs when the proportions of the various products sold are different from those in the budget.

The **sales quantity variance** shows the difference in contribution/profit because of a change in sales volume from the budgeted volume of sales.

A sales mix variance and a sales quantity variance are only meaningful where management can control the proportions of the products sold.

The units method of calculation

4.4   The sales **mix** variance is calculated as the **difference between the actual quantity sold in the standard mix** and the **actual quantity sold in the actual mix,** valued at standard margin per unit. The sales **quantity** variance is **calculated** as the **difference between the actual sales volume in the budgeted proportions and the budgeted sales volumes,** multiplied by the standard margin.

4.5   **EXAMPLE: SALES MIX AND QUANTITY VARIANCES**

Just Desserts Limited makes and sells two products, Bland Fete and Gotters Dew. The budgeted sales and profit are as follows.

	Sales Units	*Revenue* £	*Costs* £	*Profit* £	*Profit per unit* £
Bland Fete	400	8,000	6,000	2,000	5
Gotters Dew	300	12,000	11,100	900	3
				2,900	

Actual sales were 280 units of Bland Fete and 630 units of Gotters Dew. The company management is able to control the relative sales of each product through the allocation of sales effort, advertising and sales promotion expenses.

Required

Calculate the sales volume profit variance, the sales mix variance and the sales quantity variance.

4.6   **SOLUTION**

(a)

	Bland Fete	*Gotters Dew*
Budgeted sales	400 units	300 units
Actual sales	280 units	630 units
Sales volume variance in units	120 units (A)	330 units (F)
× standard margin per unit	× £5	× £3
Sales volume variance in £	£600 (A)	£990 (F)
Total **sales volume variance**	£390 (F)	

The favourable sales volume variance indicates that a potential increase in profit was achieved as a result of the change in sales volume compared with budgeted volume.

Now we will see how to analyse this favourable variance into its mix and quantity elements.

(b) When we look at the mix of sales in this example it is apparent that a bigger proportion than budgeted of the less profitable Gotters Dew has been sold, therefore the **sales mix variance** will be adverse. The method for calculating the variance is as follows.

    (i) Take the **actual total of sales** and **convert** this total into a **standard or budgeted mix,** on the assumption that sales should have been in the budgeted proportions or mix.

    (ii) The **difference between actual sales and 'standard mix'** sales for each product is then converted into a variance by **multiplying by the standard margin.**

		Units
Total quantity sold (280 + 630)		910
Budgeted mix for actual sales:	⁴/₇ Bland Fete	520
	³/₇ Gotters Dew	390
		910

	Bland Fete	*Gotters Dew*
Mix should have been	520 units	390 units
but was	280 units	630 units
Mix variance in units	240 units (A)	240 units (F)
× standard margin per unit	× £5	× £3
Mix variance in £	£1,200 (A)	£720 (F)
Total mix variance	£480 (A)	

The profit would have been £480 higher if the 910 units had been sold in the budgeted mix of 4:3.

(c) The **sales quantity variance** is calculated as follows.

	Bland Fete	*Gotters Dew*
Actual sales in budgeted mix	520 units	390 units
Budgeted sales	400 units	300 units
Quantity variance in units	120 units (F)	90 units (F)
× standard margin per unit	× £5	× £3
	£600 (F)	£270 (F)
Total quantity variance	£870 (F)	

Summary

	£
Sales mix variance	480 (A)
Sales quantity variance	870 (F)
Sales volume profit variance	390 (F)

4.7 If an organisation uses **standard marginal costing** instead of standard absorption costing then standard **contribution** rather than standard **profit margin** is used in the calculations.

4.8 The use of standard profit or contribution in the calculations enables a full **reconciliation** between the original budgeted profit and the actual profit achieved. This is the more usual way to evaluate the sales volume variance and its constituent parts, the sales mix and sales quantity variances. However, it is also possible to use the standard sales **price** to evaluate each of the variances, in place of standard profit or contribution. It would **not be possible to use the resulting variances to perform a full profit reconciliation,** but they may be useful to evaluate the **impact on sales value of the change in volume.** This evaluation may be more meaningful and useful to a manager who is focussed on sales value, such as a salesperson or marketing specialist.

Market size and market share variances

4.9 An alternative focus for the sub-division of the sales volume variance might be in terms of market size and market share.

4.10 The **market size variance** indicates the change in margin or contribution which is **caused by a change in the size of the market**. The **market share variance** indicates the change in margin or contribution which is **caused by a change in the market share achieved**.

4.11 EXAMPLE: MARKET SIZE AND MARKET SHARE VARIANCES

FJH Ltd budgeted to sell 6,000 units of X during year 1. The standard contribution per unit is £10. Actual sales for the year were 6,500 units. In examining the market conditions for year 1 it was found that industry sales were 20% higher than previously forecast.

Required

Calculate the market size and market share variances.

4.12 SOLUTION

Market size variance

Revised sales volume, given industry sales (120% × 6,000 units)	7,200	units
Original budgeted sales volume	6,000	units
	1,200	units (F)
× standard contribution per unit	× £10	
Market size variance	£12,000	(F)

The revised sales volume represents the **sales which would have been budgeted in view of the increased market size**. You may have recognised that the market size variance could be identified as a **planning** variance, that you learned about in your studies for Paper 8.

Market share variance

Actual sales volume	6,500	units
Revised sales volume, given industry sales	7,200	units
	700	units (A)
× standard contribution per unit	× £10	
Market share variance	£7,000	★(A)

The revised sales volume represents the **sales which would have been budgeted to maintain market share in view of the increased market**. The variance therefore represents the decrease in market share and could be identified as an **operational variance**.

You should be able to prove that the sum of the market size variance and the market share variance is equal to the sales volume variance.

	Sales units	
Actual sales volume	6,500	
Budgeted sales volume	6,000	
Sales volume variance in units	500	(F)
× standard contribution per unit	× £10	
Sales volume variance in £	£5,000	(F)

Check: market size variance £12,000 (F) + market share variance £7,000 (A) = £5,000 (F).

4.13 As with the sales mix and quantity variances, the market size and market share variances **can be evaluated in terms of standard selling price**. This would preclude a full profit

reconciliation, but it may be more useful for salespeople or other managers who are focussed on sales value, to highlight the effect of the volume changes on the sales revenue achievable.

Exam focus point

The pilot paper contained a multiple choice question which entailed evaluating the market size and market share variances in terms of the weighted average standard selling price.

Question 4

HYT Limited sells two products, R1 and R2, in the same market. When the original budget was set, the size of the total market was expected to be 5,000 units for the period. In retrospect the size of the total market was found to be 5,500 units.

HYT's budgeted and actual results were as follows.

	Standard selling price	Budget sales units	Actual sales units
Product R1	£32	800	850
Product R2	£14	200	300

The market size and market share variances for the period are

	Market size	Market share
A	£2,300 (F)	£1,150 (F)
B	£2,840 (F)	£1,420 (F)
C	£2,840 (F)	£3,450 (F)
D	£2,840 (A)	£1,420 (F)
E	£2,840 (A)	£3,450 (F)

Answer

The correct option is **B**.

$$\text{Weighted average standard selling price} = \frac{(£32 \times 800) + (£14 \times 200)}{1,000} = £28.40 \text{ per unit}$$

Market size variance

Budgeted market share = (800 + 200)/5,000 = 20%

Given total market sales, sales volume should have been 20% × 5,500 units =	1,100	units
Original budgeted sales volume	1,000	units
	100	units (F)
× weighted average selling price	£28.40	
Market size variance	£2,840	(F)

Market share variance

Actual sales volume	1,150	units
Revised expected sales volume, given total market sales	1,100	units
	50	units (F)
× weighted average standard selling price	£28.40	
	£1,420	(F)

Check: sales volume variance = [(850 + 300) − (800 + 200)] × £28.40 = £4,260 (F)
= £2,840 (F) + £1,420 (F)

Chapter roundup

- **Price elasticity** is a measure of the extent of change in market demand for a good in response to a change in its price. If **demand is elastic** a reduction in price would lead to a rise in total sales revenue. If **demand is inelastic** a reduction in price would lead to a fall in total sales revenue.

- In **full cost-plus pricing** the sales price is determined by calculating the full cost of the product and then adding a percentage mark-up for profit. **Marginal cost-plus pricing** involves adding a profit margin to the marginal cost of production/sales. The most important criticism of full cost-plus pricing is that it fails to recognise that since sales demand may be determined by the sales price, there will be a profit-maximising combination of price and demand. A marginal costing approach is more likely to help with identifying a profit-maximising price.

- The basic approach to pricing **special orders** is **minimum pricing**.

- Three alternative pricing strategies for **new** products are **market penetration pricing, market skimming pricing** and **premium pricing**.

- **Product differentiation** may be used to make products appear to be different and segment markets so that premium prices can be justified in some markets.

- **Optional extras** may also be used to justify premium prices, where the price premium is in excess of the cost of providing the extras.

- **Product bundling** involves selling a number of products or services as a package at a price lower than the aggregate of their individual prices.

- **Loss leaders** relate to the practice of charging a low price for one product in order to encourage consumers to buy additional products which earn higher profit margins.

- **Sales mix** and **sales quantity variances** can be calculated to show the effect on standard contribution/profit/sales revenue of changes in the relative proportions of products sold and changes in the total quantity sold, compared with budget.

- **Market size** and **market share variances** can be calculated to show the effect on standard contribution/profit/sales revenue of changes in the size of the market or in the market share achieved, compared with budget.

Quick quiz

1   The price elasticity of demand for a particular good at the current price is 1.2. Demand for this good at this price is (1) **elastic/inelastic**. If the price of the good is reduced, total sales revenue will (2) **rise/fall/stay the same.**

2   Name the four stages of the product life cycle.

3   Name one advantage, and one disadvantage of full cost-plus pricing.

4   A company knows that demand for its new product will be highly elastic. The most appropriate pricing strategy for the new product will be

Market penetration pricing

Market skimming pricing

5   A theatre offers a special deal whereby two show tickets and pre-theatre dinner can be purchased as a package for a reduced price. This pricing strategy is usually referred to as

    A   Loss leader pricing
    B   Optional extras
    C   Product bundling
    D   Price discrimination
    E   Product differentiation

6   Last period, the sales volume variance was £345 adverse and the sales mix variance was £200 favourable. What was the value of the sales quantity variance?

7   Which of the following variances could be described as planning/operational variances? Tick the correct boxes.

	Planning variance	*Operational variance*
Market share variance		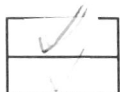
Market size variance		

Answers to quick quiz

1   (1) elastic, (2) rise

2   Introduction, growth, maturity, saturation and decline

3   Advantage = pricing rule can be delegated;
    Disadvantage = takes no account of market and demand conditions

4   Market penetration pricing

5   C

6   £545 adverse

7   Market share variance = operational;
    Market size variance = planning

Now try the question below from the Exam Question Bank

Number	Level	Marks	Time
Q6	Introductory	n/a	n/a

BPP
PUBLISHING

Chapter 5

TRANSFER PRICING

Topic List		Syllabus reference	Ability required
1	The basic principles of transfer pricing	(i)	Explain and demonstrate
2	Transfer pricing with no external market/imperfect market	(i)	Explain and demonstrate
3	Negotiated transfer prices	(i)	Explain and demonstrate
4	Using subsidies to spread risk	(i)	Explain and demonstrate
5	International transfer pricing	(i)	Explain and demonstrate

Introduction

In the previous chapter we looked at how to price the products/services that an organisation sells to an external market. We now have to consider how to price those products/services which are not sold externally but are transferred between different units of the same organisation.

You will have already learned the basic principles of transfer pricing in your studies for Paper 8 but we will begin this chapter by reviewing the basics in the first section, before going on to more advanced principles.

Learning outcomes covered in this chapter

- Explain and demonstrate transfer pricing in an international context

Syllabus content covered in this chapter

- Transfer pricing
- International transfer pricing

1 THE BASIC PRINCIPLES OF TRANSFER PRICING

1.1 **Transfer pricing** is used when divisions of an organisation need to charge other divisions of the same organisation **for goods or services they provide to them**. For example, subsidiary A of X plc might make a component that is used as part of a product made by subsidiary B of X plc, but that can also be sold to the external market, including makers of rival products to subsidiary B's product.

> ## KEY TERM
>
> A **transfer price** is 'The price at which goods or services are transferred between different units of the same company'.
>
> (CIMA *Official Terminology*)

Three problems with transfer pricing

Divisional autonomy

1.2 Transfer prices are particularly appropriate for **profit centres** because if one profit centre does work for another the size of the transfer price will affect the costs of one profit centre and the revenues of another.

1.3 However, a danger with profit centre accounting is that the business organisation will **divide into a number of self-interested segments,** each acting at times against the wishes and interests of other segments. Decisions might be taken by a profit centre manager in the best interests of his own part of the business, but against the best interests of other profit centres and possibly the organisation as a whole.

1.4 A task of **head office** is therefore to try to **prevent dysfunctional decision making** by individual profit centres. To do this, head office must reserve some power and authority for itself and so **profit centres cannot be allowed to make entirely autonomous decisions.**

1.5 Just how much authority head office decides to keep for itself will vary according to individual circumstances. **A balance** ought to be kept **between divisional autonomy** to provide incentives and motivation, and **retaining centralised authority** to ensure that the organisation's profit centres are all working towards the same target, the benefit of the organisation as a whole (in other words, **retaining goal congruence** among the organisation's separate divisions).

Divisional performance measurement

1.6 Profit centre managers tend to put their own profit performance above everything else. Since profit centre performance is measured according to the profit they earn, no profit centre will want to do work for another and incur costs without being paid for it. Consequently, profit centre managers are likely to dispute the size of transfer prices with each other, or disagree about whether one profit centre should do work for another or not. Transfer prices **affect behaviour and decisions** by profit centre managers.

Corporate profit maximisation

1.7 When there are disagreements about how much work should be transferred between divisions, and how many sales the division should make to the external market, there is presumably a **profit-maximising level of output and sales for the organisation as a whole.** However, unless each profit centre also maximises its own profit at this same level of output, there will be inter-divisional disagreements about output levels and the profit-maximising output will not be achieved.

The ideal solution

1.8 Ideally a transfer price should be set at a level that overcomes these problems.

(a) The transfer price should provide an 'artificial' selling price that enables the **transferring division to earn a return for its efforts**, and the **receiving division to incur a cost for benefits received**.

(b) The transfer price should be set at a level that enables **profit centre performance** to be **measured 'commercially'**. This means that the transfer price should be a fair commercial price.

(c) The transfer price, if possible, should encourage profit centre managers to agree on the amount of goods and services to be transferred, which will also be at a level that is consistent with the aims of the organisation as a whole such as **maximising company profits**.

In practice it is difficult to achieve all three aims.

The use of market price as a basis for transfer prices

1.9 If an **external market price exists** for transferred goods, profit centre managers will be aware of the price they could obtain or the price they would have to pay for their goods on the external market, and they would inevitably **compare** this price **with the transfer price**.

1.10 EXAMPLE: TRANSFERRING GOODS AT MARKET VALUE

A company has two profit centres, A and B. A sells half of its output on the open market and transfers the other half to B. Costs and external revenues in an accounting period are as follows.

	A	B	Total
	£	£	£
External sales	8,000	24,000	32,000
Costs of production	12,000	10,000	22,000
Company profit			10,000

Required

What are the consequences of setting a transfer price at market value?

1.11 SOLUTION

If the transfer price is at market price, A would be happy to sell the output to B for £8,000, which is what A would get by selling it externally instead of transferring it.

	A		B		Total
	£	£	£	£	£
Market sales		8,000		24,000	32,000
Transfer sales		8,000		-	
		16,000		24,000	
Transfer costs		-	8,000		
Own costs	12,000		10,000		22,000
		12,000	18,000		
Profit		4,000		6,000	10,000

Consequences

(a) A earns the same profit on transfers as on external sales. B must pay a commercial price for transferred goods, and both divisions will have their profit measured in a fair way.

(b) A will be indifferent about selling externally or transferring goods to B because the profit is the same on both types of transaction. B can therefore ask for and obtain as many units as it wants from A.

Adjusted market price

1.12 **Internal transfers** are often **cheaper** than external sales, with **savings** in selling and administration costs, bad debt risks and possibly transport/delivery costs. It would therefore seem reasonable for the **buying division to expect a discount** on the external market price. The transfer price might be slightly less than market price, so that **A and B could share the cost savings** from internal transfers compared with external sales. It should be possible to reach agreement on this price and on output levels with a minimum of intervention from head office.

The merits and disadvantages of market value transfer prices

1.13 A market-based transfer price therefore seems to be the **ideal** transfer price because the buying division is likely to benefit from a better quality of service, greater flexibility, and dependability of supply. Both divisions may benefit from cheaper costs of administration, selling and transport. A market price as the transfer price would therefore result in decisions which would be in the best interests of the company or group as a whole.

1.14 Market value as a transfer price does have certain **disadvantages**.

(a) The **market price may be a temporary one**, induced by adverse economic conditions, or dumping, or the market price might depend on the volume of output supplied to the external market by the profit centre.

(b) A transfer price at market value might, under some circumstances, **act as a disincentive to use up any spare capacity** in the divisions. A price based on incremental cost, in contrast, might provide an incentive to use up the spare resources in order to provide a marginal contribution to profit.

(c) Many products **do not have an equivalent market price** so that the price of a similar, but not identical, product might have to be chosen. In such circumstances, the option to sell or buy on the open market does not really exist.

(d) There might be an **imperfect external market** for the transferred item, so that if the transferring division tried to sell more externally, it would have to reduce its selling price.

2 TRANSFER PRICING WITH NO EXTERNAL MARKET/IMPERFECT MARKET
Pilot paper

Cost-based approaches to transfer pricing

2.1 Cost-based approaches to transfer pricing are often used in practice, because in practice the following conditions are common.

- There is **no external market** for the product that is being transferred.

- Alternatively, although there is an external market it is an **imperfect** one because the market price is affected by such factors as the amount that the company setting the transfer price supplies to it, or because there is only a limited external demand.

In either case there will **not be a suitable market price** upon which to base the transfer price.

2.2 **Actual costs** vary with volume, seasonal and other factors. Moreover, if actual costs are used as a basis for transfer prices, any inefficiency in the producing department will be passed on to the receiving department in the form of an increased transfer price. The **use of standard costs is therefore recommended**.

Transfer prices based on full cost

2.3 Under this approach, unsurprisingly, the **full cost** (including fixed overheads absorbed) that has been incurred by the supplying division in making the intermediate product is charged to the receiving division. If a **full cost plus approach** is used a **profit margin is also included** in this transfer price.

2.4 EXAMPLE: TRANSFERS AT FULL COST (PLUS)

A company has two profit centres, A and B. A can only sell half of its maximum output externally because of limited demand. It transfers the other half of its output to B which also faces limited demand. Costs and revenues in an accounting period are as follows.

	A	B	Total
	£	£	£
External sales	8,000	24,000	32,000
Costs of production in the division	12,000	10,000	22,000
Profit			10,000

There are no opening or closing stocks. It does not matter, for this illustration, whether marginal costing or absorption costing is used. For the moment, we shall ignore the question of whether the current output levels are profit-maximising and congruent with the goals of the company as a whole.

Transfer price at full cost only

2.5 If the transfer price is at full cost, A in our example would have 'sales' to B of £6,000 (£12,000 × 50%). This would be a cost to B, as follows.

	A		B		Company as a whole
	£	£	£	£	£
Open market sales		8,000		24,000	32,000
Transfer sales		6,000		-	
Total sales, inc transfers		14,000		24,000	
Transfer costs			6,000		
Own costs	12,000		10,000		22,000
Total costs, inc transfers		12,000		16,000	
Profit		2,000		8,000	10,000

The **transfer sales of A are self-cancelling with the transfer costs of B** so that total profits are **unaffected by the transfer items**. The transfer price simply spreads the total profit of £10,000 between A and B.

2.6 The obvious **drawback** to the transfer price at cost is that **A makes no profit** on its work, and the manager of division A would much prefer to sell output on the open market to earn a profit, rather than transfer to B, regardless of whether or not transfers to B would be in the best interests of the company as a whole. Division A needs a profit on its transfers in order to be motivated to supply B; therefore transfer pricing at cost is inconsistent with the use of a profit centre accounting system.

Transfer prices based on full cost plus

2.7 If the transfers are at cost plus a margin of, say, 25%, A's sales to B would be £7,500 (£12,000 × 50% × 1.25).

	A	A	B	B	Total
	£	£	£	£	£
Open market sales		8,000		24,000	32,000
Transfer sales		7,500		-	
		15,500		24,000	
Transfer costs			7,500		
Own costs	12,000		10,000		22,000
		12,000		17,500	
Profit		3,500		6,500	10,000

2.8 Compared to a transfer price at cost, **A gains some profit** at the expense of B. However, A makes a bigger profit on external sales in this case because the profit mark-up of 25% is less than the profit mark-up on open market sales. The choice of 25% as a profit mark-up was arbitrary and unrelated to external market conditions.

2.9 The transfer price **fails on all three criteria** (divisional autonomy, performance measurement and corporate profit measurement) for judgement.

(a) Arguably, the transfer price does not give A fair revenue or charge B a reasonable cost, and so their profit **performance is distorted**. It would certainly be unfair, for example, to compare A's profit with B's profit.

(b) Given this unfairness it is likely that the **autonomy** of each of the divisional managers is **under threat**. If they cannot agree on what is a fair split of the external profit a decision will have to be imposed from above.

(c) It would seem to give A an incentive to sell more goods externally and transfer less to B. This may or **may not be in the best interests of the company as a whole**.

2.10 In fact we can demonstrate that the method is **flawed from the point of view of corporate profit maximisation**. Division A's total costs of £12,000 will include an element of fixed costs. Half of division A's total costs are transferred to division B. However from the point of view of division B the cost is entirely variable.

2.11 Suppose that the cost per unit to A is £15 and that this includes a fixed element of £6, while division B's own costs are £25 (10,000 ÷ 400) per unit, including a fixed element of £10. The **total variable cost is really £9 + £15 = £24**, but from division **B's point of view** the **variable cost is £15 + £15 = £30**. This means that division B will be unwilling to sell the final product for less than £30, whereas any price above £24 would make a contribution to overall costs. Thus if external prices for the final product fall, B might be tempted to cease production.

Transfer prices based on variable cost

2.12 A variable cost approach entails charging the variable cost that has been incurred by the supplying division to the receiving division. As above, we shall suppose that A's cost per unit is £15, of which £6 is fixed and £9 variable.

	A £	A £	B £	B £	Company as a whole £	Company as a whole £
Market sales		8,000		24,000		32,000
Transfer sales		3,600		-		
		11,600		24,000		
Transfer costs	-		3,600			
Own variable costs	7,200		6,000		13,200	
Own fixed costs	4,800		4,000		8,800	
Total costs and transfers		12,000		13,600		22,000
(Loss)/Profit		(400)		10,400		10,000

2.13 This result is **deeply unsatisfactory for the manager of division** A who could make an additional £4,400 (£(8,000 – 3,600)) profit if no goods were transferred to division B. For the company overall, however, this action would cause a large fall in profit, because division B could make no sales at all.

2.14 The problem is that with a transfer price at variable cost the **supplying division does not cover its fixed costs.**

Fixed costs and transfer pricing

2.15 There are a number of ways in which the problem in Paragraph 2.14 can be overcome.

(a) Use a transfer price based on variable cost and, at the end of the period, the supplying division is credited with a share of the overall profit arising from the final sale of the transferred goods. This **dual pricing** system seems fairer but it will be necessary to determine the share of profits centrally, thus **undermining divisional autonomy.**

(b) A further variation on **dual pricing**, where an external market exists, is to credit the selling division with the market price for transfers made, but debit the buying division with the variable or marginal cost. This can be effective in avoiding dysfunctional behaviour and sub-optimal decisions, but it can be administratively cumbersome.

(c) A **two-part tariff system** can be used. Transfer prices are set at variable cost and once a year there is a **transfer of a fixed fee to the supplying division**, representing an allowance for its fixed costs. This method risks sending the message to the supplying division that it need not control its fixed costs, however, because the company will subsidise any inefficiencies. On the other hand, if fixed costs are incurred because spare capacity is kept available for the needs of other divisions, it is reasonable to expect those other divisions to pay a fee if they 'booked' that capacity in advance but later failed to utilise it. But the main problem with this approach is that it is likely to **conflict with divisional autonomy.**

Transfer pricing when there is no external market for the transferred item

2.16 If there is **no similar item sold on an external market**, and if the **transferred item** is a **major product of the transferring division**, there is a strong argument that **profit centre accounting is a waste of time.** Profit centres cannot be judged on their commercial performance because there is no way of estimating what a fair revenue for their work should be. It would be more appropriate, perhaps, to treat the transferring division as a cost centre, and to judge performance on the basis of cost variances.

2.17 If **profit centres are established**, in the **absence of a market price**, the **optimum transfer price is likely to be one based on standard cost plus**, but only provided that the **variable**

cost per unit and selling price per unit are unchanged at all levels of output. A standard cost plus price would motivate divisional managers to increase output and to reduce expenditure levels.

2.18 EXAMPLE: STANDARD COST PLUS AS A TRANSFER PRICE IN THE ABSENCE OF AN EXTERNAL MARKET

Motivate Ltd has two profit centres, P and Q. P transfers all its output to Q. The variable cost of output from P is £5 a unit, and fixed costs are £1,200 a month. Additional processing costs in Q are £4 a unit for variable costs, plus fixed costs of £800 a month. Budgeted production is 400 units a month, and the output of Q sells for £15 a unit.

Required

Determine the range of prices from which the transfer price (based on standard full cost plus) should be selected, in order to motivate the managers of both profit centres to both increase output and reduce costs.

2.19 SOLUTION

Any transfer price based on standard cost plus will motivate managers to cut costs, because favourable variances between standard costs and actual costs will be credited to the division's profits. Managers of each division will also be willing to increase output (above the budget) provided that it is profitable to do so.

(a) The **manager of P** will **increase output if the transfer price exceeds the variable cost** of £5 a unit.

(b) The **manager of Q** will **increase output if the transfer price is less than** the difference between the fixed selling price (£15) and the variable costs in Q itself. This amount of £11 (£15 – £4) is sometimes called **net marginal revenue**.

The range of prices is therefore between £5.01 and £10.99.

Check

Suppose the transfer price is £9. With absorption based on the budgeted output of 400 units what would divisional profits be if output and sales are 400 units and 500 units?

Overheads per unit are £1,200/400. The full cost of sales is £(5 + 3) = £8 in division P. In division Q, full cost is £(4 + 2) = £6, plus transfer costs of £9.

(a) At 400 units:

	P	*Q*	*Total*
	£	£	£
Sales	-	6,000	6,000
Transfer sales	3,600	-	
Transfer costs	-	(3,600)	
Own full cost of sales	(3,200)	(2,400)	(5,600)
	400	0	400
Under-/over-absorbed overhead	0	0	0
Profit/(loss)	400	0	400

(b) At 500 units:

	P	Q	Total
	£	£	£
Sales	-	7,500	7,500
Transfer sales	4,500	-	-
Transfer costs	-	(4,500)	-
Own full cost of sales	(4,000)	(3,000)	(7,000)
	500	0	500
Over-absorbed overhead	300	200	500
Profit/(loss)	800	200	1,000

Increasing output improves the profit performance of both divisions and the company as a whole, and so decisions on output by the two divisions are likely to be **goal congruent**.

2.20 To summarise the **transfer price should be set in the range** where:

variable cost in supplying division $\leq$ **selling price minus variable costs (net marginal revenue) in the receiving division**

Profit maximisation with no external market and changing costs/prices

2.21 If cost behaviour patterns change and the selling price to the external market is reduced at higher levels of output, there will be a profit-maximising level of output: to produce more than an 'optimum' amount would cause reductions in profitability.

2.22 Under such circumstances, the **ideal transfer price** is one which would **motivate profit centre managers to produce at the optimum level of output, and neither below nor above this level.**

2.23 EXAMPLE: THE PROFIT-MAXIMISING TRANSFER PRICE

MCMR Ltd has two divisions, S and T. There is no external intermediate market and so S transfers all its output to T, which finishes the work. Costs and revenues at various levels of capacity are as follows.

Output	S costs	T revenues	T costs	T net revenues	Profit
Units	£	£	£	£	£
600	600	3,190	240	2,950	2,350
700	700	3,530	280	3,250	2,550
800	840	3,866	336	3,530	2,690
900	1,000	4,180	400	3,780	2,780
1,000	1,200	4,480	480	4,000	2,800 ★
1,100	1,450	4,780	580	4,200	2,750
1,200	1,800	5,070	720	4,350	2,550

Company profits are maximised at £2,800 with output of 1,000 units. But if we wish to select a transfer price in order to establish S and T as profit centres, what transfer price would motivate the managers of S and T together to produce 1,000 units, no more and no less?

2.24 DISCUSSION AND SOLUTION

The transfer price will act as revenue to S and as a cost to T.

(a) **S will continue to produce more output until** the costs of additional production exceed the transfer price revenue, that is where the **marginal cost exceeds the transfer price**.

(b) **T will continue to want to receive more output from S until** its net revenue from further processing is not sufficient to cover the additional transfer price costs, that is where its **net marginal revenue is less than the transfer price**.

Output	Division S Marginal costs	Division T Net marginal revenues
Units	£	£
600	-	-
700	100	300
800	140	280
900	160	250
1,000	200 *	220 *
1,100	250	200
1,200	350	150

Since S will continue to produce more output if the transfer price exceeds the marginal cost of production, a **price of at least £200 per 100 units (£2 per unit) is required to 'persuade' the manager of S to produce as many as 1,000 units**. A price in excess of £250 per 100 units would motivate the manager of S to produce 1,100 units or more.

By a similar argument, T will continue to want more output from S if the net marginal revenues exceed the transfer costs from S. **If T wants 1,000 units, the transfer price must be less than £220 per 100 units**. However, if the transfer price is lower than £200 per 100 units, T will ask for 1,100 units from S in order to improve its divisional profit further.

Summary

• The total company profit is maximised at 1,000 units of output.

• Division S will want to produce 1,000 units, no more and no less, if the transfer price is between £200 to £250 per 100 units, or £2 and £2.50 per unit.

• Division T will want to receive and process 1,000 units, no more and no less, if the transfer price per unit is between £2 and £2.20.

• A transfer price must therefore be selected in the **range £2.00 to £2.20 per unit** (exclusive).

2.25 The **transfer price should therefore be set in the range** where

marginal cost in supplying division = net marginal revenue in the receiving division

Except that we use the term 'marginal' instead of 'variable', this is precisely the same solution as the one we reached in Paragraph 2.20.

Question 1

Explain how the following figures are calculated, or arrived at.

(a) Paragraph 2.23 - T net revenues
(b) Paragraph 2.24(b) - Division S marginal costs
(c) Paragraph 2.24(b) - Division T net marginal revenue
(d) Paragraph 2.24 - a transfer price of £2.10 per unit

Answer

(a) T revenues minus T costs
(b) S costs for 700 units minus S costs for 600 units (and so on)
(c) T net revenues for 700 units minus T net revenues for 600 units (and so on)
(d) See Paragraph 2.24

This exercise is to make sure that you were following the argument.

Profit maximisation with an external market and changing costs/prices

Imperfect external market

2.26 The approach is essentially the same as the one shown in paragraph 2.24, except that the supplying division may also have income, and so its marginal revenue needs to be taken into account.

2.27 EXAMPLE: PROFIT MAXIMISATION WITH AN IMPERFECT EXTERNAL MARKET

IMP Ltd makes hand-built sports cars. The company has two divisions, M and N. The output of division M can either be sold externally or transferred to division N which turns it into a version for the USA. Due to competition from Japanese car makers the US market is giving poor returns at present. Cost and marginal revenues at various levels of output are as follows.

Cars produced	M Total cost £'000	M Marginal cost £'000	M Marginal revenue £'000	N Net marginal revenue £'000
1	18	18	20 (1)	18 (2)
2	26	8	16 (3)	12 (4)
3	35	9	12 (5)	6
4	45	10	8 (6) will not be built	0
5	56	11	4	(6)
6	68	12	0	(12)
7	81	13	(4)	(18)
8	95	14	(8)	0

Required

Determine the optimal output level.

2.28 SOLUTION

Note the following.

(a) In this situation, for any individual car, **marginal revenue will be received by division M *or* net marginal revenue will be received by division N. The same car cannot be sold twice!**

(b) Marginal revenue is the extra amount received for each additional car sold into M's market (or net marginal revenue is the extra amount for additional cars in N's market). Thus the marginal revenue for three cars in M's market is £12,000 only if all three cars have been sold in M's market. If three are produced but one is sold in N's market, the marginal revenue for M for the other two is £16,000.

(c) For each car produced a decision must therefore be made as to which market to sell it in, and this will be done according to which market offers the higher marginal revenue.

(d) As shown by the numbers in brackets, the first car is sold in M's market, the second in N's, the third in M's, and the fourth and fifth in either. By the time six cars have been produced and shared out between the two markets the marginal cost has risen to £12,000. This is greater than the marginal revenue obtainable from either market (£8,000 in M, £6,000 in N).

(e) The sixth car will therefore not be built. Division M will produce five units and sell three cars itself and transfer two to division N. The transfer price must be more than £11,000 to meet M's marginal cost, but less than £12,000 otherwise division N will not buy it.

2.29 EXAMPLE: MAXIMISING PROFITS WITH SHORT SUPPLIES

Suppose that one month division M suffered a two-week strike and was only able to produce 2 cars. If it follows normal policy and transfers the second to division N, its own results for the month will be as follows.

		£'000
Sales	- own	20
	- transfers	11
		31
Total cost		26
		5

However, if division M keeps the second car and sells both in its own market it will earn £36,000 in total (£20,000 + £16,000) increasing its own divisional profit by £5,000.

From the point of view of the company this is a bad decision. If the second car is transferred to division N it can be sold for £18,000. Overall revenue and profit will increase by £2,000 ((£18,000 – 16,000)).

2.30 In other words, where there is a **capacity constraint** resulting in short supplies of the product, **a transfer price based on matching marginal cost and marginal revenue will not encourage corporate profit maximisation**.

2.31 The only way to be sure that a profit maximising transfer policy will be implemented is to **dictate the policy from the centre.**

Perfect external market

2.32 The approach is the same as that used for an imperfect external market except that marginal revenue for the supplying division is constant at the market price.

2.33 EXAMPLE: PROFIT MAXIMISATION WITH A PERFECT EXTERNAL MARKET

We will use the example IMP Ltd but this time the market price achieved by M is £10,000. The costs and marginal revenues at various levels of output are as follows.

Cars produced	M Total cost £'000	M Marginal cost £'000	M Marginal revenue £'000	N Net marginal revenue £'000
1	18	18	10 (3)	18 (1)
2	26	8	10 (4)	12 (2)
3	35	9	10	6
4	45	10	10	0
5	56	11	10	(6)
6	68	12	10	(12)
7	81	13	10	(18)
8	95	14	10	0

Marginal cost is greater than marginal revenue in either market by the fifth car, so four cars will be built, two sold by M and two transferred to be sold by N. As seen earlier, the market price will be the transfer price.

Graphical representation

2.34 A graphical representation of the IMP Ltd example with a perfect external market is shown below.

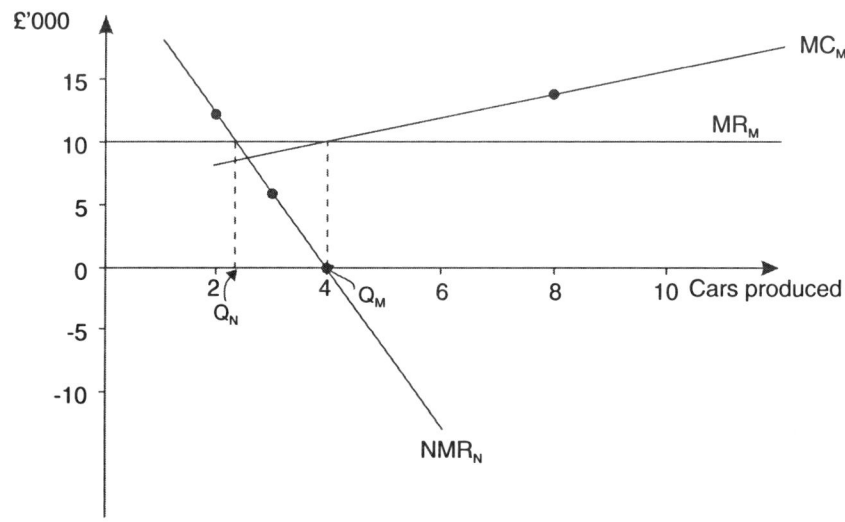

2.35 Profits are maximised when marginal cost = marginal revenue.

- **For M,** this is when $MC_M = MR_M$. M will make four cars.

- **For N,** this is when $MR_M = NMR_N$, because MR_M **is the transfer price** (which is the marginal cost to N). Only whole cars can be made and so, as Q_N is between two and three, two cars should be transferred.

2.36 Note that the graph has omitted the initial dip in MC_M (due to the fixed costs) for the sake of clarity.

Exam focus point

The pilot paper included a multiple choice question on transfer pricing. Given the transfer price and costs, it was necessary to determine the profit maximising output, ie where marginal cost = marginal revenue.

Transfer prices based on opportunity costs

Question 2

Opportunity costs were covered in chapter 1 of this text. Do you remember what they are?

Answer

An opportunity cost is the benefit forgone by choosing one alternative instead of the next best alternative.

2.37 It has been suggested that transfer prices can be set using the following rule.

> **Transfer price per unit = standard variable cost** in the producing division **plus** the **opportunity cost to the organisation as a whole for supplying the unit internally**

2.38 The **opportunity cost** will be one of the following.

(a) The maximum contribution forgone by the supplying division **in transferring internally rather than selling goods externally**

(b) The contribution forgone by **not using the same facilities** in the producing division **for their next best alternative use**

2.39 If there is **no external market** for the item being transferred, and **no alternative uses for** the division's facilities, the **transfer price = standard variable cost of production.**

If there is an **external market** for the item being transferred and **no alternative, more profitable use** for the facilities in that division, the **transfer price = the market price.**

Identifying the optimal transfer price

2.40 Throughout the chapter we have been leading up to the following guiding rules for identifying the optimal transfer price.

(a) The **ideal transfer price** should **reflect the opportunity cost** of sale to the supply division and the opportunity cost to the buying division. Unfortunately, full information about opportunity costs may not be easily obtainable in practice.

(b) Where a **perfect external market price exists and unit variable costs and unit selling prices are constant,** the **opportunity cost** of transfer will be **external market price** or **external market price less savings in selling costs.**

(c) In the **absence of a perfect external market price for the transferred item,** but when **unit variable costs are constant,** and the **sales price per unit of the end-product is constant,** the **ideal transfer price** should reflect the opportunity cost of the resources consumed by the supply division to make and supply the item and so should be at **standard variable cost + opportunity cost of making the transfer.**

(d) When **unit variable costs and/or unit selling prices are not constant,** there will be a **profit-maximising level of output** and the **ideal transfer price** will only be found by sensible **negotiation** and careful **analysis.**

(i) Establish the output and sales quantities that will optimise the profits of the company or group as a whole.

(ii) Establish the transfer price at which both profit centres would maximise their profits at this company-optimising output level.

There may be a range of prices within which both profit centres can agree on the output level that would maximise their individual profits and the profits of the company as a whole. Any price within the range would then be 'ideal'.

Question 3

You should try to learn the above rules, and refer back to the appropriate part of the chapter if you are not sure about any point. Read through the rules again and then answer these questions.

(a)   In what situation should the transfer price be the external market price?

(b)   How should the transfer price be established when there are diseconomies of scale and prices have to be lowered to increase sales volume?

(c)   What is the ideal transfer price?

(d)   In what circumstances should the transfer price be standard variable cost + the opportunity cost of making the transfer?

3   NEGOTIATED TRANSFER PRICES

3.1   A transfer price based on opportunity cost is often difficult to identify, for lack of suitable information about costs and revenues in individual divisions.

3.2   In this case it is likely that transfer prices will be set by means of negotiation. The agreed price may be finalised from a mixture of accounting arithmetic, politics and compromise.

(a)   A negotiated price might be based on market value, but with some reductions to allow for the internal nature of the transaction, which saves external selling and distribution costs

(b)   Where one division receives near-finished goods from another, a negotiated price might be based on the market value of the end product, minus an amount for the finishing work in the receiving division.

Behavioural implications

3.3   Even so, inter-departmental **disputes** about transfer prices are likely to arise and these may need the **intervention or mediation of head office** to settle the problem. Head office management may then **impose a price** which maximises the profit of the company as a whole. On the other hand, head office management might restrict their intervention to the **task of keeping negotiations in progress** until a transfer price is eventually settled. The **more head office has to impose** its own decisions on profit centres, the less **decentralisation of authority** there will be and the **less effective the profit centre system** of accounting will be for **motivating** divisional managers.

4   USING SUBSIDIES TO SPREAD RISK

4.1   A situation may arise where a large division requires a much smaller division to provide components for its product. This may require a substantial investment to be made by the smaller division, with a considerable commitment to fixed cost expenditure.

4.2   This fixed cost commitment may represent a substantial risk to the smaller division if things do not turn out as planned. On the other hand, the amounts of money involved may be relatively insignificant to the larger division and may not expose the larger company to any major risk.

4.3 This difference is due to the different **utilities** of the various sums of money for the two businesses. It may be possible to spread the risk if the larger division is willing to contribute towards the fixed cost in return for a reduction in the transfer price.

4.4 EXAMPLE: UTILITY FUNCTION

Division S has the following utilities (U) for different levels of profit or loss (P).

$U = P$ where $P \geq -£50,000$ Equation (a)

$U = 150,000 + 4P$ where $P < -£50,000$ Equation (b)

Draw the graph of the division's utility function from $P = -£100,000$ to $P = £100,000$.

4.5 SOLUTION

All figures are in thousands

When $P = 100$, $U = 100$ (using equation (a))
When $P = 0$, $U = 0$ (using equation (a))
When $P = -50$, $U = -50$ (using both equations)
When $P = -100$, $U = 150 - (4 \times 100) = -250$ (using equation (b))

This data is used to draw the graph on the following page.

The utility reduces sharply for losses greater than £50,000 because division S is extremely averse to such losses.

4.6 A knowledge of the supplying division's utility function can help to assess the suitability of a subsidised transfer pricing arrangement.

Utility function of Division S

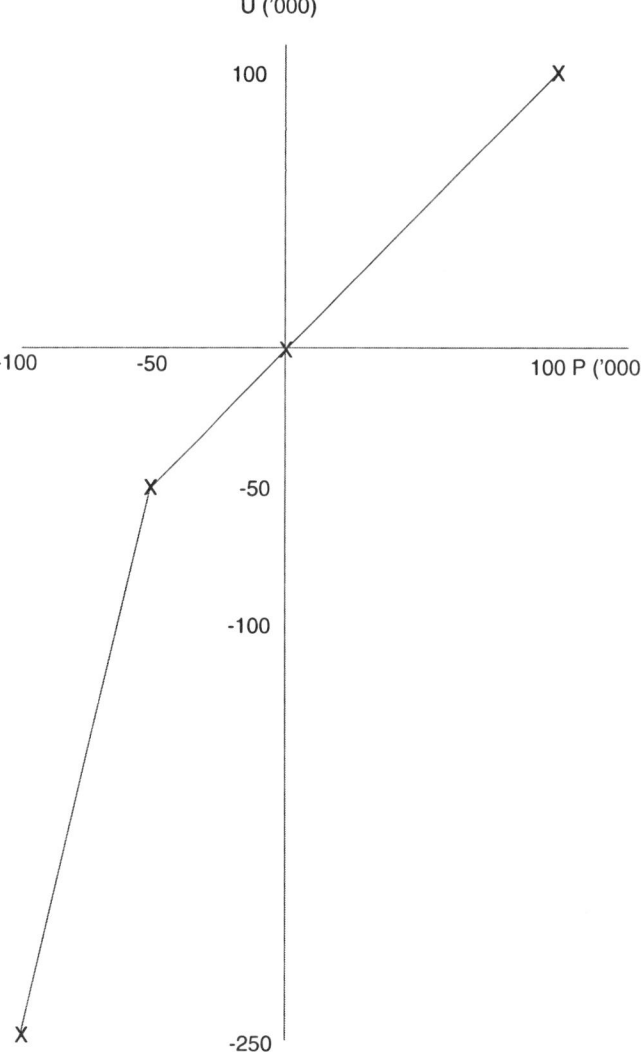

4.7 EXAMPLE: USING SUBSIDIES TO SPREAD RISK

Division S (see paragraph 4.4) has been approached by division B to supply components to B at a transfer price of £50 per unit. Relevant cost and demand data is as follows.

Variable cost per unit in division S   £30
Annual fixed costs in division S   £680,000

Annual demand	*Probability*
Units	
25,000	0.25
35,000	0.50
45,000	0.25

(a) Calculate division S's expected profit from the supply of the components to division B.

(b) Calculate division S's expected utility of profit and interpret it.

(c) Division B is prepared to assist division S by paying £385,000 towards the annual fixed costs provided this is compensated by a reduction in the transfer price, assuming demand is at its expected level. Will this arrangement be acceptable to division S?

4.8 SOLUTION

(a) Contribution per unit = £50 – £30 = £20

Expected demand $= (25,000 \times 0.25) + (35,000 \times 0.5) + (45,000 \times 0.25)$

$= 35,000$ units

Expected profit $= (35,000 \times £20) - £680,000 = £20,000$

(b)

Lowest profit = (25,000 × £20) – £680,000	= – £180,000
From equation (b) in paragraph 4.4, U = 150,000 – (4 × 180,000)	= – 570,000
Middle profit = (35,000 × £20) – £680,000	= £20,000
From equation (a) in paragraph 4.4, U	= 20,000
Highest profit = (45,000 × £20) – £680,000	= £220,000
From equation (a) in paragraph 4.4, U	= 220,000
Expected utility = (–570,000 × 0.25) + (20,000 × 0.5) + (220,000 × 0.25)	= –77,500 U

The fact that the expected utility is negative means that division S will not be prepared to supply to division B on these terms, because they are extremely averse to losses greater than £50,000.

(c) With expected demand of 35,000 units, an outlay of £385,000 towards the annual fixed costs will be compensated by a transfer price reduction of £385,000/35,000 = £11 per unit.

Revised transfer price = £50 – £11	= £39 per unit
Revised contribution = £39 – £30	= £9 per unit
Fixed costs to be borne by division S = £680,000 – £385,000	= £295,000
Lowest profit = (25,000 × £9) – £295,000	= – £70,000
From equation (b) in paragraph 4.4, U = 150,000 – (4 × 70,000)	= –130,000
Middle profit = (35,000 × £9) – £295,000	= £20,000
From equation (a)in paragraph 4.4, U	= 20,000
Highest profit = (45,000 × £9) – £295,000	= £110,000
From equation (a)in paragraph 4.4, U	= 110,000
Expected utility = (–130,000 × 0.25) + (20,000 × 0.5) + (110,000 × 0.25)	= 5,000 U

This arrangement should be acceptable to division S because it has a positive expected utility.

Question 4

In the previous example, division S could accept losses of up to £50,000 but was strongly averse to greater losses. Suppose that S's utility function changes to the following, which indicates extreme aversion to any loss.

U = P where P ≥ 0

U = 5P where P < 0

(a) Draw the graph of S's revised utility function from P = –£100,00 to P = £100,000

(b) Calculate division S's utility of profit without the fixed cost subsidy and interpret it.

(c) Will the proposed fixed cost subsidy be acceptable to S with the revised utility function?

Answer

(a)   *Data for graph*

When   P = £100,000   U = £100,000
            P = 0   U = 0
            P = −£100,000   U = −£500,000

Utility function of Division S

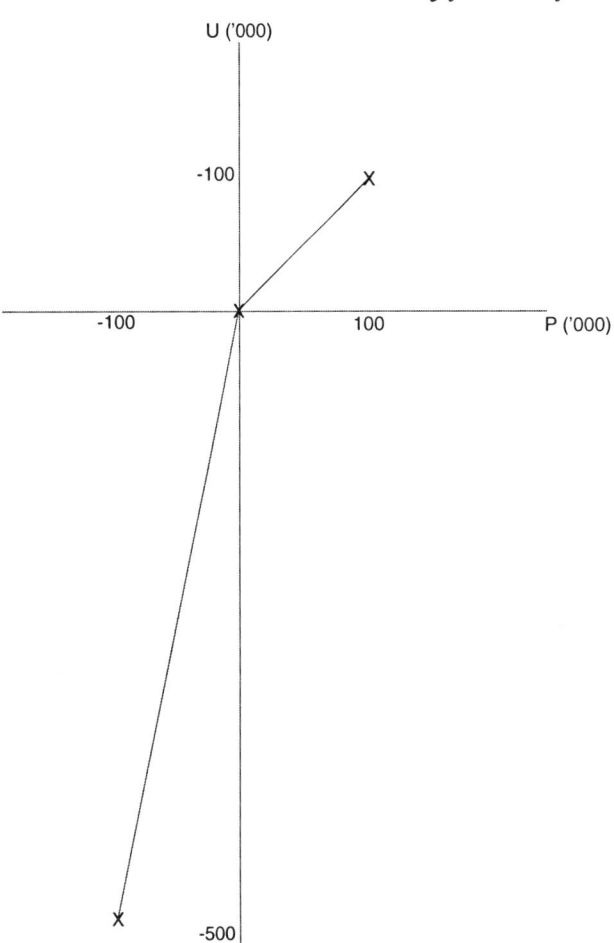

(b)   Lowest profit = −£180,000 as before, and U = (−180,000 × 5) = −900,000

The other utilities are unchanged at 20,000 and 220,000.

Expected utility = (−900,000 × 0.25) + (20,000 × 0.5) + (220,000 × 0.25) = −160,000 U

The negative utility means that division S would not be willing to supply to Division B without the subsidy.

(c)   Lowest profit = −£70,000 as before
            U   = (−70,000 × 5)
                = −350,000

The other utilities are unchanged at 20,000 and 110,000

Expected utility = (−350,000 × 0.25) + (20,000 × 0.5) + (110,000 × 0.25) = −50,000U

In this case the arrangement is not acceptable to division S because of their extreme aversion to any loss.

---

5   INTERNATIONAL TRANSFER PRICING

5.1   As we have seen, the level at which a transfer price should be set is not a straightforward decision for organisations. The situation is even less clear cut for organisations operating in

a number of countries, when even more factors need to be taken into consideration. Moreover, the manipulation of profits through the use of transfer pricing is a common area of confrontation between multinational organisations and host country governments.

Factor	Explanation
Exchange rate fluctuation	The value of a transfer of goods between profit centres in different countries could depend on fluctuations in the currency exchange rate.
Taxation in different countries	If taxation on profits is 20% of profits in Country A and 50% on profits in Country B, a company will presumably try to 'manipulate' profits (by means of raising or lowering transfer prices or by invoicing the subsidiary in the high-tax country for 'services' provided by the subsidiary in the low-tax country) so that profits are maximised for a subsidiary in Country A, by reducing profits for a subsidiary in Country B.
	Artificial attempts at reducing tax liabilities could, however, upset a country's tax officials if they discover it and may lead to some form of penalty. Many tax authorities have the power to modify transfer prices in computing tariffs or taxes on profit, although a genuine arms-length market price should be accepted.
Import tariffs	Suppose that Country A imposes an import tariff of 20% on the value of goods imported. A multi-national company has a subsidiary in Country A which imports goods from a subsidiary in Country B. In such a situation, the company would minimise costs by keeping the transfer price to a minimum value.
Exchange controls	If a country imposes restrictions on the transfer of profits from domestic subsidiaries to foreign multinationals, the restrictions on the transfer can be overcome if head office provides some goods or services to the subsidiary and charges exorbitantly high prices, disguising the 'profits' as sales revenue, and transferring them from one country to the other. The ethics of such an approach should, of course, be questioned.
Anti-dumping legislation	Governments may take action to protect home industries by preventing companies from transferring goods cheaply into their countries. They may do this, for example, by insisting on the use of a fair market value for the transfer price.
Competitive pressures	Transfer pricing can be used to enable profit centres to match or undercut local competitors.

BPP
PUBLISHING

The pros and cons of different transfer pricing bases

5.2 (a) A transfer price at **market value** is usually encouraged by the tax and customs authorities of both host and home countries as they will receive a fair share of the profits made but there are problems with its use.

   (i) Prices for the same product may vary considerably from one country to another.

   (ii) Changes in exchange rates, local taxes and so on can result in large variations in selling price.

   (iii) A division will want to set its prices in relation to the supply and demand conditions present in the country in question to ensure that it can compete in that country.

   (b) A transfer price at **cost** is usually acceptable to tax and customs authorities since it provides some indication that the transfer price approximates to the real cost of supplying the item and because it indicates that they will therefore receive a fair share of tax and tariff revenues. Cost-based approaches do not totally remove the suspicion that the figure may have been massaged because the choice of the type of cost (full actual, full standard, actual variable, marginal) can alter the size of the transfer price.

   (c) In a multinational organisation, **negotiated** transfer prices may result in overall sub-optimisation because no account is taken of factors such as differences in tax and tariff rates between countries.

Question 5

RBN is a UK parent company with an overseas subsidiary. The directors of RBN wish to transfer profits from the UK to the overseas company. They are considering changing the level of the transfer prices charged on goods shipped from the overseas subsidiary to UK subsidiaries and the size of the royalty payments paid by UK subsidiaries to the overseas subsidiary.

In order to transfer profit from the UK to the overseas subsidiary, the directors of RBN should

A   increase both the transfer prices and royalty payments
B   increase the transfer prices but decrease the royalty payments
C   decrease the transfer prices but increase the royalty payments
D   decrease both the transfer prices and royalty payments
E   allow the subsidiaries to agree their own transfer prices and royalty payments

Answer

The correct option is **A**.

To increase the overseas subsidiary's profit, the transfer price needs to be higher (since it is the overseas subsidiary doing the selling) and the royalty payments by the UK subsidiaries to the overseas subsidiary company should also be higher. Both would add to the overseas subsidiary's revenue without affecting its costs.

5.3 A recent study by Ernst and Young of 210 multinationals found that 49% were being investigated over transfer pricing, while 83% had been involved in a transfer pricing dispute at some time.

   'Transfer pricing is big business ... The figures involved are sometimes huge. During the 1992 presidential campaign, Bill Clinton claimed that $45bn in tax revenue could be raised from foreign-based enterprises operating in the US which were unfairly allocating their profits by transfer pricing distortions.'   (J Kelly, *Financial Times,* 23 November 1995)

Case examples

The following descriptions are taken from Christopher Pass's article 'Transfer Pricing in Multinational Companies' which appeared in the September 1994 edition of *Management Accounting*.

'In 1993 Nissan agreed to pay 'penalty taxes' of Y17bn (£106m) to the US Internal Revenue Services (IRS) following an IRS investigation which concluded that Nissan had avoided US taxes by transferring part of its US profits to Japan in the early 1990s. The IRS's main contention was that Nissan had set transfer prices on its passenger cars and trucks imported from Japan at 'unrealistically' high levels and as a result declared lower profits in the US than it should have done. What constitutes a 'fair' or 'realistic' transfer price is, as we have indicated above, open to question. In the USA, the common Japanese practice of charging relatively low prices to build market share over the longer term is viewed with some scepticism and hence has raised suspicions regarding 'unfair' transfer pricing practices.

The NTA alleged that many US and European concerns had deliberately under-recorded profits earned in Japan both by charging 'excessive' transfer prices to their local subsidiaries for materials imported from their parent companies, and by levying 'excessive' royalty payments on their Japanese subsidiaries.

The NTA imposed a penalty tax of Y15bn (£96m) on Cola-Cola for 'unfair' transfer pricing practices and for applying excessive brand and marketing royalty payments transferred to its US parent company over the period 1990-92; while Ciba-Geigy was charged a penalty tax of Y5.7bn (£38m) and Roche Y10bn (£64m) for engaging in manipulative transfer pricing over a similar three year period. Hoechst has been 'fined' an undisclosed amount which it is appealing against before a Japan-Germany inter-governmental tax authority.'

Chapter roundup

- Transfer prices are a way of promoting **divisional autonomy**, ideally without prejudicing the **measurement of divisional performance** or discouraging **overall corporate profit maximisation**.

- Transfer prices should be set at a level which ensures that profits for the organisation as a whole are maximised.

- If **variable costs and market prices are constant**, regardless of the volume of output, a **market-based transfer price** is the ideal transfer price. If there is **no external market** for the transferred item the optimum transfer price is likely to be one based on **standard cost plus**.

- When **unit costs and prices are not constant at all levels of output**, there will be a profit-maximising level above which total revenue will start to decline. The ideal transfer price is one which motivates profit centre managers to produce at the optimum level of output for the organisation. This level may be below full capacity. The transfer price set should enable individual divisions to maximise their profits at this level of output. The transfer price which achieves this is unlikely to be market based or cost based.

- Where goods are transferred internally by a **supply division which also has an outside market** for its product, the optimum **transfer price is one based on opportunity cost** so that there is not a more profitable opportunity for an individual division. The problem with this approach is that it entails collecting all the relevant divisional data centrally and imposing a transfer price, undermining divisional autonomy.

- If divisional managers are allowed to **negotiate transfer prices** with each other, the agreed price may be finalised from a mixture of accounting arithmetic, politics and compromise.

- A consideration of the supplying division's **utility function** can assist in assessing the acceptability of a transfer price with **subsidies to spread risk.**

- Problems associated with currency exchange rates, taxation, import tariffs, exchange control, anti-dumping legislation and competitive pressures arise **with transfer pricing in multinational companies**.

BPP
PUBLISHING

Quick quiz

1 What three criteria should a transfer price ideally fulfil?

2 Name one advantage and one disadvantage of a market based transfer price

3 Division P transfers it output to division Q at variable cost. Once a year P charges a fixed fee to Q, representing an allowance for P's fixed costs. This type of transfer pricing system is commonly known as

    A   Dual pricing
    B   Negotiated transfer pricing
    C   Opportunity cost based transfer pricing
    D   Two-part tariff transfer pricing
    E   Subsidised transfer pricing

4 Profits are maximised when marginal cost is equal to marginal revenue. True or false?

5 When transfer prices are based on opportunity costs, how are opportunity costs determined?

6 Taxation on profits in country C is charged at a higher rate than in country D. When goods are transferred from a subsidiary in country C to a subsidiary in country D it would be beneficial, from the point of view of the whole organisation, to charge a (1) **higher/lower** transfer price so that the total taxation cost for the organisation is (2) **higher/lower**.

Answers to quick quiz

1   (1)   Should reward the transferring division and be a reasonable cost for the receiving division.
    (2)   Should enable the measurement of profit centre performance.
    (3)   Should encourage output at the level which maximises profits of the whole organisation.

2   *Advantage:* fairness; *disadvantage:* equivalent market price for an identical product may not exist.

3   D

4   True

5   *Either* the contribution forgone by the supplying division in transferring internally rather than selling externally, *or* the contribution forgone by not using the relevant facilities for their next best alternative use.

6   (1)   Lower
    (2)   Lower

Now try the question below from the Exam Question Bank

Number	Level	Marks	Time
7	Introductory	n/a	n/a

Part B
Costing and accounting systems

Chapter 6

RELATING COSTS TO COST OBJECTS

Topic list		Syllabus reference	Ability required
1	The nature of costs	(ii)	Apply and evaluate
2	Activity based costing	(ii)	Apply and evaluate
3	Customer profitability analysis	(ii)	Apply and evaluate
4	Direct product profitability	(ii)	Apply and evaluate
5	Activity based management (ABM)	(ii)	Apply and evaluate
6	Behavioural aspects – overhead allocation (Japanese)	(ii)	Apply and evaluate

Introduction

The next two chapters consider the costing and accounting systems section of the syllabus. This chapter will deal with the tricky problem of the treatment of costs in these systems and the following chapter with costing and accounting systems to suit particular manufacturing and operations systems.

You have probably already encountered **activity based costing** (ABC) in your earlier studies but we will be studying the topic in more detail and considering how it can also be used by service and retail organisations.

Customer profitability analysis and **direct product profitability** will probably be new to you. In some organisations it is just as important to determine the cost of serving different categories of customers as it is to cost products.   Customer profitability analysis (CPA) is a system devised to do this. Direct product profitability (DPP) is a system used in retail organisations in order to trace as many costs as possible directly to the product.

The basic activity-based cost analysis has been broadened in recent years and now provides a number of new approaches to management accounting which go under the general term **activity based management** (ABM).

The chapter will end with a consideration of the **behavioural aspects** raised by spreading costs on different bases. This is also referred to in the syllabus as 'overhead allocation (Japanese)'

Learning outcomes covered in this chapter

- Apply and evaluate activity-based costing and activity-based management

- Apply and evaluate direct product profitability

- Apply and evaluate alternative costing and accounting systems: overhead allocation (Japanese), absorption costing, marginal costing, activity based costing

Syllabus content covered in this chapter

- Activity-based costing and activity-based management
- Customer profitability analysis
- Direct product profitability
- Behavioural aspects of alternative costing systems

Exam focus point

The examiner has stated that 'The CIMA examination scheme is cumulative and many IDEC examination questions draw heavily on material introduced in FMAF and IMPM .... IDEC syllabus and examination are by no means 'free standing'.'

For this reason you will encounter 'knowledge brought forward' boxes which summarise those topics covered in earlier syllabuses which are relevant to the IDEC exam. If, having read through the list of points, you are still unsure of the topic, it might be advisable to work through the BPP *Passcards* for the appropriate paper.

Knowledge brought forward from Papers 2 and 8

Cost object – any item for which separate cost measurement is required eg a product or customer.

Cost pool - a collection of individual cost items.

Direct cost – one that can be traced directly to a cost object, possibly via a cost pool.

Indirect cost – one that cannot be traced conveniently or economically to a cost pool and a cost object.

Traditional absorption costing

Absorption costing is a three-stage process (allocation, apportionment, absorption).

- *Allocation* is the process by which whole cost items are charged directly to a cost unit or cost centre.

- *Apportionment* involves two steps, general overhead apportionment and service overhead cost apportionment.

- In the *absorption* stage, overheads are absorbed into products on the basis of estimated/budgeted figures, using a *predetermined overhead absorption rate (OAR)* for the following reasons.

  ° Many overheads are not known until the end of a period and to wait until then to calculate overhead absorption rates would produce unacceptable delays in invoicing, pricing, stock valuations and so on.

  ° Because of random fluctuations in overheads from, for example, month to month, absorption rates calculated on a monthly basis would vary, which would produce misleading information for costing purposes and would be administratively and clerically inconvenient to deal with.

  OARs are calculated as *budgeted overheads allocated and apportioned to production cost centres ÷ budgeted activity level* (hours, units etc) on which the rate is to be based.

- **Possible absorption bases** (the fairest should be chosen)

  ° Rate per unit (if all units are identical)
  ° Direct labour hour rate (labour-intensive production departments)
  ° Machine hour rate (machine-intensive production departments)
  ° Percentage of direct material cost/direct labour cost/prime cost

- The choice of overhead absorption basis is significant in determining the cost of individual units produced since it affects the relative share of overhead costs borne by each product.

- Using the predetermined OAR, the total cost of production is established as follows and therefore includes some absorbed overhead and *not* a share of actual overhead expenditure

  Actual direct materials
  + actual direct labour
  + actual direct expenses
  + overheads (*actual* no. of units/labour hours/machine hours etc × *predetermined OAR*)

- **Under-/over-absorbed overhead will usually occur**

  ○ Overhead incurred > overhead absorbed ⇒ under-absorbed overhead = adjusted with a debit entry in P&L a/c

  ○ Overhead incurred < overhead absorbed ⇒ over-absorbed overhead = adjusted with a credit entry in P&L a/c

- **Reasons for under/over absorption**

  ○ Actual o/hds ≠ budgeted o/hds (expenditure variance)
  ○ Actual activity level ≠ budgeted activity level (volume variance)
  ○ Actual o/hds and activity level ≠ budgeted o/hds and activity level

Principles of marginal costing

- Marginal cost = variable cost

- Contribution = sales revenue − variable (marginal) cost of sales

- Marginal costing

  ○ Only variable costs are charged as cost of sales

  ○ Closing stocks are valued at marginal (variable) production cost

  ○ Fixed costs are treated as period costs, are deducted from profit and hence are charged in full against profit of the period in which they are incurred

  ○ If the volume of sales rises/falls by one item, profit will rise/fall by the contribution earned from the item

  ○ Contribution per unit is constant at all levels of output and sales (whereas profit per unit varies)

- *The valuation of stock*

  ○ In marginal costing, closing stocks are valued at marginal production cost (usually the total of direct materials, direct labour and variable production overhead).

  ○ In absorption costing, closing stocks are valued at full production cost and include a share of fixed production overheads.

- *The calculation of profit*

  ○ In marginal costing, fixed costs are charged *in full* against the profit of the period in which they are incurred.

  ○ In absorption costing, the cost of sales in a period will *include* some fixed overheads incurred in a previous period (in opening stock values) but will *exclude* some fixed overheads incurred in the current period (carried forward in closing stock values as a charge against profit of a subsequent accounting period).

- *Differences in profit*

  ○ If there is any change in the level of stocks in the period, so that opening and closing stock values are different, marginal costing and absorption costing give different figures for profit.

BPP PUBLISHING

- ° *If sales exceed production*, reported profits will be *lower with absorption costing* than with marginal costing. The reason is that stock levels are reduced and, with absorption costing, some fixed overheads will be released from stock and charged against sales for the period.

- ° *If production exceeds sales,* reported profits will be *higher with absorption costing* than with marginal costing. The reason is that stock levels are increased and, with absorption costing, some of the period's fixed overheads will be carried forward in stock to be matched against the sales revenue of future periods.

- ° The difference in reported profits is calculated as the difference between the fixed production overhead included in the opening and closing stock valuations using absorption costing.

- ° In the long run, total profit will be the same whichever costing method is used because in the long run, total costs will be the same by either method of accounting. Different accounting conventions merely affect the profit of individual accounting periods.

- *Arguments in favour of absorption costing*

  - ° Fixed production costs are incurred in order to make output and so it is only 'fair' to charge all output with a share of these costs

  - ° Closing stock will be valued in accordance with SSAP 9

  - ° Appraising products in terms of contribution gives no indication of whether fixed costs are being covered

- **Arguments in favour of marginal costing**

  - ° Absorption costing information is irrelevant when making short-run decisions

  - ° It is simple to operate

  - ° There are no arbitrary fixed cost apportionments

  - ° Fixed costs in a period will be the same regardless of the level of output and so it makes sense to charge them in full as a cost of the period

  - ° It is realistic to value closing stock items at the (directly attributable) cost to produce an extra unit

  - ° Under/over absorption is avoided

  - ° Absorption costing gives managers the wrong signals. Goods are produced, not to meet demand, but to absorb allocated overheads. Absorption costing profit may therefore be increased merely by producing in excess of sales. Production in excess of demand in fact increases the overheads (for example warehousing) the organisation must bear

Activity based costing

You will probably have some prior knowledge of this technique from paper 8, but because you need a detailed knowledge for this syllabus in order to be able to 'apply and evaluate' the technique, we will study the topic from basics

Exam focus point

It is unlikely that a large proportion of Section A MCQs will be on this area of the syllabus. The topics are more likely to be dealt with in Sections B, C and D of the exam. The compulsory question in the May 1999 MAA exam (similar to IDEC) was a reasonably straightforward question on ABC.

1   THE NATURE OF COSTS

1.1   Over the years the definition of direct and indirect costs appears to have changed. This is because material and labour costs have become a much smaller part of the total cost and expenses have become a much greater proportion. Traditionally virtually all these other expenses were called 'indirect' and were either not related to cost objects or if they were they were related via rather unsatisfactory absorption rates such as direct labour hours. Referring to all these costs 'overheads', meaning that they are indirect and therefore not caused by cost objects, such as products, is misleading.

1.2   The absorption of 'indirect' costs into product costs on a direct labour basis does not recognise the causal factors of overheads in the modern business environment.

1.3   So called **'indirect' costs** have become a **greater proportion of total production costs**, and the **direct labour cost proportion has declined**, in some cases to less than ten per cent of the total cost. This has resulted in a large volume of costs being spread on the basis of the behaviour of a small volume of costs – **any inaccuracy is magnified**.

1.4   **Most costs are fixed in the short term** rather than variable, and so **marginal costing is not a particularly appropriate** costing convention to use. Some method of absorption costing is preferred by the majority of companies - hence the development of ABC and the other systems described in this chapter.

1.5   Most costs can be analysed between the following.

- **Short-term variable costs,** that vary with the volume of production

- **Long-term variable costs,** that are fixed in the short-term and do *not* vary with the volume of production, but that do **vary with a different measure of activity**

1.6   It has been suggested that **long-term variable costs** are **related** to the **complexity** and **diversity of production** rather than to simple volume of output. For example, costs for support services such as set-ups, stock handling, expediting (progress chasing) and scheduling do not increase with the volume of output. They are fixed in the **shorter term** but they vary in the **longer term** according to the **range and complexity of product items manufactured**. If another product or product variation is added to the range the **support activities** will become more **complex.** If a single product is made some support activities, such as production scheduling, will not exist.

1.7   The problem of producing a small number of products in volume against producing a large variety of products in small runs is known as *volume versus variety* and can be expressed graphically.

BPP
PUBLISHING

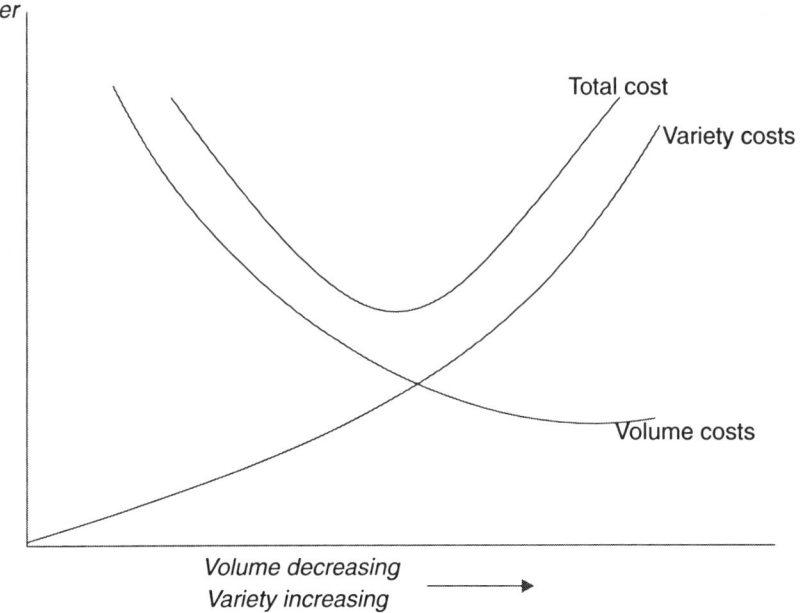

1.8 **Long production runs** (volume) **reduce some costs, short production runs** (variety) **increase some costs.** Research has shown that when volume doubles, the average cost per unit decreases by 15% to 25% (the experience curve effect, 75% to 85% of previous cost). Stalk & Hout (1990) found that when the variety of products manufactured doubles the average unit costs rise by 20% to 35%. When a company adopts the modern philosophy and **manufactures in variety,** therefore, **costs of support activities increase** and **emphasis is inevitably put on controlling these costs,** such as minimising production scheduling and set-up costs. In **order to control costs some attempt must be made to relate these costs to products via their causal factors in as accurate a way as possible.**

2 ACTIVITY BASED COSTING   Pilot paper

2.1 Activity based costing (ABC) has been developed as an alternative costing system to traditional overhead absorption costing.

- More **accurate product costs** can be obtained.
- The cost of serving individual or different categories of customers can be determined.
- Better long-term decisions will be made.

KEY TERM

Activity based costing (ABC) is an approach to costing that focusses on activities as the fundamental cost objects. It uses the cost of these activities as the basis for assigning costs to other cost objects such as products, services or customers.

2.2 The ABC approach is to relate costs to the factors that cause or 'drive' them to be incurred in the first place and to change subsequently. These factors are called 'cost drivers'.

Cost drivers and cost pools

> **KEY TERM**
>
> A **cost driver** is 'Any factor which causes a change in the cost of an activity, eg the quality of parts received by an activity is a determining factor in the work required by that activity and therefore affects the resources required. An activity may have multiple cost drivers associated with it.'   (CIMA *Official Terminology*)

2.3   **Examples of activity-based cost drivers**

Support department costs	Possible cost driver
Set-up costs	Number of production runs
Production scheduling	Number of production runs
Material handling	Number of production runs
Inspection costs	Number of inspections or inspection hours
Raw materials inventory handling etc	Number of purchase orders delivered
Despatch costs	Number of customer orders delivered

All of the costs associated with a particular cost driver (for example production runs) would be grouped into cost pools.

2.4   Miller and Vollman ('The Hidden Factory', *Harvard Business Review*, 1985) provided a useful system for analysing the activities (transactions) which cause costs to be incurred.

Types of transaction	Detail
Logistical transactions	Those activities concerned with organising the flow of resources throughout the manufacturing process.
Balancing transactions	Those activities which ensure that demand for and supply of resources are matched.
Quality transactions	Those activities which relate to ensuring that production is at the required level of quality.
Change transactions	Those activities associated with ensuring that customers' requirements (delivery date, changed design and so on) are met.

Professor Kaplan commented ('Relevance regained', *Management Accounting*, September 1988) as follows (with BPP's emphasis).

> 'Our task is to **dissect these activities**, find out how much is being spent on them and **come up with a quantity measure that can be related to a finished product**. These measures will be things like how many items are being inspected, how many purchase orders are being produced, how many engineering changes are being processed, how much material is being moved, how many set-up hours are being delivered, how many customer calls are being made.
>
> Remarkably, the old traditional methods of cost accounting never had quantity measures related to overhead. We had quantity measures for labour, we had quantity measures for direct material, but **overhead was always a big glob of money to be allocated**. That's exactly the wrong way to think about it. The **goal is to think about what are the quantities of overhead that are being delivered**.'

2.5   In order to understand how ABC operates in detail it is necessary to understand fully the meaning of cost drivers.

KEY TERMS

Cost drivers can be subdivided

A **resource cost driver** is a measure of the quantity of resources consumed by an activity. It is used to assign the **cost of a resource to an activity** or cost pool.

An **activity cost driver** is a measure of the frequency and intensity of demand placed on activities by cost objects. It is used to **assign activity costs to cost objects.**

2.6   In **traditional absorption costing** overheads are first related to **cost centres** and then to **cost objects,** ie products. In **ABC** overheads are first related to **activities** or grouped into cost pools (depending on the terminology preferred) and then related to the **cost objects,** eg products. (Unlike traditional absorption costing ABC has other cost objects such as customers – this will be discussed later). **The two processes** are, therefore, **very similar,** but the first stage is different as ABC uses activities instead of cost centres (functional departments). Like traditional absorption costing **ABC rates** are also **calculated in advance,** usually for **a year ahead.**

ABC calculations

2.7   The different stages in ABC calculations are illustrated and described below.

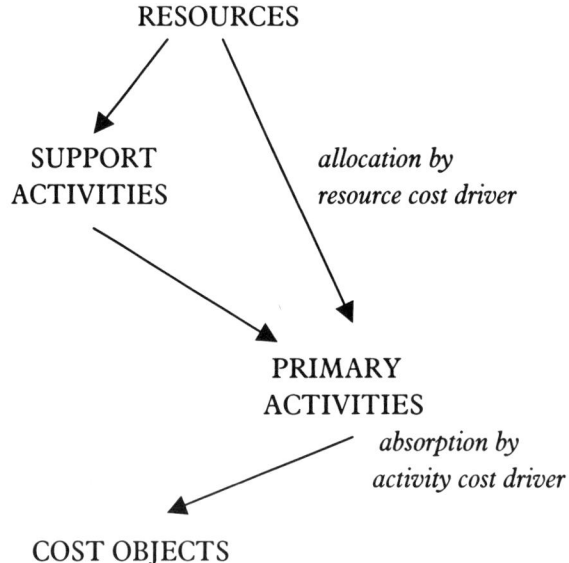

KEY TERMS

Primary activities are those performed directly for products, services or customers.

Support activities create the environment that enables the primary activities to be performed, eg the activities of the human resources department.

Step 1. **Identify the different activities**. The number of activities may range from, say, 20 to 150. There is an **accuracy/cost trade-off**. In 'The Design of Costing Systems' (1998) Cooper & Kaplan expressed it this way: '*The goal is **not to have the most accurate cost system**...(it) should be to **have the best cost system**, one that **balances the cost of errors** made from inaccurate estimates **with the cost of measurement**'*. This effect is demonstrated in the following graph.

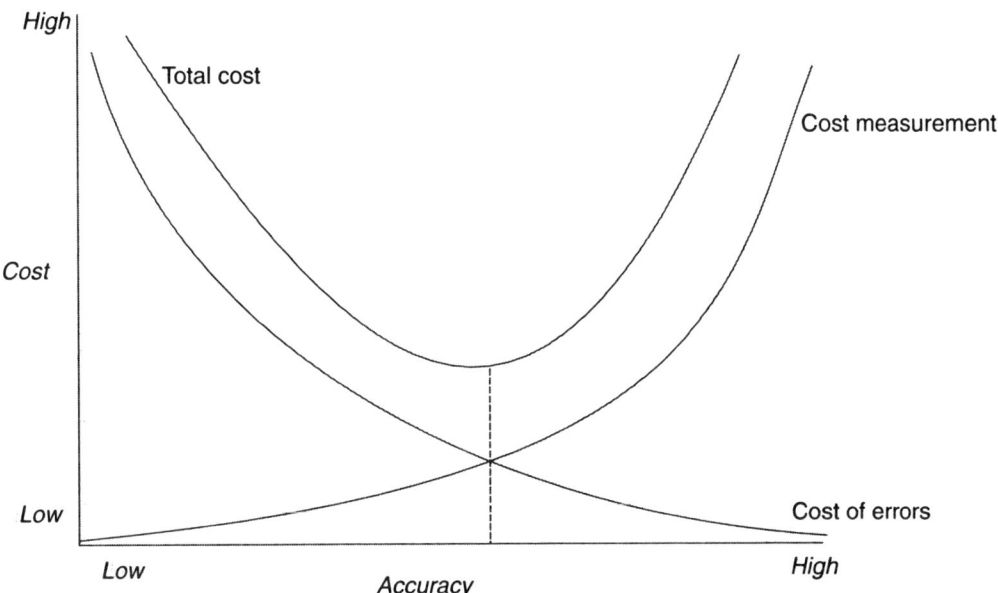

Step 2. **Relate the overheads to the activities,** both primary and support, that caused them. This creates 'cost pools'. This will be done using **resource cost drivers that reflect causality.**

Step 3. **Spread the support activities across the primary activities** based on some suitable cost driver, which reflects the use of the support activity.

Step 4. **Determine the activity cost drivers** that will be used to relate the overheads collected in the cost pools to the cost objects. This is done by selecting the **factor that drives the consumption of the activity.**

Step 5. **Calculate activity cost driver rates.**

$$\text{Activity cost driver rate} = \frac{\text{Total cost of activity}}{\text{Activity driver}}$$

The **activity driver rate** can be used to **cost products**, as in traditional absorption costing, but it can also cost **other cost objects** such as **customers** or groups of customers. The possibility of **costing objects other than products** is part of the **benefit of ABC**. The activity cost driver rates will be multiplied by the different amounts of each activity that each cost object consumes.

2.8 **Activities fall into four different categories,** known as the **manufacturing cost hierarchy.** The categories are useful because they help to determine the type of activity cost driver required. The categories are these.

Unit level activities	The costs of some activities are strongly correlated to the number of units produced.
Batch level activities	The costs of some activities are driven by the number of batches of units produced.
Product level activities	The costs of some activities (sometimes once only activities) are driven by the creation and maintenance of a product line. For

BPP
PUBLISHING

example product design, creation and up-keep of technical drawings, product advertising and promotion.

Facility level activities Some costs cannot be related to a particular product line, instead they are related to maintaining the buildings and facilities. These costs cannot be related to cost objects with any degree of accuracy and are often excluded from ABC calculations for this reason.

2.9 The following example illustrates how traditional cost accounting techniques could result in a misleading and inequitable division of costs between low-volume and high-volume products, and demonstrates that ABC may provide a more meaningful allocation of costs.

2.10 EXAMPLE: ACTIVITY BASED COSTING

Suppose that Cooplan Ltd manufactures four products, W, X, Y and Z. Output and cost data for the period just ended are as follows.

	Output units	Number of production runs in the period	Material cost per unit £	Direct labour hours per unit	Machine hours per unit
W	10	2	20	1	1
X	10	2	80	3	3
Y	100	5	20	1	1
Z	100	5	80	3	3
		14			

Direct labour cost per hour	£5

Overhead costs	£
Short run variable costs	3,080
Set-up costs	10,920
Expediting and scheduling costs	9,100
Materials handling costs	7,700
	30,800

Required

Prepare unit costs for each product using traditional costing and ABC.

2.11 SOLUTION

Using a **conventional absorption costing approach** and an absorption rate for overheads based on either direct labour hours or machine hours, the product costs would be as follows.

	W £	X £	Y £	Z £	Total £
Direct material	200	800	2,000	8,000	
Direct labour	50	150	500	1,500	
Overheads *	700	2,100	7,000	21,000	
	950	3,050	9,500	30,500	44,000
Units produced	10	10	100	100	
Cost per unit	£95	£305	£95	£305	

* £30,800 ÷ 440 hours = £70 per direct labour or machine hour.

Using **activity based costing** and assuming that the number of production runs is the cost driver for set-up costs, expediting and scheduling costs and materials handling costs and

that machine hours are the cost driver for short-run variable costs, unit costs would be as follows.

	W	X	Y	Z	Total
	£	£	£	£	£
Direct material	200	800	2,000	8,000	
Direct labour	50	150	500	1,500	
Short-run variable overheads (W1)	70	210	700	2,100	
Set-up costs (W2)	1,560	1,560	3,900	3,900	
Expediting, scheduling costs (W3)	1,300	1,300	3,250	3,250	
Materials handling costs (W4)	1,100	1,100	2,750	2,750	
	4,280	5,120	13,100	21,500	44,000
Units produced	10	10	100	100	
Cost per unit	£428	£512	£131	£215	

Workings

1	£3,080 ÷ 440 machine hours =	£7 per machine hour
2	£10,920 ÷ 14 production runs =	£780 per run
3	£9,100 ÷ 14 production runs =	£650 per run
4	£7,700 ÷ 14 production runs =	£550 per run

Summary

Product	Traditional costing Unit cost	ABC Unit cost	Difference per unit	Difference in total
	£	£	£	£
W	95	428	+ 333	+3,330
X	305	512	+ 207	+2,070
Y	95	131	+ 36	+3,600
Z	305	215	− 90	−9,000

The figures suggest that the traditional volume-based absorption costing system is flawed.

(a) It **under-allocates overhead costs to low-volume products** (here, W and X) and **over-allocates overheads to higher-volume products** (here Z in particular).

(b) It **under-allocates overhead costs to smaller-sized products** (here W and Y with just one hour of work needed per unit) and **over allocates overheads to larger products** (here X and particularly Z).

2.12 **ABC** traces the appropriate amount of input to each product. However, it is **important** to realise that although **ABC should be** a **more accurate** way of relating overheads to products **it is not a perfect system** and **product costs** could still be **inaccurate** as it is based on a number of assumptions.

The merits of activity based costing

2.13 As the above example illustrates, there is nothing difficult about ABC. Once the necessary information has been obtained it is similar to traditional absorption costing. This **simplicity** is part of its appeal. Further merits of ABC are as follows.

(a) The **complexity** of many businesses has **increased,** with wider product ranges, shorter product life cycles, the greater importance of quality and more complex production processes. ABC **recognises this complexity** with its **multiple cost drivers,** many of which are transaction-based rather than volume-based.

(b) In modern manufacturing systems, overhead functions include a lot of non-factory-floor activities such as product design, quality control, production planning, sales order planning and customer service. ABC is **concerned with all overhead costs,** including

the costs of these functions, and so it takes cost accounting beyond its 'traditional' factory floor boundaries.

(c) Many companies sell products at a loss, subsidising their customers because they do not understand the true cost of the product. In today's **competitive** environment, companies must be able to **assess product profitability realistically.** To do this, they must have a good understanding of what drives overhead costs. ABC gives a meaningful analysis of costs which should provide a suitable basis for decisions about pricing, product mix, design and production.

(d) ABC helps with **cost reduction** because it provides an insight into causal activities and allows organisations to consider the possibility of **outsourcing particular activities,** or even of moving to different areas in the industry value chain. This is discussed later in the chapter under activity based management.

(e) Many **costs are driven by customers** (delivery costs, discounts, after-sales service and so on), but traditional cost accounting does not account for this. Companies may be trading with certain customers at a loss but may not realise it because costs are not analysed in a way that would reveal the true situation. ABC can be **used in conjunction with customer profitability analysis (CPA),** discussed later in this chapter, to determine more accurately the profit earned by serving particular customers.

(f) ABC can be used by **service and retail organisations.** This will be discussed later in the chapter. Many service and retail businesses have characteristics very similar to those required for the successful application of ABC in modern manufacturing industry.

   ° A highly **competitive** market

   ° **Diversity** of products, processes and customers

   o **Significant overhead costs** which are not easily assigned to individual products

   ° **Demands placed on overhead resources** by individual products and customers, which are **not proportional to volume.**

   If ABC were to be used in a hotel, for example, attempts could be made to identify the activities required to support each guest by category and the cost drivers of those activities. The cost of a one-night stay midweek by a businessman could then be distinguished from the cost of a one-night stay by a teenager at the weekend. Such information may prove invaluable for customer profitability analysis.

Criticisms of ABC

2.14 Activity based costing has some serious flaws and concern is now growing that ABC is seen by many as a panacea for management accounting ills, despite that fact that its suitability for all environments remains unproven.

(a) The **cost** of obtaining and interpreting the new information may be considerable. **ABC should not be introduced unless it can provide additional information** for management to use in planning or control decisions.

(b) Some arbitrary **cost apportionment** may still be required at the cost pooling stage for items like rent, rates and building depreciation. If an ABC system has many cost pools the amount of apportionment needed may be greater than ever.

(c) Many **overheads relate neither to volume or to complexity**. The ability of a **single cost driver** to fully explain the cost behaviour of all items in its associated pool is **questionable**.

(d) There will have to be a **trade off between accuracy, the number of cost drivers and complexity**.

(e) ABC tends to **burden low-volume (new) products** with a punitive level of overhead costs and hence threatens opportunities for successful innovation if it is used without due care.

(f) Some people have questioned the fundamental assumption that activities cause cost, they suggest **that decisions cause cost or the passage of time causes cost** - or that there may be **no clear cause of cost**.

Wider uses of ABC

2.15 The **information** provided by **analysing activities** can **support** the management functions of **planning, control and decision making**, provided it is used carefully and with full appreciation of its implications.

Planning

2.16 Before an ABC system can be implemented, management must **analyse** the **organisation's activities**, determine the **extent of their occurrence**, and establish the **relationship between activities, products/services and their cost**. This can be used as a basis for **forward planning and budgeting**. You learned about activity-based budgeting in your studies for Paper 8.

Control

2.17 Knowledge of activities also provides an **insight into the way in which costs are structured and incurred in service and support departments**. Traditionally it has been difficult to control the costs of such departments because of the lack of relationship between departmental output levels and departmental cost. With ABC, however, it is possible to **control or manage the costs by managing the activities which underlie them** using a number of key performance measures which must be monitored if costs and the business generally are to be controlled.

Decision making

2.18 Many of **ABC's supporters** claim that it can assist with **decision making** because it provides accurate and reliable cost information. This is a **contentious issue** among accountants. Many 'purists' consider that **marginal costing** alone provides the correct information on which to **make short-term decisions such as the following.**

- Pricing
- Make or buy decisions
- Promoting or discontinuing products or parts of the business
- Developing and designing changed products.

2.19 **ABC establishes a long-run product cost** and because it provides data which can be used to evaluate different business possibilities and opportunities it is particularly suited for the types of decision listed in paragraph 2.18. Those decisions have long-term implications and **average cost** is probably **more important** than **marginal cost** in many circumstances. **An**

BPP PUBLISHING

ABC cost is an average cost, but it is **not always a true cost** because some costs such as depreciation are usually arbitrarily allocated to products. An ABC cost is therefore **not a relevant cost for all decisions.**

2.20   Raiborn *et al* explain how a product cost is determined using an ABC approach.

> 'Traditionally, accounting has assumed that if costs did not vary with changes in production at the unit level, those costs were fixed rather than variable. Such an assumption is not true. Batch level, product level, and organisational level costs are all variable, but these types of costs vary for reasons other than changes in production volume. For this reason, to determine an accurate estimate of product or service cost, costs should be accumulated at each successively higher level of costs. Because unit, batch and product level costs are all related to units of products (merely at different levels), these costs can be gathered together at the product level to match with the revenues generated by product sales. Organisational level costs, however, are not product related and, thus, should only be subtracted in total from net product revenues.'

Question 1

List briefly the reasons why ABC is particularly suitable in a modern business environment and any situations where it is not appropriate.

Answer

Reasons for suitability

(a)   Most modern organisations tend to have a high level of overhead costs, especially relating to support services such as maintenance and data processing. ABC, by the use of carefully chosen cost drivers, traces these overheads to product lines in a more logical and less arbitrary manner than traditional absorption costing.

(b)   The determination and use of cost drivers helps to measure and improve the efficiency and effectiveness of support departments.

(c)   Many costs included in general overheads can actually be traced to specific JIT lines and/or product lines using ABC. This improves product costing and cost management because the costs are made the responsibility of the line manager.

(d)   ABC forces the organisation to ask such searching questions as 'What causes the demand for the activity?', 'What does the department achieve?', 'Does it add value?' and so on.

(e)   ABC systems may encourage reductions in throughput time and inventory and improvements in quality.

Unsuitable situations

(a)   A number of businesses have recently been split into several small autonomous sections. In this situation there may be no need for a sophisticated costing system such as ABC because staff should be aware of cost behaviour.

(b)   ABC can work against modern manufacturing methods such as JIT. JIT seeks to reduce set-up time so that very small batches can be made economically.

(c)   The aim of set-up time reduction is to allow more set-ups, not just to reduce set-up costs. The use of a cost driver based on the number of set-ups will therefore work against JIT principles as it will tend to encourage larger batches.

2.21   **Using ABC in service and retail organisations**

ABC was **first introduced in manufacturing organisations** but it can equally well be used in **other types of organisation.**   For example the management of the Post Office in the USA recently introduced ABC. They analysed their activities for cash processing as follows.

Unit activities	Possible cost driver
Accept cash	Number of transactions
Processing of cash by bank	Number of transactions

Batch activities

'Close out' and supervisor review of clerk	Number of 'close outs'
Deposits	Number of deposits
Review and transfer of funds	Number of accounts

Product activities

Maintenance charges for bank accounts	Number of accounts
Reconciling bank accounts	Number of accounts

2.22 **Retail organisations** are considered in more detail in the context of direct product profitability in section 4 of this chapter, but they too **can use ABC**.

2.23 **Examples of activities and drivers in retail organisations**

Activities	Possible cost driver
Procure goods	Number of orders
Receive goods	Number of orders or pallets
Store goods	Volume of goods
Pick goods	Number of packs
Handle returnables/recyclables	Volume of goods

3 CUSTOMER PROFITABILITY ANALYSIS

3.1 The use of **activities** as cost pools in ABC systems allows organisations to arrange costs in a variety of different ways. This makes it possible to build up costs for **individual customers or groups of customers** on an activity basis so that their relative profitability can be assessed. Whether individual customers or groups of customers are used largely depends on the number of customers. A manufacturing company supplying six companies would cost each customer separately, but a supermarket or bank would cost groups of similar customers. UK banks divide their customers into categories such as single and 30ish, married with young children, older couples with spending money, etc. and give each category a colourful 'fruity' name such as plum or lemon.

3.2 **Marketing departments** should be aiming to attract and retain profitable customers but in order to do this they need to know **which customers are profitable and how much can be spent on retaining them**. The costing system must provide the necessary answers.

> **KEY TERM**
>
> **Customer profitability analysis (CPA)** is the analysis of the revenue streams and service costs associated with specific customers or customer groups.
>
> (CIMA *Official Terminology*)

3.3 **Customer revenues** are cash flows from customers. They are influenced by different factors, mainly **allowances and discounts**.

(a) Some types of customer **store and distribute goods** (eg wholesalers) or promote the goods in return for an allowance.

(b) By giving a discount the company may **encourage bulk orders,** which may be cheaper to provide and may result in higher sales volume.

Case example

The USA company *General Electric*, which manufactures and sells refrigerators, etc, used to give substantial discounts to customers who placed large orders. This did not result in customers buying more products, instead GE's sales orders bunched in particular weeks of the year. In turn this led to an uneven production and distribution flow, which increased costs. The company found that, by removing the discounts while at the same time guaranteeing swift delivery, order size decreased and profits increased.

3.4 **Examples of the build up of customer costs using an activity based system**

Activity	Cost driver
Order taking	Number of orders taken
Sales visits	Number of sales visits
Emergency orders	Number of rushed orders
Delivery	Miles travelled
Product handling	Number of pallets or part-pallets handled
After sales service and support	Number of visits
Product repairs and service	Number of repair visits

3.5 There is no set format for a **customer profitability statement**, but it would normally be similar to the one below. Note that financing costs have been included.

	£'000	£'000
Revenue at list prices		100
Less: discounts given		8
Net revenue		92
Less: cost of goods sold		50
Gross margin		42
Less: customer specific costs (such as those in paragraph 3.4)	28	
financing costs:		
credit period	3	
customer specific inventory	2	
		33
Net margin from customer		9

Question 2

Seth Ltd supplies shoes to Narayan Ltd and Kipling Ltd. Each pair of shoes has a list price of £50 and costs Seth Ltd £25. As Kipling buys in bulk it receives a 10% trade discount for every order for 100 pairs of shoes or more. Narayan receives a 15% discount irrespective of order size, because that company collects the shoes, thereby saving Seth Ltd any distribution costs. The cost of administering each order is £50 and the distribution cost is £1,000 per order. Narayan makes 10 orders in the year, totalling 420 pairs of shoes, and Kipling places 5 orders for 100 pairs. Which customer is the most profitable for Seth Ltd?

Answer

It can be shown that Seth Ltd earns more from supplying Narayan, despite the larger discount percentage.

	Kipling	*Narayan*
	£	£
Revenue	25,000	21,000
Less: discount	2,500	3,150
Net revenue	22,500	17,850
Less: cost of shoes	(12,500)	(10,500)
customer transport cost	(5,000)	-
customer administration cost	(250)	((500)
Net gain	4,750	6,850

The difference on a unit basis is considerable.

Number of pair of shoes sold	500	420
Net gain per pair of shoes sold	£9.50	£16.31
Net gain per £1 of sales revenue	£0.19	£0.32

3.6 In order to analyse different customers it may be useful to review non-financial data:

	Customer		
	X	*Y*	*Z*
Number of purchase orders	10	20	30
Number of sales visits	5	5	5
Number of deliveries	15	20	55
Distance per delivery	50	20	70
Number of emergency orders	1	0	4

Customer Y may be the cheapest to serve because of the number of deliveries per order, the lower distance travelled and the lack of emergency orders.

3.7 When a **customer profitability analysis** is first carried out it is often found that something close to **Pareto's rule** applies. This is illustrated in the following diagram where **20 of the 100** customers generate approximately **80%** of the company's total margin. As 50 of the 100 customers generate 100% of the total margin, resources appear to be wasted serving the remaining 50 customers.

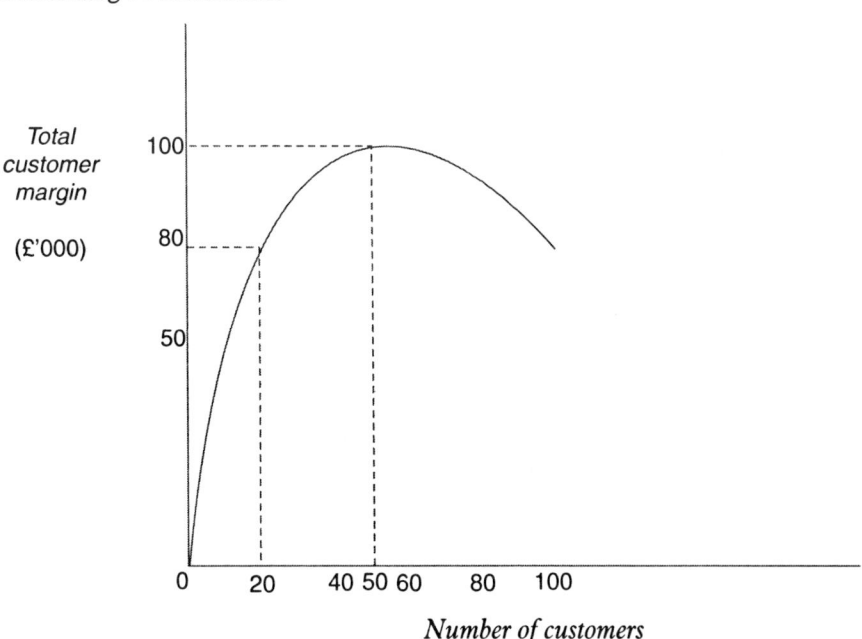

3.8 In order to produce a chart such as that above customers need to be **ranked** according to their **relative profitability** to the company. A bar chart, such as that below, produces an alternative view and may prove more useful for the marketing department.

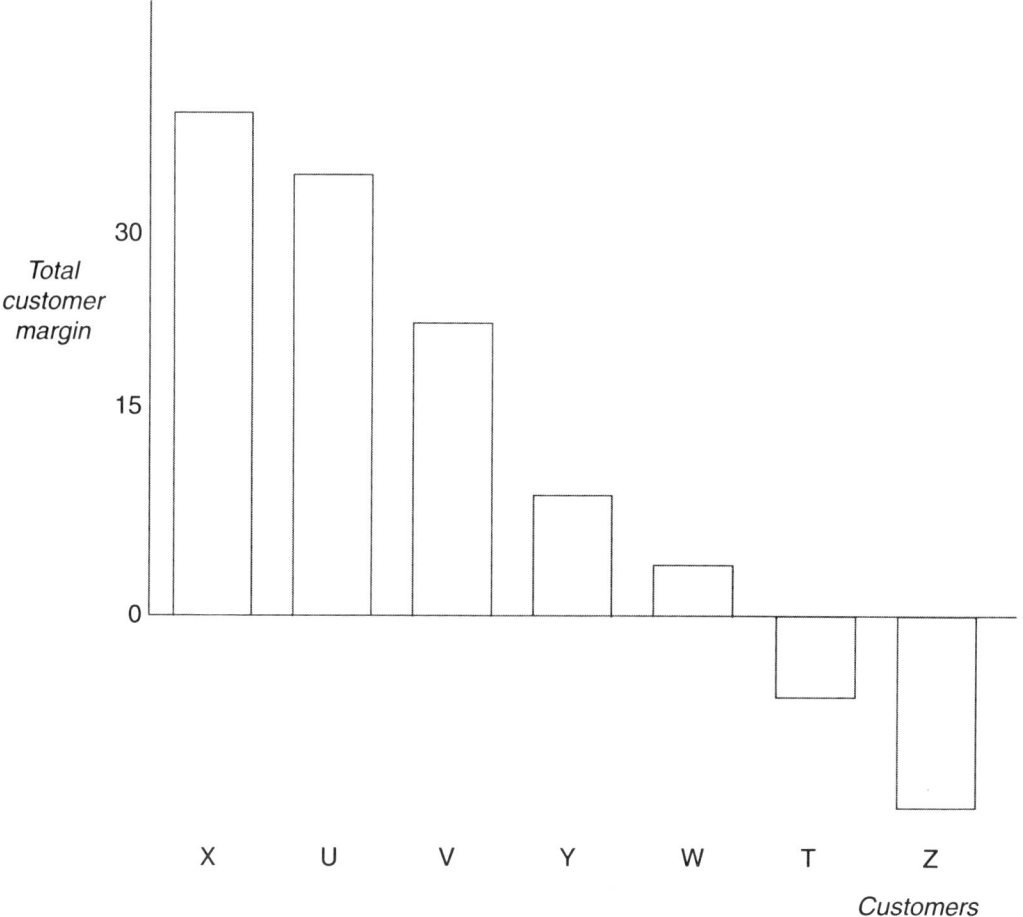

3.9 **It is not possible to 'cost' future dealings with customers accurately** because the number and size of orders and rush orders is likely to be unpredictable. It is, however, possible to gain a **broad idea of the amount of profit that can be expected from a particular category of customer.** Customers can be categorised in the following grid.

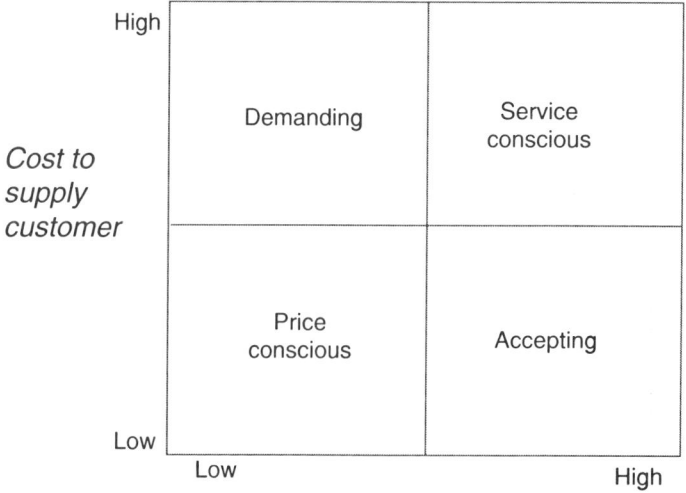

3.10 The aim is to **attract as many accepting customers as possible**. Such customers will have a low 'cost to supply' perhaps because they are located close by, or do not place rush orders, etc. and are prepared to accept a high price. **Many large retail organisations fall into the demanding category** because they expect the supplier to deal with rush orders, change production methods to suit them, etc. It is undesirable for a **small supplier to be tied to a large demanding customer** who has the power to threaten the withdrawal of its custom if the supplier does not acquiesce.

3.11 **Customers** can also be **costed over their expected 'life cycle'** and expected future cash flows relating to the customer may be discounted. This is illustrated in the next chapter. It is rarely possible to accurately predict the life cycle of a particular customer unless contracts are awarded for a specific time period. Nevertheless the information is valuable as the longer the customer remains with the organisation the more profitable the customer becomes. This is valuable information and may show the importance of creating and retaining loyal customers.

4 DIRECT PRODUCT PROFITABILITY   Pilot paper

4.1 Direct product profitability is a costing system used by retail businesses.

> **KEY TERM**
>
> **Direct Product Profit (DPP)** is the contribution a product category makes to fixed costs and profits. It is calculated by deducting direct product costs (such as warehousing and transport) from the product's gross margin.

4.2 Direct product profitability was first defined in 1963 in a McKinsey study and was further developed during the 1960s by Harvard Business School. It was not until EPOS (electronic point of sale) tills and electronic scanning were introduced in the late 1980s that the detailed data was available to allow DPP to be used fully. Work has been carried out by a number of industry organisations in different countries to produce unified industry DPP models with common standards for cost treatment; these include the Institute of Grocery Distribution in the UK and the Food Marketing Institute in the USA.

4.3 Prior to the introduction of DPP retail organisations relied on **gross margin** (sales revenue less purchase price) per product group and **sales per square metre** as profitability measures. Gross margin includes none of the organisation's own costs and so it provides little information for controlling and planning resources. As some product categories consume more of the organisation's resources than others, some attempt ought to be made to **relate these direct costs to the products**.

Direct Product Profit is calculated as follows.

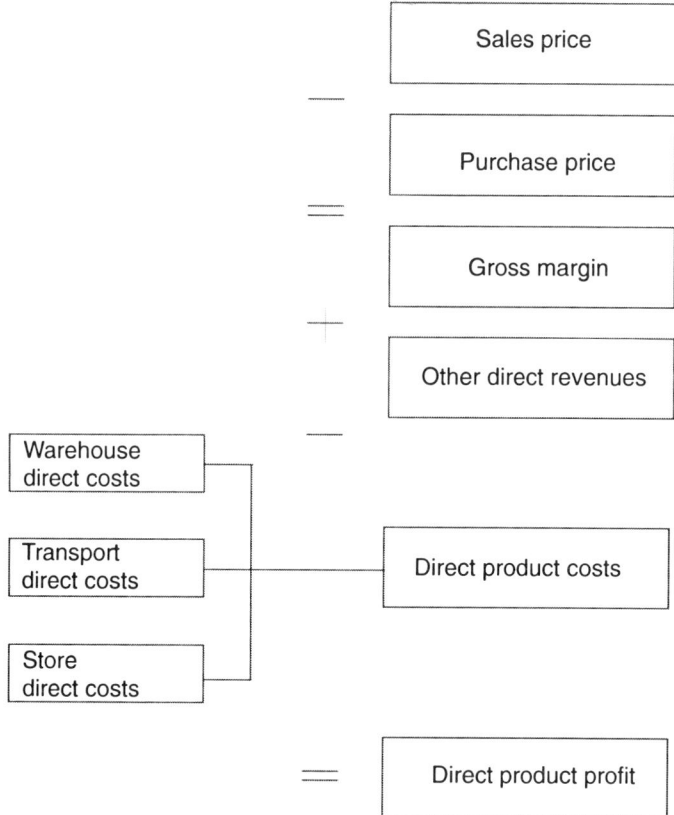

What are other direct revenues?

4.4   They occur occasionally, for example if the retailer receives a discount from the manufacturer for point of sale promotion.

What are direct product costs?

4.5   Costs that can be **directly attributed** to the handling and storing of individual products.

Direct product cost	Examples
Warehouse direct costs	offloading, unpacking, picking and sorting, space costs, inventory financing costs
Transport direct costs	fuel, depreciation of vehicle, driver's salary, vehicle servicing
Store/supermarket direct costs	receiving and inspecting, moving, shelf filling, space costs, inventory financing costs

Direct product costs may also include other product specific costs such as retailer brand development costs.

4.6   Rather confusingly direct product cost also contains **part of the indirect cost** that can be apportioned to the product, based on one or more **product characteristics**. For example, the **cost of shelf space** is apportioned by means of the **physical volume** of the product. All other costs, for example Head Office costs, are not included.

4.7   In practice each product would be charged with a number of different costs, The following example deals only with the space costs in the store.

4.8 EXAMPLE: DPP

A supermarket group has estimated that its store space cost is £0.50 per cubic metre per day.

Its product range includes the following products.

- Six-packs of lager – volume: 0.01 cubic metres, days in store: 5
- Detergent – volume: 0.005 cubic metres, days in store: 4
- Double roll of kitchen paper – volume: 0.185 cubic metres, days in store: 3.

4.9 SOLUTION

The space costs would be allocated as follows.

Lager £0.50 × 0.01 × 5 = £0.025 per pack
Detergent £0.50 × 0.005 × 4 = £0.01 per pack
Kitchen paper £0.50 × 0.0185 × 3 = £0.278 per pack

4.10 The results show the need to achieve a high turnover with bulky low price goods. Refrigerated items would carry a higher space cost due to the cost of refrigeration.

4.11 Benefits of using DPP

- Detailed information is provided on the **profitability** of an **individual product**.

- Products can be **ranked** according to product profitability.

- **Diagnostic capabilities**. Why did a product under perform? Was the stock turn acceptable?

- Profitable product lines can be identified and given more **prominent shelf space**.

- Leads to a mutual understanding of **product and supply chain** costs and improves supplier retailer relationships.

4.12 Comparison of DPP and gross margin

In 1990 Touche Ross Management Consultants carried out a study of detergent products which highlighted the inadequacy of using gross margin. The first chart below shows the gross margin per week of eight detergent products and the first subsequent chart shows the DPP per week for the same products. The difference is dramatic; decisions made on the basis of gross margin in this instance were likely to be incorrect.

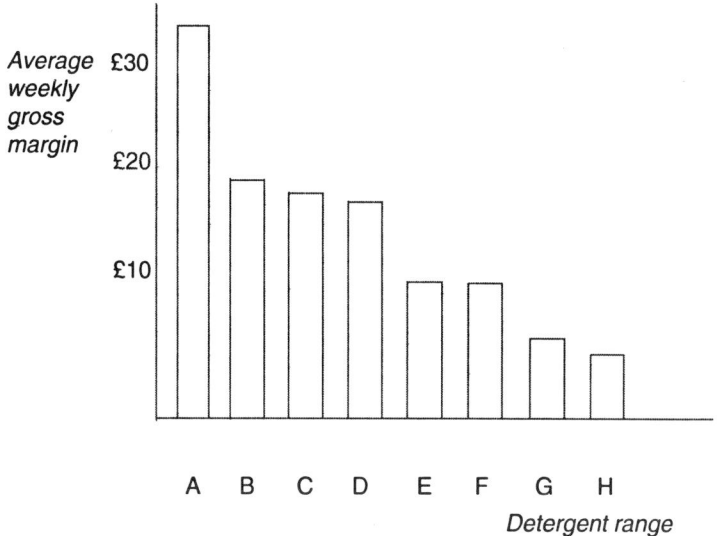

BPP
PUBLISHING

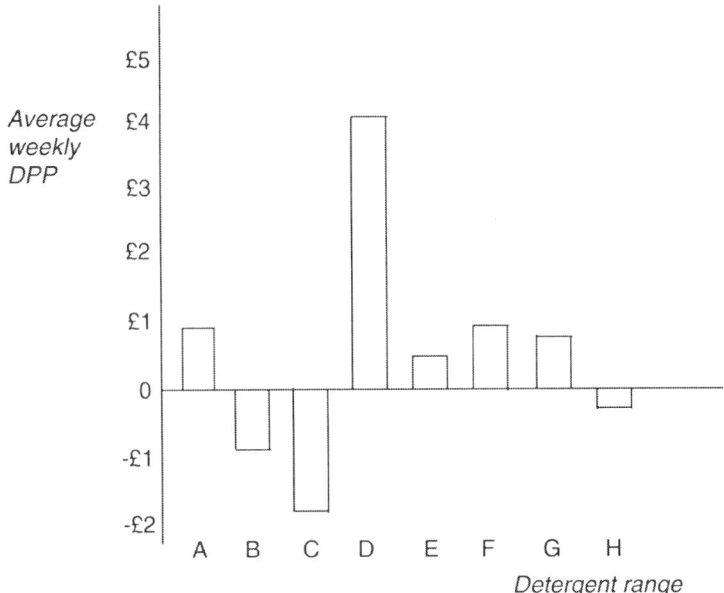

Exam focus point

The Pilot paper contains a full 25 mark question on DPP

5 ACTIVITY-BASED MANAGEMENT (ABM)

5.1 Once the **building blocks of activities** have been created it is possible to use them as the **basis** for a number of **different costing systems**, such as **customer profitability analysis**, according to the organisation's needs.

5.2 Only 15 to 20 years ago Kaplan was arguing that a single **costing system was not sufficient** because it was called on to **meet a number of different needs**. Once **data** had been aggregated in one particular way for one particular purpose it **could not be dis-aggregated** for another purpose, so an organisation needed a number of costing systems. Historically this was not possible because of the cost of creating them. The **use of ABC, where activities are used as building blocks,** allows **a single costing system** to meet a number of **different needs**.

What is ABM?

5.3 This chapter has described ABC and several related techniques or systems which supply long-run product/customer cost information for management. The information can be used in decision making and to aid planning and control. **ABC has developed into activity-based management (ABM)** – but **what is ABM?** It is more than an extension of ABC. It is not simply a costing tool that supports process management. **It is a process management tool**. Over the years a number of different definitions have been put forward.

KEY TERM

Activity based management (ABM) is a 'System of management which uses activity-based cost information for a variety of purposes including cost reduction, cost modelling and customer profitability analysis'. *(CIMA Official Terminology)*

5.4   'ABM is the management of activities to improve the value received by the customer and to increase the profit achieved by providing this value.' *Norm Raffish & Peter Turney, Glossary of Activity-based Management, Journal of Cost Management, Fall 1991.*

- ABM measures the effectiveness of the key business processes and activities and identifies how they can be improved to reduce costs and to increase value to customers.

- ABM improves management focus by allocating resources to key value-added activities to maintain the company's competitiveness.

5.5   Clark and Baxter (*Management Accounting*, June 1992) provide a description which appears to include every management accounting buzzword of the 1990s. The emphasis is BPP's.

> 'The aim of activity-based management (ABM) is to provide management with a method of introducing and **managing 'process and organisational change'**.
>
> It focuses on activities within a process, decision-making and planning relative to those activities and the need for continuous improvement of all organisational activity. Management and staff must determine which activities are critical to success and decide how these are to be clearly defined across all functions.
>
> Everyone must co-operate in defining:
>
> - cost pools;
> - cost drivers;
> - key performance indicators.
>
> They must be trained and **empowered** to act; all must be fairly treated and success recognised.
>
> Clearly, ABM and employee empowerment take a critical step forward beyond ABC by recognising the contribution that people make as the key resource in any organisation's success.
>
> - It nurtures good communication and team work.
> - It develops quality decision-making.
> - It leads to quality control and continuous improvement.
>
> Some accountants do not appear to understand that ABM provides an essential link to total quality management (**TQM**) and its concepts of 'continuous improvement'.
>
> ABM helps deliver:
>
> - improved quality;
> - increased customer satisfaction;
> - lower costs;
> - increased profitability.
>
> It provides accountants and other technical managers with a meaningful path into the business management team.'

5.6   Perhaps the clearest and most concise definition is offered by Kaplan *et al* in *Management Accounting.*

> '...the management processes that use the information provided by an activity-based cost analysis to improve organisational profitability. Activity-based management (ABM) includes performing activities more efficiently, eliminating the need to perform certain activities that do not add value for customers, improving the design of products, and developing better relationships with customers and suppliers. The goal of ABM is to enable customer needs to be satisfied while making fewer demands on organisational resources.'

Benefits of using an ABM approach

5.7   When it is first used **ABM may give management a sudden revelation allowing them to improve the effectiveness of the organisation.** Top management may have a set picture of the business in their mind which is reinforced each month or quarter by the aggregation and grouping of the figures they receive in performance and control reports. Very few companies had considered collecting the costs for each activity before the late 1980s. When this was done management gained another perspective on the business, rather like looking at a three-dimensional model from a completely new angle. This allowed them to see the weaknesses in the existing procedures.

5.8 **Activities** themselves **can be examined and the value they add can be assessed.** Non-profitable activities can be reduced, scrapped or outsourced.

5.9 **Sometimes non-value added activities arise because of inadequacies in existing processes.** The National Health Service (NHS) is a classic example of this. Some heart patients on the NHS wait up to four months for critical heart surgery. During this time they are likely to be severely ill on a number of occasions and have to be taken to hospital where they spend the day receiving treatment that will temporarily relieve the problem. This non-value added activity is totally unnecessary and is dependent on an inadequate process: that of providing operations when required.

(a) Customer complaints services can be viewed in the same way: eliminate the source of complaints and the need for the department greatly reduces.

(b) **Setting up machinery for a new production run is a non-value added cost.** If the number of components per product can be reduced the number of different components made will reduce and therefore set up time will also reduce.

5.10 ABM can to be **used strategically to build up value along the industry value chain** and to take action to move from activities/areas which are not so profitable to activities/areas which are more profitable.

5.11 In an article in *Management Accounting*, March 2000, Jane Gibbon discussed the implementation of ABM at Lloyds TSB and described the main outputs of the system.

(a) **Blueprints and maps** which provided a full understanding of operational processes and the means to measure improvement to those processes.

(b) **A common activity model** which compared common activities across the business to identify total cost and define best practice.

(c) **A support activity model** which was used to understand and improve non-operational or business sustaining areas that tended not to have traditional measurements.

6 BEHAVIOURAL ASPECTS - OVERHEAD ALLOCATION (JAPANESE)

6.1 If you thought that the **key reason** for selecting an overhead absorption base was always to **cost products or customers,** think again. Overhead absorption rates are often used to **influence behaviour.**

6.2 Most organisations measure a department or a division's performance and the manager of that department is held responsible to a greater or lesser extent. Where strong pressure is put on managers to achieve performance measures managers tend to try to influence them. For example, a manager might not release manufactured goods for sale in one month because manufacturing targets have already been met and the goods in question will give the department a head start in the next month.

6.3 **Top management** may attempt to **influence the behaviour** of lower levels of management by providing specific measures. The **overhead absorption rate** is one key measure which can be manipulated.

6.4 If a **direct labour cost percentage** is used line managers will strive to keep **labour costs down**. For example, if the overhead rate is 300% of labour cost and the manager takes on a new member of staff at an annual salary of £20,000, the total cost to the department will be £80,000 (£20,000 + £20,000 x 300%).

6.5 In the UK 20 to 30 years ago top management seemed preoccupied with direct labour costs and used traditional absorption costing to keep their labour costs down. In particular they did not like adding new staff to the payroll because it was then very difficult to cut staff. They would rather pay overtime at time and a half. Today **direct labour costs have decreased** as a percentage of total cost and it **makes little sense** to **spread 60% of costs** (overhead) **on the basis of 10%** labour costs, if an accurate system for calculating product costs is required.

6.6 In **Japan direct labour hours** are often used as an overhead absorption base. *Hiromoto* uses *Hitachi's* VCR plant as an illustration. Despite being highly automated direct labour hours were used to absorb overheads. This was done because management's policy was to automate as far as possible (replacing staff with automated processes) and using a direct labour rate encouraged managers to **shed labour** wherever possible in favour of automation.

6.7 *Hiromoto* also provides other examples of using overhead rates to encourage a particular type of behaviour. For example, product costs depend on the number and type of components. A product which is well designed in terms of manufacturing construction so that it uses **less components** will be **cheaper to produce**. A product using standard components and/or components used in the company's other products will also be cheaper to produce. Who makes these crucial decisions? Normally the **designers**. It is possible for management to influence their actions through overhead absorption rates if overheads are related to products on the basis of the **number of component parts** they contain. Hitachi's refrigeration plant uses this method to influence the behaviour of their product designers and ultimately the cost of manufacture.

6.8 Some companies split their annual **stock holding costs evenly** between the number of components held so that each component line might bear a charge of say, £5,000. If 10,000 units were used during the year the product would bear a cost of 50p for that particular component. If only 100 units were used the stock holding cost of that component per product would be £50. There would be a strong incentive for designers to use standard components.

6.9 The question arises as to whether this **'influencing' type of behaviour** is **unethical**. Swierings and Weick in *Organisations and Society* (1987) thought it was: 'spreading overheads on direct labour...may be regarded as being unethical if it is done to force managers to control labour costs'. If the aim is to reduce product costs which will increase sales volume and profits, it can be argued that it is in the **interest of the majority of stakeholders**. This presupposes that top management have the right knowledge to make the correct decisions. Sometimes cross-functional 'new product' teams may have superior knowledge of relative costs and customer expectations.

Chapter roundup

- **Absorption costing** is a three-stage process (allocation, apportionment, absorption).

- **Activity based costing (ABC)** is one method of accounting for overheads which is considered to be more accurate and has become very popular in recent years.

- ABC relates overhead/resource costs to the primary and secondary activities that cause or drive them. This is done using **resource cost drivers**. The costs of primary activities are related to cost units using an **activity cost driver**. Ensure that you are aware of the merits and problems of ABC.

- **Customer profitability analysis** uses an activity based approach to relate revenues and costs to groups of customers in order to assess their relative profitability.

- **Direct product profit** is the method used by food retailers in particular for relating direct product costs to product categories. It is much more meaningful than the use of gross margin to assess product profitability.

- **Activity based management (ABM)** has been defined as 'the management processes that use the information provided by an activity-based cost analysis to improve organisational profitability'. ABM includes performing activities more efficiently, eliminating the need to perform certain activities that do not add value for customers, improving the design of products, and developing better relationships with customers and suppliers. The goal of ABM is to enable customer needs to be satisfied while making fewer demands on organisational resources.

- There are **behavioural aspects** to all areas of management accounting as there are wherever people interact. They can be an important consideration when determining overhead absorption methods and rates. Traditional absorption costing continues to be used by some companies for behavioural reasons. For example the use of labour hour rates may encourage managers to keep labour costs to a minimum.

Quick quiz

1   Fill in the blanks in the statements below, using the words in the box.

- Customer profitability analysis is the analysis of (1)..~~revenues~~..and (2)~~costs~~.. associated with specific customers or customer groups.

- DPP is the contribution a product category makes to (3)..~~profit~~.. and (4)..~~fixed costs~~..that results from deducting direct product costs such as (5)~~transport~~.., (6)..~~warehousing~~.., and (7)..~~store costs~~....

- ABM is a system of management which uses activity-based cost information for a variety of purposes including (8)~~cost reduction~~, (9)..~~cost modelling~~..and (10)....................

- Overhead absorption rates can be used to influence behaviour to reduce the cost of   (11) .... or (12)...........

> Customer profitability analysis
> Warehousing
> Revenue streams
> Profit
> Direct labour
> Service costs
> Cost modelling
> Fixed costs
> Store costs
> Transport
> Bought-in components
> Cost reduction

2   The cost driver for quality inspection is likely to be batch size.   True/False

3   ABC is not a system that is suitable for use by service organisations.   True/False

4   Which of these are categories of direct product cost?

     Warehouse costs
     Production labour costs
     Transport costs
     Raw material costs
     Store costs

5   One of the following is incorrect as a description of part of the ABC process:

     A   Costs should be collected together for each cost driver.

     B   Transactions undertaken by support department personnel are appropriate cost drivers for long-term variable overheads.

     C   Longer-term production overhead costs are partly driven by volume of output.

     D   Longer-term production overhead costs are partly driven by the complexity and diversity of production work.

     E   Short-term variable overhead costs should normally be traced to products using volume related cost drivers.

Answers to quick quiz

1   1   Revenue streams
     2   Service costs
     3   Fixed costs
     4   Profit
     5   Warehousing
     6   Transport
     7   Store costs
     8   Cost reduction
     9   Cost modelling
     10   Customer profitability analysis
     11   Direct labour
     12   Bought-in components

2   True - assuming that the first items in each batch are inspected

3   False - it is highly suitable

4   Warehouse, transport and store costs

5   C   Short-term variable overhead costs are driven by volume of output but longer-term costs, such as set-up costs, design, etc are driven by the number of different products ie diversity.

Now try the question below from the Exam Question Bank

Number	Level	Marks	Time
Q8	Introductory	n/a	n/a
Q9	Introductory	n/a	n/a
Q10	Examination (pilot)	25	45 mins
Q11	Examination (pilot)	25	45 mins

BPP PUBLISHING

Chapter 7

COSTING SYSTEMS FOR MODERN MANUFACTURING

Topic list	Syllabus reference	Ability required
1 Modern manufacturing methods	(ii)	Apply and evaluate
2 The theory of constraints	(ii)	Apply and evaluate
3 Throughput accounting	(ii)	Apply and evaluate
4 Backflush accounting	(ii)	Apply and evaluate
5 Target costing	(ii)	Apply and evaluate
6 Life cycle costing	(ii)	Apply and evaluate
7 The emperor's new clothes?	(ii)	Apply and evaluate

Introduction

The chapter starts by reminding you of modern developments in manufacturing and business practice, in particular the JIT approach, and then continues by looking at techniques that have been developed to suit modern practices.

The theory of constraints (TOC) and throughput accounting (TA) will probably be new to you and you are unlikely to have met them in practice. They are techniques ideally suited to the modern production environment where production is an immediate response to customer demand. These systems attempt to maximise the net return on sales. They are also applicable in service industries where bottleneck processes can be identified and alleviated.

Backflush accounting is an accounting system that has been specifically designed for use with JIT systems where stock is at a minimum. It cannot be used in other circumstances. Its main advantage is the simplification it brings.

The chapter goes on to look at ways of planning and controlling costs over the life cycle of the cost object – product, service or customer. The first topic dealt with is **target costing** which is a system that the West imported from Japan for achieving a target cost derived from a predetermined selling price and a required profit margin. This system effectively controls costs in advance of production. **Life cycle costing** itself is a rather general term and it can relate both to products/services and to customers. Both aspects are dealt with, starting with the need to identify and control costs at the development stage because they influence costs incurred later.

The chapter ends by considering the relevance and significance of the concepts and techniques covered in section (ii) of the syllabus (this chapter and chapter 6). You'll have to make your own mind up as to the value of these techniques.

Learning outcomes covered in this chapter

- Apply and evaluate alternative costing and accounting systems: backflush accounting, throughput accounting, integrated/interlocking accounting (Note: detailed accounting entries are not required)

- Apply and evaluate target costing

- Apply and evaluate life cycle costing

Syllabus content covered in this chapter

- Just-in-time and backflush accounting

- Theory of constraints and throughput accounting

- Target costing

- Life cycle costing

Knowledge brought forward from Paper 8

The modern business environment and techniques such as JIT

This chapter will consider modern costing systems that are designed to fit with modern manufacturing methods required by the modern business environment. You will need to have a good background knowledge of modern manufacturing and operating systems in order to understand why the costing systems described are used and the benefits they can bring. The first section gives you a brief reminder of the subject, but a deeper knowledge would be an advantage.

Value engineering & analysis and functional analysis

Knowledge of these techniques is required as value engineering and functional analysis are used when target costs are first set and value analysis is used to reduce costs below established target costs.

Interlocking accounts

- Two ledgers are maintained, a financial ledger and a cost ledger, and each is an independent double entry system.

The principal accounts in the cost ledger are as follows.

- Materials/stores control a/c

- Wages control a/c

- Production overhead control a/c

- Work in progress control a/c

- Finished goods control a/c

- Sales a/c

- Cost of sales a/c

- Administration o/hd control a/c

- Selling and distribution o/hd control a/c

- Under-/over-absorbed o/hd a/c (absorption costing)

- Costing profit and loss a/c

- Cost ledger control account (CLCA) (the account in which any non-costing (cash, debtors, creditors etc) sides of double entries are entered)

A reconciliation has to be performed between the cost ledger profit and the financial ledger profit, the difference between the profits arising for various reasons.

- Values of opening and closing stocks
- Items appearing in the financial ledger only
    - ° Income
        - – Interest/Dividends
        - – Discounts
        - – Profits on disposal of fixed assets
    - ° Appropriations of profit
        - – Donations
        - – Income tax
        - – Dividends
    - ° Expenditure
        - – Interest
        - – Discounts
        - – Losses on disposal of fixed assets
- Depreciation method
- Items appearing in the cost ledger only will generally be 'notional costs' (rent on owned premises)

Integrated system

In this system, the financial and cost ledgers are combined in one self-balancing ledger. There is therefore no need to reconcile the cost and financial profits and no need to operate a cost ledger control account since all those accounts it represents in an interlocking system are included in the one ledger of an integrated system.

Advantages

- Saves administrative effort and expense
- Less confusing

Disadvantages

- One set of books to fulfil two purposes
- More detailed analysis of costs required

1   MODERN MANUFACTURING METHODS

1.1   Nowadays **many customers demand goods immediately**. If they cannot obtain goods from one company when they require them they will go elsewhere. This means that most organisations must be capable of meeting customer demand immediately or very quickly. In order to do this **information, production and delivery systems must be properly linked and be as immediate as possible**.

1.2   Traditionally in the West manufacturing organisations strove for long production runs that minimised machinery set-up time, as it was thought that this lowered the cost per unit of the component or product. But this tactic increases some costs, such as production scheduling and stock holding costs, and is also very expensive in terms of space. It also ignores the fact that what gets measured gets controlled.

1.3   Therefore if set-up times are not critical, because long production runs attempt to minimise their effect on the overall cost, they will not be measured and over the years they will escalate. This escalation can be dramatic: organisations which switch to **just in time (JIT)** systems have been able to drive set-up times down from two hours to, say, five minutes.

Some of this decrease may be due to the purchase of smaller and simpler machines that are easier to change over.

1.4 Traditional systems compartmentalise costs and benefits by splitting them according to function and cost centre. Whenever this happens, all costs associated with a particular action or decision are unlikely to be viewed together making it difficult to judge the effectiveness of the decision. For example the production cost per unit per batch may not be considered at the same time as the cost of holding a unit of stock for one day.

1.5 JIT is the name given to the main type of immediate production system. It was 'invented' by Toyota, who have refined the method over many years. Its use is now widespread and a number of organisations throughout the world have adopted JIT.

1.6 JIT systems are often linked with manufacturing methods where they bring the added benefit of the virtual elimination of stock. They can also be used very effectively by service and retail organisations for cutting costs and meeting customer needs more immediately. For example, the supermarket industry has long adopted this approach with constant deliveries and shelf restocking.

2 THE THEORY OF CONSTRAINTS

2.1 The use of a JIT operating system, whether in a manufacturing or service organisation requires a different type of costing system. **Throughput accounting** is a technique that has been developed to deal with this. The name was first coined in the late 1980s when *Galloway and Waldron* developed the system in the UK. Throughput accounting is based on the concept of the **theory of constraints** (TOC) which was formulated by Goldratt and Cox in the U.S.A. in 1986. Its key financial concept is to turn materials into sales as quickly as possible thereby maximising the net cash generated from sales. This is to be achieved by striving for balance in production processes, therefore evenness of production flow is also an important aim.

> **KEY TERMS**
>
> **Theory of constraints (TOC)** is an approach to production management which aims to maximise sales revenue less material and variable overhead cost. It focuses on factors such as bottlenecks which act as constraints to this maximisation.
>
> **Bottleneck resource or binding constraint** – an activity which has a lower capacity than preceding or subsequent activities, thereby limiting throughput.
>
> *CIMA Official Terminology*

2.2 **One process will inevitably act as a bottleneck** (or limiting factor) and constrain throughput – this is known as the **binding constraint** in TOC terminology. Steps should be taken to remove this by buying more equipment, improving production flow, etc. But ultimately there will always be a binding constraint, unless capacity is far greater than sales demand or all processes are totally in balance, which is unlikely even if it is a goal to be aimed for.

2.3 **Output through the binding constraint should never be delayed or held up otherwise sales will be lost.** To avoid this happening **a buffer stock should be built up immediately prior to the bottleneck** or binding constraint. **This is the only stock that the business should hold,** with the exception of possibly a very small amount of finished goods stock and raw materials that are consistent with the JIT approach.

2.4 **Operations prior to the binding constraint should operate at the same speed as the binding constraint**, otherwise work in progress (other than the buffer stock) will be built up. According to TOC, stock costs money in terms of storage space and interest costs, therefore stock is not desirable. In a traditional production system an **organisation will often pay staff a bonus to produce as many units as possible**. TOC views this as inefficient since the organisation is paying extra to build up stock which then costs money to store until it is required.

KEY TERMS

Throughput contribution = Sales revenue – material cost

Conversion cost = all operating costs except material cost (ie all costs except totally variable costs)

Investment cost = stock, equipment, building costs ,etc.

2.5 **The aim is to maximise throughput contribution while keeping conversion and investment costs to the minimum.** So if a strategy for increasing throughput contribution is being considered it will only be accepted if conversion and investment costs increase by a lower amount than the contribution. It is important to realise that **TOC is not an accounting system it is a production system**.

3 THROUGHPUT ACCOUNTING

3.1 The concept of throughput accounting has been developed as an **alternative system of cost and management accounting in a JIT environment**.

KEY TERM

'**Throughput accounting** (TA) is an approach to accounting which is largely in sympathy with the JIT philosophy. In essence, TA assumes that a manager has a given set of resources available. These comprise existing buildings, capital equipment and labour force. Using these resources, purchased materials and parts must be processed to generate sales revenue. Given this scenario the most appropriate financial objective to set for doing this is the maximisation of throughput (Goldratt and Cox, 1984) which is defined as: sales revenue *less* direct material cost.'

(Tanaka, Yoshikawa, Innes and Mitchell, *Contemporary Cost Management*)

3.2 TA is based on three concepts.

(a) *Concept 1.* In the short run, **most costs in the factory (with the exception of materials costs) are fixed.** Because TA differentiates between fixed and variable costs it is often compared with marginal costing and **some people argue that there is no difference between marginal costing and throughput accounting.** In marginal costing direct labour costs are usually assumed to be variable costs. Years ago this assumption was true, but employees are not usually paid piece rate today and they are not laid off for part of the year when there is no work, and so labour cost is not truly variable. If this is accepted the two techniques are identical in some respects, but **marginal costing is generally thought of as being purely a short-term decision-making technique** while **TA, or at least TOC, was conceived with the aim of**

changing manufacturing strategy to achieve evenness of flow. **It is therefore much more than a short-term decision technique.**

Because TA combines all conversion costs together and does not attempt to examine them in detail it is particularly suited to use with ABC, which examines the behaviour of these costs and assumes them to be variable in the long-run.

(b) *Concept 2.* In a JIT environment, all stock is a 'bad thing' and the **ideal inventory level is zero.** Products should not be made unless there is a customer waiting for them. This means **unavoidable idle capacity must be accepted in some operations,** but not for the operation that is the bottleneck of the moment. There is one exception to the zero stock policy, and that is that stock should be held prior to the bottleneck process, ie a buffer stock should be held.

(c) *Concept 3.* **Profitability is determined by the rate at which 'money comes in at the door'** (that is, sales are made) and, in a JIT environment, this depends on how quickly goods can be produced to satisfy customer orders. Since the goal of a profit-orientated organisation is to make money, stock must be sold for that goal to be achieved.

The **buffer stock and any other work in progress or finished goods stock** should be **valued at material cost only** until the output is eventually sold, so that **no value will be added and no profit earned until the sale takes place.** Producing output just to add to work in progress or finished goods stock creates no profit, and so should not be encouraged. This method of stock valuation should help in this regard.

Question 1

How are these concepts a direct contrast to the fundamental principles of conventional cost accounting?

Answer

Conventional cost accounting	Throughput accounting
Stock is an asset.	Stock is *not* an asset. It is a result of unsynchronised manufacturing and is a barrier to making profit.
Costs can be classified either as direct or indirect.	Such classifications are no longer useful.
Product profitability can be determined by deducting a product cost from selling price.	Profitability is determined by the rate at which money is earned.
Profit is a function of costs.	Profit is a function of throughput as well as costs.

Bottleneck resources

3.3 The aim of modern manufacturing approaches is to match production resources with the demand for them. This implies that there are **no constraints, termed bottleneck resources** in TA, within an organisation. The throughput philosophy entails the identification and elimination of these bottleneck resources. Where they cannot be eliminated **production must be limited to the capacity of the bottleneck resource in order to avoid the build-up of work in progress.** If a rearrangement of existing resources or buying-in resources does not alleviate the bottleneck, investment in new equipment may be necessary. The **elimination of one bottleneck is likely to lead to the creation of another** at a previously satisfactory location, however. The management of bottlenecks therefore becomes a primary concern of the manager seeking to increase throughput.

3.4 There are other factors that might limit throughput other than a lack of production resources (bottlenecks).

- The existence of an non-competitive selling price
- The need to deliver on time to particular customers, which may disrupt normal production flow.
- The lack of product quality and reliability, which may cause large amounts of rework or an unnecessary increase in production volume.
- Unreliable material suppliers, which will lead to poor quality products that require rework.

Throughput measures

3.5 In a throughput environment, **production priority** must be given to the products best able to generate throughput, that is those **products that maximise throughput contribution per minute when using the bottleneck resource.** (This is similar in concept to maximising contribution per unit of limiting factor.) Such product rankings are for **short-term production scheduling only**. In throughput accounting, bottlenecks should be eliminated and so rankings may change quickly. Customer demand can, of course, cause the bottleneck to change at short notice too.

3.6 Products can be ranked according to **the throughput accounting ratio (TA ratio)**.

$$\text{TA ratio} = \frac{\text{throughput contribution per factory hour}}{\text{conversion cost per factory hour}}$$

Where, throughput contribution per factory hour = (sales – material cost) per hour.

For example:	Product A £ per hour	Product B £ per hour
Sales price	100	150
Material cost	(40)	(50)
Conversion cost	(50)	(50)
Profit	10	50
TA ratio	$\frac{60}{50} = 1.2$	$\frac{100}{50} = 2.0$

Profit will be maximised by manufacturing as much of product B as possible.

3.7 It can be seen from the example above that the **TA ratio** is **similar in concept to contribution per unit of limiting factor.** (Assuming materials were the only variable cost, contribution and throughput would be identical and there would be no difference between traditional contribution analysis and throughput analysis.) The TA ratio can be **used to assess the relative earning capabilities of different products** and hence can help with decision making.

Is it good or bad?

3.8 TA is seen by some as **too short term**, as all costs other than direct material are regarded as fixed. This is not true. But it does **concentrate on direct material costs** and does nothing for the control of other costs. These characteristics make throughput accounting a **good complement for ABC,** as ABC focuses on labour and overhead costs.

3.9 **TA attempts to maximise throughput whereas traditional systems attempt to maximise profit.** By attempting to maximise throughput an organisation could be producing in excess of the profit-maximising output.

3.10 TA helps direct attention to:

- bottlenecks
- the key elements in making profits
- inventory reduction
- reducing the response time to customer demand
- the aim of evenness of production flow.

Case examples

(a) An article in *Management Accounting* in April 1992 describes a case study of *Garrett Automotive* that adopted TA with the particular aim of managing and alleviating bottlenecks in the production process and moving towards 'evenness of flow'. When the project started one particular manufacturing area had three machines with the following outputs:

Machine A 30 units per hour

Machine B 18 units per hour

Machine C 80 units per hour

The production system was certainly not in balance.

As a result of the initial analysis machine D was moved to assist B and this increased capacity at this point to 21 units per hour. Then machine E was purchased very cheaply and this increased output at B to 26 units per hour. (Machine E paid for itself in just five weeks.) Machine C was due for replacement shortly afterwards and it was replaced with a new and cheaper machine that produced just 26 units per hour. These three changes raised output from 2,025 units to 2,700 units per week and greatly increased profit.

Changing the production process brought considerable financial benefits and changed the reporting emphasis to the critical need to adhere to production schedules and to 'first-time capability' (getting it right first time). The monthly management report was reduced from more than forty pages to five pages and it was made available if requested to all employees. It forced management accounting staff to get back to understanding what is actually happening on the shop floor and to be inventive about performance measures.

(b) An article in the *Harvard Business Review* September-October 1996 cites the instance of *Pratt & Whitney* the jet engine manufacturer, which had ten computer controlled grinding machines that were used to shape cast blades. The machines cost $80M and were technical marvels, grinding a blade in just three minutes. They were fed and unloaded by robots but it took eight hours to change the machines so that they could grind a different sort of blade. In addition each blade had to be encased in a special metal alloy to prevent it fracturing during grinding and this was difficult to remove after the process. Twenty two members of staff were required to maintain the complicated computerised control system. As a result of all this, each blade took ten days to pass through the grinding department.

After studies, eight simple grinding machines that did not require the blades to be encased in metal were purchased to replace the computer controlled machines. The time it took to change from grinding one type of blade to the next took just 100 seconds with these machines and it only took the labour of one full-time and one part-time member of staff to feed and control the machines. Processing time increased from three minutes to 75 minutes, however, but this was not a major disadvantage. The factory space required was halved and the time for a blade to pass through the grinding department fell from ten days to 75 minutes.

3.11 EXAMPLE: THROUGHPUT ACCOUNTING

Corrie Ltd produces three products, X, Y and Z. The capacity of Corrie's plant is restricted by process alpha. Process alpha is expected to be operational for eight hours per day and can produce 1,200 units of X per hour, 1,500 units of Y per hour, and 600 units of Z per hour.

Selling prices and material costs for each product are as follows.

Product	Selling price	Material cost	Throughput contribution
	£ per unit	£ per unit	£ per unit
X	150	70	80
Y	120	40	80
X	300	100	200

Conversion costs are £720,000 per day.

Requirements

(a) Calculate the profit per day if daily output achieved is 6,000 units of X, 4,500 units of Y and 1,200 units of Z.

(b) Determine the efficiency of the bottleneck process given the output in (a).

(c) Calculate the TA ratio for each product.

(d) In the absence of demand restrictions for the three products, advise Corrie Ltd's management on the optimal production plan.

3.12 SOLUTION

(a) Profit per day = throughput contribution – conversion cost

$$= [(£80 \times 6,000) + (£80 \times 4,500) + (£200 \times 1,200)] - £720,000$$

$$= £360,000$$

(b)

Product	Minutes in alpha per unit	Minutes in alpha per day
X	60/1,200 = 0.05	6,000 × 0.05 = 300
Y	60/1,500 = 0.04	4,500 × 0.04 = 180
Z	60/600 = 0.10	1,200 × 0.10 = 120
		600

Total hours = 600 minutes ÷ 60 = 10 hours

Hours available = 8, hours produced = 10, ∴ Efficiency = 125%

(c) TA ratio = throughput contribution per factory hour/conversion cost per factory hour

Conversion cost per factory hour = £720,000/8 = £90,000

Product	Throughput contribution per factory hour	Cost per factory hour	TA ratio
X	£80 x (60 ÷ 0.05 mins) = £96,000	£90,000	1.07
Y	£80 x (60 ÷ 0.04 mins) = £120,000	£90,000	1.33
Z	£200 x (60 ÷ 0.10 mins) = £120,000	£90,000	1.33

(d) An attempt should be made to remove the restriction on output caused by process alpha's capacity. This will probably result in another bottleneck emerging elsewhere. The extra capacity required to remove the restriction could be obtained by working overtime, making process improvements or product specification changes. Until the volume of throughput can be increased, output should be concentrated upon products Y and Z (greatest TA ratios), unless there are good marketing reasons for continuing the current production mix.

Case example

In 'Accounting for Throughput' (*Management Accounting,* May 1996), Dugdale and Jones discuss the consequences of introducing throughput ideas into the accounting, production and marketing functions of a particular company. The emphasis is BPP's.

(a) 'Measures of efficiency and overhead recovery were no longer considered useful ... The danger of traditional measures causing sub-optimal behaviour was now recognised and the **key measure became 'schedule adherence'** ... The use of schedule adherence was later accompanied by the introduction of a **throughput profit and loss account** ... [which was] extremely simple.

	£
Sales revenue	X
Less: Materials	(X)
Materials price and exchange variances	X
Throughput	X
Less: Expense	(X)
Net profit	X

Gradually other measures were added to cell managers' monthly accounting packages - **days' inventory on-hand, manufacturing cycle time, cost of quality, customer due-date performance**.'

(b) '... most [cell managers] thought that schedule adherence was a good measure but its credibility depended on the creation of **realistic schedules** ... Without such [financially-based] measures [of departmental performance], many managers considered that they were operating in a measurement vacuum in which they had insufficient information ... It may be that this [creating new local performance measures] is an intractable problem in accounting for throughput.'

(c) 'Whilst there was some disagreement about the use of throughput measures in production there were no such reservations in **marketing**... the move towards marginal cost pricing [throughput accounting being a form of marginal costing, only material costs being treated as variable] and away from absorbed costs and gross margin targets was an unmitigated success.'

Throughput accounting in service and retail industries

3.13 Sales staff have always preferred to use a marginal costing approach so that they can use their discretion on discounts, etc and retail organisations have traditionally thought in terms of sales revenue less the bought in price of goods. Therefore the throughput accounting approach is nothing new to them.

3.14 Throughput accounting can be used very effectively in support departments and service industries to highlight and remove bottlenecks. For example, if there is a delay in processing a potential customer's application business can be lost or the potential customer may decide not to proceed. Sometimes credit rating checks are too detailed, slowing the whole procedure unnecessarily and delaying acceptance from say 24 hours to eight days.

3.15 A similar problem could occur in hospitals where work that could be done by nurses has to be carried out by doctors. Not only does this increase the cost of the work but it may well cause a bottleneck by tying up a doctor's time unnecessarily.

4 BACKFLUSH ACCOUNTING

4.1 Backflush accounting is the name given to the method of keeping cost accounts which is employed where **backflush costing** is used. The two terms are almost interchangeable.

4.2 Traditional costing systems use **sequential tracking** (also known as synchronous tracking) to track costs sequentially as products pass from raw materials to work in progress, to finished goods and finally to sales. In other words material costs are charged to WIP when materials are issued to production, direct labour and overhead costs are charged in a similar way as the cost is incurred or very soon after.

4.3 If a production system such as JIT is used, sequentially tracking means that all entries are made at almost the same moment and so a different accounting system can be used. In backflush costing/accounting costs are calculated and charged when the product is sold, or when it is transferred to the finished goods store.

KEY TERM

Backflush costing is 'A method of costing, associated with a JIT production system, which applies cost to the output of a process. Costs do not mirror the flow of products through the production process, but are attached to the output produced (finished goods stock and cost of sales), on the assumption that such backflushed costs are a realistic measure of the actual costs incurred.' (CIMA *Official Terminology*)

4.4 The CIMA definition omits to say that **budgeted or standard costs are used to work backwards to 'flush' out manufacturing costs** for the units produced. (Hence the rather unattractive name for the system!) The application of standard costs to finished goods units, or to units sold, is used in order to calculate cost of goods sold thereby simplifying the costing system and creating financial savings. **In a true backflush accounting system all records of materials used and work in progress** are no longer required as material cost can be calculated from either finished goods or goods sold.

4.5 Backflush costing runs counter to the principle enshrined in SSAP 9, and the staple of cost accounting for decades, that stock and WIP should be accounted for by calculating cost and net realisable value of '**each item of stock separately**'. The substantial **reduction in stocks that is a feature of JIT** means that stock valuation is less relevant and therefore the costing system can be simplified to a considerable extent. Johnson & Kaplan wrote, in the 1980s, that **management rarely requires a value** to **be placed on stock for internal management purposes**, the value is only required for external reporting.

4.6 Backflush costing is therefore appropriate where organisations try their utmost **to keep stocks to the very minimum**. Under these circumstances the **recording** of every little increase in stock value, as each nut and bolt is added, is simply an expensive and **non-value-added activity** that should be eliminated.

KEY TERMS

Backflush accounting is a cost accounting system which focuses on the output of the organisation and then works backwards to allocate costs between cost of goods sold and stock. *Horngren (1999)*

Trigger point is the point at which the physical activity triggers an entry in the accounts which flushes out cost.

4.7 EXAMPLE: WORKING BACKWARDS FROM OUTPUT

To take a **very simplified example**, if backflush costing is used, the management accountant might extract the following information from the monthly accounting transaction records and production records.

Orders completed and despatched in July	196 units
Orders prepared in advance 1 July	3 units
Orders prepared in advance 31 July	2 units
Scrapped items	5 units
Conversion costs in the month	£250,000
Material costs in the month	£475,000

This is enough to place a value on stocks and production as follows.

	Units		£
B/f	(3)	Conversion costs	250,000
Despatched	196	Material costs	475,000
Scrapped	5	Total costs	725,000
C/f	2		
Units produced	200		

Cost per unit is £725,000 divided by 200 units = £3,625

In this case a single process account could be drawn up as follows.

	Dr (£)	Cr (£)
Stock b/fwd (3 × £3,625)	10,875	
Materials	475,000	
Conversion costs	250,000	
To finished goods (196 × £3,625)		710,500
Losses etc written off to P& L (5 × £3,625)		18,125
Stock c/fwd (2 × £3,625)		7,250
	735,875	735,875

4.8 Traditional management accountants might argue:

(a) that the figure for **losses** here is **inaccurate**. They would say that in reality the faulty goods would have been scrapped when only partially complete and it is wrong to value them at the same cost as a fully finished good unit;

(b) using this approach, the figure for stocks b/fwd and c/fwd will not tie up with the accounts for last month and next month, because the material and conversion costs may be different.

4.9 **Modern** management accountants might reply as follows.

(a) **Losses** represent only about 2% of total cost and are **not material**. In any case putting a value to them is less important than improving the quality of **production** procedures (on the basis of TQM practices and **non-financial** production information) to ensure that they do not occur again.

(b) **Finished good stocks represent between 1% and 2% of total cost and are immaterial.** Slight discrepancies in valuation methods of b/fwds and c/fwds will amount to a *fraction* of a percentage, and can be written off in the month as a small **variance.**

(c) Even with computers the **cost of tracing units** every step of the way through production - with 'normal' and 'abnormal losses', equivalent units and numerous process accounts - **is simply not worth it, in terms of the benefit derived** from the information it provides.

Variants of backflush costing

4.10 There are several variants of backflush accounting, which are explained below. Bear in mind the following points.

(a) **Trigger points determine when the entries are made in the accounting system.** There will be either one or two trigger points that trigger entries in the accounts:

(i) when materials are purchased/received, and

(ii) when goods are completed or when they are sold.

In a true JIT system where no stocks are held the first trigger, when raw materials are purchased, is unnecessary.

(b) **Actual conversion costs are recorded as incurred,** just as in conventional recording systems. **Conversion costs are applied to products at the second trigger point based on a standard cost.** It is assumed that any conversion costs not applied to products are carried forward and disposed of at the period end.

4.11 EXAMPLE: ACCOUNTING ENTRIES AT DIFFERENT TRIGGER POINTS

The transactions for period 8 20X1 for Clive Ltd are as follows.

Purchase of raw materials	£24,990
Conversion costs incurred	£20,580
Finished goods produced (used in methods 2 & 3 only)	4,900 units
Sales	4,850 units

There are no opening stocks of raw materials, WIP or finished goods. The standard cost per unit is made up of £5.10 for materials and £4.20 for conversion costs. The figures have been chosen so that, for simplicity, no variances arise.

4.12 SOLUTION FOR 1 TRIGGER POINT – when goods are sold (method 1)

This is the simplest method of backflush costing. There is only one **trigger point and that is when the entry to the cost of goods sold account is required** when the goods are sold. (This method assumes that units are sold as soon as they are produced.)

			£	£
(a)	DEBIT	Conversion costs	20,580	
	CREDIT	Expense creditors		20,580
	Being the actual conversion costs incurred			
(b)	DEBIT	Cost of sales (4,850 × £9.30)	45,105	
	CREDIT	Creditors (4,850 × £5.10)		24,735
	CREDIT	Conversion costs (4,850 × £4.20)		20,370
	Being the standard cost of goods sold			

4.13 SOLUTION FOR 1 TRIGGER POINT – when goods are completed (method 2)

This is very similar to the solution above but in this instance **the trigger is** the completion of a unit and its **movement into finished goods store.** The accounting entries are as follows.

			£	£
(a)	DEBIT	Conversion costs	20,580	
	CREDIT	Expense creditors		20,580
	Being the actual conversion costs incurred			

			£	£
(b)	DEBIT	Finished goods stock (4,900 × £9.30)	45,570	
	CREDIT	Creditors (4,900 × £5.10)		24,990
	CREDIT	Conversion costs (4,900 × £4.20)		20,580
	Being the standard cost of goods produced			
(c)	DEBIT	Cost of sales (4,850 × £9.30)	45,105	
	CREDIT	Finished goods stock		45,105
	Being the standard cost of goods sold			

The end of period finished goods stock balance is £465 (50 × £9.30).

4.14 SOLUTION FOR 2 TRIGGER POINTS – (method 3)

There are two trigger points, the first when materials and components are received and the other at the point of transfer to finished goods.

			£	£
(a)	DEBIT	Raw materials	24,990	
	CREDIT	Creditors		24,990
	Being the purchase of raw materials on credit			
(b)	DEBIT	Conversion costs	20,580	
	CREDIT	Expense creditors		20,580
	Being the incurring of conversion costs			
(c)	DEBIT	Finished goods stock (4,900 × £9.30)	45,570	
	CREDIT	Raw materials		24,990
	CREDIT	Conversion costs		20,580
	Being the cost of goods produced			
(d)	DEBIT	Cost of sales (4,850 × £9.30)	45,105	
	CREDIT	Finished goods stock		45,105
	Being the cost of goods sold			

4.15 Note that the WIP account is eliminated using all methods. In a JIT system the vast majority of manufacturing costs will form part of the cost of sales and will not be deferred in closing stock values. In such a situation the amount of work involved in tracking costs through WIP, cost of sales and finished goods is unlikely to be justified. This considerably reduces the volume of transactions recorded in the internal accounting system.

4.16 The successful operation of backflush costing rests upon predictable levels of efficiency and stable material prices and usage. In other words there should be insignificant cost variances.

Possible problems with backflush costing

4.17 (a) **It is only appropriate for JIT operations** where production and sales volumes are approximately equal.

(b) Some people claim that it **should not** be used **for external reporting** purposes. If, however, **stocks are low** or are practically **unchanged** from one accounting period to the next, operating income and stock valuations derived from backflush accounting will **not be materially different** from the results using conventional systems. Hence, in such circumstances, backflush accounting is acceptable for external financial reporting.

(c) It is **vital** that adequate production controls exist so that **cost control during the production process is maintained**.

Advantages of backflush costing

4.18
- It is much **simpler**, as there is no separate accounting for WIP

    - Even the **finished goods** account is **unnecessary**, as we demonstrated in the first example in paragraph 4.12.

    - The number of **accounting entries should be greatly reduced**, as are the supporting vouchers, documents and so on.

    - The system should **discourage** managers from **producing simply for stock** since working on material does not add value until the final product is completed or sold.

5 TARGET COSTING

Product design

5.1 In order to compete effectively in today's competitive market, organisations need to **continually redesign their products** with the result that **product life cycles** have become much **shorter**. The **planning, design and development stages of a product's cycle** are therefore **critical to an organisation's cost management process**. Cost reduction at this stage of a product's life cycle, rather than during the production process, is one of the most important ways of reducing product cost.

Case example

General Motors estimate that 70% of the cost of manufacturing truck transmissions is determined in the design stage. Estimates for other companies and products often exceed 80%.

5.2 Examples of costs that are determined at the design stage
- The number of different components
- Whether the components are standard or not
- The ease of changing over tools

The role of the management accountant in the design process

5.3 Having established that the planning, development and design stages of a product's life cycle are critical, you may be wondering what contribution the management accountant can make to the cost management process. *Nixon, Innes and Rabinowitz* list a wide variety of activities with which the management accountant can help. (The emphasis is BPP's.)

- **determining** which **designs minimise** assembly and service times (and hence costs)

- **evaluating** the **impact of different design** possibilities on the **cost** of developing, producing, owning and operating the product

- **appraising alternatives** (including outsourcing**) to resolve** technical, management and time scheduling **problems**

- **balancing the inherent tensions** that exist among the needs of customers, designers, developers, suppliers, operations, financiers and top management

- making explicit much of the tacit corporate knowledge that affects the filtering of ideas and proposals in the early 'fuzzy front end' of NPD [new product design]

- **making the 'go/no go' expenditure decisions** that the product development process entails

- **developing a performance measurement system** that enables managers to objectively assess the performance of individual products and the contribution of departments' activities to the attainment of competitive and corporate strategic objectives

- **helping the design teams communicate with senior management**, communicating not only the value of the work done within design teams but also the resources required to achieve product success.

5.4   Japanese companies developed target costing as a response to the problem of controlling and reducing costs over the product life cycle.

KEY TERM

Target cost is 'A product cost estimate derived by subtracting a desired profit margin from a competitive market price. This may be less than the planned initial product cost, but will be expected to be achieved by the time the product reaches the mature production stage.'

(CIMA *Official Terminology*)

'Target cost management has been defined as a system that is effective in managing costs in new-product design and development stages. It has also been viewed as allowing the production cost of a proposed product to be identified so that when sold it generates the desired profit level. ... Target cost management has also been viewed as playing a useful role in enabling an enterprise to set and support the attainment of cost levels to effectively reflect its planned financial performance. ...What appears to be evident is that there are almost as **many conceptions of target costing** as there are companies deploying the approach and there are probably many **companies engaging in various aspects of target cost management without referring to the term**.

Target cost management has been posited to assist in the pursuit of product development time reduction, as well as the quality definition for a new product and cost containment generally. It has therefore been perceived as a managerial tool simultaneously to **address time, quality and cost issues**.'

(A Bhimani and H Okano, 'Targeting excellence: target cost management at Toyota in the UK', *Management Accounting,* June 1995 (with BPP's emphasis))

Case example

'When Toyota developed the Lexus to compete with BMW, Mercedes and Jaguar, it employed two basic concepts: reverse engineering and target costing. In essence, it sought to produce a car with BMW 7-series attributes at a BMW 5-series price. Cost was the dominant design parameter that shaped the development of the Lexus, as it was later with Nissan's Infiniti.

The response from Mercedes Benz, one of the competitors who lost market share through this strategy, was to acknowledge that its cars were over-engineered and too expensive and to change its product-development process to determine target product costs from competitive market prices.

(B Nixon, J Innes and J Rabinowitz, *Management Accounting for Design,* Management Accounting, September 1997)

5.5   Target costing requires managers to change the way they think about the relationship between cost, price and profit.

(a)   The **traditional approach** is to **develop a product, determine the expected standard production cost** of that product and **then set a selling price** (probably based on cost)

with a resulting profit or loss. Costs are controlled through variance analysis at monthly intervals.

(b) The **target costing approach** is to develop a **product concept** and the primary specifications for performance and design and then to **determine the price customers would be willing to pay** for that concept. The **desired profit margin is deducted from the price leaving a figure that represents total cost.** This is the target cost and the product must be capable of being produced for this amount otherwise the product will not be manufactured. **During the product's life the target cost will constantly be reduced** allowing the price to decrease and so continuous cost reduction techniques must be employed.

5.6 Products that are **varieties of existing products** or **new brands of existing products** enter an already established market and therefore a competitive **price should be fairly easy to set.** There is no existing market price for **new products,** however and so **market research** will probably be used to assist in price setting. Many Japanese companies use **functional analysis** and **pricing by function** in such circumstances.

KEY TERMS

Functional analysis is 'an analysis of the relationships between product functions, their perceived value to the customer and their cost of provision'.

Value analysis is 'a systematic interdisciplinary examination of factors affecting the cost of a product or service, in order to devise means of achieving the specified purpose most economically at the required standard of quality and reliability'.

Value engineering is 'an activity which helps to design products which meet customer needs at the lowest cost while assuring the required standard of quality and reliability'. (CIMA *Official Terminology*)

5.7 In functional analysis a product is viewed as a collection of individual functions, for each of which the customer will be willing to pay a price. By splitting the product into a number of functions (reliability, looks and so on) and valuing each function at a price that customers will be willing to pay, an overall price can be established. **Selling price will also be affected by factors such as the stage in the product life cycle, expected sales volume and the price charged by rivals** in the market.

The target costing process

5.8 The target costing process consists of three main stages.

Step 1. **Analyse the external environment** to ascertain what customers require and what competitors are producing. Determine the product concept, the price customers will be willing to pay and thus the target cost.

Step 2. **Split the total target cost into broad cost categories** such as development, marketing, manufacturing, etc. **Then split up the manufacturing target cost per unit across the different functional areas of the product. Design the product so that each functional product area can be made within the target cost.** If a functional product area cannot be made within the target cost the targets for the other areas will be reduced, or the product will be redesigned or scrapped. The product will be developed in an atmosphere of **continuous** improvement using value engineering techniques and close collaboration with suppliers, to enhance the product (in terms of service, quality, durability and so on) and reduce costs.

Step 3. Once it is decided that it is feasible to meet the total target cost, detailed cost sheets will be prepared and processes formalised.

5.9 It is possible that management may decide to go ahead and manufacture a product whose target cost is well below the currently attainable cost, determined by current technology and processes. If this is the case management will **set benchmarks for improvement** towards the target costs, by specified dates.

5.10 **Options available to reduce costs**

- **Training** staff in more efficient techniques
- Using **cheaper staff**
- Acquiring new, more **efficient technology**
- Cutting out **non-value-added activities**

5.11 Even if the product can be produced within the target cost the story does not end there. **Once the product goes into production target costs will gradually be reduced.** These reductions will be incorporated into the budgeting process. This means that cost savings must be actively sought and made continuously. Value analysis will be used to reduce costs if and when targets are missed.

Case examples

(a) The following comments appeared in an article in the *Financial Times* in January 1993. (Emphasis is BPP's.)

'Mercedes-Benz, one of the world's most prestigious and tradition-laden carmakers, has taken its time to wake up to the daunting dimensions of the challenges it faces in the **rapidly-changing world car market** of the 1990s.

The company has accepted that radical changes in the world car market mean that Mercedes-Benz will no longer be able to demand premium prices for its products based on an image of effortless superiority and a content of the ultimate in automotive engineering.

Instead of developing the ultimate car and then charging a correspondingly sky-high price as in the past, Mercedes-Benz is taking the dramatic and radical step of moving to '**target pricing'. It will decide what the customer is willing to pay** in a particular product category - priced against its competitors - it will **add its profit margin** and then the real work will begin to **cost every part and component to bring in the vehicle at the target price.**

The following extracts are from an article which appeared three months later.

'The marketing motto for the Mercedes-Benz compact C-class is that it offers customers more car for their money.

It is the first practical example of the group's new pricing policy. The range embodies a principle new to Mercedes which states that **before any work starts a new product will be priced according to what the market will bear and what the company considers an acceptable profit. Then each component and manufacturing process will be costed to ensure the final product is delivered at the target price.**

Under the old system of building the car, adding up the costs and then fixing a price, the C-class would have been **between 15 per cent and 20 per cent dearer** than the 10-year-old outgoing 190 series, Mr Vöhringer said.

Explaining the practical workings of the new system, he explained that project groups for each component and construction process were instructed without exception to increase productivity by between 15 and 25 per cent. And they had to reach their targets in record time.

One result was that development time on the new models was cut to 40 months, about a third less than usual. But the most important effect, according to Mr Vöhringer, has been to **reduce** the **company's cost disadvantages** *vis-à-vis* **Japanese competitors in this class from 35 per cent to only 15 per cent.**'

(b) The following extracts from Bhimani's and Okano's article (with BPP's emphasis) illustrate the way in which the Japanese target cost management approach has been introduced at Toyota in the UK.

'...the target cost for the model essentially reflects the difference between the target price and the target profit. The **target** price is **established** primarily by TMC [Toyota Motor Corporation in Japan] which first obtains input on **expected European sales** from TMME [Toyota Motor Europe Marketing and Engineering]. The **target profit** is a **function of Toyota's long-term strategy for the European market** as well as commercial viability considerations concerning TMUK [Toyota Motor Manufacturing UK Ltd].

It is in fact the Department of Purchasing which is more directly engaged in pursuing target costs. ... One role of this department is to identify European **producers** of sub-components who are **able to meet TMUK's stringent product specification criteria**. From a total of 2,000 potential suppliers approached in the period 1989-91, approximately 160 will ultimately become the core base of parts manufacturers. It is these model parts which provide the focus of target cost management activities at TMUK. Suppliers' prototypes are assessed in the UK and in Japan for approval as a starting point, **but suppliers are expected to generate ideas for cost reduction and operational improvements**. An important part of the target cost management exercise is to undertake **inspection visits** by members of the Purchasing Department's staff and the Technical Support segment's 'Supplier Parts Tracking Team'. These periodic visits are carried out to check plant and facilities layout of suppliers with a **view to pinpointing cost reduction and quality enhancement possibilities**.

Summary

5.12 Bhimani and Okano's article provides a useful summary of this important technique.

'... target cost management has been seen as an activity which is aimed at reducing lifecycle costs of new products, while ensuring speedy quality, reliability and other customer requirements, by examining all ideas for cost reduction at the product planning, research and development process.'

Exam focus point

Target costing has yet to feature in an exam despite being on the old syllabus as well and so it could be included in the paper you will be facing.

6 LIFE CYCLE COSTING

What are life cycle costs?

6.1 Product life cycle costs are incurred **from the design stage through development to market launch, production and sales, and their eventual withdrawal from the market**. The component elements of a product's cost over its life cycle could therefore include the following.

- **Research & development costs**

    o design
    o testing
    o production process and equipment

- **Technical data cost.** Cost of purchasing any technical data required.

- **Training costs** including initial operator training and skills updating.

- **Production costs**

- **Distribution costs**. Transportation and handling costs.

- **Marketing costs**
  - ° customer service
  - ° field maintenance
  - ° brand promotion

- **Inventory costs**. Holding spare parts, warehousing and so on

- **Retirement and disposal costs**. Costs occurring at the end of the product's life

6.2 Life cycle costs can apply to services as well as to physical products, and to customers and projects.

6.3 **Traditional management accounting systems** are based on the financial accounting year and tend to dissect the product's life cycle into a series of annual sections. This means that management accounting systems do not accumulate costs over the entire life cycle. They **do not**, therefore, **assess a product's profitability over its entire life** but rather on a periodic basis.

6.4 **Life cycle costing**, on the other hand, **tracks and accumulates actual costs and revenues** attributable to each product **over the entire product life cycle.** Hence the total profitability of any given product can be determined.

KEY TERM

Life cycle costing is 'the profiling of cost over a product's life, including the pre-production stage'.

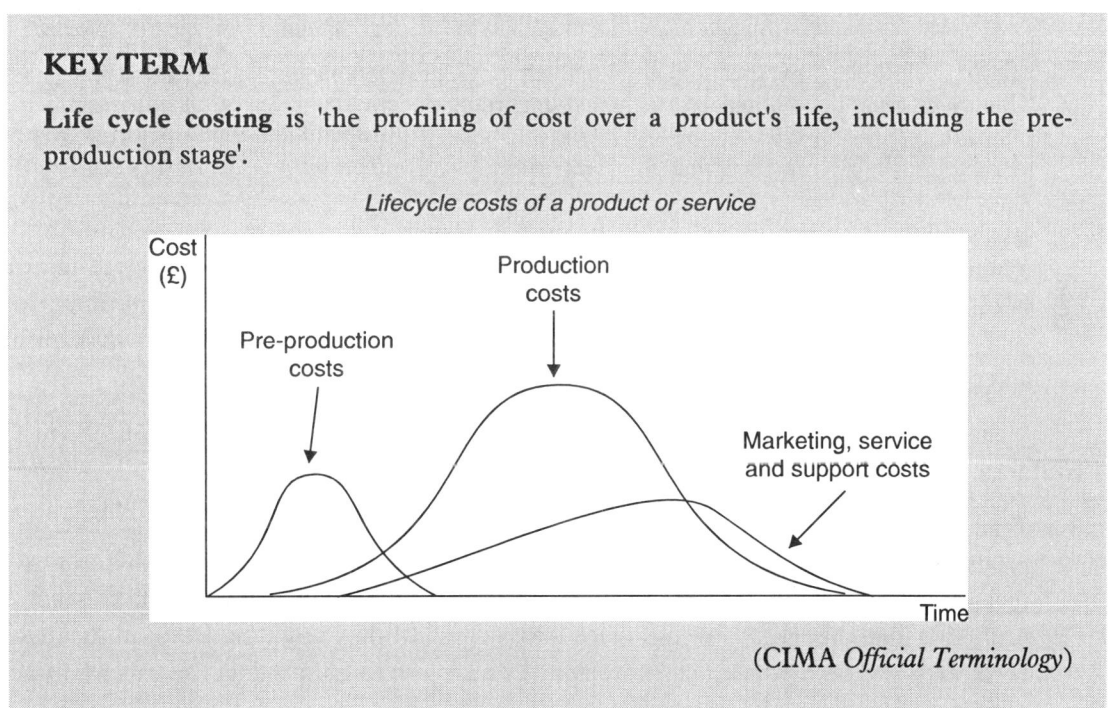

Lifecycle costs of a product or service

(CIMA *Official Terminology*)

The product life cycle

6.5 **Every product goes through a life cycle**, the curve of which resembles the generic curve in the following diagram.

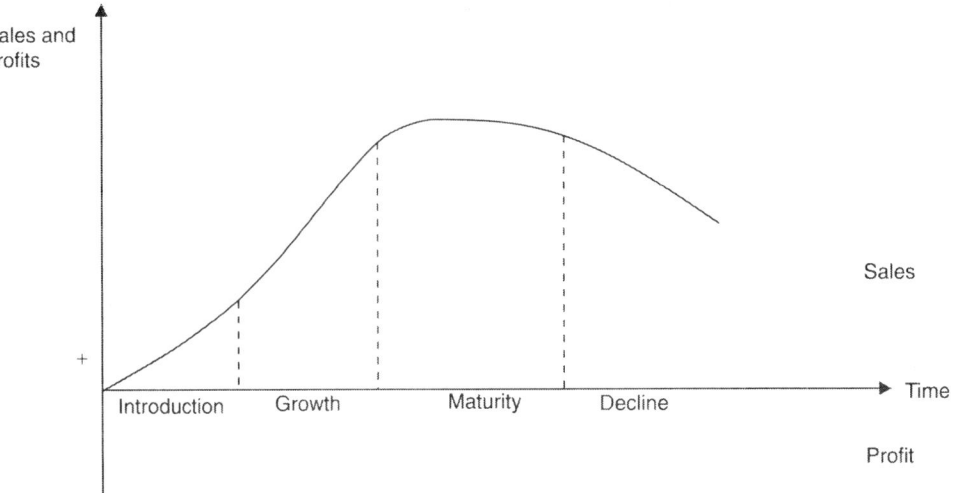

6.6 The horizontal axis measures the duration of **the life cycle**, which **can last** from, say, **18 months to several hundred years**. Children's crazes or fad products have very short lives while some products, such as binoculars (invented in the eighteenth century) can last a very long time. It is important to know where the product is in its life cycle, as this will affect the returns that are expected and the appropriate management action.

Performance measure	Stage in the life cycle			
	Introduction	*Growth*	*Maturity*	*Decline*
Cash	net user	net user	generator	generator
Return on capital	not important	not important	important	important
Growth	vital	vital	grow with new uses	negative growth
Profit	not expected	important	important	very important

6.7 If a product is **in the introductory or growth stages it cannot be expected to be a net generator of cash** as all the cash it generates will be used in expansion through increased sales, etc. As the product moves from maturity towards decline, it is of **prime importance** that the product still **generates a profit and cash** and that its **return on capital** is acceptable.

Problems with traditional accounting systems

6.8 Traditional accounting systems tend not to relate research and development costs to the products that caused them. Instead they write off these costs on an annual basis against the revenue generated by existing products. This makes the existing products seem less profitable than they really are and there is a danger that they might be scrapped too quickly. If research and development costs are not related to the causal product the true profitability of that product cannot be assessed.

6.9 Traditional management accounting systems usually total **all non-production costs** and record them as a period expense. With life cycle costing these costs are traced to individual products over complete life cycles.

(a) The total of these costs for each individual product can therefore be reported and compared with revenues generated in the future.

(b) The visibility of such costs is increased.

(c) **Individual product profitability can be more fully understood** by attributing *all* costs to products.

(d) As a consequence, **more accurate feedback information** is available on the organisation's success or failure in developing new products. In today's competitive environment, where the ability to produce new and updated versions of products is paramount to the survival of an organisation, this information is vital.

Maximising the return over the product life cycle

6.10 There are a number of ways the return can be increased over a product's life.

(a) **Design costs out of products**. Between 70% to 90% of a product's life cycle costs are determined by decisions made early in the life cycle, at the design or development stage. Careful design of the product and manufacturing and other processes will keep cost to a minimum over the life cycle.

(b) **Minimise the time to market**. This is the time from the conception of the product to its launch. More products come onto the market nowadays and development times have been reduced over the years. Competitors watch each other very carefully to determine what types of products their rivals are developing. If an organisation is launching a new product it is vital to get it to the market place as soon as possible. This will give the product as long a period as possible without a rival in the market place and this should mean that the market share is increased in the long run. Furthermore the life span may not proportionally lengthen if the product's launch is delayed and so sales may be permanently lost. It is not unusual for the product's overall profitability to fall by 25% if the launch is delayed by six months. This means that it is usually worthwhile incurring extra costs to keep the launch on schedule or to speed up the launch.

(c) **Minimise break-even time** (BET). A short BET is very important in keeping an organisation liquid. The sooner the product is launched the quicker the research and development costs will be repaid, providing the organisation funds to develop further products.

(d) **Maximise the length of the life span**. Product life cycles are not predetermined; they are set by the actions of management and competitors. Once developed, some products lend themselves to a number of different uses; this is especially true of materials, such as plastic, PVC, nylon and other synthetic materials. The life cycle of the material is then a series of individual product curves nesting on top of each other as shown below.

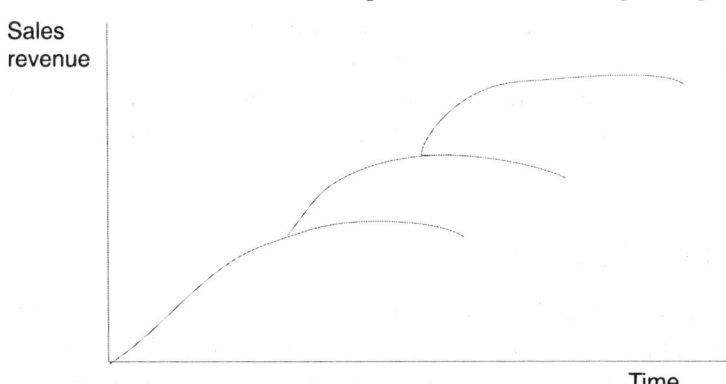

By entering different national or regional markets one after another an organisation may be able to maximise revenue. This allows resources to be better applied, and sales in each market are maximised. On the other hand in today's fast moving world an organisation could lose out to a competitor if it failed to establish an early presence in a particular market.

BPP PUBLISHING

Service and project life cycles

6.11 A service organisation will also have products that have life cycles. The only difference being that the R & D stages will not exist in the same way and will not have the same impact on subsequent costs. However, the **different processes that go to form the complete service** are important and **consideration should be given in advance to how to carry them out and arrange them so as to minimise cost.**

6.12 Products that take years to produce or come to fruition are usually called projects, and discounted cash flow calculations are invariably used **to cost them over their life cycle in advance.** The projects need to be **monitored** very carefully **over their life** to make sure that they **remain on schedule and that cost overruns are not being incurred.** We will study this in more detail in chapter 8.

Customer life cycle

6.13 Customers also have life cycles, and an organisation will wish to maximise the return from a customer over their life cycle. The aim is to **extend the life cycle of a particular customer** or decrease the 'churn' rate, as the Americans say. This means encouraging customer loyalty. For example, supermarkets and other retail outlets have recently begun issuing loyalty cards that offer discounts to loyal customers who return to the shop and spend a certain amount with the organisation. As existing customers tend to be more profitable than new ones they should be retained wherever possible.

6.14 **Customers become more profitable over their life cycle.** The profit can go on increasing for a period of between approximately 4 and 20 years. For example, if you open a bank account, take out insurance or invest in a pension, the company involved has to set up the account, run checks, etc. The initial cost is high and the company will be keen to retain your business so that it can recoup this cost. Once customers get used to their supplier they tend to use them more frequently, and so there is a double benefit in holding on to customers. For example, you may use the bank to purchase shares on your behalf, or you may take out a second insurance policy with the same company, and so on.

6.15 The projected cash flows over the full lives of customers or customer segments can be analysed to highlight the worth of customers and the importance of customer retention. It may take a year or more to recoup the initial costs of winning a customer, and we will see in the next chapter that this could be referred to as the **payback period** of the investment in the customer. The investment in the customer and the consequent returns can be analysed in the same way as the investment in the capital projects that we will be reviewing in chapter 8.

7 THE EMPEROR'S NEW CLOTHES?

7.1 The techniques we have looked at in this and the previous chapter, are relatively new and may appear to solve a lot of problems. But in the late 1990s a number of articles and letters in *Management Accounting* questioned whether they were in fact **radical/new ideas or just a case of 'the emperor's new clothes'.** This was the title of Tony Mock's article (*Management Accounting*, October 1995) in which he looked at the topics examined in CIMA's management accounting syllabuses. (The emphasis is BPP's.)

> 'I would suggest that, whilst one or two of these ideas have improved the information available to management and contributed to an increase in the profitability of organisations, several [world class manufacturing, synchronous manufacturing, **throughput accounting, life cycle costing and backflush accounting**] are merely established techniques given a new gloss.'

7.2   Bob Scarlett, the examiner at the time, responded to these comments in 'In defence of management accounting applications' (*Management Accounting*, January 1996).

> 'At the root of much traditional management accounting practice is the assumption of a simple model of cost behaviour. Costs are assumed either to vary in proportion with output volume or to be fixed ... It may be that this simple model correctly represents the way things were in the manufacturing sector at one time ... However, it is equally possible that traditional management accounting practices were always based on an oversimplified understanding of the way the world works ...

> ...an increase in product diversity, a shortening in product lifecycles, the widespread adoption of robotics and information technology in manufacturing operations and the advent of world markets in products and components as a result of the erosion of barriers to trade ... have a profound influence on the way in which manufacturing operations incur costs. This in turn impacts on the way in which costs should be collated and reported ... It is these factors that have promoted consideration of new approaches ... The thrust of all these techniques or approaches is that they seek to deploy a more sophisticated understanding of cost behaviour than that found in much traditional management accounting ...

> Exploration of 'modern' management accounting techniques ... gives all sorts of insights into how business operations work and what accounting is all about. This is so even though those modern techniques may not be currently in common practical use - and may be subject to serious criticism. Current thinking and discussion about management accounting are therefore an important element in the MAA syllabus - and will continue to be.'

7.3   In 'The changing practice of management accounting' (*Management Accounting*, March 1996), Robin Cooper argued that the **growing importance of cost management is significantly changing the practice of management accounting.** He was referring to the professional institute in the USA when he wrote:

'If they fail to take these steps [of radically altering the skills taught as a preface to qualifying] the CMA could easily cease to be viewed as a useful certification and thousands of career management accountants will be ill-prepared to adapt to the changes in the practice of management accounting that are currently occurring'.

7.4   Letters in both the April and May 1996 editions of *Management Accounting* felt that 'there was much in the article that sounded very familiar' and the 'skill set' that Professor Cooper says must be acquired was one that every management accountant is, in the UK, presently trained in. **'Cost management, that is made to seem something new, is pretty old hat...'**

7.5   You, of course, are perfectly at liberty to **decide for yourself** whether the topics we have been looking at are 'radical ideas or just a case of the emperor's new clothes' but it may be worth bearing in mind a comment made by Bob Scarlett.

> 'Reliable research has indicated that employers increasingly seek the services of 'thinking accountants' who understand the logic and limitations of the techniques they practise.'

Exam focus point

The topics covered in this chapter are unlikely to be a major element in the MCQs in the examination paper. They lend themselves more to calculation or essay questions.

Chapter roundup

- **Modern business methods** strive to meet customer demands as quickly as possible by manufacturing in short production runs.

- **Theory of constraints** is a set of concepts developed in the USA with a view to identifying the binding constraints in a production system and striving for evenness of production flow so that the organisation works as effectively as possible. No stocks should be held, except prior to the binding constraint.

- **Throughput accounting** is the accounting system developed in the UK, which is based on the theory of constraints and JIT. It measures the throughput contribution per factory hour. It is very similar to marginal costing but can be used to make longer-term decisions about production equipment/capacity.

- **Backflush accounting** is a method of accounting that can be used with JIT production systems. It saves a considerable amount of time as it avoids having to make a number of accounting entries that are required by a traditional system.

- **Target costing** is a pro-active cost control system. The target cost is calculated by deducting the target profit from the predetermined selling price, based on customers' views. Functional analysis, value engineering and value analysis are used to change production methods and/or reduce expected costs so that the target cost is met.

- **Life cycle costing** involves a number of techniques that assist in the planning and control of a product's life cycle costs by monitoring spending and commitment to spend during a product's life cycle. Its aim is to minimise cost and maximise sales revenue over the life of the product.

Quick quiz

1   **Fill in the blanks** in the statements below, using the words in the box. Some words may be used twice.

- The theory of constraints is an approach to production management which aims to maximise (1)............ less (2)........ and (3).......... It focuses on factors such as (4)................ which act as (5)....................

- Throughput contribution = (6)............. minus (7) ....

- TA ratio = (8) .... per factory hour ÷ (9) ....per factory hour

- Target costing was developed by the Japanese as a response to the problem of (10) .... and (11) ....costs over the (12).............

    - Product life cycle
    - Variable overhead costs
    - Bottlenecks
    - Material costs
    - Controlling
    - Sales revenue
    - Throughput contribution
    - Constraints
    - Conversion cost
    - Reducing

2   Backflush accounting is a cost accounting system which focuses on the (13) input/output of an organisation and then works (14) forwards/backwards to allocate costs between cost of goods sold and stock.

3   The point at which a physical activity causes an entry in the accounts which flushes out cost in a backflush system is known as the (15) ....

4   Life cycle costing is the profiling of cost over a product's production life.   True/False

5   A company manufacturing a single product operates a backflush accounting system with two trigger points, one of which is cost of sales. The standard cost of materials is £10 per unit and the standard conversion cost is £15 per unit. At the beginning of the period there are no stocks of any sort, and this is a fairly regular state of affairs. During the period 2,020 units were completed and 2,000 units were sold. What is the balance on the finished goods account at the end of the period?

A   £700   Dr
B   £700   Cr
C   zero
D   £400   Dr
E   £400   Cr

Answers to quick quiz

1	1	Sales revenue
	2	Material costs
	3	Variable overhead costs
	4	Bottlenecks
	5	Constraints
	6	Sales revenue
	7	Material costs
	8	Throughput acontribution
	9	Conversion cost
	10	Controlling
	11	Reducing
	12	Product life cycle
2	13	Output
	14	Backwards
3	15	Trigger point

4   False - it includes development costs, etc, prior to production and any dismantling costs, etc when production costs have ceased.

5   C   As cost of sales is a trigger point the second trigger point must be raw materials purchased. It would be extremely unusual to operate trigger points at finished goods *and* cost of sales in a backflush accounting system and as stock is not normally held there would be no point

Now try the question below from the Exam Question Bank

Number	Level	Marks	Time
12	Introductory	n/a	n/a
13	Introductory	n/a	n/a

BPP PUBLISHING

Part C
Investment appraisal

Chapter 8

INVESTMENT APPRAISAL: BASIC PRINCIPLES

Topic list		Syllabus Reference	Ability required
1	The capital budgeting process	(iii)	Explain
2	The payback method	(iii)	Evaluate
3	The accounting rate of return method	(iii)	Evaluate
4	The net present value method	(iii)	Evaluate
5	The internal rate of return method	(iii)	Evaluate
6	NPV and IRR compared	(iii)	Evaluate
7	DCF: additional points	(iii)	Evaluate
8	Discounted payback	(iii)	Evaluate

Introduction

In the next two chapters we will be examining the appraisal of projects which involve the **outlay of capital**.

Capital expenditure differs from day to day revenue expenditure for two reasons.

- Capital expenditure often involves a **bigger outlay of money**.

- The **benefits** from capital expenditure are likely to **accrue over a long period of time**, usually well over one year and often much longer. In such circumstances the benefits cannot all be set against costs in the current year's profit and loss account.

For these reasons any proposed capital expenditure project should be **properly appraised**, and found to be worthwhile, before the decision is taken to go ahead with the expenditure.

We will be examining the capital budgeting process as well as a number of **capital investment appraisal techniques**. Some of the techniques involve **discounting** cash flows which you will have encountered at an introductory level in Paper 3(c), but we will review the basics again in this chapter.

Learning outcomes covered in this chapter

- **Explain** the capital budgeting process

- **Evaluate** projects using investment appraisal techniques

- **Evaluate** alternative investment appraisal techniques

- **Discuss** the relevance of qualitative factors

- **Discuss** post-completion appraisal

Syllabus content covered in this chapter

- Capital budgeting process
- Investment appraisal techniques
- Post-completion appraisal

Exam focus point

Three out of the eight questions in the multiple choice section of the pilot paper were concerned with investment appraisal techniques. The examiner has stated that in future the multiple choice questions will be largely on investment appraisal. It is therefore vital that you study this chapter and the next very carefully. Ensure that you can apply all the techniques quickly and accurately in a variety of situations.

1 THE CAPITAL BUDGETING PROCESS

1.1 We have seen in the introduction to this chapter that capital expenditure often involves the outlay of **large sums of money**, and that any expected **benefits may take a number of years to accrue**. For these reasons it is vital that capital expenditure is subject to a rigorous process of appraisal and control.

1.2 The first stages in the capital budgeting process involve identifying and locating the funds for investment, and identifying possible projects for investment. The detail of these stages is outside the scope of your Paper 9 syllabus, so we will focus on explaining the next five stages in the capital budgeting process.

- Evaluate the projects
- Consider any qualitative factors
- Approve the projects, if appropriate
- Monitor and control the progress of the approved projects
- Perform a post-completion appraisal

Evaluate the projects

1.3 Each proposal must be subject to **detailed screening and evaluation**. To begin with, a number of key questions such as those below might be asked before any numerical or financial analysis is undertaken at all. Only if the project passes this initial screening will more detailed financial analysis begin.

- What is the purpose of the project?
- Does it 'fit' with the organisation's long-term objectives?
- Is it a mandatory investment, for example to conform with safety legislation?
- What resources are required and are they available, eg money, capacity, labour?
- Do we have the necessary management expertise to guide the project to completion?
- Does the project expose the organisation to unnecessary risk?
- How long will the project last and what factors are key to its success?
- Have all possible alternatives been considered?

1.4 The financial analysis will involve the application of the organisation's preferred appraisal techniques. We will be studying these techniques in detail in this chapter and the next. In many projects some of the financial implications will be extremely difficult to quantify, but

every effort must be made to do so, in order to have a formal basis for planning and controlling the project.

The type of question that will be addressed at this stage

1.5
- What cash flows/profits will arise from the project and when?
- Has inflation been considered in the determination of the cash flows?
- What are the results of the financial appraisal?
- Has any allowance been made for risk, and if so, what was the outcome?

1.6 Some types of project, for example a marketing investment decision, may give rise to cash inflows and **returns which are so intangible and difficult to quantify that a full financial appraisal may not be possible**. In this case more weight may be given to a consideration of the qualitative factors.

Qualitative factors

1.7 Financial analysis of capital projects is obviously vital because of the amount of money involved and the length of time for which it is tied up. However a consideration of **qualitative factors** is also relevant to the decision, ie factors which are difficult or impossible to quantify. We have already seen that qualitative factors would be considered in the **initial screening stage**, for example in reviewing the project's 'fit' with the organisation's overall objectives and whether it is a mandatory investment. There is a very wide range of other qualitative factors that may be relevant to a particular project.

- What are the implications of not undertaking the investment, eg adverse effect on staff morale, loss of market share?

- Will acceptance of this project lead to the need for further investment activity in future?

- What will be the effect on the company's image?

- Will the organisation be more flexible as a result of the investment, and better able to respond to market and technology changes?

Project approval

1.8 Once the project has been subject to all the appropriate stages of analysis, **formal approval** can be given for its commencement. A suitably qualified manager will be charged with responsibility for the progress of the project and it should be given **senior management backing**.

Monitoring the progress of the project

1.9 During the project's progress, **project controls should be applied** to ensure the following.

- Capital spending does not exceed the amount authorised
- The implementation of the project is not delayed
- The anticipated benefits are eventually obtained

1.10 The first two items are probably easier to control than the third, because the controls can normally be applied soon after the capital expenditure has been authorised, whereas monitoring the benefits will span a longer period of time.

BPP PUBLISHING

Controls over excess spending

1.11 There are a number of controls which organisations can implement to ensure that capital spending does not exceed the amount authorised.

(a) The **authority to make capital expenditure decisions** must be **formally assigned**. For example, all spending over £250,000, say, must be authorised by, for example, the holding company's board of directors, spending over £100,000 and up to £250,000, say, must be authorised by, for example, the subsidiary company's board of directors, while spending over £10,000 and up to £100,000, say, could be authorised by heads of departments.

(b) Capital expenditure decisions should be **documented** and approval of the project should specify the **manager authorised** to carry out the expenditure (and hence responsible for the successful implementation of the project), the **amount of expenditure** authorised and the **period of time** in which the expenditure should take place.

(c) **Some overspending** above the amount authorised- say 5% or 10% - **might be allowed**. If the required expenditure exceeds the amount authorised by more than this amount, a fresh submission for reauthorisation of the project should be required. It would be bad management to approve spending of £1 million, and then to allow an overspending to £1.5 million to go by unchecked and without comment!

(d) There should be a total capital budget, and the authorisation of any **capital expenditure which would take total spending above the budget should be referred** to, for example, board level for approval.

Control over delays

1.12 If there is a delay in carrying out the project and the capital expenditure has not taken place before the stated deadline is reached, the project should be **resubmitted for fresh authorisation,** and the proposer should be asked to **explain the reasons for the delay.**

Control over the anticipated benefits

1.13 Further control can be exercised over capital projects by ensuring that the anticipated benefits do actually materialise, the benefits are as big as anticipated and running costs do not exceed expectation.

1.14 A **difficulty** with control measurements of capital projects is that most **projects are 'unique' with no standard or yardstick to judge them against** other than their own appraisal data. Therefore if actual costs were to exceed the estimated costs, it might be impossible to tell just how much of the variance is due to bad estimating and how much is due to inefficiencies and poor cost control.

1.15 In the same way, if benefits are below expectation, is this because the original estimates were optimistic, or because management has been inefficient and failed to get the benefits they should have done?

1.16 Many capital projects such as the purchase of replacement assets and marketing investment decisions **do not have clearly identifiable costs and benefits**. The incremental benefits and costs of such schemes can be estimated, but it would need a very sophisticated management accounting system to be able to identify and measure the actual benefits and many of the costs. Even so, some degree of monitoring and control can still be exercised by means of a **post-completion appraisal** or audit review.

Post-completion appraisal

> ### KEY TERM
>
> A **post-completion audit** is 'An objective and independent appraisal of the measure of success of a capital expenditure project in progressing the business as planned. The appraisal should cover the implementation of the project from authorisation to commissioning and its technical and commercial performance after commissioning. The information provided is also used by management as feedback which aids the implementation and control of future projects.' (CIMA *Official Terminology*)

Why perform a post-completion appraisal or audit?

1.17 Post-completion audit checking cannot reverse the decision to incur the capital expenditure, because the expenditure will already have taken place. However, it does have a certain control value.

   (a) The **threat** of the post-completion audit will **motivate managers** to work to achieve the promised benefits from the project.

   (b) If the audit takes place before the project life ends, and if it finds that the benefits have been less than expected because of management inefficiency, steps can be taken to **improve efficiency**. Alternatively, it will **highlight those projects which should be discontinued**.

   (c) It can help to **identify** managers who have been **good performers** and those who have been poor performers.

   (d) It might identify weaknesses in the forecasting and estimating techniques used to evaluate projects, and so should help to **improve** the discipline and quality of **forecasting** for future investment decisions.

   (e) Areas where improvements can be made in methods which should help to achieve **better results in general from capital investments** might be revealed.

   (f) The **original estimates may be more realistic** if managers are aware that they will be monitored, but post-completion audits **should not be unfairly critical**.

Which projects should be audited?

1.18 It may be too expensive to audit all capital expenditure projects, and so managers may need to select **a sample** for a post-completion audit. The selection will depend on the probability that the audit of any particular project will produce benefits, which is obviously difficult to determine.

1.19 Generally size is likely to be the best guide as to which projects should be audited. However, **managers should perceive that every capital expenditure project has a chance of being the subject of a detailed post-completion audit**.

   A reasonable **guideline** might be to **audit all projects above a certain size, and a random selection of smaller projects**.

1.20 A post-completion audit does not need to focus on all aspects of an investment, but should **concentrate on those aspects which have been identified as particularly sensitive or critical to the success of a project**. The most important thing to remember is that post-

completion audits are time-consuming and costly and so **careful consideration should be given to the cost-benefit trade-off** arising from the post-completion audit results.

When should projects be audited?

1.21 If the audit is carried out too soon, the information may not be complete. On the other hand, if the audit is too late then management action will be delayed and the usefulness of the information is greatly reduced.

1.22 There is no correct answer to the question of when to audit, although Jan Gadella (*Management Accounting,* November 1986) suggests that in practice most companies perform the post-completion audit **approximately one year after the completion of the project.**

Problems with post-completion audits

1.23 There are a number of problems with post-completion audits.

   (a) There are many **uncontrollable factors** which are outside management control in long-term investments, such as environmental changes.

   (b) It **may not be possible** to **identify separately the costs and benefits** of any particular project.

   (c) Post-completion audit can be a **costly** and **time-consuming** exercise.

   (d) Applied punitively, post-completion audit exercises may lead to **managers becoming over cautious** and unnecessarily **risk averse.**

   (e) The **strategic effects** of a capital investment project **may take years** to materialise and it may in fact **never be possible** to identify or quantify them effectively.

1.24 Despite the growth in popularity of post-completion audits, you should bear in mind the possible **alternative** control processes.

   (a) **Teams** could manage a project from beginning to end, control being used **before** the project is started and **during** its life, rather than at the end of its life.

   (b) **More time could be spent choosing projects** rather than checking completed projects.

1.25 Now that we have discussed all the stages involved in the capital budgeting process, we will return to study in detail the stage that many managers consider to be the most important: the financial appraisal. We will begin with what is probably the most straightforward appraisal technique: the payback method.

2 THE PAYBACK METHOD

KEY TERM

Payback is 'The time required for the cash inflows from a capital investment project to equal the cash outflows'. (CIMA *Official Terminology*)

2.1 When **deciding between two or more competing projects,** the usual decision is to **accept the one with the shortest payback.**

2.2 Payback is often used as a '**first screening method**'. By this, we mean that when a capital investment project is being subjected to financial appraisal, the first question to ask is: 'How long will it take to pay back its cost?' The organisation might have a target payback, and so it would reject a capital project unless its payback period were less than a certain number of years.

2.3 However, a project should not be evaluated on the basis of payback alone. Payback should be a *first* screening process, and if a project gets through the payback test, it ought **then to be evaluated with a more sophisticated project appraisal technique**.

2.4 You should note that when payback is calculated, we take **profits before depreciation**, because we are trying to estimate the *cash* returns from a project and profit before depreciation is likely to be a **rough approximation of cash flows**.

Why is payback alone an inadequate project appraisal technique?

2.5 Look at the figures below for two mutually exclusive projects (this means that only one of them can be undertaken).

	Project P	*Project Q*
Capital asset	£60,000	£60,000
Profits before depreciation		
Year 1	£20,000	£50,000
Year 2	£30,000	£20,000
Year 3	£40,000	£5,000
Year 4	£50,000	£5,000
Year 5	£60,000	£5,000

2.6 Project P pays back in year 3 (about one quarter of the way through year 3). Project Q pays back half way through year 2. **Using payback alone** to judge projects, **project Q would be preferred. But the returns from project P over its life are much higher than the returns from project Q**. Project P will earn total profits before depreciation of £140,000 on an investment of £60,000, whereas Project Q will earn total profits after depreciation of only £25,000 on an investment of £60,000.

Disadvantages of the payback method

2.7 There are a number of serious drawbacks to the payback method.

(a) It **ignores the timing of cash flows** within the payback period, the cash flows after the end of payback period and therefore the total project return.

(b) It **ignores the time value of money** (a concept incorporated into more sophisticated appraisal methods). This means that it does not take account of the fact that £1 today is worth more than £1 in one year's time. An investor who has £1 today can either consume it immediately or alternatively can invest it at the prevailing interest rate, say 10%, to get a return of £1.10 in a year's time.

2.8 There are also other disadvantages.

(a) The method is **unable to distinguish between projects with the same payback period**.

(b) The **choice of any cut-off payback period** by an organisation is **arbitrary**.

(c) It may lead to excessive **investment in short-term projects**.

(d) It takes account of the risk of the timing of cash flows but **does not take account of the variability of those cash flows**.

Advantages of the payback method

2.9 The use of the payback method does have advantages, especially as an initial screening device.

- Long payback means **capital is tied up**
- Focus on early payback can **enhance liquidity**
- **Investment risk is increased** if payback is longer
- **Shorter term forecasts** are likely to be **more reliable**
- The calculation is **quick** and **simple**
- Payback is an **easily understood** concept

3 THE ACCOUNTING RATE OF RETURN METHOD

KEY TERMS

The accounting rate of return (ARR) method (also called the return on capital employed (ROCE) method or the return on investment (ROI) method) of appraising a project is to estimate the accounting rate of return that the project should yield. If it exceeds a target rate of return, the project will be undertaken. The CIMA *Official Terminology* definition is $\dfrac{\text{Average annual profit from an investment} \times 100}{\text{Average investment}}$

3.1 Unfortunately there are several different definitions of ARR.

$$\text{ARR} = \frac{\text{Estimted total profits}}{\text{Estimated initial investment}} \times 100\%$$

$$\text{ARR} = \frac{\text{Estimted average profits}}{\text{Estimated initial investment}} \times 100\%$$

3.2 There are arguments in favour of each of these definitions. The most important point is, however, that the **method selected should be used consistently**. For **examination** purposes we recommend the **first definition** unless the question clearly indicates that some other one is to be used.

Note that this is the only appraisal method that we will be studying that **uses profit** instead of cash flow. If you are not provided with a figure for profit, **assume that net cash inflow minus depreciation equals profit**.

3.3 EXAMPLE: THE ACCOUNTING RATE OF RETURN

A company has a target accounting rate of return of 20% (using the CIMA definition above), and is now considering the following project.

Capital cost of asset	£80,000
Estimated life	4 years
Estimated profit before depreciation	
Year 1	£20,000
Year 2	£25,000
Year 3	£35,000
Year 4	£25,000

The capital asset would be depreciated by 25% of its cost each year, and will have no residual value.

Required

Assess whether the project should be undertaken.

3.4 SOLUTION

The annual profits after depreciation, and the mid-year net book value of the asset, would be as follows.

Year	Profit after depreciation £	Mid-year net book value £	ARR in the year %
1	0	70,000	0
2	5,000	50,000	10
3	15,000	30,000	50
4	5,000	10,000	50

As the table shows, the ARR is low in the early stages of the project, partly because of low profits in Year 1 but mainly because the net book value of the asset is much higher early on in its life. So the project does not achieve the target ARR of 20% in its first two years, but exceeds it in years 3 and 4. So should it be undertaken?

When the **ARR from a project varies from year to year**, it makes sense to **take an overall or 'average' view of the project's return**. In this case, we should look at the return as a whole over the four-year period.

	£
Total profit before depreciation over four years	105,000
Total profit after depreciation over four years	25,000
Average annual profit after depreciation	6,250
Original cost of investment	80,000
Average net book value over the four year period ((80,000 + 0)/2)	40,000

The project would not be undertaken because its ARR is 6,250/40,000 = 15.625% and so it would fail to yield the target return of 20%.

The ARR and the comparison of mutually exclusive projects

3.5 The ARR method of capital investment appraisal can also be used to compare two or more projects which are mutually exclusive. The project with the highest ARR would be selected (provided that the expected ARR is higher than the company's target ARR).

3.6 EXAMPLE: THE ARR AND MUTUALLY EXCLUSIVE PROJECTS

Arrow Ltd wants to buy a new item of equipment. Two models of equipment are available, one with a slightly higher capacity and greater reliability than the other. The expected costs and profits of each item are as follows.

	Equipment item X	Equipment item Y
Capital cost	£80,000	£150,000
Life	5 years	5 years
Profits before depreciation	£	£
Year 1	50,000	50,000
Year 2	50,000	50,000
Year 3	30,000	60,000
Year 4	20,000	60,000
Year 5	10,000	60,000
Disposal value	0	0

ARR is measured as the average annual profit after depreciation, divided by the average net book value of the asset.

Required

Decide which item of equipment should be selected, if any, if the company's target ARR is 30%.

3.7 SOLUTION

	Item X	Item Y
	£	£
Total profit over life of equipment		
Before depreciation	160,000	280,000
After depreciation	80,000	130,000
Average annual profit after depreciation	16,000	26,000
(Capital cost + disposal value)/2	40,000	75,000
ARR	40%	34.7%

Both projects would earn a return in excess of 30%, but since **item X would earn a bigger ARR, it would be preferred to item Y**, even though the profits from Y would be higher by an average of £10,000 a year.

The drawbacks and advantages to the ARR method of project appraisal

3.8 The ARR method has the serious **drawback** that it **does not take account of the timing of the profits from a project**. Whenever capital is invested in a project, money is tied up until the project begins to earn profits which pay back the investment. Money tied up in one project cannot be invested anywhere else until the profits come in. Management should be aware of the benefits of early repayments from an investment, which will provide the money for other investments.

3.9 There are a number of other disadvantages.

- It is **based on accounting profits** which are **subject to a number of different accounting treatments**

- It is a **relative measure** rather than an absolute measure and hence **takes no account of the size of the investment**

- It **takes no account of the length of the project**

- Like the payback method, it **ignores the time value of money**

3.10 There are, however, **advantages** to the ARR method.

- It is quick and **simple** to calculate

- It involves a **familiar concept** of a percentage return

- Accounting profits can be **easily calculated from financial statements**

- It **looks at the entire project life**

- Managers and investors are accustomed to thinking in terms of profit, and so an appraisal method which **employs profit** may therefore be more **easily understood**

4 THE NET PRESENT VALUE METHOD

Discounting

4.1 Suppose that a company has £10,000 to invest, and wants to earn a return of 10% (compound interest) on its investments. This means that if the £10,000 could be invested at 10%, the value of the investment with interest would build up as follows.

(a)	After 1 year	$£10,000 \times (1.10)$	$= £11,000$
(b)	After 2 years	$£10,000 \times (1.10)^2$	$= £12,100$
(c)	After 3 years	$£10,000 \times (1.10)^3$	$= £13,310$

and so on.

4.2 This is **compounding**. The formula for the future value of an investment plus accumulated interest after n time periods is $V = X(1 + r)^n$

where   V is the future value of the investment with interest
X is the initial or 'present' value of the investment
r is the compound rate of return per time period, expressed as a proportion (so 10% = 0.10, 5% = 0.05 and so on)
n is the number of time periods.

4.3 **Discounting starts with the future value, and converts a future value to a present value.** For example, if a company expects to earn a (compound) rate of return of 10% on its investments, how much would it need to invest now to have the following investments?

(a)   £11,000 after 1 year
(b)   £12,100 after 2 years
(c)   £13,310 after 3 years

4.4 The answer is £10,000 in each case, and we can calculate it by discounting. The discounting formula to calculate the present value of a future sum of money at the end of n time periods is $X = V/(1+r)^n$.

(a)   After 1 year, $£11,000 \times 1/1.10 = £10,000$
(b)   After 2 years, $£12,100 \times 1/1.10^2 = £10,000$
(c)   After 3 years, $£13,310 \times 1/1.10^3 = £10,000$

> ## KEY TERM
>
> **Present value** is 'The cash equivalent now of a sum of money receivable or payable at a future date'. *(CIMA Official Terminology)*

4.5 The **timing of cash flows is taken into account by discounting them.** The effect of discounting is to **give a bigger value per £1 for cash flows that occur earlier**: £1 earned

BPP PUBLISHING

after one year will be worth more than £1 earned after two years, which in turn will be worth more than £1 earned after five years, and so on.

Question 1

Spender Ltd expects the cash inflow from an investment to be £40,000 after 2 years and another £30,000 after 3 years. Its target rate of return is 12%.

Required

(a) Calculate the present value of these future returns.
(b) Explain what this present value signifies.

Answer

(a)

Year	Cash flow £	Discount factor 12%	Present value £
2	40,000	$\dfrac{1}{(1.12)^2} = 0.797$	31,880
3	30,000	$\dfrac{1}{(1.12)^3} = 0.712$	21,360
		Total PV	53,240

(b) The present value of the future returns, discounted at 12%, is £53,240. This means that if Spender Ltd can invest now to earn a return of 12% on its investments, it would have to invest £53,240 now to earn £40,000 after 2 years plus £30,000 after 3 years.

KEY TERM

Discounted cash flow is 'The discounting of the projected net cash flows of a capital project to ascertain its present value. The methods commonly used are:

- yield, or internal rate of return (IRR), in which the calculation determines the return in the form of a percentage;

- net present value (NPV), in which the discount rate is chosen and the present value is expressed as a sum of money;

- discounted payback, in which the discount rate is chosen, and the payback is the number of years required to repay the original investment.'

4.6 We will be looking at these methods in the remainder of this chapter.

4.7 DCF looks at the **cash flows** of a project, **not the accounting profits**. Like the payback technique of investment appraisal, DCF is concerned with liquidity, not profitability. Cash flows are considered because they show the costs and benefit of a project when they actually occur. For example, the capital cost of a project will be the original cash outlay, and not the notional cost of depreciation which is used to spread the capital cost over the asset's life in the financial accounts.

The net present value method

4.8 The NPV method therefore **compares the present value of all the cash inflows** from a project **with the present value of all the cash outflows** from a project. The **NPV** is thus calculated as the **PV of cash inflows minus the PV of cash outflows**.

(a) If the **NPV is positive**, it means that the cash inflows from a project will yield a return in excess of the cost of capital, and so the **project should be undertaken** if the cost of capital is the organisation's target rate of return.

(b) If the **NPV is negative,** it means that the cash inflows from a project will yield a return below the cost of capital, and so the **project should not be undertaken** if the cost of capital is the organisation's target rate of return.

(c) If the **NPV is exactly zero,** the cash inflows from a project will yield a return which is exactly the same as the cost of capital, and so if the cost of capital is the organisation's target rate of return, the **project will be only just worth undertaking**.

4.9 EXAMPLE: NPV

Slogger Ltd has a cost of capital of 15% and is considering a capital investment project, where the estimated cash flows are as follows.

Year	Cash flow
	£
0 (ie now)	(100,000)
1	60,000
2	80,000
3	40,000
4	30,000

Required

Calculate the NPV of the project, and assess whether it should be undertaken.

4.10 SOLUTION

Year	Cash flow	Discount factor	Present value
	£	15%	£
0	(100,000)	1.000	(100,000)
1	60,000	$1/(1.15) = 0.870$	52,200
2	80,000	$1/1.15^2 = 0.756$	60,480
3	40,000	$1/1.15^3 = 0.658$	26,320
4	30,000	$1/1.15^4 = 0.572$	17,160
		NPV =	56,160

(*Note*. The **discount factor for any cash flow 'now' (time 0) is always = 1,** regardless of what the cost of capital is.)

The **PV of cash inflows exceeds the PV of cash outflows** by £56,160, which means that the project will earn a DCF yield in excess of 15%. It should therefore be **undertaken.**

Timing of cash flows: conventions used in DCF

4.11 Discounting reduces the value of future cash flows to a present value equivalent and so is clearly concerned with the timing of the cash flows. As a general rule, the following guidelines may be applied.

(a) **A cash outlay to be incurred at the beginning of an investment project ('now') occurs in time 0.** The **present value of £1 now, in time 0, is £1** regardless of the value of r. This is common sense.

(b) A **cash flow** which occurs **during the course of a time period** is **assumed to occur** all at once at the **end of the time period** (at the end of the year). Receipts of £10,000 during time period 1 are therefore taken to occur at the end of time period 1.

(c) A **cash flow** which occurs **at the beginning of a time period** is **taken to occur at the end of the previous time period.** Therefore a cash outlay of £5,000 at the beginning of time period 2 is taken to occur at the end of time period 1.

Discount tables for the PV of £1

4.12 The discount factor that we use in discounting is $1/(1+r)^n = (1+r)^{-n}$. Instead of having to calculate this factor every time we can use **tables.** Discount tables for the present value of £1, for different values of r and n, are **shown in the Appendix at the back of this Study Text.** Use these tables to work out your own solution to the following exercise.

Question 2

LCH Limited manufactures product X which it sells for £5 per unit. Variable costs of production are currently £3 per unit, and fixed costs 50p per unit. A new machine is available which would cost £90,000 but which could be used to make product X for a variable cost of only £2.50 per unit. Fixed costs, however, would increase by £7,500 per annum as a direct result of purchasing the machine. The machine would have an expected life of 4 years and a resale value after that time of £10,000. Sales of product X are estimated to be 75,000 units per annum. LCH Limited expects to earn at least 12% per annum from its investments.

Required

Decide whether LCH Limited should purchase the machine. Ignore taxation.

Answer

Savings are 75,000 × (£3 − £2.50) = £37,500 per annum.

Additional costs are £7,500 per annum.

Net cash savings are therefore £30,000 per annum. (Remember, depreciation is not a cash flow and must be ignored as a 'cost'.)

The first step in calculating an NPV is to establish the relevant costs year by year. All future cash flows arising as a direct consequence of the decision should be taken into account.

It is assumed that the machine will be sold for £10,000 at the end of year 4.

Year	Cash flow	PV factor	PV of cash flow
	£	12%	£
0	(90,000)	1.000	(90,000)
1	30,000	0.893	26,790
2	30,000	0.797	23,910
3	30,000	0.712	21,360
4	40,000	0.636	25,440
		NPV =	+7,500

The NPV is positive and so the project is expected to earn more than 12% per annum and is therefore acceptable.

Annuity tables

4.13 In the previous exercise, the calculations could have been simplified for years 1-3 as follows.

$$
\begin{array}{l}
30{,}000 \times 0.893 \\
+\ 30{,}000 \times 0.797 \\
+\ 30{,}000 \times 0.712 \\
\hline
=\ 30{,}000 \times 2.402
\end{array}
$$

> ### KEY TERM
>
> An **annuity** is a constant cash flow from year to year.

4.14 Where there is a **constant cash flow from year to year** (in this case £30,000 per annum for years 1-3) it is quicker to calculate the present value by adding together the discount factors for the individual years. These total factors could be described as 'same cash flow per annum' factors, **'cumulative present value' factors** or **'annuity' factors**. They are **shown in the table for cumulative PV of £1 factors which is shown in the Appendix at the back of this Study Text** (2.402, for example, is in the column for 12% per annum and the row for year 3). If you have not used them before, check that you can understand annuity tables by trying this question.

Question 3

(a) What is the present value of £1,000 in contribution earned each year from years 1-10, when the required return on investment is 11%?

(b) What is the present value of £2,000 costs incurred each year from years 3-6 when the cost of capital is 5%?

Answer

(a) The PV of £1,000 earned each year from year 1-10 when the required earning rate of money is 11% is calculated as follows.

   £1,000 × 5.889 = £5,889

(b) The PV of £2,000 in costs each year from years 3-6 when the cost of capital is 5% per annum is calculated as follows.

$$
£2{,}000 \times \left[\begin{array}{lr}
\text{PV of £1 per annum for years 1 - 6 at 5\%} & = 5.076 \\
\text{Less PV of £1 per annum for years 1 - 2 at 5\%} & = \underline{1.859} \\
\text{PV of £1 per annum for years 3 - 6} & = \underline{3.217}
\end{array} \right]
$$

   PV = £2,000 × 3.217 = £6,434

4.15 EXAMPLE: NPV INCLUDING USE OF ANNUITY TABLES

Elsie Limited is considering the manufacture of a new product which would involve the use of both a new machine (costing £150,000) and an existing machine, which cost £80,000 two years ago and has a current net book value of £60,000. There is sufficient capacity on this machine, which has so far been under-utilised. Annual sales of the product would be 5,000 units, selling at £32 per unit. Unit costs would be as follows.

	£
Direct labour (4 hours at £2 per hour)	8
Direct materials	7
Fixed costs including depreciation	9
	24

The project would have a five-year life, after which the new machine would have a net residual value of £10,000. Because direct labour is continually in short supply, labour resources would have to be diverted from other work which currently earns a contribution of £1.50 per direct labour hour. The fixed overhead absorption rate would be £2.25 per hour (£9 per unit) but actual expenditure on fixed overhead would not alter. Working capital requirements would be £10,000 in the first year, rising to £15,000 in the second year and remaining at this level until the end of the project, when it will all be recovered.

Required

Assess whether the project is worthwhile, given that the company's cost of capital is 20%. Ignore taxation.

4.16 SOLUTION

The relevant cash flows are as follows.

Year 0	Purchase of new machine	£150,000

		£
Years 1-5	Contribution from new product (5,000 units × £(32 – 15))	85,000
	Less contribution forgone (5,000 × (4 × £1.50))	30,000
		55,000

The project requires £10,000 of working capital at the end of year 1 and a further £5,000 at the start of year 2. Increases in working capital reduce the net cash flow for the period to which they relate. When the working capital tied up in the project is 'recovered' at the end of the project, it will provide an extra cash inflow (for example debtors will eventually pay up).

All other costs, which are past costs, notional accounting costs or costs which would be incurred anyway without the project, are not relevant to the investment decision.

The NPV is calculated as follows.

Year	Equipment	Working capital	Contribution	Net cash flow	Discount factor	PV of net cash flow
	£	£	£	£	20%	£
0	(150,000)	(10,000)		(160,000)	1.000	(160,000)
1		(5,000)		(5,000)	0.833	(4,165)
1-5			55,000	55,000	2.991	164,505
5	10,000	15,000		25,000	0.402	10,050
					NPV =	10,390

The NPV is positive and the project is worthwhile, although there is not much margin for error. Some risk analysis of the project is recommended.

Annual cash flows in perpetuity

4.17 It can sometimes be useful to calculate the **cumulative present value of £1 per annum** for every year in perpetuity (that is, **forever**).

> **KEY TERM**
>
> A **perpetuity** is an annuity that lasts forever.

4.18 When the cost of capital is r, the cumulative PV of £1 per annum in perpetuity is **£1/r**. For example, the PV of £1 per annum in perpetuity at a discount rate of 10% would be £1/0.10 = £10.

Similarly, the PV of £1 per annum in perpetuity at a discount rate of 15% would be £1/0.15 = £6.67 and at a discount rate of 20% it would be £1/0.20 = £5.

Question 4

An organisation with a cost of capital of 14% is considering investing in a project costing £500,000 that would yield cash inflows of £100,000 pa in perpetuity.

Required

Assess whether the project should be undertaken.

Answer

Year	Cash flow	Discount factor	Present value
	£	14%	£
0	(500,000)	1.00	(500,000)
1 - ∞	100,000	1/0.14 = 7.14	714,000
		Net present value	214,000

The NPV is positive and so the project should be undertaken.

4.19 You might well wonder what is the use of cash flows in perpetuity. This surely is an impractical and nonsensical notion? **Cash flows in perpetuity** do actually have **two practical uses**.

(a) They are **used in the calculation of a company's cost of capital.**

(b) They **indicate the maximum value of the cumulative present value factor of £1 per annum.** For example, we can say that the maximum present value of £1 pa for any period of time at a discount rate of 10% is £1/0.1 = £10. The longer the period of time under review, and the more years that are in the project period, the closer the cumulative PV factor of £1 pa will get to £10 at a 10% discount rate.

   (i)   The PV factor of £1 pa at 10% for years 1 to 15 is £7.606
   (ii)   The PV factor of £1 pa at 10% for years 1 to 20 is £8.514
   (iii) The PV factor of £1 pa at 10% for years 1 to 30 is £9.427
   (iv)   The PV factor of £1 pa at 10% for years 1 to 50 is £9.915

   As you can see, the cumulative PV gets closer to the limit of £10 as time progresses and the limit has almost been reached by year 50, and even by year 30. Knowing what the limit is might help with project analysis when capital projects extend over a long period of time and certainly it can provide a very useful yardstick and 'ready-reckoner' for managers who must carry out DCF evaluations as a regular part of their job.

4.20 In the next chapter we will see a practical example of the application of the present value of an annuity.

Net terminal value

KEY TERM

Net terminal value (NTV) is the cash surplus remaining at the end of a project after taking account of interest and capital repayments.

4.21 The NTV discounted at the cost of capital will give the NPV of the project.

4.22 EXAMPLE: THE NET TERMINAL VALUE

A project has the following cash flows.

Year	£
0	(5,000)
1	3,000
2	2,600
3	6,200

The project has an NPV of £4,531 at the company's cost of capital of 10% (workings not shown).

Required

Calculate the net terminal value of the project.

4.23 SOLUTION

The net terminal value can be determined directly from the NPV, or by calculating the cash surplus at the end of the project.

Assume that the £5,000 for the project is borrowed at an interest rate of 10% and that cash flows from the project are used to repay the loan.

	£
Loan balance outstanding at beginning of project	5,000
Interest in year 1 at 10%	500
Repaid at end of year 1	(3,000)
Balance outstanding at end of year 1	2,500
Interest year 2	250
Repaid year 2	(2,600)
Balance outstanding year 2	150
Interest year 3	15
Repaid year 3	(6,200)
Cash surplus at end of project	6,035

The net terminal value is £6,035.

Check

NPV = £6,035 × 0.751 (discount factor for year 3) = £4,532

Allowing for the rounding errors caused by three-figure discount tables, this is the correct figure for the NPV.

Assumptions in the NPV model

4.24 • Forecasts are assumed to be certain.

• Information is assumed to be freely available and costless.

• The discount rate is a measure of the opportunity cost of funds which ensures wealth maximisation for *all* individuals and companies.

Question 5

A project has the following forecast cash flows.

Year	£
0	(280,000)
1	149,000
2	128,000
3	84,000
4	70,000

Using two decimal places in all discount factors, what is the net present value of the project at a cost of capital of 16.5%?

A £27, 906   B £29,270   C £32,195   D £33,580   E £35,120

Answer

The correct option is **D**.

There are no present value tables for 16.5%, therefore you need to calculate your own discount factors, using discount factor = $1/(1 + r)^n$ where r = cost of capital and n = number of years.

Year	16.5% factor		Cash flow £	Present value £
0		1.00	(280,000)	(280,000)
1	$\dfrac{1}{(1+0.165)}$	0.86	149,000	128,140
2	$\dfrac{1}{(1+0.165)^2}$	0.74	128,000	94,720
3	$\dfrac{1}{(1+0.165)^3}$	0.63	84,000	52,920
4	$\dfrac{1}{(1+0.165)^4}$	0.54	70,000	37,800
			Net present value	33,580

---

5   THE INTERNAL RATE OF RETURN METHOD

5.1   The **IRR method** of project appraisal is to **calculate the exact DCF rate of return which the project is expected to achieve,** in other words the **rate at which the NPV is zero.**

If the **expected rate of return (the IRR yield or DCF yield) exceeds a target rate of return, the project would be worth undertaking** (ignoring risk and uncertainty factors).

> **KEY TERM**
>
> The **internal rate of return (IRR)** is 'The annual percentage return achieved by a project, at which the sum of the discounted cash inflows over the life of the project is equal to the sum of the discounted cash outflows'. (CIMA *Official Terminology*)

5.2   Without a computer or calculator program, an estimate of the internal rate of return is made using either a graph or using a hit-and-miss technique known as the interpolation method.

Graphical approach

5.3   The easiest way to estimate the IRR of a project is to **find the project's NPV at a number of costs of capital** and **sketch a graph of NPV against discount rate**. You can then use the sketch to estimate the **discount rate at which the NPV is equal to zero (the point where the curve cuts the axis)**.

5.4   EXAMPLE: GRAPHICAL APPROACH

A project might have the following NPVs at the following discount rates.

Discount rate	NPV
%	£
5	5,300
10	2,900
15	(1,700)
20	(3,200)

This could be sketched on a graph as follows.

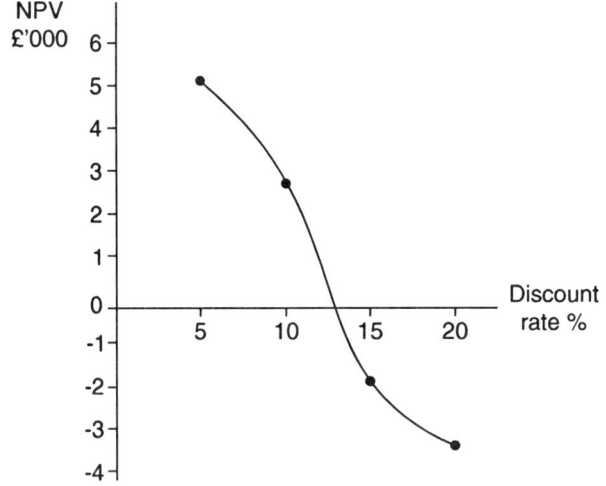

The IRR can be **estimated as 13%**. The NPV should then be **recalculated using this interest rate**. The resulting NPV **should be equal to, or very near, zero. If it is not, additional NPVs at different discount rates should be calculated, the graph resketched and a more accurate IRR determined.**

Interpolation method

5.5   If we were to draw a graph of a 'typical' capital project, with a negative cash flow at the start of the project, and positive net cash flows afterwards up to the end of the project, we could draw a graph of the project's NPV at different costs of capital. It would look like this.

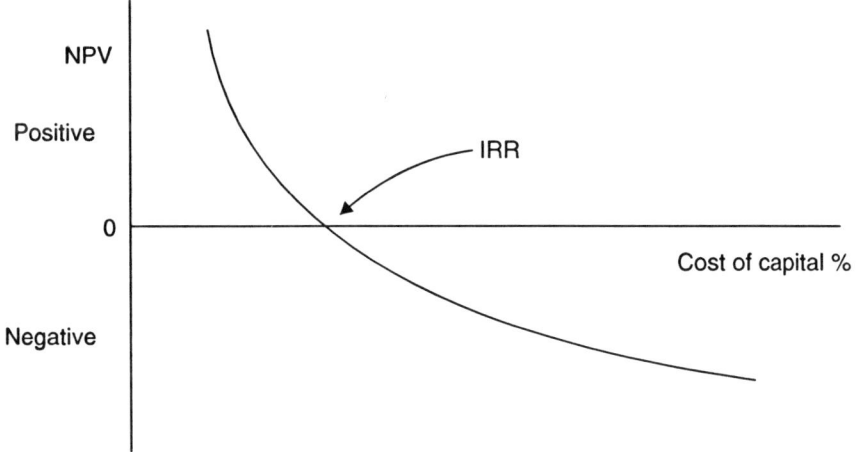

5.6   If we determine **a cost of capital where the NPV is slightly positive, and another cost of capital where it is slightly negative,** we can **estimate the IRR - where the NPV is zero - by drawing a straight line between the two points** on the graph that we have calculated.

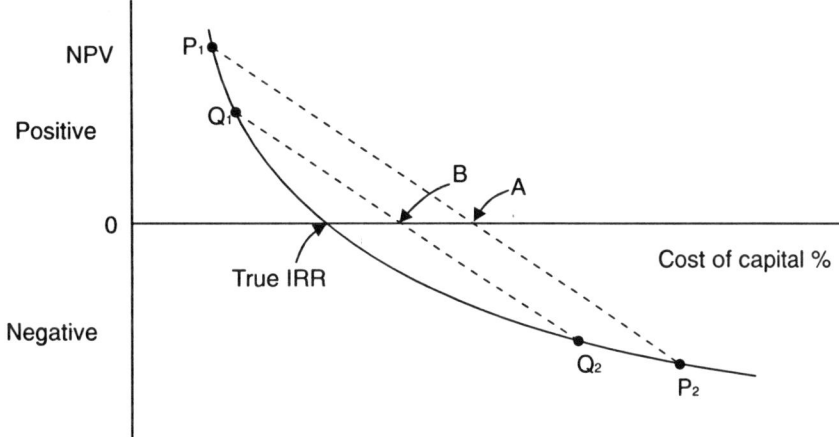

- If we **establish the NPVs at the two points P,** we would estimate the **IRR** to be at **point A**.

- If we **establish the NPVs at the two points Q,** we would estimate the **IRR** to be at **point B**.

The **closer our NPVs are to zero, the closer our estimate will be to the true IRR.**

5.7   The **interpolation method assumes that the NPV rises in linear fashion between the two NPVs close to 0.** The real rate of return is therefore assumed to be on a straight line between the NPV at point Q_1 and the NPV at point Q_2.

5.8   The **formula** to apply is as follows.

$$\text{IRR}=\text{A}+\left[\frac{\text{P}}{\text{P}+\text{N}}\times(\text{B}-\text{A})\right]\%$$

where   A is the (lower) rate of return with a positive NPV
             B is the (higher) rate of return with a negative NPV
             P is the amount of the positive NPV
             N is the absolute value of the negative NPV

BPP
PUBLISHING

5.9   EXAMPLE: THE IRR METHOD AND INTERPOLATION

A company is trying to decide whether to buy a machine for £80,000 which will save costs of £20,000 per annum for 5 years and which will have a resale value of £10,000 at the end of year 5.

Required

If it is the company's policy to undertake projects only if they are expected to yield a DCF return of 10% or more, ascertain whether this project be undertaken.

5.10   SOLUTION

The first step is to calculate two net present values, both as close as possible to zero, using rates for the cost of capital which are whole numbers. One NPV should be positive and the other negative.

Choosing rates for the cost of capital which will give an NPV close to zero (that is, rates which are close to the actual rate of return) is a hit-and-miss exercise, and several attempts may be needed to find satisfactory rates. **As a rough guide**, try starting at a **return figure which is about two thirds or three quarters of the ARR.**

Annual depreciation would be £(80,000 – 10,000)/5 = £14,000.

The **ARR** would be (20,000 – depreciation of 14,000)/(½ of (80,000 + 10,000)) = 6,000/45,000 = 13.3%

Two thirds of this is 8.9% and so we can start by trying 9%.

Try 9%.	*Year*	*Cash flow*	*PV factor*	*PV of cash flow*
		£	9%	£
	0	(80,000)	1.000	(80,000)
	1-5	20,000	3.890	77,800
	5	10,000	0.650	6,500
			NPV	4,300

This is **fairly close to zero**. It is also **positive**, which means that the **real rate of return** is **more than 9%**. We can use 9% as one of our two NPVs close to zero, although for greater accuracy, we should try 10% or even 11% to find an NPV even closer to zero if we can. As a guess, it might be worth trying 12% next, to see what the NPV is.

Try 12%.	*Year*	*Cash flow*	*PV factor*	*PV of cash flow*
		£	12%	£
	0	(80,000)	1.000	(80,000)
	1-5	20,000	3.605	72,100
	5	10,000	0.567	5,670
			NPV	(2,230)

This is **fairly close to zero** and **negative**. The **real rate of return** is therefore **greater than 9%** (positive NPV of £4,300) but **less than 12%** (negative NPV of £2,230).

Note. **If the first NPV is positive, choose a higher rate for the next calculation to get a negative NPV. If the first NPV is negative, choose a lower rate for the next calculation.**

So   IRR = $9 + \left[\frac{4,300}{4,300+2,230} \times (12-9) \right]\%$ = 10.98%, say 11%

If it is company policy to undertake investments which are expected to yield 10% or more, this project would be undertaken.

Question 6

Find the IRR of the project given below and state whether the project should be accepted if the company requires a minimum return of 17%.

Time		£
0	Investment	(4,000)
1	Receipts	1,200
2	'	1,410
3	'	1,875
4	'	1,150

Answer

The total receipts are £5,635 giving a total profit of £1,635 and average profits of £409. The average investment is £2,000. The ARR is £409 ÷ £2,000 = 20%. Two thirds of the ARR is approximately 14%. The initial estimate of the IRR that we shall try is therefore 14%.

		Try 14%		Try 16%	
Time	Cash flow	Discount factor	PV	Discount factor	PV
	£	14%	£	16%	£
0	(4,000)	1.000	(4,000)	1.000	(4,000)
1	1,200	0.877	1,052	0.862	1,034
2	1,410	0.769	1,084	0.743	1,048
3	1,875	0.675	1,266	0.641	1,202
4	1,150	0.592	681	0.552	635
		NPV	83	NPV	(81)

The IRR must be less than 16%, but higher than 14%. The NPVs at these two costs of capital will be used to estimate the IRR.

Using the interpolation formula

$$IRR = 14\% + \left[\frac{83}{83+81} \times (16\% - 14\%) \right] = 15.01\%$$

The IRR is, in fact, exactly 15%.

The project should be rejected as the IRR is less than the minimum return demanded.

The IRR of an annuity

5.11 Suppose an investment now of £100,000 will produce inflows of £30,000 over the next four years. We know that the IRR is the discount rate which produces at NPV of zero. **At the IRR (rate r) the PV of inflows must therefore equal the PV of outflows.**

∴ £100,000 = PV of £30,000 for years 1 to 4 at rate r
∴ £100,000 = (cumulative PV factor for years 1 to 4 at rate r) × £30,000
∴ £100,000/£30,000 = cumulative PV factor for years 1 to 4 at rate r
∴ 3.333 = cumulative PV factor for years 1 to 4 at rate r

5.12 We can now **look in cumulative PV tables along the line for year 4 to find a discount factor which corresponds to 3.333. The corresponding rate is the IRR.** The nearest figure is 3.312 and so the IRR of the project is approximately 8%.

The IRR of a perpetuity

5.13 Suppose an investment of £25,000 will produce cash flows in perpetuity of £2,000. Using the **same reasoning** as in Paragraph 5.11:

£25,000 = PV of £2,000 in perpetuity

$$\therefore \pounds25{,}000 = \pounds2{,}000/r \text{ (where } r = IRR)$$

$$\therefore r = \frac{\pounds2{,}000}{\pounds25{,}000} = 0.08 = 8\%$$

6 NPV AND IRR COMPARED

6.1 Advantages of IRR method

(a) The main advantage is that the information it provides is more **easily understood** by managers, especially non-financial managers. It is fairly easy to understand the meaning of 'The project will be expected to have an initial capital outlay of £100,000, and to earn a yield of 25%. This is in excess of the target yield of 15% for investments'. It is not so easy to understand the meaning of 'The project will cost £100,000 and have an NPV of £30,000 when discounted at the minimum required rate of 15%'.

(b) A **discount rate does not have to be specified** before the IRR can be calculated. A hurdle discount rate is simply required to which the IRR can be compared.

6.2 Disadvantages of IRR method

(a) If managers were given information about both **ROCE (or ROI) and IRR**, it might be easy to get their relative **meaning and significance mixed up.**

(b) It **ignores the relative size of investments**. Both the following projects have a IRR of 18%.

	Project A	*Project B*
	£	£
Cost, year 0	350,000	35,000
Annual savings, years 1-6	100,000	10,000

Clearly, project A is bigger (ten times as big) and so more 'profitable' but if the only information on which the projects were judged were to be their IRR of 18%, project B would be made to seem just as beneficial as project A, which is not the case.

(c) **When discount rates are expected to differ over the life of the project, such variations can be incorporated easily into NPV calculations, but not into IRR calculations.**

(d) There are **problems** with using the IRR **when the project has non-conventional cash flows** (see Paragraphs 6.3 to 6.6) or when **deciding between mutually exclusive projects** (see Paragraphs 6.7 to 6.10).

Non-conventional cash flows

6.3 The projects we have considered so far have had **conventional cash flows (an initial cash outflow followed by a series of inflows)** and in such circumstances the NPV and IRR methods give the same accept or reject decision. When flows vary from this they are termed non-conventional. The following project has non-conventional cash flows.

Year	Project X
	£'000
0	(1,900)
1	4,590
2	(2,735)

6.4 Project X above has two IRRs as shown by the diagram which follows.

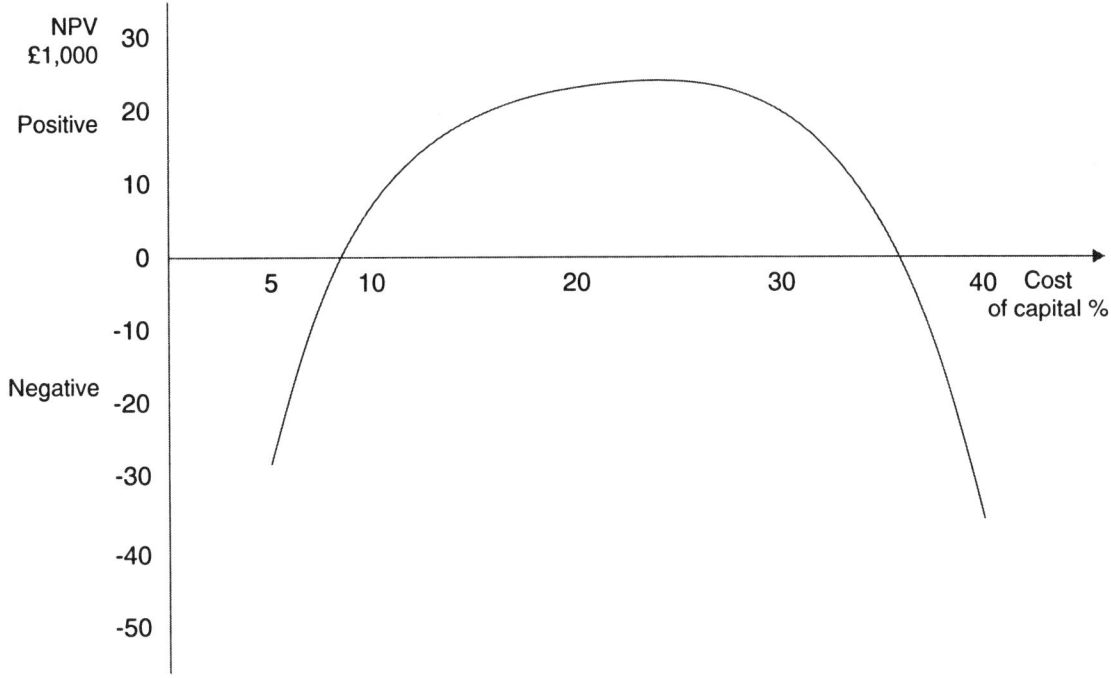

Suppose that the required rate of return on project X is 10% but that the IRR of 7% is used to decide whether to accept or reject the project. The project would be rejected since it appears that it can only yield 7%. The diagram shows, however, that **between rates of 7% and 35% the project should be accepted**. Using the IRR of 35% would produce the correct decision to accept the project. **Lack of knowledge of multiple IRRs** could therefore lead to serious **errors in the decision** of whether to accept or reject a project.

6.5   In general, if the sign of the net cash flow changes in successive periods (inflow to outflow or vice versa), it is possible for the calculations to produce **as many IRRs as there are sign changes**.

6.6   The use of the **IRR** is therefore **not recommended** in circumstances in which there are **non-conventional cash flow patterns** (unless the decision maker is aware of the existence of multiple IRRs). The NPV method, on the other hand, gives clear, unambiguous results whatever the cash flow pattern.

Mutually exclusive projects

6.7   The IRR and NPV methods give conflicting rankings as to which project should be given priority. Let us suppose that a company with a cost of capital of 16% is considering two mutually exclusive options, option A and option B. The cash flows for each are as follows

Year		Option A £	Option B £
0	Capital outlay	(10,200)	(35,250)
1	Net cash inflow	6,000	18,000
2	Net cash inflow	5,000	15,000
3	Net cash inflow	3,000	15,000

The NPV of each project is calculated below.

		Option A		Option B	
Year	Discount factor	Cash flow	Present value	Cash flow	Present value
		£	£	£	£
0	1.000	(10,200)	(10,200)	(35,250)	(35,250)
1	0.862	6,000	5,172	18,000	15,516
2	0.743	5,000	3,715	15,000	11,145
3	0.641	3,000	1,923	15,000	9,615
		NPV =	+610	NPV = +	1,026

The **DCF yield (IRR) of option A is 20%, while the yield of option B is only 18%** (workings not shown.)

On a **comparison of NPVs, option B would be preferred,** but on a **comparison of IRRs, option A would be preferred.**

6.8 **The preference should go to option B.** This is because the **differences in the cash flows** between the two options, when discounted at the cost of capital of 16%, shows that the present value of the incremental benefits from option B compared with option A exceed the PV of the incremental costs. This can be re-stated in the following ways.

- The **NPV of the differential cash flows (option B cash flows minus option A cash flows) is positive,** and so it is worth spending the extra capital to get the extra benefits.

- The **IRR of the differential cash flows exceeds the cost of capital 16%,** and so it is worth spending the extra capital to get the extra benefits.

Year	Option A cash flow	Option B cash flow	Difference	Discount factor	Present value of difference
	£	£	£	16%	£
0	(10,200)	(35,250)	(25,050)	1.000	(25,050)
1	6,000	18,000	12,000	0.862	10,344
2	5,000	15,000	10,000	0.743	7,430
3	3,000	15,000	12,000	0.641	7,692
				NPV of difference	416

The **NPV of the difference,** not surprisingly, **is also the difference between the NPV of option A (£610) and the NPV of option B (£1,026).**

The **IRR of the differential cash flows** (workings not shown) **is a little over 18%.**

6.9 It must be stressed that the investment represented by (B – A) is a notional one, but the inflows from this notional project would be enjoyed by the company if project B were accepted and would be lost if project A were accepted.

6.10 **Mutually exclusive investments do not have to be considered over equal time periods.** For example, suppose an organisation has two investment options, one lasting two years and one lasting four years. The two options can be compared and the one with the highest NPV chosen. If, however, the investment is an asset which is required for four years, the organisation will have to re-invest if it chooses the two-year option. In such circumstances the investment options should be compared over a similar period of time. We will be looking at how to do this in the next chapter.

7   DCF: ADDITIONAL POINTS

The time value of money

7.1   DCF is a project appraisal technique that is based on the concept of the time value of money, that £1 earned or spent sooner is worth more than £1 earned or spent later. Various reasons could be suggested as to **why a present £1 is worth more than a future £1**.

(a)   **Uncertainty.** The business world is full of risk and uncertainty, and although there might be the promise of money to come in the future, it can never be certain that the money will be received until it has actually been paid. This is an important argument, and risk and uncertainty must always be considered in investment appraisal. But this argument does not explain why the discounted cash flow technique should be used to reflect the time value of money.

(b)   **Inflation.** Because of inflation it is common sense that £1 now is worth more than £1 in the future. It is important, however, that the problem of inflation should not confuse the meaning of DCF, and the following points should be noted.

(i)   If there were no inflation at all, discounted cash flow techniques would still be used for investment appraisal.

(ii)   Inflation, for the moment, has been completely ignored.

(iii)   It is obviously necessary to allow for inflation.

(c)   **An individual attaches more weight to current pleasures than to future ones, and would rather have £1 to spend now than £1 in a year's time.** Individuals have the choice of consuming or investing their wealth and so the return from projects must be sufficient to persuade individuals to prefer to invest now. Discounting is a measure of this time preference.

(d)   Money is invested now to make profits (more money or wealth) in the future. **Discounted cash flow techniques** can therefore be used to **measure** either of two things.

(i)   **What alternative uses of the money would earn (NPV method)** (assuming that money can be invested elsewhere at the cost of capital)

(ii)   **What the money is expected to earn (IRR method)**

Future cash flows: relevant costs

7.2   The cash flows to be considered are those which arise as a consequence of the investment decision under evaluation. It therefore follows that any costs incurred in the past, or any committed costs which will be incurred regardless of whether or not an investment is undertaken, are not relevant cash flows. They have occurred, or will occur, whatever investment decision is taken.

7.3   To a management accountant, it might be apparent that the annual profits from a project can be calculated as the incremental contribution earned minus any incremental fixed costs which are cash items of expenditure (that is, ignoring depreciation and so on).

7.4   There are, however, other cash flows to consider. These might include the following.

(a)   The extra **taxation** that will be payable on extra profits, or the reductions in tax arising from capital allowances or operating losses in any year.

(b) The **residual value or disposal value of equipment at the end of its life, or its disposal cost**.

(c) **Working capital**. If a company invests £20,000 in working capital and earns cash profits of £50,000, the net cash receipts will be £30,000. Working capital will be released again at the end of a project's life, and so there will be a cash inflow arising out of the eventual realisation into cash of the project's stocks and debtors in the final year of the project.

7.5 **Finance-related cash flows**, on the other hand, are normally **excluded** from project appraisal exercises because the discounting process takes account of the time value of money, that is the opportunity cost of investing the money in the project. The cash inflow from, say, a loan could be included but then the cash outflows of the interest payments and the loan repayment would also have to be included. These flows would all be discounted at the cost of capital, (which we assume is the same as the cost of the loan) and they would reduce to a zero net present value. They would therefore have had no effect on the NPV and are thus deemed irrelevant to the appraisal.

7.6 Finance-related cash flows are **only relevant if they incur a different rate of interest from that which is being used as the discount rate**. For example, a company may be offered a loan at a preferential rate below that which it uses for its discount rate and so the inclusion and discounting of the loan's cash flows produces a differential NPV.

8 DISCOUNTED PAYBACK

8.1 The payback method of a project was described earlier in this chapter. Payback can be combined with DCF, and a discounted payback period calculated.

KEY TERM

The **discounted payback period** is the time it will take before a project's cumulative NPV turns from being negative to being positive.

8.2 For example if we have a cost of capital of 10% and a project with the cash flows shown below, we can calculate a discounted payback period.

Year	Cash flow	Discount factor	Present value	Cumulative NPV
	£	10%	£	£
0	(100,000)	1.000	(100,000)	(100,000)
1	30,000	0.909	27,270	(72,730)
2	50,000	0.826	41,300	(31,430)
3	40,000	0.751	30,040	(1,390)
4	30,000	0.683	20,490	19,100
5	20,000	0.621	12,420	31,520
		NPV =	31,520	

The discounted payback period is early in year 4.

8.3 A company can set a target discounted payback period, and choose not to undertake any projects with a discounted payback period in excess of a certain number of years, say five years.

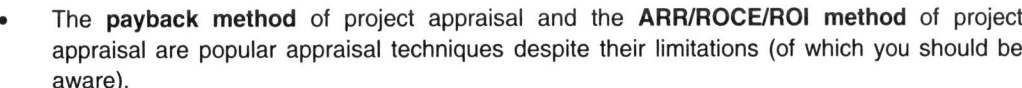

Chapter roundup

- The **payback method** of project appraisal and the **ARR/ROCE/ROI method** of project appraisal are popular appraisal techniques despite their limitations (of which you should be aware).

- There are two methods of using **DCF** to appraise investment projects, the NPV method and the IRR/DCF yield method.

- The **NPV method** of project appraisal is to accept projects with a positive NPV. Ensure that you are aware of the three conventions concerning the timings of cash flows.

- An **annuity** is a constant cash flow for a number of years. A **perpetuity** is a constant cash flow forever.

- The **IRR method** of project appraisal is to accept projects whose IRR (the rate at which the NPV is zero) exceeds a target rate of return. The IRR is estimated either from a graph or using interpolation. The formula to apply is IRR = A + [(P/(P + N)) × (B − A)]%.

- There are advantages and disadvantages to each appraisal method. Make sure that you can discuss them.

- Payback can be combined with DCF and a **discounted payback period** calculated. This is the time it will take before a project's cumulative NPV turns from being negative to being positive.

- **DCF** methods of appraisal have a number of **advantages** over other appraisal methods.

  ○ The time value of money is taken into account.
  ○ The method takes account of all of a project's cash flows.
  ○ It allows for the timing of cash flows.
  ○ There are universally accepted methods of calculating the NPV and IRR.

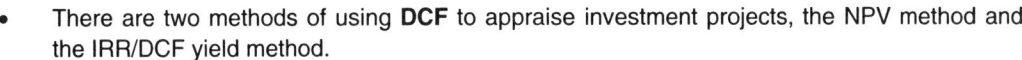

Quick quiz

1   Name five possible problems in performing a post-completion audit.

2   In what ways does the requirement for a shorter payback period reduce risk and uncertainty?

3   The accounting rate of return method of investment appraisal uses accounting profits before depreciation charges. True or false? *f*

4   In a discounted cash flow exercise, what is the discount factor (to 3 decimal places) for year 4 when the cost of capital is 11.5%?   *0 - 647* ✓

5   What is the present value of a cash inflow of £3,000 each year from years 1 - 5, when the required return on investment is 12%?   *10815* ✓

6   With a cost of capital of 13%, what is the present value of £2,500 received every year in perpetuity?   *(9230* ✓

7   For a certain project, the net present value at a discount rate of 15% is £3,670, and at a rate of 18% the net present value is negative at (£1,390). What is the internal rate of return of the project?

   A 15.7%   B 16.5%   C 16.6%   D 17.2% ✓

8   Which of the following items are included in the cash flows when determining the net present value of a project?

		Included	Not included
(a)	The disposal value of equipment at the end of its life	✓	
(b)	Depreciation charges for the equipment		✓
(c)	Research costs incurred prior to the appraisal		✓
(d)	Interest payments on the loan to finance the investment	✗	✓

unc of diff
rate to coc.

9   Name four major advantages of the DCF method of investment appraisal.

 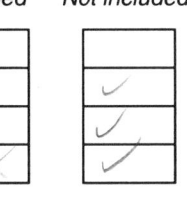

Answers to quick quiz

1. (a) Many factors are uncontrollable in long-term investments
   (b) May not be possible to identify costs and benefits separately
   (c) Can be costly and time-consuming
   (d) May lead to managers becoming risk averse
   (e) May take years for strategic effects of project to materialise

2. Longer term forecasts tend to be less reliable

3. False

4. $1/(1 + 0.115)^4 = 0.647$

5. £3,000 × 3.605 = £10,815

6. £2,500/0.13 = £19,231

7. 15% + {(3,670/[3,670 + 1,390]) × 3%} = 17.2%. The answer is D.

8. (a) Included

   (b) Not included (non-cash)

   (c) Not included (past cost)

   (d) Not usually included, unless the loan incurs a different rate of interest from that which is being used as the discount rate

9. Takes account of time value of money; all relevant cash flows are considered; allows for timing of cash flows; universally accepted methods exist for calculation of NPV and IRR.

Now try the question below from the Exam Question Bank

Number	Level	Marks	Time
Q14	Introductory	25	45 mins

Chapter 9

FURTHER ASPECTS OF INVESTMENT APPRAISAL

Topic list	Syllabus Reference	Ability required
1 Mutually exclusive projects with unequal lives	(iii)	Evaluate
2 Sensitivity analysis	(iii)	Apply
3 Project abandonment values	(iii)	Calculate
4 Life cycle costing and project appraisal	(iii)	Apply and evaluate
5 Allowing for inflation	(iii)	Prepare cash flows
6 Allowing for taxation	(iii)	Prepare cash flows

Introduction

This chapter builds on the knowledge gained in the previous chapter and looks at a number of related project appraisal topics.

In the first part of this chapter we will be looking at **appraising projects with unequal lives**, and within this context we will study **replacement theory**, which is concerned with deciding when, and how frequently, an asset should be replaced as opposed to the simple 'invest/do not invest' decisions we looked at in Chapter 8.

Because project appraisal involves estimating future cash flows, projects will always be (to varying degrees) **risky** simply because the future is risky. **Sensitivity analysis** is one method of assessing the risk associated with a project and this will form the subject of the second part of the chapter.

We then take a look at how to decide whether a project should be **abandoned** or not. The chapter concludes by looking at how to incorporate the effects of **taxation** and **inflation** into investment decisions.

Learning outcomes covered in this chapter

- **Prepare** project cash flows that take account of taxation and inflation
- **Evaluate** mutually exclusive projects with unequal lives
- **Apply** sensitivity analysis to cash flows
- **Calculate** abandonment values

Syllabus content covered in this chapter

- Taxation
- Inflation
- Unequal lives
- Project abandonment
- Sensitivity analysis
- Life cycle costing

---

1 MUTUALLY EXCLUSIVE PROJECTS WITH UNEQUAL LIVES

1.1 All of the discounted cash flow examples that we have seen so far have involved a choice between projects with equal lives. However if managers are deciding between projects with different time spans a direct comparison of the NPV generated by each project would not be valid.

1.2 For example if an organisation decides to invest in a project with a shorter life it may then have the opportunity to invest in a new project in the future sooner than if a longer term project is accepted. This should be taken into account in the analysis in order to be able to make direct comparisons between projects with unequal lives.

Annualised equivalents

1.3 Annualised equivalents are used to **enable a comparison to be made between the net present values of projects with different durations.**

1.4 EXAMPLE: ANNUALISED EQUIVALENTS

A company has the opportunity to invest in either project G or project H. The forecast cash flows from the projects are as follows.

		Project G	*Project H*
		£'000	£'000
Capital cost		(200)	(143)
Cash inflows:	year 1	90	100
	year 2	120	80
	year 3	50	-

The company's cost of capital is 12%. Which project should be accepted?

1.5 SOLUTION

		Project G		
Year	*Cash flow*		*PV factor*	*PV of cash flow*
	£		12%	£
0	(200,000)		1.000	(200,000)
1	90,000		0.893	80,370
2	120,000		0.797	95,640
3	50,000		0.712	35,600
			NPV =	11,610

Project H

Year	Cash flow	PV factor	PV of cash flow
	£	12%	£
0	(143,000)	1.000	(143,000)
1	100,000	0.893	89,300
2	80,000	0.797	63,760
		NPV =	10,060

1.6 These NPVs **cannot be compared directly** because they each relate to a different number of years. In order to make a comparison we must convert each NPV to an **annualised equivalent cost**. In other words, we convert the project's NPV into an equivalent annual annuity stream over its expected life. We do this by using **cumulative discount factors** that you met in the last chapter.

	Project G	*Project H*
NPV at 12%	£11,610	£10,060
Cumulative 12% discount factor	÷ 2.402	÷ 1.69
Annualised equivalent	£4,833	£5,953

Project H is offering an equivalent annual annuity of £5,953 which is higher than that offered by project G, therefore project H is preferable.

Replacement theory

1.7 As well as assisting with decisions between particular assets, DCF techniques combined with annualised equivalents can be used to assess **when** and **how frequently an asset should be replaced**.

Identical replacement

1.8 When an asset is to be replaced by an **'identical' asset**, the problem is to decide the optimum interval between replacements. As the asset gets older, it may cost more to maintain and operate, its residual value will decrease, and it may lose some productivity/operating capability.

1.9 EXAMPLE: REPLACEMENT OF AN IDENTICAL ASSET

James Ltd operates a machine which costs £25,000 to buy and has the following costs and resale values over its four year life.

	Year 1	*Year 2*	*Year 3*	*Year 4*
	£	£	£	£
Running costs (cash expenses)	7,500	10,000	12,500	15,000
Resale value (end of year)	15,000	10,000	7,500	2,500

The organisation's cost of capital is 10%.

Required

Assess how frequently the asset should be replaced.

1.10 SOLUTION

To begin, it is necessary to **calculate the present value of costs for each replacement cycle, but over one cycle only.**

Year	Replace every year		Replace every 2 years		Replace every 3 years		Replace every 4 years	
	Cash flow	PV at 10%	Cash flow	PV at 10%	Cash flow	PV at 10%	Cash flow	PV at 10%
	£	£	£	£	£	£	£	£
0	(25,000)	(25,000)	(25,000)	(25,000)	(25,000)	(25,000)	(25,000)	(25,000)
1	7,500	6,818	(7,500)	(6,818)	(7,500)	(6,818)	(7,500)	(6,818)
2			0	0	(10,000)	(8,260)	(10,000)	(8,260)
3					(5,000)	(3,755)	(12,500)	(9,388)
4							(12,500)	(8,538)
PV of cost over one replacement cycle		(18,182)		(31,818)		(43,833)		(58,004)

These **costs are not comparable, because they refer to different time periods, whereas replacement is continuous.** We need to convert each of them to an equivalent annual cost.

Given a discount rate of 10%, the equivalent annual cost is calculated as follows.

	Replace every year	Replace every 2 years	Replace every 3 years	Replace every 4 years
PV of cost over one replacement cycle	£18,182	£31,818	£43,833	£58,004
Cumulative PV factor	÷ 0.909	÷ 1.736	÷ 2.487	÷ 3.170
Annualised equivalent cost	£20,002	£18,328	£17,625	£18,298

The **optimum replacement policy** is the one with the **lowest equivalent annual cost**, every three years.

Question 1

A company is deciding whether to replace company cars after a three, four or five year cycle. The relevant cash flows are as follows.

	Year	Three-year cycle £	Four-year cycle £	Five-year cycle £
Capital cost	0	(6,000)	(6,000)	(6,000)
Running costs	1	(280)	(280)	(280)
Running costs	2	(1,090)	(1,090)	(1,090)
Running costs	3	(1,120)	(1,120)	(1,120)
Trade in value	3	1,000	-	-
Running costs	4		(1,590)	(1,590)
Trade in value	4		700	-
Running costs	5			(1,260)
Trade in value	5			300
NPV at 15% *		(7,146.6)	(8,313.68)	(9,191.2)

* The workings are not shown, but as an exercise you could check the NPV calculations yourself.

What is the optimum replacement policy for company cars?

Answer

	Three-year cycle	Four-year cycle	Five-year cycle
NPV at 15%	£(7,146.6)	£(8,313.68)	£(9,191.2)
Cumulative 15% discount factor	÷ 2.283	÷ 2.855	÷ 3.352
Annualised equivalent cost	£3,130	£2,912	£2,742

The **lowest annualised equivalent cost** results from a five year cycle, therefore the company should replace its cars every five years.

Non-identical replacement

1.11   When a machine is to be replaced by a machine of a different type, there is a different replacement problem. The decision has to be made as to **when** the existing asset should be replaced rather than how frequently it should be replaced.

1.12   EXAMPLE: NON-IDENTICAL REPLACEMENT

Suppose that James Ltd's machine (in our example in Paragraph 1.9) is a new machine, and will be introduced to replace a non-identical existing machine which is nearing the end of its life and has a maximum remaining life of only three years. The organisation wishes to decide when is the best time to replace the old machine, and estimates of relevant costs have been drawn up as follows.

Year	Resale value of current machine £	Extra expenditure and opportunity costs of keeping the existing machine in operation during the year £
0	8,500	n/a
1	5,000	9,000
2	2,500	12,000
3	0	15,000

Required

Calculate the best time to replace the existing machine.

1.13   SOLUTION

The costs of the new machine will be those given in Paragraph 1.9, so that the optimum replacement cycle for the new machine will already have been calculated as three years, with an equivalent annual cost of £17,625 (Paragraph 1.10).

The best time to replace the existing machine will be the option which gives the lowest NPV of cost in perpetuity, for both the existing machine and the machine which eventually replaces it.

We saw in the last chapter that the present value of an annuity, £a per annum, in perpetuity is a/r, where r is the cost of capital.

This formula may be used to calculate the PV of cost in perpetuity of the new machine. In our example, PV of cost = £17,625/0.1 = £176,250.

The new machine will have a PV of cost in perpetuity of £176,250 from the start of the year when it is eventually purchased.

The present value relates to the beginning of the year when the first annual cash flow occurs, so that if replacement occurs now, the first annuity is in year 1, and the PV of cost relates to year 0 values. If replacement occurs at the end of year 1 the first annuity is in year 2, and the PV of cost relates to year 1, and so on.

The total cash flows of the replacement decision may now be presented as follows. These cash flows show the **PV of cost in perpetuity of the new machine**, the **running costs of the existing machine**, and the **resale value of the existing machine**, at the **end of year 0, 1, 2 or 3 as appropriate**.

Year	Replace now £	Replace in 1 year £	Replace in 2 years £	Replace in 3 years £
0	(176,250)	–	–	–
	8,500			
1	–	(176,250)		
		(9,000)	(9,000)	(9,000)
		5,000		
2	–	–	(176,250)	
			(12,000)	(12,000)
			2,500	
3	–	–	–	(176,250)
				(15,000)

The PVs of each replacement option are as follows.

	Year	Cash flow £	Discount factor 10%	Present value £
Replace now	0	(176,250)		
		8,500		
		(167,750)	1.000	(167,700)
Replace in one year	1	(176,250)		
		(9,000)		
		5,000		
		(180,250)	0.909	(163,847)
Replace in two years	1	(9,000)	0.909	(8,181)
	2	(185,750)	0.826	(153,430)
				(161,611)
Replace in three years	1	(9,000)	0.909	(8,181)
	2	(12,000)	0.826	(9,912)
	3	(191,250)	0.751	(143,629)
				(161,722)

The marginally **optimum policy** would be to replace the existing machine in two years' time, because this has the **lowest total PV of cost in perpetuity**.

2   SENSITIVITY ANALYSIS   Pilot paper

Risk

2.1   In general risky projects are those whose future cash flows, and hence the project returns, are likely to be variable - the greater the variability, the greater the risk. The problem of **risk is more acute with capital investment decisions** than other decisions because estimates of costs and benefits might be for up to 20 years ahead, and such long-term estimates can at best be approximations.

Why are projects risky?

2.2   A decision about whether or not to go ahead with a project is based on expectations about the future. Forecasts of cash flows (whether they be inflows or outflows) that are likely to arise following a particular course of action are made. These forecasts are made, however, on the basis of what is expected to happen given the present state of knowledge and the future is, by definition, uncertain. Actual cash flows are almost certain to differ from prior expectations. It is this **uncertainty about a project's future income and costs that give rise to risk in business generally and investment activity in particular**.

Using sensitivity analysis

2.3 Sensitivity analysis is one method of analysing the risk surrounding a capital expenditure project and enables an **assessment** to be made of **how responsive the project's NPV is to changes in the variables that are used to calculate that NPV.**

2.4 The NPV could depend on a number of uncertain independent variables.

- Estimated selling price
- Estimated sales volume
- Estimated cost of capital
- Estimated initial cost

- Estimated operating costs
- Estimated benefits
- Estimated length of project

The margin of error approach to sensitivity analysis

2.5 This basic approach involves **calculating the project's NPV under alternative assumptions to determine how sensitive it is to changing conditions, thereby indicating those variables to which the NPV is most sensitive (critical variables)** and the **extent to which those variables may change before the investment decision would change** (ie a **positive NPV becoming a negative NPV).**

Once these critical variables have been identified, management should review them to assess whether or not there is a strong possibility of events occurring which will lead to a change in the investment decision. Management should also pay particular attention to controlling those variables to which the NPV is particularly sensitive, once the decision has been taken to accept the investment.

Exam focus point

The pilot paper contained a straightforward sensitivity analysis question in the multiple choice section of the paper. Make sure that you practise the technique so that you can quickly identify the critical variables.

2.6 EXAMPLE: SENSITIVITY ANALYSIS

Kenney Ltd, which has a cost of capital of 8%, is considering a project. The 'most likely' cash flows associated with the project are as follows.

Year	0	1	2
	£'000	£'000	£'000
Initial investment	(7,000)		
Variable costs		(2,000)	(2,000)
Cash inflows (650,000 units at £10 per unit)		6,500	6,500
Net cashflows	(7,000)	4,500	4,500

Required

Measure the sensitivity of the project to changes in variables.

2.7 SOLUTION

The PVs of the cash flow are as follows.

BPP PUBLISHING

Year	Discount factor 8%	PV of initial investment £'000	PV of variable costs £'000	PV of cash inflows £'000	PV of net cash flow £'000
0	1.000	(7,000)			(7,000)
1	0.926		(1,852)	6,019	4,167
2	0.857		(1,714)	5,571	3,857
		(7,000)	(3,566)	11,590	1,024

The project has a positive NPV and would appear to be worthwhile. The **changes in cash flows which would need to occur for the project to only just breakeven (and hence be on the point of being unacceptable) are as follows.**

(a) **Initial investment.** The initial investment can rise by £1,024,000 before the investment breaks even. The initial investment may therefore increase by 1,024/7,000 = 14.6%.

(b) **Sales volume.** We know that the present value of the cash inflows less the present value of the variable costs will have to fall to £7,000,000 for the NPV to be zero.

We need to find the net cash flows in actual values. As the cash flows are equal each year, cumulative discount tables can be used. The discount factor for 8% for year 1 and year 2 is 1.783. If the discount factor is divided into the required present value of £7,000,000 we get an annual cash flow of £3,925,968. Given that the most likely net cash flow is £4,500,000, the net cash flow may decline by approximately £574,032 each year before the NPV becomes zero. Total sales revenue may therefore decline by £831,930 (assuming net cash flow is 69% (4,500/6,500) of sales). At a selling price of £10 per unit this represents 83,193 units. Alternatively we may state that sales volume may decline by 12.8% before the NPV becomes negative.

(c) **Selling price.** When sales volume is 650,000 units per annum, total sales revenue can fall to £5,925,968 (£(6,500,000 – 574,032) per annum before the NPV becomes negative. This assumes that total variable costs and sales volume remain unchanged. This represents a selling price of £9.12 per unit, which represents a 8.8% reduction in the selling price.

(d) **Variable costs.** The total variable cost can increase by £574,032, or £0.88 per unit. This represents an increase of 28.6%.

(e) **Cost of capital.** We need to calculate the IRR of the project. Let us try discount rates of 15% and 20%.

Year	Net cash flow £'000	Discount factor 15%	PV £'000	Discount factor 20%	PV £'000
0	(7,000)	0.870	(6,090)	0.833	(5,831)
1	4,500	0.756	3,402	0.694	3,123
2	4,500	0.658	2,961	0.579	2,606
			NPV = 273		NPV = (102)

IRR = 0.15 + [(273/(273 + 102)) × (0.20 – 0.15)] = 18.64%

The cost of capital can therefore increase by 133% before the NPV becomes negative.

The elements to which the NPV appears to be **most sensitive** are the **selling price** followed by the **sales volume,** and it is therefore important for management to pay particular attention to these factors so that they can be carefully monitored.

Question 2

Nevers Ure Ltd has a cost of capital of 8% and is considering a project with the following 'most-likely' cash flows.

Year	Purchase of plant £	Running costs £	Savings £
0	(7,000)		
1		2,000	6,000
2		2,500	7,000

Required

Measure the sensitivity (in percentages) of the project to changes in the levels of expected costs and savings.

Answer

The PVs of the cash flows are as follows.

Year	Discount factor 8%	PV of plant cost £	PV of' running costs £	PV of savings £	PV of net cash flow £
0	1.000	(7,000)			(7,000)
1	0.926		(1,852)	5,556	3,704
2	0.857		(2,143)	5,999	3,856
		(7,000)	(3,995)	11,555	560

The project has a positive NPV and would appear to be worthwhile. The changes in cash flows which would need to occur for the project to break even (NPV = 0) are as follows.

(a) Plant costs would need to increase by a PV of £560, that is by (560/7,000) × 100% = 8%
(b) Running costs would need to increase by a PV of £560, that is by (560/3,995) × 100% = 14%
(c) Savings would need to fall by a PV of £560, that is by (560/11,555) × 100% = 4.8%

2.8   **Weaknesses of the margin of error approach to sensitivity analysis**

(a)   The method requires that changes in each key variable are isolated but management is more interested in the combination of the effects of changes in two or more key variables. Looking at factors in isolation is unrealistic since they are often interdependent.

(b)   Sensitivity analysis does not examine the probability that any particular variation in costs or revenues might occur.

Exam focus point

The pilot paper contained a 25-mark question on investment appraisal which provided a fairly large volume of data concerning the proposed purchase of a new machine. The requirement was to prepare 'detailed calculations' that showed whether the machine should be bought. The model solution contained an outline sensitivity analysis as well as a detailed NPV calculation. Therefore you must be prepared to perform sensitivity analysis **even when the question does not specifically request it.**

The certainty-equivalent approach

2.9   In this approach the **expected cash flows** of the project are **converted to riskless equivalent amounts**. The **greater the risk** of an expected cash flow, the **smaller the 'certainty-equivalent' value** (for receipts) or the **larger the certainty equivalent value (for payments).**

2.10 EXAMPLE: CERTAINTY-EQUIVALENT APPROACH

Dark Ages Ltd, whose cost of capital is 10%, is considering a project with the following expected cash flows.

Year	Cash flow £	Discount factor 10%	Present value £
0	(9,000)	1.000	(9,000)
1	7,000	0.909	6,363
2	5,000	0.826	4,130
3	5,000	0.751	3,755
		NPV	+5,248

The project would seem to be clearly worthwhile. However, because of the uncertainty about the future cash receipts, the management decides to reduce them to 'certainty-equivalents' by taking only 70%, 60% and 50% of the years 1, 2 and 3 cash flows respectively. (Note that this method of risk adjustment allows for different risk factors in each year of the project.)

Required

On the basis of the information set out above, assess whether the project is worthwhile.

2.11 SOLUTION

The risk-adjusted NPV of the project is as follows.

Year	Cash flow £	Discount factor 10%	PV £
0	(9,000)	1.000	(9,000)
1	4,900	0.909	4,454
2	3,000	0.826	2,478
3	2,500	0.751	1,878
		NPV =	(190)

The project is too risky and should be rejected.

2.12 The **disadvantage** of the certainty-equivalent approach is that the amount of the adjustment to each cash flow is decided **subjectively**.

Use of different cost of money rates

2.13 A fairly straightforward way in which organisations can attempt to take account of risk is to use a **higher cost of money rate for higher-risk projects** and a lower rate for lower-risk projects. Higher-risk projects would therefore have to generate larger positive cash flows to be accepted.

2.14 Alternatively, **riskier projects can be assessed over a shorter length of time**, so that they have to generate larger positive cashflows than those deemed less risky.

2.15 The obvious **disadvantage** of such approaches is that they are **subjective**, because someone must decide what is high risk and what is low risk.

Introducing probability

2.16 In the example in Paragraph 2.7, attention was drawn to the selling price, which only needed to fall by 8.8% before the project's NPV became negative. A fuller understanding of the impact of the selling price on the attractiveness of the project may therefore be required.

The original NPV was calculated using the 'most likely' selling price, no probability of occurrence having been assigned to this figure. If a **full probability distribution** of selling price were to be drawn up, however, it would indicate the level of confidence that management could have in the original estimate and the probability of other selling prices occurring.

Obviously, it is far more demanding to draw up a full probability distribution than to provide a 'most likely' figure to which no probability has to be attached.

2.17 A probability distribution for the selling price could be as follows.

Probability (p)	Price (P)	pP
	£	
0.2	9	1.80
0.5	10	5.00
0.2	11	2.20
0.1	12	1.20
	EV of selling price =	10.20

2.18 The **NPV could be recalculated using the EV of the selling price (£10.20) or** alternatively the **NPV could be calculated using each price and then the expected value of the NPVs calculated** (using the probabilities 0.2, 0.5, 0.2 and 0.1).

2.19 Such additional information gives management a much greater **awareness** of the financial consequences to the project if **the 'most likely' price proves not to be the actual price.** They are then in a much better position to decide whether or not to proceed with the project. (Don't forget that the outcome of the project depends on the performance of all of the variables, however, not just (for example) the selling price.)

Diagrammatic approach to sensitivity analysis

2.20 We can use a **graph** either to **show how sensitive a project is to changes in a key variable** or to **compare the sensitivities of two or more projects to changes in a key variable.**

2.21 Suppose that an organisation wishes to compare two machines (A and B), both of which produce product X. The machines' initial costs, annual fixed running costs and variable cost of producing one unit of product X are different. Annual demand for product X varies unpredictably between 0 and 10,000 units. The selling price of product X is regulated by government and so is fixed at a certain level, whatever the demand.

2.22 The NPV of investments in machines A and B at the highest and lowest demand levels are as follows.

	NPVs	
Demand pa	*Machine A*	*Machine B*
Units	£'000	£'000
0	(1)	(4)
10,000	8	11

2.23 If we plot these four points we can **see how the NPV changes as demand for product X changes**. Note that the NPV does not change in a linear fashion with changes in other variables but **we can plot straight lines to approximate to the curvilinear behaviour** that would be evident if we calculated the NPV at more demand levels.

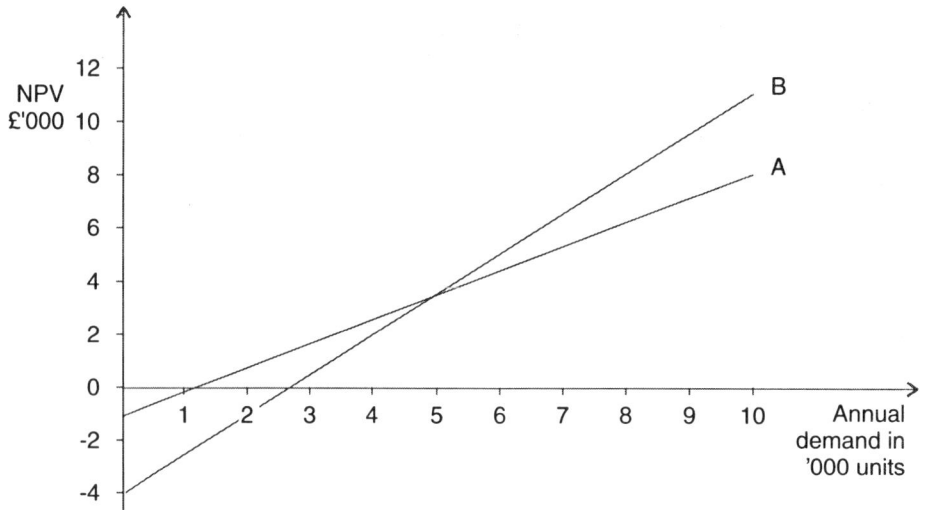

(a) The two lines cross at demand of 5,000 units so **machine B returns a higher NPV in 50% of the possible outcomes that could arise.**

(b) On the other hand, machine A crosses the horizontal axis at around 1,100 units. This means that in **approximately 89% of the possible outcomes, machine A would produce a positive NPV.** Contrast this with machine B, where only about 73% of outcomes result in a positive NPV.

(c) The point at which the **two lines cross** is the point at which the **two machines are equally viable.**

Sensitivity to changes in discount rate

2.24 In all our examples we have assumed, for simplicity, a constant rate of interest. Changes in interest rates can be easily accommodated in NPV calculations but they are not so easily incorporated into IRR calculations since an IRR reflects an average rate of return over a project's life. In **periods of great discount rate volatility** the **NPV method should** therefore **be used.**

2.25 In situations of **non-conventional cash flows** a graph can help show the sensitivity of projects to changes in discount rates. Take the following two projects with non-conventional cash flows.

Time	Project Y £'000	Project Z £'000
0	1,920	1,700
1	(4,800)	(4,800)
2	3,000	3,300
NPV @ 10%	£34,800	£62,600

If the projects were **mutually exclusive Project Z would be chosen.** However **if interest rates were not likely to be stable the graph below would illustrate the relative sensitivity of the projects.** (This kind of graph can be sketched by calculating the NPV of the projects at various discount rates but the calculations have not been shown here.)

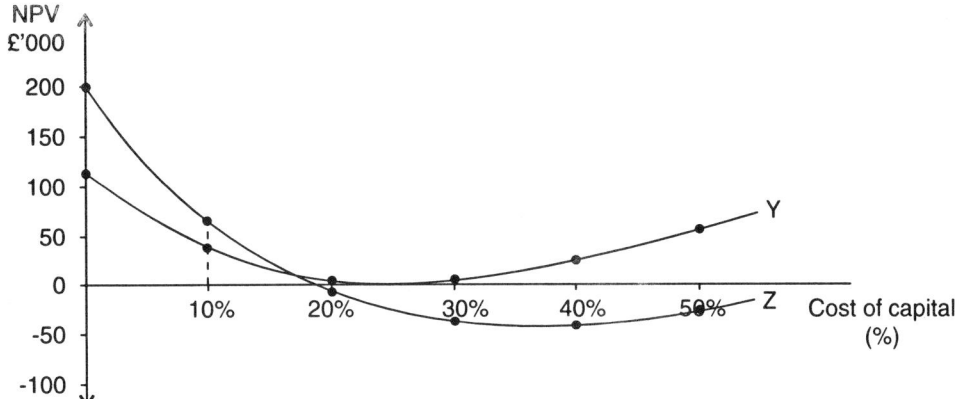

2.26 The graph shows that project **Y will remain profitable at any interest rate**, but project **Z would not be worthwhile if interest rates increased beyond about 18%** (unless they then increased to something over 50%). Therefore if one wished to avoid all risk, project Y would be favourable.

3 PROJECT ABANDONMENT VALUES

3.1 Initial project appraisals are based on forecasts of cash inflows and outflows and a decision is made on the basis of these forecasts. These forecasts are subject to uncertainty, however, and the assumptions upon which the original estimates were based become invalid: demand may not be at the level anticipated, costs may have increased due to labour or material shortages and so on.

3.2 Therefore as part of the **post-completion audit** discussed in chapter 8, the following factors should be considered at each stage of a project's life.

(a) The NPV of the cash flows associated with abandoning the project. Many cash flows could be relevant.

    (i) Redundancy payments
    (ii) Sale of machinery
    (iii) **Opportunity cost** of tying up funds if there is a more profitable use for them.

(c) The option with the highest NPV (continue or abandon) should be selected.

3.3 EXAMPLE: ABANDONING PROJECTS

When EFG Ltd carried out the initial appraisal for project P, it contained the following forecast cash flows.

Year	0	1	2	3	4	5
Cash flow (£'000)	(1,000)	(700)	(400)	900	1,500	1,600

It is now the end of year 0 and the investment is about to be made for year 1. The actual cash outflow for year 0 amounted to £1,300,000 and it seems likely that the required investment in year 1 will be £1,000,000. The estimates of the projected cash flows for years 2 to 5 have not altered.

Another company has offered to take over the project from EFG Ltd immediately for a consideration of £1,400,000. If EFG did abandon the project they would be obliged to make redundancy payments of £100,000.

EFG's cost of capital is 12%

Should project P be abandoned?

3.4 SOLUTION

The £1,300,000 already spent in year 0 is a sunk cost that is not relevant to the abandonment decision (although the post-completion audit process should investigate the reasons for the overspending, to prevent such an occurrence in future.)

The NPV of the future cash flows associated with continuing the project should be calculated, starting again with a 'new' year 0.

Year	Cash flow	12% factor	Present value
X	£'000		£'000
0	(1,000)	1.000	(1,000)
1	(400)	0.893	(357)
2	900	0.797	717
3	1,500	0.712	1,068
4	1,600	0.636	1,018
Net present value of the decision to continue			1,446

The present value of abandoning the project $\quad$ = £1,400,000 - £1,00,000

$\qquad\qquad\qquad\qquad\qquad\qquad\qquad\qquad$ = £1,300,000

This is lower than the net present value of the cash flows to be generated by continuing, therefore the project should not be abandoned.

3.5 The decision to continue with the project in this example relied heavily on management predictions that the forecast cash flows for the remainder of the project were still reliable. In view of the errors in their forecasts for the original years 0 and 1 this may seem rather doubtful.

3.6 It may be difficult for managers who are heavily involved with a project to admit that early problems are likely to continue. For this reason it is important that abandonment reviews are carried out objectively, preferably overseen by a manager who was not involved in the initial appraisal.

4 LIFE CYCLE COSTING AND PROJECT APPRAISAL

4.1 You studied life cycle costing in chapter 7. We will now return and look further at the concept in the context of project appraisal.

4.2 The **life cycle costs of a capital asset** can be grouped into three broad categories.

(a) **Initial costs**

(i) **If the asset is constructed 'in-house'** these include research and development, design specifications, manufacturing, quality control and testing, design modifications, and recruitment and training of operations staff and maintenance engineers.

(ii) **If the asset is purchased from a supplier** these include acquisition, installation, commissioning, obtaining spares, recruitment and training of operations staff and maintenance engineers, and purchase of auxiliary maintenance equipment.

(b) The **operating costs** for an item of capital equipment include not just operator costs and maintenance costs, but also indirect materials, tools, and costs of support services such as materials handling and quality control. The following may also be included.

(i) The **cost of lost production during downtime** due to preventive maintenance work or breakdown repairs

(ii) The **cost of poor performance**, if the equipment produces poor-quality output

(iii) The **cost of low utilisation**, because the equipment did not meet the original specifications exactly and so cannot be used for everything it was initially intended

(c) **Disposal costs** can be significant for a fixed asset, because the asset must be demolished or dismantled and removed, and the site made good for other use. These costs may be offset by the disposal value of the asset.

Maintainability and availability of capital assets

4.3 Two concepts useful for life cycle costing are **maintainability** (a measure of the ease with which an asset can be given routine maintenance, or repaired if it breaks down) and **availability** (the percentage of the time for which an asset is capable of performing a specified function to a specified standard of performance).

4.4 Given these definitions, an asset **availability breakeven chart** can then be drawn, to show how profitability might vary with asset availability, since a higher availability should result in higher output and sales.

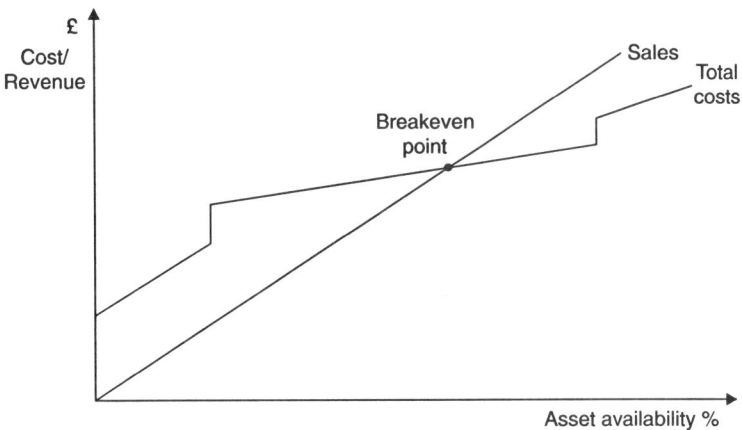

4.5 All too often, however, the following statement applies.

'Asset acquisition appraisals concentrate on the earning capacity of the investment in terms of the return on capital invested or the period required to recover the capital outlay. This emphasis is justified. But the **determination of earning capacity is a function not only of the investment, but also of the utilisation obtained and the cost of maintaining the asset**. All too frequently, the reliability and availability of a physical asset are regarded as constants' (Department of Industry).

Optimising life cycle costs

4.6 To optimise life cycle costs for a capital asset, it is therefore necessary to **optimise the trade-off** between acquisition costs, commissioning costs, operating costs, maintenance costs, disposal costs and so on over the economic lives of each asset option.

(a) If a company is trying to select which of two alternative items of capital equipment to buy, item A or item B, it should not make the decision on the basis of which has a cheaper purchase price. This would be a buy-now, pay-later attitude, because the **cheaper item might cost more to operate and maintain, and might be worth much less on eventual disposal.**

(b)   Suppose that a company is trying to choose between two machines, X and Y. Machine X costs more, but is known to be more reliable than Y. This means that the expected capacity utilisation of X should be higher. The decision maker should **make a trade-off between the higher purchase cost and the greater capacity utilisation**. This is the sort of decision that might for example face hospital management (is it worth paying more for an item of equipment that will be used on more patients over its economic life?).

4.7   The trade-off between capital costs, maintenance costs and disposal costs or value can be important for the **design of a product**, as well as the purchase of capital equipment. For example, suppose that a computer manufacturer makes computers which it sells with a one-year guarantee.

(a)   It might be worth increasing manufacturing costs by, say, 2%, in order to improve the computer's reliability and so reduce the costs of repairs given under the customer guarantee.

(b)   It might also be worth improving the computer's reliability and design specifications in order to improve its life-expectancy and/or improve its disposal value for customers.

Life cycle costing and management control

4.8   Once life cycle costing has been used for capital investment appraisal, the aim of life-cycle management should then switch to control. Expected costs may be allocated to specific stages in the **product life cycle**, and as the asset evolves through its life cycle and through each stage of its development or use, **cost figures should be gathered** for what the various costs are, and these should be **compared with the expected costs**. Where there is excess spending over the expected level, the variance should be reported, and **corrective action** should be taken where appropriate.

4.9   **Control action** might consist of action to reduce costs of the existing asset, but it will also include the following types of action.

- Action to improve the design or specifications for future capital purchases.

- Action to **improve the life cycle costing techniques** that are being used, so that future capital asset purchase decisions will be better

5   ALLOWING FOR INFLATION   Pilot paper

5.1   So far we have not considered the effect of **inflation** on the appraisal of capital investment proposals. As the inflation rate increases so will the minimum return required by an investor. For example, you might be happy with a return of 5% in an inflation-free world, but if inflation was running at 15% you would expect a considerably greater yield.

5.2   EXAMPLE: INFLATION (1)

A company is considering investing in a project with the following cash flows.

Time	Actual cash flows
	£
0	(15,000)
1	9,000
2	8,000
3	7,000

The company requires a minimum return of 20% under the present and anticipated conditions. Inflation is currently running at 10% a year, and this rate of inflation is expected to continue indefinitely. Should the company go ahead with the project?

5.3   Let us first look at the company's required rate of return. Suppose that it invested £1,000 for one year on 1 January, then on 31 December it would require a minimum return of £200. With the initial investment of £1,000, the total value of the investment by 31 December must therefore increase to £1,200. During the course of the year the purchasing value of the pound would fall due to inflation. We can restate the amount received on 31 December in terms of the purchasing power of the pound at 1 January as follows.

Amount received on 31 December in terms of the value of the pound at 1 January

$$= \frac{£1,200}{(1.10)^1} = £1,091$$

5.4   In terms of the value of the pound at 1 January, the company would make a profit of £91 which represents a rate of return of 9.1% in 'today's money' terms. This is known as the **real rate of return**. The required rate of 20% is a **money rate of return** (sometimes called a **nominal rate of return**). The money rate measures the return in terms of the pound which is, of course, falling in value. The real rate measures the return in constant price level terms.

The two rates of return and the inflation rate are linked by an equation.

FORMULA TO LEARN

(1 + money rate) = (1 + real rate) × (1 + inflation rate)

where all the rates are expressed as proportions.

In our example,

(1 + 0.20) = (1 + 0.091) × (1 + 0.10) = 1.20

Exam focus point

A multiple choice question in the pilot paper required a straightforward application of this formula. Easy marks - if you have learned the formula!

5.5   We must decide **which rate** to use for discounting, the **real rate** or the **money rate**. The rule is as follows.

(a)   If the cash flows are expressed in terms of the **actual number of pounds** that will be received or paid on the various future dates, we **use the money rate for discounting**.

(b)   If the cash flows are expressed in terms of the **value of the pound at time 0 (that is, in constant price level terms), we use the real rate**.

5.6   The cash flows given in Paragraph 5.2 are expressed in terms of the actual number of pounds that will be received or paid at the relevant dates. We should, therefore, discount them using the money rate of return.

BPP PUBLISHING

Time	Cash flow £	Discount factor 20%	PV £
0	(15,000)	1.000	(15,000)
1	9,000	0.833	7,497
2	8,000	0.694	5,552
3	7,000	0.579	4,053
			2,102

The project has a positive net present value of £2,102.

5.7 The future cash flows can be re-expressed in terms of the value of the pound at time 0 as follows, given inflation at 10% a year.

Time	Actual cash flow £	Cash flow at time 0 price level	£
0	(15,000)		(15,000)
1	9,000	$9,000 \times \dfrac{1}{1.10}$ =	8,182
2	8,000	$8,000 \times \dfrac{1}{(1.10)^2}$ =	6,612
3	7,000	$7,000 \times \dfrac{1}{(1.10)^3}$ =	5,259

5.8 The cash flows expressed in terms of the value of the pound at time 0 can now be discounted using the real rate of 9.1%.

Time	Cash flow £	Discount factor 9.1%	PV £
0	(15,000)	1.00	(15,000)
1	8,182	$\dfrac{1}{1.091}$	7,500
2	6,612	$\dfrac{1}{(1.091)^2}$	5,555
3	5,259	$\dfrac{1}{(1.091)^3}$	4,050
		NPV	2,105

5.9 The NPV is the same as before (and the present value of the cash flow in each year is the same as before) apart from rounding errors with a net total of £3.

The advantages and misuses of real values and a real rate of return

5.10 Although it is recommended that **companies should discount money values at the money cost of capital,** there are some advantages of using real values discounted at a real cost of capital.

(a) **When all costs and benefits rise at the same rate of price inflation, real values are the same as current day values,** so that no further adjustments need be made to cash flows before discounting. In contrast, when money values are discounted at the money cost of capital, the prices in future years must be calculated before discounting can begin.

(b) The government or nationalised industries might prefer to set a real return as a target for investments, as being more suitable to their particular situation than a commercial money rate of return.

Costs and benefits which inflate at different rates

5.11 Not all costs and benefits will rise in line with the general level of inflation. In such cases, we can apply the money rate to inflated values to determine a project's NPV.

5.12 **EXAMPLE: INFLATION (2)**

Rice Ltd is considering a project which would cost £5,000 now. The annual benefits, for four years, would be a fixed income of £2,500 a year, plus other savings of £500 a year in year 1, rising by 5% each year because of inflation. Running costs will be £1,000 in the first year, but would increase at 10% each year because of inflating labour costs. The general rate of inflation is expected to be 7½% and the company's required money rate of return is 16%. Is the project worthwhile? Ignore taxation.

5.13 **SOLUTION**

The cash flows at inflated values are as follows.

Year	Fixed income £	Other savings £	Running costs £	Net cash flow £
1	2,500	500	1,000	2,000
2	2,500	525	1,100	1,925
3	2,500	551	1,210	1,841
4	2,500	579	1,331	1,748

The NPV of the project is as follows.

Year	Cash flow £	Discount factor 16%	PV £
0	(5,000)	1.000	(5,000)
1	2,000	0.862	1,724
2	1,925	0.743	1,430
3	1,841	0.641	1,180
4	1,748	0.552	965
			+ 299

The NPV is positive and the project would seem therefore to be worthwhile.

6 **ALLOWING FOR TAXATION**   **Pilot paper**

6.1 So far, in looking at project appraisal, we have ignored **taxation**. However, payments of tax, or reductions of tax payments, are cash flows and ought to be considered in DCF analysis. Typical assumptions which may be stated in questions are as follows.

(a) Corporation tax is payable in the year following the one in which the taxable profits are made. Thus, if a project increases taxable profits by £10,000 in year 2, there will be a tax payment, assuming tax at 30%, of £3,000 in year 3.

   This is not always the case in examination questions. Always follow the instructions given and look out for questions which state that tax is payable in the same year as that in which the profits arise.

(b) Net cash flows from a project should be considered as the taxable profits arising from the project (unless an indication is given to the contrary).

> ## Exam focus point
>
> An investment appraisal question in the pilot paper described taxation as payable 'in the seventh and tenth months of the year in which the profit is earned, and in the first and fourth months of the following year.' The company used DCF techniques with annual breaks (which is the method you have learned) therefore half of the tax was a cash outflow in the year in which profits were earned. The remaining half of the tax was a cash outflow in the following year. It is very straightforward as long as you follow the instructions carefully.

Capital allowances

6.2 Capital allowances are used to reduce taxable profits, and the consequent reduction in a tax payment should be treated as a cash saving arising from the acceptance of a project. Writing down allowances are generally allowed on the cost of **plant and machinery** at the rate of 25% on a **reducing balance** basis. Thus if a company purchases plant costing £80,000, the subsequent writing down allowances would be as follows.

Year		Capital allowance £	Reducing balance £
1	(25% of cost)	20,000	60,000
2	(25% of RB)	15,000	45,000
3	(25% of RB)	11,250	33,750
4	(25% of RB)	8,438	25,312

When the plant is eventually sold, the difference between the sale price and the reducing balance amount at the time of sale will be treated as a taxable profit if the sale price exceeds the reducing balance, and as a tax allowable loss if the reducing balance exceeds the sale price. Examination questions often assume that this loss will be available immediately, though in practice the balance less the sale price continues to be written off at 25% a year as part of a pool balance unless the asset has been de-pooled.

The cash saving on the capital allowances (or the cash payment for the charge) is calculated by multiplying the allowance (or charge) by the corporation tax rate.

6.3 Assumptions about capital allowances could be simplified in an exam question. For example, you might be told that capital allowances can be claimed at the rate of 25% of cost on a straight line basis (that is, over four years), or a question might refer to 'tax allowable depreciation', so that the capital allowances equal the depreciation charge.

6.4 There are two possible assumptions about the time when capital allowances start to be claimed.

(a) It can be assumed that the first claim for capital allowances occurs at the start of the project (at year 0) and so the first tax saving occurs one year later (at year 1).

(b) Alternatively it can be assumed that the first claim for capital allowances occurs later in the first year, so the first tax saving occurs one year later, that is, year 2.

6.5 You should state clearly which assumption you have made. Assumption (b) is more prudent, because it defers the tax benefit by one year, but assumption (a) is also perfectly feasible. It is very likely, however that an examination question will indicate which of the two assumptions is required.

6.6 You also need to be sure that you start off with the correct balance on which to calculate the capital allowances. For example, in addition to the original capital costs of a machine, it

may be possible to claim capital allowances on the costs of installation, such as the labour and overhead costs of removing an old machine and levelling the area for the new machine. Remember to state your assumptions concerning this type of item.

6.7 EXAMPLE: TAXATION

A company is considering whether or not to purchase an item of machinery costing £40,000 in 20X5. It would have a life of four years, after which it would be sold for £5,000. The machinery would create annual cost savings of £14,000.

The machinery would attract writing down allowances of 25% on the reducing balance basis which could be claimed against taxable profits of the current year, which is soon to end. A balancing allowance or charge would arise on disposal. The rate of corporation tax is 30%. Tax is payable one year in arrears. The after-tax cost of capital is 8%. Assume that tax payments occur in the year following the transactions.

Should the machinery be purchased?

6.8 SOLUTION

The first capital allowance is claimed against year 0 profits.

Cost: £40,000

Year	Allowance	Reducing balance (RB)	
	£	£	
(0) 20X5 (25% of cost)	10,000	30,000	(40,000 – 10,000)
(1) 20X6 (25% of RB)	7,500	22,500	(30,000 – 7,500)
(2) 20X7 (25% of RB)	5,625	16,875	(22,500 – 5,625)
(3) 20X8 (25% of RB)	4,219	12,656	(16,875 – 4,219)
(4) 20X9 (25% of RB)	3,164	9,492	(12,656 – 3,164)

	£
Sale proceeds, end of fourth year	5,000
Less reducing balance, end of fourth year	9,492
Balancing allowance	4,492

6.9 Having calculated the allowances each year, the tax savings can be computed. The year of the cash flow is one year after the year for which the allowance is claimed.

Year of claim	Allowance	Tax saved	Year of tax payment/saving
	£	£	
0	10,000	3,000	1
1	7,500	2,250	2
2	5,625	1,688	3
3	4,219	1,266	4
4	7,656	2,297	5
	35,000 ⋆		

⋆ Net cost £(40,000 – 5,000) = £35,000

These tax savings relate to capital allowances. We must also calculate the extra tax payments on annual savings of £14,000.

6.10 The net cash flows and the NPV are now calculated as follows.

Year	Equipment £	Savings £	Tax on savings £	Tax saved on capital allowances £	Net cash flow £	Discount factor 8%	Present value of cash flow £
0	(40,000)				(40,000)	1.000	(40,000)
1		14,000		3,000	17,000	0.926	15,742
2		14,000	(4,200)	2,250	12,050	0.857	10,327
3		14,000	(4,200)	1,688	11,488	0.794	9,121
4	5,000	14,000	(4,200)	1,266	11,066	0.735	8,134
5			(4,200)	2,297	(1,903)	0.681	(1,296)
							2,028

The NPV is positive and so the purchase appears to be worthwhile.

An alternative and quicker method of calculating tax payments or savings

6.11 In the above example, the tax computations could have been combined, as follows.

Year	0 £	1 £	2 £	3 £	4 £
Cost savings	0	14,000	14,000	14,000	14,000
Capital allowance	10,000	7,500	5,625	4,219	7,656
Taxable profits	(10,000)	6,500	8,375	9,781	6,344
Tax at 30%	3,000	(1,950)	(2,512)	(2,934)	(1,903)

6.12 The net cash flows would then be as follows.

Year	Equipment £	Savings £	Tax £	Net cash flow £
0	(40,000)			(40,000)
1		14,000	3,000	17,000
2		14,000	(1,950)	12,050
3		14,000	(2,512)	11,488
4	5,000	14,000	(2,934)	11,066
5			(1,903)	(1,903)

The net cash flows are exactly the same as calculated previously in Paragraph 6.9.

Taxation and DCF

6.13 The effect of taxation on capital budgeting is theoretically quite simple. Organisations must pay tax, and the effect of undertaking a project will be to increase or decrease tax payments each year. These incremental tax cash flows should be included in the cash flows of the project for discounting to arrive at the project's NPV.

6.14 When taxation is ignored in the DCF calculations, the discount rate will reflect the pre-tax rate of return required on capital investments. When taxation is included in the cash flows, a post-tax required rate of return should be used.

Question 3

A company is considering the purchase of an item of equipment, which would earn profits before tax of £25,000 a year. Depreciation charges would be £20,000 a year for six years. Capital allowances would be £30,000 a year for the first four years. Corporation tax is at 30%.

What would be the annual net cash inflows of the project:

(a) for the first four years;
(b) for the fifth and sixth years,

242

assuming that tax payments occur in the same year as the profits giving rise to them, and there is no balancing charge or allowance when the machine is scrapped at the end of the sixth year?

Answer

(a)

	Years 1-4	Years 5-6
	£	£
Profit before tax	25,000	25,000
Add back depreciation	20,000	20,000
Net cash inflow before tax	45,000	45,000
Less capital allowance	30,000	0
	15,000	45,000
Tax at 30%	4,500	13,500

Years 1 - 4 Net cash inflow after tax £45,000 – £4,500 = £40,500

(b)   Years 5 - 6 Net cash inflow after tax = £45,000 – £13,500 = £31,500

Question 4

A company is considering the purchase of a machine for £150,000. It would be sold after four years for an estimated realisable value of £50,000. By this time capital allowances of £120,000 would have been claimed. The rate of corporation tax is 30%.

The cash flow arising as a result of the tax implications of the sale of the machine at the end of the four years is

A   £6,000 inflow
B   £6,000 outflow
C   £15,000 outflow
D   £20,000 outflow
E   £24,000 outflow

Answer

The correct option is **B**.

There will be a balancing charge on the sale of the machine of £(50,000 – (150,000 – 120,000)) = £20,000. This will give rise to a tax payment of 30% × £20,000 = £6,000.

If you chose A you got the calculations correct but the direction of the cash flow was wrong.

Option C is 30% taxation on the estimated sales value. The revenue from the actual sale is not taxed directly, but any remaining balancing charge will be taxable.

If you chose option D you forgot to calculate the 30% corporation tax on the balancing charge of 20%.

Chapter roundup

*   **Annualised equivalents** are used to enable a comparison to be made between the net present value of projects with different durations.

*   When an asset is being replaced with an **identical asset** the **equivalent annual cost method** can be used. When an **asset** is being replaced with a **non-identical asset** the decision is **when to replace** the asset **rather than how frequently**. The **present value of an annuity in perpetuity** must be calculated.

*   **Sensitivity analysis** is one technique for incorporating risk into project appraisal. It assesses how responsive the project's NPV is to changes in the variables used to calculate that NPV. One particular approach to sensitivity analysis, the certainty-equivalent approach, involves the conversion of the expected cash flows of the project to riskless equivalent amounts.

*   Projects need to be **abandoned** if the expected net proceeds from abandonment are greater than the expected net proceeds from continuing.

*   **Life cycle costing** is a technique which takes account of the total cost of owning an asset during its economic life.

*   **Inflation** is a feature of all economies, and it must be accommodated in investment appraisal.

*   (1+ money rate of return) = (1 + real rate of return) × (1 + rate of inflation)

*   **Real cash flows** (ie adjusted for inflation) should be discounted at a real discount rate.

*   **Money cash flows** should be discounted at a money discount rate.

*   The **money** rate of return is sometimes called the **nominal** rate of return.

*   **Taxation** is a major practical consideration for businesses. It is vital to take it into account in making decisions.

*   **Capital allowances** details should be checked in any question you attempt.

*   If **taxation is ignored** in the project cash flows, the discount rate should be the **pre-tax** cost of capital. When **taxation is included** in the cash flows, the **after tax** cost of capital should be used.

Quick quiz

1   The net present value of the costs of operating a machine for the next three years is £10,724 at a cost of capital of 15%. What is the equivalent annual cost of operating the machine?

2   What is the cost of operating the machine in perpetuity?

3   Sensitivity analysis allows for uncertainty in project appraisal by assessing the probability of changes in the decision variables. True or false?

4   Which of these projects displays a non-conventional pattern of cash flows

Time	Project D	Project E
	£'000	£'000
0	1,150	(4,800)
1	(2,800)	1,700
2	1,800	890

5   What is the relationship between the money rate of return, the real rate of return and the rate of inflation?

6   The money cost of capital is 11%. The expected annual rate of inflation is 5%. What is the real cost of capital?

7   A company wants a minimum real return of 3% a year on its investments. Inflation is expected to be 8% a year. What is the company's minimum money cost of capital?

8   A company is appraising an investment that will save electricity costs. Electricity prices are expected to rise at a rate of 15% per annum in future, although the general inflation rate will be 10% per annum. The money cost of capital for the company is 20%. What is the appropriate discount rate to apply to the forecast actual money cash flows for electricity?

A 20.0%   B 22.0%   C 26.5%   D 32.0%   E 35.0%

9   State three ways in which taxation might affect the forecast cash flows in an investment appraisal.

Answers to quick quiz

1   £10,724/2.283 = £4,697

2   £4,697/0.15 = £31,313

3   False

4   Project D

5   (1 + money rate) = (1 + real rate) × (1 + inflation rate)

6    $\dfrac{1.11}{1.05}$ = 1.057. The real cost of capital is 5.7%

7   1.03 × 1.08 = 1.1124. The money cost of capital is 11.24%

8   A; the money rate of 20% is applied to the money cash flows

9   (1)   Profits and losses on projects may be subject to corporation tax and payments of taxation are cash outflows

    (2)   Capital expenditure may attract capital allowances, and savings in taxation payments are cash savings/inflows

    (3)   Taxation may affect the timing of cash flows

Now try the questions below from the Exam Question Bank

Number	Level	Marks	Time
15	Examination	25	45 mins
16	Examination	20	36 mins
17	Examination (Pilot)	25	45 mins

Chapter 10

INVESTMENT CENTRES AND PERFORMANCE APPRAISAL

Topic list	Syllabus reference	Ability required
1 Investment centres	(iii)	Discuss
2 Return on investment (ROI)	(iii)	Calculate and evaluate
3 ROI and decision making	(iii)	Discuss
4 Residual income (RI)	(iii)	Calculate and evaluate

Introduction

In the last two chapters we looked at one of the most important management accounting techniques, discounted cashflow analysis. In particular, we concentrated on its use as a method of project appraisal.

In the past, other methods of appraisal were used more frequently than DCF analysis. Such methods were adapted from those used to appraise published financial reports. In this chapter we consider two such methods: **return on investment (ROI)** and **residual income (RI)**. These techniques are used to appraise both managerial performance within a system of **responsibility accounting** and **investment centres**, and individual projects. Although possibly easier to understand, RI and ROI are quite seriously flawed when compared with DCF.

Learning outcomes covered in this chapter

- **Discuss** investment centres

- **Calculate** return on investment and residual income

- **Evaluate** return on investment and residual income

- **Discuss** the behavioural implications of return on investment and residual income

Syllabus content covered in this chapter

- Return on investment

- Residual income

1   INVESTMENT CENTRES

Divisionalisation

1.1 In general a large organisation can be **structured in one or two ways: functionally** (all activities of a similar type within a company, such as production, sales, research, are placed under the control of the appropriate departmental head) or **divisionally** (split into divisions in accordance with the products which are made or services which are provided).

1.2   Divisional managers are therefore responsible for all operations (production, sales and so on) relating to their product, the functional structure being applied to each division. It is quite possible, of course, that only part of a company is divisionalised and activities such as administration are structured centrally on a functional basis with the responsibility of providing services to *all* divisions.

Decentralisation

1.3   In general, a **divisional structure will lead to decentralisation** of the decision-making process and divisional managers may have the freedom to set selling prices, choose suppliers, make product mix and output decisions and so on. Decentralisation is, however, a matter of degree, depending on how much freedom divisional managers are given.

Advantages of divisionalisation

1.4   (a)   Divisionalisation can **improve** the **quality of decisions** made because divisional managers (those taking the decisions) have good knowledge of local conditions and should therefore be able to make more informed judgements. Moreover, with the personal incentive to improve the division's performance, they ought to take decisions in the division's best interests.

       (b)   **Decisions should be taken more quickly** because information does not have to pass along the chain of command to and from top management. Decisions can be made on the spot by those who are familiar with the product lines and production processes and who are able to react to changes in local conditions quickly and efficiently.

       (c)   The authority to act to improve performance should **motivate divisional managers**.

       (d)   Divisional organisation **frees top management** from detailed involvement in day-to-day operations and allows them to devote more time to strategic planning.

       (e)   Divisions provide **valuable training grounds for future members of top management** by giving them experience of managerial skills in a less complex environment than that faced by top management.

       (f)   In a large business organisation, the **central head office will not have the management resources or skills to direct operations closely enough itself**. Some authority must be delegated to local operational managers.

Disadvantages of divisionalisation

1.5   (a)   A danger with divisional accounting is that the **business organisation will divide into a number of self-interested segments, each acting at times against the wishes and interests of other segments**. Decisions might be taken by a divisional manager in the best interests of his own part of the business, but against the best interest of other divisions and possibly against the interests of the organisation as a whole.

              A task of **head office** is therefore to try to **prevent dysfunctional decision making** by individual divisional managers. To do this, head office must reserve some power and authority for itself so that divisional managers cannot be allowed to make entirely independent decisions. A **balance** ought to be kept **between decentralisation** of authority to provide incentives and motivation, **and retaining centralised authority** to ensure that the organisation's divisions are all working towards the same target, the benefit of the organisation as a whole (in other words, **retaining goal congruence** among the organisation's separate divisions).

BPP
PUBLISHING

KEY TERM

Goal congruence is '... the state which leads individuals or groups to take actions which are in their self-interest and also in the best interest of the entity'.

(CIMA *Official Terminology*)

(b) It is claimed that the **costs of activities that are common** to all divisions such as running the accounting department **may be greater** for a divisionalised structure than for a centralised structure.

(c) **Top management,** by delegating decision making to divisional managers, may **lose control** since they are not aware of what is going on in the organisation as a whole. (With a good system of performance evaluation and appropriate control information, however, top management should be able to control operations just as effectively.)

Responsibility accounting

1.6 The creation of divisions allows for the operation of a system of responsibility accounting.

KEY TERM

Responsibility accounting is a system of accounting that segregates revenues and costs into areas of personal responsibility in order to monitor and assess the performance of each part of an organisation.

1.7 There are three types of responsibility accounting unit, or responsibility centre.

KEY TERM

A **responsibility centre** is 'A department or organisational function whose performance is the direct responsibility of a specific manager'. (CIMA *Official Terminology*)

1.8 In the weakest form of **decentralisation** a system of cost centres might be used. As decentralisation becomes stronger the responsibility accounting framework will be based around profit centres. In its **strongest form investment centres are used.**

Type of responsibility centre	Manager has control over ...	Principal performance measurement
Cost centre	Controllable costs	Variance analysis Efficiency measures
Revenue centre	Revenues only	Revenues
Profit centre	Controllable costs Sales prices (including transfer prices)	Profit
Contribution centre	As for profit centre except that expenditure is reported on a marginal cost basis	Contribution
Investment centre	Controllable costs Sales prices (including transfer prices) Output volumes Investment in fixed and current assets	Return on investment Residual income Other financial ratios

What are investment centres?

1.9 Where a divisional manager of a company is **allowed some discretion about the amount of investment undertaken** by the division, assessment of results by profit alone (as for a profit centre) is clearly inadequate. The profit earned must be related to the amount of capital invested. Such divisions are sometimes called investment centres for this reason. Performance is measured by **return on capital employed (ROCE),** often referred to as **return on investment (ROI)** and other subsidiary ratios, or by **residual income (RI).**

> ### KEY TERM
>
> An **investment centre** is 'A profit centre with additional responsibilities for capital investment and possibly for financing, and whose performance is measured by its return on investment'. (CIMA *Official Terminology*)

1.10 Managers of **subsidiary companies will often be treated as investment centre** managers, accountable for profits and capital employed. Within each subsidiary, the major divisions might be treated as profit centres, with each divisional manager having the authority to decide the prices and output volumes for the products or services of the division. Within each division, there will be departmental managers, section managers and so on, who can all be treated as cost centre managers. All managers should receive regular, periodic performance reports for their own areas of responsibility.

1.11 The amount of **capital employed** in an investment centre should consist only of **directly attributable fixed assets and working capital.**

   (a) Subsidiary companies are often required to remit spare cash to the central treasury department at group head office, and so directly attributable working capital would normally consist of stocks and debtors less creditors, but minimal amounts of cash.

   (b) If an investment centre is apportioned a share of head office fixed assets, the amount of capital employed in these assets should be recorded separately because it is not directly attributable to the investment centre.

Controllable costs and uncontrollable costs

> ### KEY TERM
>
> A **controllable cost** is 'A cost which can be influenced by its budget holder'.
> (CIMA *Official Terminology*)

1.12 Responsibility accounting attempts to associate costs, revenues, assets and liabilities with the managers most capable of controlling them. As a system of accounting, it therefore distinguishes between controllable and uncontrollable costs.

   (a) Most **variable costs** within a department are thought to be **controllable in the short term** because managers can influence the efficiency with which resources are used, even if they cannot do anything to raise or lower price levels.

   (b) Many **fixed costs are uncontrollable** (or committed) **in the short term**, although some fixed costs **may be discretionary**.

(c) **Many fixed costs are directly attributable** to a department or profit centre in that although they are fixed (in the short term) within the relevant range of output, a drastic reduction in the department's output, or closure of the division entirely, would reduce or remove these costs.

(d) **Assets and liabilities** are only **controllable to the extent** that the investment centre manager has **authority to increase or reduce them**.

Question 1

Over what type of decision is head office likely to retain control?

Answer

Head office might retain certain 'powers' over the following.

- Company financing decisions
- The appointment of senior personnel
- Product line closure or departmental closure decisions
- Administration of centralised departments, such as the computer department
- Approval for all major capital expenditure proposals
- Monitoring overall results and settling inter-departmental disputes

2 RETURN ON INVESTMENT (ROI)

2.1 The performance of an investment centre is usually monitored using either or both of return on investment (ROI) (also known as return on capital employed (ROCE)) and residual income (RI).

2.2 ROI is generally regarded as the **key performance measure**. There are two main reasons for its **widespread use**.

(a) It **ties in directly with the accounting process**, and is identifiable from the profit and loss account and balance sheet.

(b) Even more importantly, ROI is the **only measure of performance** available (apart from residual income) by which the return on investment for a **division** or **company as a single entire unit** (or collection of assets) **can be measured**.

KEY TERM

Return on investment (ROI) (or return on capital employed (ROCE)) shows how much profit has been made in relation to the amount of capital invested and is calculated as (profit/capital employed) × 100%.

2.3 For example, suppose that a company has two investment centres A and B, which show results for the year as follows.

	A £	B £
Profit	60,000	30,000
Capital employed	400,000	120,000
ROI	15%	25%

Investment centre A has made double the profits of investment centre B, and in terms of profits alone has therefore been more 'successful'. However, B has achieved its profits with a

much lower capital investment, and so has earned a much higher ROI. This suggests that B has been a more successful investment than A.

Measuring ROI

2.4 ROI can be measured in different ways.

Profit after depreciation as a % of net assets employed

2.5 This is probably the **most common method**, but it does present a problem. If an investment centre maintains the same annual profit, and keeps the same assets without a policy of regular fixed asset replacement, its ROI will increase year by year as the assets get older. This **can give a false impression of improving performance over time**.

2.6 For example, the results of investment centre X, with a policy of straight-line depreciation of assets over a 5-year period, might be as follows.

Year	Fixed assets at cost £'000	Depreciation in the year £'000	NBV (mid year) £'000	Working capital £'000	Capital employed £'000	Profit £'000	ROI
0	100			10	110		
1	100	20	90	10	100	10	10.0%
2	100	20	70	10	80	10	12.5%
3	100	20	50	10	60	10	16.7%
4	100	20	30	10	40	10	25.0%
5	100	20	10	10	20	10	50.0%

This table of figures is intended to show that an investment centre can **improve its ROI** year by year, simply **by allowing its fixed assets to depreciate**, and there could be a **disincentive to** investment centre managers to **reinvest in new or replacement assets**, because the centre's ROI would probably fall.

Question 2

A new company has fixed assets of £460,000 which will be depreciated to nil on a straight line basis over 10 years. Working capital will consistently be £75,000, and annual profit will consistently be £30,000. ROI is measured as return on net assets.
Required

Calculate the company's ROI in years 2 and 6.

Answer

Year 2 - 6.4%
Year 6 - 10.6%

2.7 A further disadvantage of measuring ROI as profit divided by net assets is that, for similar reasons, it is not **easy to compare** fairly the **performance of investment centres**.

2.8 For example, suppose that we have two investment centres.

	Investment centre P		Investment centre Q	
	£	£	£	£
Working capital		20,000		20,000
Fixed assets at cost	230,000		230,000	
Accumulated depreciation	170,000		10,000	
Net book value		60,000		220,000
Capital employed		80,000		240,000
Profit		£24,000		£24,000
ROI		30%		10%

Investment centres P and Q have the same amount of working capital, the same value of fixed assets at cost, and the same profit. But P's fixed assets have been depreciated by a much bigger amount (presumably P's fixed assets are much older than Q's) and so P's ROI is three times the size of Q's ROI. The conclusion might therefore be that P has performed much better than Q. This comparison, however, would not be 'fair', because the **difference in performance might be entirely attributable to the age of their fixed assets.**

2.9 The arguments for using net book values for calculating ROI

(a) It is the '**normally accepted**' method of calculating ROI.

(b) Firms are continually buying new fixed assets to replace old ones that wear out, and so on the whole, the **total net book value** of all fixed assets together **will remain fairly constant** (assuming nil inflation and nil growth).

Profit after depreciation as a % of gross assets employed

2.10 Instead of measuring ROI as return on net assets, we could measure it as return on gross assets. This would **remove the problem of ROI increasing over time as fixed assets get older**.

2.11 If a company acquired a fixed asset costing £40,000, which it intends to depreciate by £10,000 pa for 4 years, and if the asset earns a profit of £8,000 pa after depreciation, ROI might be calculated on net book values or gross values, as follows.

Year	Profit	NBV(mid-year value)	ROI based on NBV	Gross value	ROI based on gross value
	£	£		£	
1	8,000	35,000	22.9%	40,000	20%
2	8,000	25,000	32.0%	40,000	20%
3	8,000	15,000	53.3%	40,000	20%
4	8,000	5,000	160.0%	40,000	20%

The ROI based on **net book value** shows an **increasing trend over time**, simply because the asset's value is falling as it is depreciated. The ROI based on gross book value suggests that the asset has **performed consistently** in each of the 4 years, which is probably a more valid conclusion.

Question 3

Repeat Question 2, measuring ROI as return on gross assets.

Answer

Year 2 - 5.6%
Year 6 - 5.6%

2.12 However, using gross book values to measure ROI has its **disadvantages**. Most important of these is that measuring ROI as return on gross assets ignores the age factor, and **does not distinguish between old and new assets**.

(a) **Older fixed assets** usually **cost more to repair and maintain,** to keep them running. An investment centre with old assets may therefore have its profitability reduced by repair costs, and its ROI might fall over time as its assets get older and repair costs get bigger.

(b) **Inflation** and **technological change alter the cost of fixed assets**. If one investment centre has fixed assets bought ten years ago with a gross cost of £1 million, and another investment centre, in the same area of business operations, has fixed assets bought very recently for £1 million, the quantity and technological character of the fixed assets of the two investment centres are likely to be very different.

Tangible and intangible assets

2.13 The management accountant is free to capitalise or expense intangible assets. When significant expenditure on an **intangible asset** (such as an advertising campaign) which is expected to provide future benefits is expensed, profits will be reduced and ROI/RI artificially depressed. In the future, the investment should produce significant cash inflows and the ROI/RI will be artificially inflated. **Such expenditure** should therefore be **capitalised so as to smooth out performance measures and to eradicate the risk of drawing false conclusions from them.**

2.14 A **comparison of the performance of manufacturing divisions and service divisions** should be **treated with caution**. The majority of a **manufacturing division's assets** will be **tangible** and therefore are **automatically capitalised** whereas the treatment of a **service division's** mostly **intangible assets** is **open to interpretation**.

Constituent elements of the investment base

2.15 Although we have looked at how the investment base should be valued, we need to consider its appropriate constituent elements.

(a) If a **manager's performance is being evaluated**, only those **assets** which can be **traced directly to the division** and are **controllable by the manager should be included**. Head office assets or investment centre assets controlled by head office should not be included. So, for example, only those cash balances actually maintained with an investment centre itself should be included.

(b) If it is the **performance of the investment centre that is being appraised**, a **proportion of the investment in head office assets would need to be included** because an investment centre could not operate without the support of head office assets and administrative backup.

Profits

2.16 We have looked at how to define the asset base used in the calculations but what about profit? If the **performance of the investment centre manager is being assessed** it should seem reasonable to **base profit on the revenues and costs controllable by the manager** and exclude service and head office costs except those costs specifically attributable to the investment centre. If it is the **performance of the investment centre that is being assessed, however, the inclusion of general service and head office costs would seem reasonable.**

3 ROI AND DECISION MAKING

New investments

3.1 If investment centre performance is judged by ROI, we should expect that the managers of investment centres will probably decide to undertake new capital investments **only if these new investments are likely to increase the ROI of their centre.**

3.2 Suppose that an investment centre, A, currently makes a return of 40% on capital employed. The manager of centre A would probably only want to undertake new investments that promise to yield a return of 40% or more, otherwise the investment centre's overall ROI would fall.

3.3 For example, if investment centre A currently has assets of £1,000,000 and expects to earn a profit of £400,000, how would the centre's manager view a new capital investment which would cost £250,000 and yield a profit of £75,000 pa?

	Without the new investment	*With the new investment*
Profit	£400,000	£475,000
Capital employed	£1,000,000	£1,250,000
ROI	40%	38%

The **new investment** would **reduce the investment centre's ROI** from 40% to 38%, and so the investment centre manager would probably decide **not to undertake** the new investment.

3.4 If the group of companies of which investment centre A is a part has a target ROI of, say, 25%, the new investment would presumably be seen as **beneficial for the group as a whole**. But even though it promises to yield a return of 75,000/250,000 = 30%, which is above the group's target ROI, it would still make investment centre A's results look worse. The manager of investment centre A would, in these circumstances, be motivated to do not what is best for the organisation as a whole, but what is **best for his division.**

The target return for a group of companies

3.5 If a group of companies sets a target return for the group as a whole, it might be **group policy** that investment projects should **only go ahead if** the project promises to **earn at least the target return**. For example, group policy might be as follows.

(a) There should be no new investment by any subsidiary in the group unless it is expected to earn at least a 15% return.

(b) Similarly, no fixed asset should be disposed of if the asset is currently earning a return in excess of 15% of its disposal value.

(c) Investments which promise a return of 15% or more ought to be undertaken (provided that the degree of uncertainty or risk in the project is acceptable).

3.6 A problem with such a policy is that even if investment decisions are based on a target DCF rate of return, actual performance can only be measured on the basis of an accounting ROI, which is by no means the same thing.

3.7 Suppose that an investment in a fixed asset would cost £100,000 and make a profit of £11,000 p.a. after depreciation. The asset would be depreciated by £25,000 p.a. for four years. It is group policy that investments must show a minimum return of 15%.

3.8 The DCF net present value of this investment would just about be positive, and so the investment ought to be approved if group policy is adhered to.

Year	Cash flow (profit before dep'n) £	Discount factor 15%	Present value £
0	(100,000)	1.000	(100,000)
1	36,000	0.870	31,320
2	36,000	0.756	27,216
3	36,000	0.658	23,688
4	36,000	0.572	20,592
		NPV	2,816

3.9 However, if the investment is measured year by year according to the accounting ROI it has earned, we find that its return is less than 15% in year 1, but more than 15% in years 2, 3 and 4.

Year	Profit £	NBV of equipment (mid-year value) £	ROI
1	11,000	87,500	12.6%
2	11,000	62,500	17.6%
3	11,000	37,500	29.3%
4	11,000	12,500	88.0%

3.10 In view of the low accounting ROI in year 1, should the investment be undertaken or not?

(a) Strictly speaking, **investment decisions should be based on DCF yield**, and should not be guided by short term accounting ROI.

(b) Even if accounting ROI is used as a guideline for investment decisions, **ROI should be looked at over the full life of the investment, not just in the short term**. In the short term (in the first year or so of a project's life) the accounting ROI is likely to be low because the net book value of the asset will still be high.

DCF v ROI

3.11 In spite of the superiority of DCF yield over accounting ROI as a means of evaluating investments, and in spite of the wisdom of taking a longer term view rather than a short-term view with investments, it is nevertheless an uncomfortable fact that the consideration of short-run accounting **ROI does often influence investment decisions**.

3.12 In our example, it is conceivable that the group's management might disapprove of the project because of its low accounting ROI in year 1. This approach is short-sighted, but it nevertheless can make some sense to a company or group of companies which has to **show a satisfactory profit and ROI in its published accounts each year**, to keep its shareholders satisfied with performance.

3.13 A similarly misguided decision would occur where a divisional manager is worried about the low ROI of his division, and decides to **reduce his investment by scrapping some machinery** which is not currently in use. The reduction in both depreciation charges and assets would **immediately improve the ROI**. When the machinery is eventually required the manager would then be **obliged to buy new equipment**. Such a situation may seem bizarre, but it does occur in real life.

3.14 **ROI should not be used to guide management decisions** but there is a difficult motivational problem. If management performance is measured in terms of ROI, any decisions which benefit the company in the long term but which reduce the ROI in the immediate short term would reflect badly on the manager's reported performance. In other words, **good investment decisions would make a manager's performance seem worse than if the wrong investment decision were taken instead.**

3.15 EXTENDED EXAMPLE: ROI AND DECISION-MAKING

At the end of 20X3, Division S (part of a group) had a book value of fixed assets of £300,000 and net current assets of £40,000. Net profit before tax was £64,000.

The fixed assets of Division S consist of five separate items each costing £60,000 which are depreciated to zero over 5 years on a straight-line basis. For each of the past years on 31 December it has bought a replacement for the asset that has just been withdrawn and it proposes to continue this policy. Because of technological advances the asset manufacturer has been able to keep his prices constant over time. The group's cost of capital is 15%.

Required

Assuming that, except where otherwise stated, there are no changes in the above data, deal with the following separate situations.

(a) Division S has the opportunity of an investment costing £60,000, and yielding an annual profit of £10,000.

    (i)   Calculate its new ROI if the investment were undertaken.

    (ii)   State whether you would recommend that the investment be undertaken.

(b) Division S has the opportunity of selling, at a price equal to its written-down book value of £24,000, an asset that currently earns £3,900 p.a.

    (i)   Calculate its new ROI if the asset were sold.

    (ii)   State, with brief reasons, whether you would recommend the sale of the asset.

3.16 SOLUTION IN GENERAL

The question does not state whether capital employed should include a valuation of fixed assets at gross historical cost or at net book value. It is assumed that net book value is required. It is also assumed that the fixed asset which has just been bought as a replacement on 31 December 20X3 has not been depreciated at all.

Exam focus point

It is worth stating assumptions such as these at the start of a solution to questions of this sort. If the problem has not been properly defined, clarify your own assumptions and definitions for the benefit of the marker of your exam script!

The gross book value of the 5 fixed asset items is $5 \times £60,000 = £300,000$.

	£
Net book value of asset just bought on 31.12.X3	60,000
NBV of asset bought 1 year earlier	48,000
NBV of asset bought 2 years earlier	36,000
NBV of asset bought 3 years earlier	24,000
NBV of asset bought 4 years earlier	12,000
NBV of all 5 fixed assets at 31.12.X3	180,000
Net current assets	40,000
Total capital employed, Division S	220,000

3.17 SOLUTION TO PART (a)

Part (i)

Begin with a comparison of the existing ROI (which is presumably the typical ROI achieved each year under the current policy of asset replacement) and the ROI with the new investment.

Existing ROI $= (64/220) \times 100\% = 29.1\%$

For the ROI with the new investment it is assumed that the full asset cost of £60,000 should be included in the capital employed, although the asset will obviously be depreciated over time. It is also assumed that the additional profit of £10,000 is net of depreciation charges.

ROI with new investment $= ((64 + 10)/(220 + 60)) \times 100\% = 26.4\%$

If the investment centre manager based his investment decisions on whether an investment would increase or reduce his ROI, he would not want to make the additional investment. This investment has a **marginal ROI** of $(10/60) \times 100\% = 16.7\%$, which is **above the group's cost of capital but below Division S's current ROI** of 29.1%. Making the investment would therefore lower the Division's average ROI.

This example **illustrates the weakness of ROI as a guide to investment decisions.** An investment centre manager might want an investment to show a good ROI from year 1, when the new investment has a high net book value. In the case of Division S, the average net book value of the asset over its full life will be 50% of £60,000 = £30,000, and so the average ROI on the investment over time will be $(£10,000/£30,000) \times 100\% = 33.3\%$.

Presumably, however, the Division S manager would not want to wait so long to earn a good ROI, and wants to protect his division's performance in the short run as well as the long run.

Part (ii)

The question is clearly calling for a recommendation about the investment, and in the absence of full information, two approaches to a solution could be taken.

(a) The investment's year 1 ROI of 16.7% exceeds the group's cost of capital of 15% and so it is likely to be a worthwhile investment.

(b) If we assumed a project life of 5 years, which is the same as the life of the other fixed assets, and a nil residual value, the annual cash flow required to achieve an IRR of 15% would be (using DCF tables) $(£60,000/3.352) = £17,900$ p.a.

The investment would yield an annual profit of £10,000 after depreciation of £12,000 p.a. and so **annual cash profits** would be £22,000. This **exceeds the minimum needed for a 15% yield,** and so the investment should go ahead.

3.18 SOLUTION TO PART (b)

Part (b) of the question deals with a disinvestment proposal, compared to an acquisition in part (a). The same basic principles apply.

The **ROI if the asset is sold** is $((64 - 3.9)/(220 - 24)) \times 100\% = 30.7\%$

This compares favourably with the Division's current average ROI of 29.1%, and so if the manager of Division S made his divestment decisions on the basis of ROI, he would **presumably decide to get rid of the asset.**

However, the decision would be misguided, because **decisions should not be based on the short-term effects on ROI**.

The asset which would be sold earns a ROI of (3.9/24) × 100% = 16.3%, which is higher than the group's cost of capital, but lower than the Division S average.

On the assumption that the asset would earn £3,900 after depreciation for the two remaining years of its life, its ROI next year would be (3.9/12) × 100% = 32.5%.

More importantly, the **cash flows** involved in the decision would be as follows.

Cash profits = £3,900 + £12,000 (depreciation) = £15,900 p.a.

Year	Cash flow	Discount factor	Present value
	£	15%	£
0	(24,000)*	1.000	(24,000)
1 - 2	15,900	1.626	25,853
		NPV	1,853

* Sale price forgone if asset is not sold

The correct decision is not to sell the asset because the NPV is positive.

4   RESIDUAL INCOME (RI)

4.1   An alternative way of measuring the performance of an investment centre, instead of using ROI, is residual income (RI). **Residual income is a measure of the centre's profits after deducting a notional or imputed interest cost**.

- The centre's profit is **after deducting depreciation** on capital equipment.

- The imputed cost of capital might be the organisation's cost of borrowing or its weighted average cost of capital.

> **KEY TERM**
>
> **Residual income (RI)** is 'Pretax profits less an imputed interest charge for invested capital. Used to assess divisional performance'.   (CIMA *Official Terminology*)

Question 4

A division with capital employed of £400,000 currently earns a ROI of 22%. It can make an additional investment of £50,000 for a 5 year life with nil residual value. The average net profit from this investment would be £12,000 after depreciation. The division's cost of capital is 14%.

Required

Calculate the residual income before and after the investment.

Answer

	Before investment	After investment
	£	£
Divisional profit	88,000	100,000
Imputed interest		
(400,000 × 0.14)	56,000	
(450,000 × 0.14)		63,000
Residual income	32,000	37,000

The advantages and weaknesses of RI compared with ROI

4.2 The advantages of using RI

(a) Residual income will **increase** when investments earning above the cost of capital are undertaken and investments earning below the cost of capital are eliminated.

(b) Residual income is **more flexible** since a different cost of capital can be applied to investments with **different risk** characteristics.

4.3 The **weakness** of RI is that it **does not facilitate comparisons** between investment centres nor **does it relate the size of a centre's income to the size of the investment.**

RI versus ROI: marginally profitable investments

4.4 Residual income will increase if a new investment is undertaken which earns a profit in excess of the imputed interest charge on the value of the asset acquired. Residual income will go up even if the investment only just exceeds the imputed interest charge, and this means that 'marginally profitable' investments are likely to be undertaken by the investment centre manager.

In contrast, when a manager is judged by ROI, a marginally profitable investment would be less likely to be undertaken because it would reduce the average ROI earned by the centre as a whole.

4.5 EXAMPLE: RESIDUAL INCOME AND DECISION MAKING

In the previous example in Paragraph 3.15, **whereas ROI would have worsened with the new investment opportunity (part (a)) and improved with the disinvestment (part (b)), residual income would have done the opposite** - improved with the new investment and worsened with the disinvestment.

The figures would be:

(a) *Part (a)*

	Without new investment £	*Investment* £	*With new investment* £
Profit before notional interest	64,000	10,000	74,000
Notional interest (14% of £340,000)	47,600	8,400*	56,000
	16,400	1,600	18,000

* 14% of £60,000

If the manager of Division S were **guided by residual income** into making decisions, he would **approve the new investment.** This happens to **coincide with the recommendation that a DCF analysis** would produce, and so the manager would make the **right decision,** albeit on a less satisfactory basis.

(b) *Part (b)*

	Without disinvestment £	*Disinvestment* £	*With disinvestment* £
Profit before notional interest	64,000	3,900	60,100
Notional interest	47,600	3,360 *	44,240
Residual income	16,400	540	15,860

*14% of £24,000

If the investment centre manager is guided by residual income, he would decide to **keep the asset** instead of selling it off. Again, this would **coincide with the recommendation based on DCF analysis**, and so the investment centre manager would make the **right decision** but for the wrong reason.

4.6 Residual income **does not always point to the right decision,** because notional interest on accounting capital employed is not the same as DCF yield on cash investment. However, residual income is **more likely than ROI to improve when managers make correct investment/divestment decisions,** and so is probably a 'safer' basis than ROI on which to measure performance.

4.7 EXAMPLE: ROI VERSUS RESIDUAL INCOME

Suppose that Department H has the following profit, assets employed and an imputed interest charge of 12% on operating assets.

	£	£
Operating profit	30,000	
Operating assets		100,000
Imputed interest (12%)	12,000	
Return on investment		30%
Residual income	18,000	

Suppose now that an additional investment of £10,000 is proposed, which will increase operating income in Department H by £1,400. The effect of the investment would be:

	£	£
Total operating income	31,400	
Total operating assets		110,000
Imputed interest (12%)	13,200	
Return on investment		28.5%
Residual income	18,200	

If the Department H manager is made responsible for the department's performance, he would **resist the new investment if he were to be judged on ROI**, but would **welcome the investment if he were judged according to RI**, since there would be a marginal increase of £200 in residual income from the investment, but a fall of 1.5% in ROI.

The marginal investment offers a return of 14% (£1,400 on an investment of £10,000) which is above the 'cut-off rate' of 12%. Since the original return on investment was 30%, the marginal investment will reduce the overall divisional performance. Indeed, any marginal investment offering an accounting rate of return of less than 30% in the year would reduce the overall performance.

Conclusion

4.8 Residual income should **not be used as a means of making asset purchasing decisions**; nevertheless, it may be a **useful** alternative to ROI where there is a **conflict between** investment decisions indicated by a **positive NPV** in discounted cash flow, and the **resulting reduction in divisional ROI which 'reflects badly' on management performance.**

Exam focus point

Examination questions on residual income may focus on the sort of behavioural aspects of investment centre measurement that we have discussed above, for example why it is considered necessary to use residual income to measure performance rather than ROI, and why residual income might influence an investment centre manager's investment decisions differently.

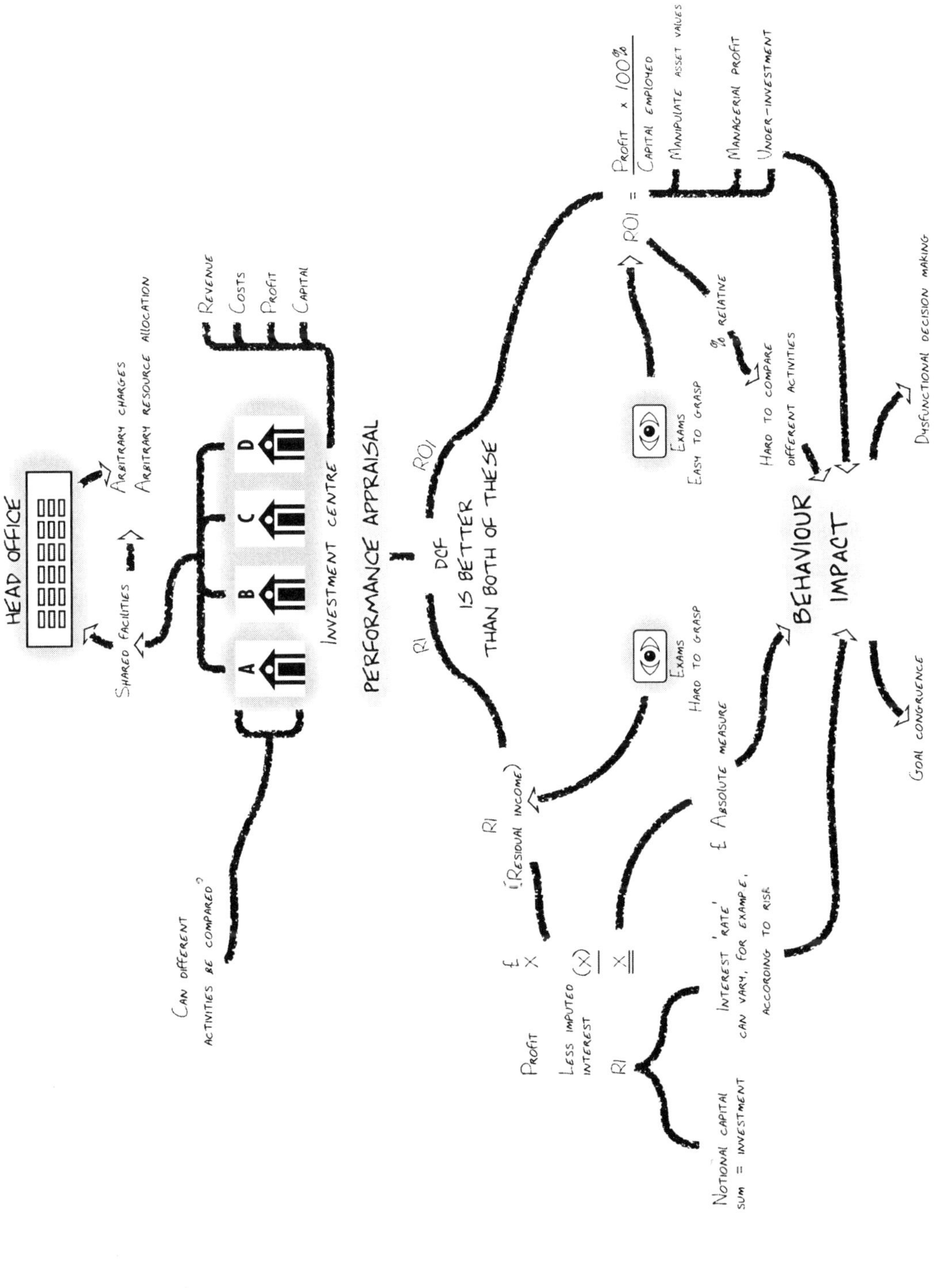

HEAD OFFICE

Arbitrary charges

Arbitrary resource allocation

Shared facilities

Revenue
Costs
Profit
Capital

Investment centre

A B C D

Can different activities be compared?

PERFORMANCE APPRAISAL

RI   DCF   ROI

IS BETTER THAN BOTH OF THESE

RI (Residual income)

Exams   Hard to grasp

£ Absolute measure

Profit   £ X
Less imputed interest   (X)
RI   X

Interest 'rate' can vary, for example, according to risk

Notional capital sum = investment

BEHAVIOUR IMPACT

Goal congruence

ROI

Exams   Easy to grasp

% relative

Hard to compare different activities

$ROI = \dfrac{Profit}{Capital\ employed} \times 100\%$

Manipulate asset values

Managerial profit

Under-investment

Dysfunctional decision making

Chapter roundup

- **Responsibility accounting** is the term used to describe decentralisation of authority, with the performance of the decentralised units measured in terms of accounting results.

- With a system of responsibility accounting there are three types of **responsibility centre: cost centre; profit centre; investment centre**.

- An **investment centre** manager has responsibility for capital investment in the centre.

- There are a number of advantages and disadvantages to **divisionalisation**. The principal disadvantage is that it can lead to dysfunctional decision making and a lack of goal congruence.

- The performance of an investment centre is usually measured as **return on investment (ROI)** or **residual income (RI).**

- There is no generally agreed method of calculating ROI and it can have **behavioural implications** and lead to dysfunctional decision making when used as a guide to investment decisions. It focuses attention on short-run performance whereas investment decisions should be evaluated over their full life.

- RI can sometimes give results that avoid the **behavioural** problem of **dysfunctionality**. Its weakness is that it does not facilitate comparisons between investment centres nor does it relate the size of a centre's income to the size of the investment.

Quick quiz

1   List five advantages of divisionalisation.

2   Over which of the following can an investment centre manager exercise control?

   (a)   Controllable costs in the division
   (b)   Selling prices of the division's output
   (c)   The division's output volumes
   (d)   Investment in the division's fixed assets and working capital

3   What could be the behavioural impact of measuring divisional performance using ROI based on profits as a % of net assets employed?

4   An investment centre with capital employed of £570,000 is budgeted to earn a profit of £119,700 next year. A proposed fixed asset investment of £50,000, not included in the budget at present, will earn a profit next year of £8,500 after depreciation. The company's cost of capital is 15%. What is the budgeted ROI and residual income for next year, both with and without the investment?

	ROI	*Residual income*
Without investment	....	....
With investment	....	....

5   'The use of residual income in performance measurement will avoid dysfunctional decision making because it will always lead to the correct decision concerning capital investments.' True or false?

Answers to quick quiz

1   Better quality decisions; quicker decision-making; motivate divisional managers; free top management from day-to-day decision making; managing a division represents a training opportunity for future senior managers; resource requirements may be less with local operational management

2   All of them

3   ROI measured on this basis will increase as an asset gets older and its book value reduces. Therefore this could create a disincentive to investment centre managers to reinvest in new or replacement assets

4
	ROI	Residual income
Without investment	21.0%	£34,200
With investment	20.7%	£35,200

5   False

Now try the question below from the Exam Question Bank

Number	Level	Marks	Time
18	Examination	25	45 mins

BPP
PUBLISHING

Part D
New developments

Chapter 11

THE HISTORY AND DEVELOPMENT OF MANAGEMENT ACCOUNTING

Topic List		Syllabus reference	Ability required
1	International management accounting issues	(iv)	Discuss
2	A comparison of management and financial accounting	(iv)	Compare and contrast
3	History of management accounting in the West	(iv)	Discuss
4	Developments in management accounting	(iv)	Discuss and evaluate

Introduction

This chapter looks at management accounting **as it is today**, how it has **developed over time** and how it may **develop in the future**.

It starts by considering the **different practices in management accounting today in three key regions of the world**: 'the West', 'Europe' and the Far East. The chapter goes on to compare and contrast management accounting and financial accounting.

The next section looks at the **history of management accounting** and how it has developed in the UK and the West during the last few centuries. Finally **recent developments** in management accounting are considered.

Learning outcomes covered in this chapter

- **Discuss** the history of management accounting

- **Compare and contrast** management accounting and financial accounting

- **Evaluate** management accounting for the modern business environment

- **Discuss** international business developments

- **Discuss** international management accounting issues and developments

Syllabus content covered in this chapter

- Management accounting

- Principles of financial accounting

- History of management accounting

- International business developments

- International management accounting issues and developments

Exam focus point

The examiner has stated that 'there will be no MCQ questions on this section of the syllabus. It will be examined by written/essay questions only'.

KNOWLEDGE BROUGHT FORWARD FROM PAPERS 6, 7 AND 8

This chapter assumes that you are familiar with the purposes of financial accounting: its rules, concepts and reporting framework. Only a general knowledge of the subject is required for the Paper 9 syllabus, rather than a detailed recollection of, for example, UK and International Accounting Standards. You may be required to compare financial and management accounting in terms of approach, standards, etc.

You should also be familiar with the modern business environment, resource planning systems and JIT, which you studied in paper 8.

1 INTERNATIONAL MANAGEMENT ACCOUNTING ISSUES

Introduction

1.1 There is no such thing as a single universal management accounting system, or even a single set of systems. Management accounting systems have developed to suit management styles, organisation structures, production methods, etc., and these in turn are usually dependent on cultural factors. Therefore despite the fact that the world is shrinking as communication systems rapidly improve, management accounting systems still vary from country to country and from industry to industry according to social, political and legal practices.

1.2 These differences in practices can be subtle, social differences or more obvious differences created by government, legal requirements, etc. For example, **the methods of raising finance in the West**, which are based on capital markets, **encourage a greater concentration on standardised** financial measures and diversified organisation structures than, say, the Japanese method which is dominated by the banks. As a consequence management will use particular management accounting practices and measures, geared to suit shareholder requirements, which in turn will influence management decision making and control systems.

1.3 **On the social side**, a study into organisational behaviour in Taiwan and Australia carried out by *Chow et al* (1999) found differences that are consistent with cultural characteristics. A consistent theme emerging from Taiwanese responses was a sense of collective responsibility on the part of business colleagues to share information for the good of the company, even if doing so was potentially disadvantageous for the person concerned. The Australian responses did not show this tendency and the response depended on the personality, management style, etc. of the individual.

1.4 We will now look briefly at some of the major **differences in the management accounting systems of different groups of countries**. The areas chosen are the '**West**', **Europe and the Far East**. The differences depend on historical factors as well as on existing cultural differences.

The 'West'

1.5 This group of countries is led by the **USA** and the **UK,** but it also includes countries such as **Canada, Australia, Sweden, Holland and Switzerland**. The UK has directly influenced Canada and Australia, and the other three countries have big multi-national companies that operate within the 'West's' capital markets. **The management accounting systems used by this group of countries are heavily influenced by financial accounting**; this will become clearer when we discuss the history of management accounting in the 'West' later in the chapter. The dominance of financial accounting in the 'West' during the twentieth century has had a number of effects.

(a) The need to provide a value for stock in the financial accounts has led to a distortion and simplification of costing systems.

    (i) **Overhead absorption methods** have rarely produced accurate product costs.

    (ii) **Distribution, marketing and administration costs have tended to be ignored** and accounted for in aggregate as they cannot be traced to products/stock for financial accounting purposes.

(b) Until recently **service and retail organisations had poor, underdeveloped management accounting systems** because of the financial accounting requirements for stock. As none of the overheads in service and retail organisations were production overheads, they were not traced to cost objects until DPP (direct product profit) was developed in the late 1980s. Financial accounting cannot be blamed for this state of affairs. The blame must be borne by management accountants.

(c) Because of the dominance of financial accounting throughout the twentieth century **there is strong emphasis in the 'West' on** the *financial* control side of management accounting, i.e. **control through variances** on a monthly basis, **as opposed to control** *through operations* which occurs in other parts of the world.

Europe (excluding those countries above)

1.6 France in particular has had a government-regulated system which defines cost and asset categories in terms of rigid numerical codes for financial accounting purposes. This chart of accounts is known as the *Plan Comptable Général (PCG)* and over time it has also developed into a government-specified numerical cost classification for cost accounts. It could be argued that this type of over-regulation for internal purposes, if that is what it is, breeds a particular type of accepting, compliant mind; but this would probably be unfair.

1.7 The code consists of a single number which represents a major category such as fixed assets or purchases and expenses, followed by two digits which represent a more detailed account code describing the item in that category.

1.8 Germany has a broadly similar chart, the *Industrie Kontenrahmen (IKR)* and countries such as Belgium, Italy, Portugal and Spain have adopted a similar (but different) chart of accounts to that of France.

1.9 One of the most striking features of the systems in these countries is that the qualification of 'management accountant' does not always exist.

- Spain has only had a management accounting association (the ACODI) since 1990.
- There is no word in the French language for a management accountant.
- In 'Europe' the work of a management accountant is usually carried out by an individual with an economics or engineering degree.

1.10 This gives internal management accounting a completely different slant and ties it in with systems and operations rather than with accounting. For example, in France the main control mechanism is the *tableau de bord*, which translates as 'a control panel'. **The tableau de bord contains detailed information, much of which is non-financial,** devised in order to control the day to day operations of the organisation. Each organisation will create its own unique system to meet its specific needs.

1.11 The legal requirements for published financial accounts developed rather differently in 'Europe', therefore absorption costing was allowed to develop in a different way. Organisations in **France and Germany**, for example, **have had sophisticated systems for absorbing overheads, very similar to ABC, for about 50 years**. There are **other differences in German practice**.

(a) **It is usual to depreciate assets beyond zero,** i.e. depreciation continues in the cost accounts even though the asset has been fully written down. The continuing depreciation in departmental accounts **influences decision making, as it becomes more advantageous to replace older equipment because it always carries a depreciation charge**.

(b) **Notional interest on capital is charged in the profit and loss account.**

(c) **The profit and loss account is based on output generated** rather than on sales achieved during the period.

(d) **The majority of German companies use a management accounting system based on marginal costing principles**. By comparison, in the UK less than a quarter of companies uses such a system.

(e) **The key performance measures are return on sales, fixed asset productivity and the value of goods produced.**

1.12 These are just some of the major differences between UK systems and those used in the rest of Europe. However, they serve to illustrate how different management accounting concepts and systems can be in different cultures. Therefore it is not easy to **implement a pan-European system**, but many multi-nationals may wish to do so.

1.13 A prerequisite of any system would be to establish data definitions and procedures and a standard set of 'chart of accounts' for all subsidiaries to use. But this may conflict with normal national procedures, both cultural and regulatory. Any management accounting system must suit the local staff who need to use it for planning and control purposes, as well as the management at Head Office who wish to view figures presented in a standard format.

1.14 Recent developments in IT and IS have made it possible today to allow subsidiaries to use their own systems and to change the format for Head Office purposes and for annual reporting.

The Far East

1.15 There are considerable differences in accounting systems in the Far East. Our discussion will consider mainly Japanese systems.

1.16 China is completely different because it is a state-controlled, planned economy. This means that the government influences an organisation's sales income, costs and subsidies. The government fixes labour costs for the year ahead and dictates how much profit can be distributed. As a result it is impossible to isolate which aspects of an organisation's performance are under its own control and which are under the control of the state.

1.17   Chinese financial statements are not split into asset and cash movements and revenue items (balance sheet and profit and loss) as they are in the West.

1.18   The Chinese also use standards for internal purposes but they are changed infrequently, say every two or three years, and so control of production costs is limited.

1.19   Financial accounting systems have not influenced management accounting practices in the Far East to the same extent as in the 'West'. This is because funds have been provided by banks, which are often part of the conglomerate organisation, and they have been prepared to invest for the long-term.

1.20   In Japan an increasing amount of long-term capital is being raised on the stock exchange, but at present there are only about 3,000 quoted companies that are required to prepare financial accounts to comply with Securities and Exchange Law. This means that most **Japanese financial accounts are prepared under the Commercial Code, and are drawn up with taxation in mind** rather than for the benefit of shareholders. This is because companies receive certain tax allowances only if this is done. Although tax requirements have influenced financial accounting practices to some extent in the 'West', the impact in Japan has been much greater. For example, depreciation shown in the accounts is invariably taken to be the maximum allowed under the tax system.

1.21   **Overhead absorption systems** developed in a similar way to the 'West', but for different reasons.

   (a)   They **are often used to influence employee behaviour** as was discussed in chapter 6. (They have also been used for this purpose in the UK but management and management accountants have not always been quite so open about this purpose and have hidden behind the excuse of stock valuation.)

   (b)   In Japan and Korea ROCE and earnings per share are not the key measures that they are in the 'West' because most finance is provided by banks. **The key financial measure is usually return on sales (ROS).**

1.22   **Management accounting systems in Japan developed in quite a different way to the 'West' after the Second World War.**

   (a)   The aim of the Japanese is to learn from the West but to develop their own systems rather than copying the methods of the West.

   (b)   The government has encouraged the success of Japanese companies and has created a regulatory framework to enhance, rather than hinder, that success. As a consequence there has been much more **emphasis on the efficiency of production processes**; and tools such as quality circles and fishbone diagrams have been used for this purpose.

   (c)   **The management accounting techniques that have been developed post war include target costing and value analysis.** Value analysis has been widely used in Japan from the 1950s onwards. In the UK and USA, after early unsuccessful trials (due to misuse), value analysis went out of fashion until more recently.

1.23   **The Japanese use matrices to build up costs**, which were first introduced early in the twentieth century. Matrices are simple **mathematical tableaux** that have an input area, an operative area and an output area. These matrices are building blocks that total to form a product cost. An input, such as material price, may be multiplied by a product material usage given in the operative area and the result written in the output area. For example £2 per kilo x 3 kilos = £6. This output will then appear as an input in the same matrix, or in another, until the product cost is determined.

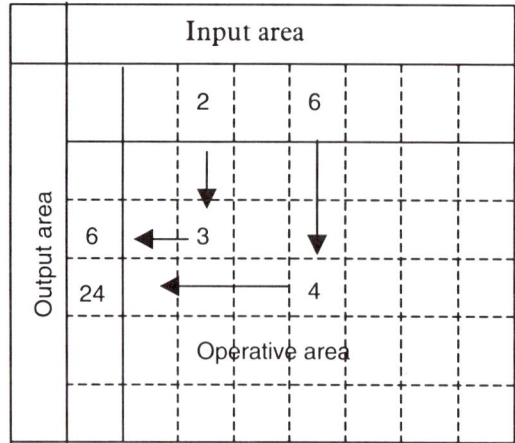

2   A COMPARISON OF MANAGEMENT AND FINANCIAL ACCOUNTING

2.1   In the previous section you learned that management accounting in the USA and UK has been heavily influenced by financial accounting. This has led to an unhealthy over-use of financial information in monthly reporting and a rigid adherence to the financial year as the time period for reporting. It has also encouraged management accountants to use historical costs rather than future predicted costs and to adopt a cautious conservative approach rather than a realistic one.

Over-use of financial information for control purposes

2.2   Events can be measured in terms of cause and effect. The **cause triggers the event and the effect is the consequence or result**. In order to control effectively, 'causes' must be sought for poor performance, and then these causes must be understood and controlled. **It is rarely useful to report only the effect to those who are to do the 'controlling'**. Yet financial information does just this: it reports the effect and not the cause.

2.3   An adverse variance, for example, is the effect of some event, or events, which could be an increase in material price per unit, the inefficient use of materials, the use of a different grade of labour, etc. **A variance does not identify the cause of overspending it simply shows the effect of the variation**. A variance is not always capable of doing even this, as it aggregates data and this can hide or confuse several different 'causes'.

Time period

2.4   **The need to report to shareholders on an annual basis artificially 'chops up' the business into inappropriate time periods**. With hindsight time periods that tie in with economic cycles could be used but these are going to cover periods of, say, five years or longer. They would be of little help for management who are looking to determine future products, markets, etc.

2.5   In reality **a business consists of a series of products/projects which have different start and stop dates,** making the business an ongoing venture. From management's point of view it is often better to consider time periods based on product life cycles and phases. Target costing is one of the new techniques that does not use standard time periods, except when management tie it in to a six-monthly or annual budget. The only advantage that can be put forward in favour of measuring in terms of quarters and years is that **most businesses have seasonal variations which can usefully be monitored and compared on a year to year basis**. The analysis of trends can help management to predict future figures and values.

Cautious, conservative approach

2.6 There is a certain amount of pressure for a company to produce good annual results which improve wherever possible from year to year. This may encourage short-termism and a conservative approach to investing in long-term projects. Most small businesses succeed in growing because their owners are prepared to take risks. Sometimes the risks taken are not successful and the business fails, but if they succeed the business does well and grows. **A manager or owner who is not prepared to take risks will gradually find that the business diminishes relative to the competition.** This is not to say that management should take unreasonable risks or risk everything on a single project.

2.7 **There are two types of risk: business and financial.** It is unusual to expose a business to both types of risk at the same time, but one or other is usually perfectly acceptable. Managers will often be unwilling to take financial risk, such as exchange rate risk, because this is an area in which they do not specialise. They are specialists at running that particular type of business and so they are much more comfortable taking business risks.

2.8 In order to aid management, management accountants must prepare a realistic picture of future events and must be able to cope with expressing risk and uncertainty in financial terms. In contrast financial accounting requires a relatively conservative approach for reporting to external shareholders.

Historical cost

2.9 In the past management accounting has encompassed many techniques which are backward looking and reactive, e.g. variance accounting. Target costing does a similar job but it is a forward looking, proactive technique. Monthly reporting statements are also backward looking and do little to control events: they are too late, and are often given to people who are not directly in a position to control day to day events. Historical cost is rarely useful for planning the future of the organisation or controlling future events.

Regulation

2.10 **Financial reporting/accounting is regulated by means of UK and international accounting standards. Some countries also have a certain amount of regulation for management or cost accounting.** We have already mentioned the standard cost classifications promulgated by the different regulatory authorities in Europe. In Japan the government introduced an act in 1937 called *Manufacturing Cost Accounting Semi-principles*. This was similar to the *Grundplan des Selbstkostenrechnung*, which was published by the German Department of Economic Rationality before the Second World War. The Japanese followed the first Act with *Outlines of Cost Accounting in the Army* (1939) and *Semi-principles of Cost Accounting in the Navy* (1940).

2.11 **These acts expressed principles rather than regulations.** Regulation usually occurs in internal management processes when the government exerts a high degree of control over business. In countries such as Russia and China, where government influence has been strong, areas of company management have been limited and management accounting systems have not developed properly as a result. Furthermore a closed system does not allow outside, foreign influences to penetrate; this occurred in Spain under General Franco. Spanish organisations have had to catch up in terms of management procedures and management accountancy in the last 25 years following the opening up of the country after Franco's death.

3 HISTORY OF MANAGEMENT ACCOUNTING IN THE 'WEST'

Pre-twentieth century

3.1 The Institute of Cost and Works Accountants (now known as CIMA) was formed in 1919. The same year a similar management accounting body was formed in the USA. What cost accounting systems existed before this time? Were there cost accountants before this date?

3.2 **Cost accounting systems definitely existed before the twentieth century,** but our knowledge of them today is limited. This is because the majority of organisations, even today, do not reveal internal processes and do not preserve documents that illustrate their internal workings. However, one or two organisations have preserved their records for hundreds of years, and recently a considerable amount of research has been carried out so that a reasonably detailed picture can be gleaned of cost accounting practices in these organisations.

3.3 On the other hand **cost accountants did not exist** as a separate category of worker prior to the twentieth century. **The owners and clerks of the business kept detailed records, which were the cost accounts, and the owners used these to make decisions about cost and price.**

3.4 Cost accounting has been carried out for many centuries in one form or another. **The earliest records are to be found in the Mediterranean** where clay tablets were used and have been preserved. **Clay tablets** of different sizes, dating from the third millennium BC, have been found in **Mesopotamia. The largest of these acted as accounts, and recorded the production and distribution of various quantities of bread and jars of beer** rationed to various people. **Budgets and actual data over several years were recorded on these tablets,** according to *Mattessich* (1998). Some foremen had been given budgets, which they exceeded. This may indicate tight budgeting based on standards because **norms based on, say, female labour days for milling grain were formulated and adhered to.** Any labour deficits were charged to the foreman, who had to pay himself. On occasions his house was forfeit: a drastic penalty for exceeding the budget! **Other tablets appear to show the planned growth in a herd of cows over a period of ten years.** The plan included expected quantities for calves, bulls, dairy fat and cheese.

3.5 *The Hudson Bay Trading Company* was formed by royal charter in Charles II's reign in order to trade around the Hudson Bay area of North America. Their archives run from 1670 to 1914 and include much interesting information. The company **kept accounts to determine the cost of furs acquired from each district so that a profit per district could be calculated.** A memorandum written in 1843 by *Edward Roberts* describes the purpose of the accounting records. He stated that the profitability of the different districts indicated the 'merit' of managers. This shows that from an early stage **cost accounting information was being used to cost products and to assess the performance of managers.** A use which middle managers are constantly aware of today but which top management constantly tend to deny.

3.6 *The Hudson Bay Trading Company's* records show that **profits were calculated by using past costs** and purchase prices of furs **compared with actual prices** obtained from the sale and auction of the furs in England. The sale could occur between six months and two years after their acquisition in Canada. **A cash budgeting system had to be used,** based on stocks held, in order to assess the finance necessary to cover the large inventory holding. Once a train system was established in Canada in 1885 the stock-holding period dropped to three months, and no doubt cash flow was considerably improved.

3.7 **By 1823 the recording of actual costs had become so onerous that an average or standard cost was used.** Apparently very few of the company's clerks were sufficiently competent to go into the 'necessary fractional calculations with accuracy' and so standard costs were adopted in order to 'simplify and facilitate the business'. This meant that a **standard transport cost was charged based on the distance of the trading district from the Canadian port.** By 1880 these standard costs had caused a problem; the prices of some products were out of line with those offered by competitors and the standards had to be reconsidered.

3.8 *The Boulton and Watts Soho Foundry* was another famous business for which records still survive. The business was founded in Birmingham in 1775 by *James Watt*, who invented an efficient steam engine, and *Matthew Boulton*, a manufacturer of metal ornaments. **By 1794 the business consisted of a Foundry which had three departments**: the foundry itself which cast the engines, a smithy which manufactured parts in wrought iron and a fitting department which fitted parts together. **There was also the Manufactory that assembled the engines** to the specific requirements of customers. **Both parts of the business were expected to make a profit** and the Foundry could take on outside work to increase its profit. **The different departments were also treated as profit centres and transfer prices were used** when goods were transferred between the departments.

3.9 **Originally *Boulton and Watt* charged a yearly premium for their engines rather than setting a single selling price.** The premium was one-third of the savings in coal usage that resulted from the use of their efficient engine over the old atmospheric stream engine. The premium was based on the number of stokes the engine made, which was recorded on a counter developed by *Watts*. Spare parts were paid for separately. By the 1790s the customer could pay for the machine outright. **The price was equivalent to five years' premium. Cost records show that this was very similar to a price based on cost plus 50%.** Later, due to competition, the price was modified to cost plus 40% for London customers and cost plus 33% for customers in the rest of the country. **Costs were determined on a type of standard cost system.** There was a standard cost for a standard type of machine and costs were added or subtracted according to the specific parts required in the specification of the particular machine.

3.10 According to *Johnson and Kaplan*, Lyman Mills, a USA textile company operating in the 1850s **had developed quite a sophisticated system for apportioning overheads**, using bases such as the horsepower of water turbines, the number of looms and floor space. The system developed so that by the 1880s a full absorption costing system for overheads was in place. Many businesses in the UK seem to have developed similar systems by the end of the nineteenth century.

3.11 Therefore by the time the twentieth century dawned a number of companies in the UK were using quite sophisticated costing systems which included a number of basic methods and techniques.

- Standard costing
- Budgets and cash budgets
- Overhead absorption costing systems
- Systems for assessing the performance of individuals
- Systems for pricing

The twentieth century and the influence of the USA

3.12 **The USA became the dominant creative force in management accounting techniques for most of the twentieth century.** The rise of giant organisations such as *Du Pont* and *General Motors* made it necessary to develop new cost accounting techniques. For example, it appears that **ROI was first used** at *Du Pont* **in the first decade of the twentieth century.** **Flexible budgets were first introduced** at *General Motors* **in the 1920s.** The key problem facing management in these large organisations was to manage them from the centre but at the same time to develop responsibility systems that allowed the lower levels of management to run day to day affairs.

3.13 **By the 1920s,** following the introduction of legislation to control published accounts, **financial accounting had become the dominant influence on recording systems in the USA and UK.** This meant that **company recording systems were set up to provide information for financial accounting,** rather than information that would help management run the business. Because the cost accounting information drawn from cost accounts was now proving inadequate for decision-making purposes, there was a sort of academic backlash against this during the 1930s.

3.14 **A group of economists** at the *London School of Economics* **suggested that opportunity costs should be used in cost accounting for decision-making.** A decade later, *William Vatter* at the University of Chicago suggested that **only relevant costs should be used when making decisions.**

3.15 By the 1940s, therefore, all the short-term decision-making techniques used today were in place. But **until the advent of advanced IT techniques it was impossible to provide a variety of information systems.** This meant that cost accounts continued in their traditional form and if other information was needed it had to be obtained on an ad hoc basis.

3.16 This was costly and took time; as a consequence managers sometimes made do with the existing information. Management probably knew that the information they were using was inadequate but that did not always matter as **figures are often used not so much to make the decision but as a means to justify the decision after the event.** If the decision proves wrong the manager only needs to produce the figures and say "I made the decision on the basis of these" to safeguard his position. Furthermore it would be very unsettling to have to admit that the figures being produced by the system were not adequate for decision-making.

3.17 Therefore management as a group did not face up to the problem. *E. Devons* (1970), writing about the *British Air Ministry* in the 1950s, suggested that there was self-deception in the Ministry and that figures were used as a justification of actions. He was writing about an organisation that knowingly made decisions based on faulty figures due to poor or incorrect collection techniques. The data was collected and processed by inexperienced junior staff, who were incapable of the job. But the same principle could be applied to an inadequate system that did not provide the figures required. Devons said that **'figures gave the processes by which decisions were reached, an apparent air of scientific rationality'** and that **'to have recognised the inadequacy of the figures would have meant admitting that policy decisions were not being taken on a rational basis'.** It seems that it may have been too difficult for an individual to suggest that the figures were inadequate or for the management team as a group to admit it.

3.18 **The words 'management accounting' were first used in 1950.** At that time it was recognised that management accounting encompassed two areas: planning the future of the business and controlling day to day operations. But the new terminology made little difference to the nature of the work or to practising cost or management accountants.

3.19 There were, however, two major developments during the 1950s that were to have far reaching consequences. The first was the **introduction of mathematical and statistical models**. These arrived under the guise of **operations research**, which was developed in the UK by a group of mathematicians and physicists. The models work by singling out an area of business operations and viewing it in isolation. This technique may help to simplify the problem so that the human mind can cope with it, but it assumes that a small area of the business operates independently from the rest.

3.20 This is clearly faulty reasoning and has been shown to be erroneous over and over again. For example the creator of the model may select two dependent items to consider, but may hold all parameters and other items constant. For instance, if a decision is to be made concerning the optimum production batch size, set up costs are assumed to be fixed i.e. unchangeable. This is clearly untrue, as many of the organisations that have employed JIT have found that set-up costs reduce very quickly, and ways of reducing set-up time are sought under management pressure.

3.21 The second major development in the 1950s was **the introduction of discounted cash flow** that was first discussed by *Joel Dean* in 1954. There is no doubt that this was a major development, and a timely one, because **investment in machinery and equipment was becoming a major cost** for most businesses as labour decreased in importance. It also provided a 'nice little model' or set of figures on which management could hang the responsibility for making investment decisions.

3.22 Perhaps it is unfair to make the generalisation that during the 1960s top management became divorced from the day to day operations of the business and no longer had hands-on control. But this is how it appears: they seem to have managed through figures rather than by face to face contact. This had the effect of allowing middle managers to build in budgetary and process slack and to devise schemes for making figures, or ratios, look good.

3.23 For example, if annual production targets had been met by the end of month 11, in month 12 production would not be acknowledged as finished goods stock and not released for sale until the following year.

3.24 A technique which is not so widely used today, **zero based budgeting (ZBB), was introduced in the 1970s** to try to cope with, and correct, the creation of slack. Again it was 'managing through figures'. It required a budget to be justified from scratch on each occasion. Therefore a manager could not assume that because he had a department of ten staff, who all appeared to be doing useful work, this situation would continue in the following year. He had to justify the position in financial terms and bid for scarce funds in a contest with other managers. Naturally this was a very time consuming procedure and although it was taken up quite widely in the USA, and to some extent in the UK, it did not remain popular for very long. It could argued that ZBB was yet another set of figures for top management to hide behind when making awkward decisions about the future of the organisation.

3.25 This was also the decade when five-year corporate plans, that were almost as detailed as the annual budget, were produced. They caused a reduction of flexibility in planning and resulted in mountains of paperwork.

BPP PUBLISHING

4   DEVELOPMENTS IN MANAGEMENT ACCOUNTING   Pilot paper

4.1   During the 1980s global competition grew and companies were forced to reconsider their strategies for gaining competitive advantage. Many companies identified that **meeting customer needs was paramount**. This meant two things.

- Meeting customer requirements in terms of quality and features
- Meeting customer needs as quickly as possible.

4.2   Systems such as **value analysis** and **total quality management** were developed to help achieve the first requirement. The second requirement was met by creating **fast cycle systems**. This meant adopting **JIT techniques** and introducing computer systems to relay orders placed with retail outlets to manufacturing as quickly as possible.

4.3   Management information systems should always be developed to suit the particular business. If a JIT system was to be used the management information systems needed to change because control information had to be immediate. This did not necessarily mean a more complicated system. Sometimes systems were simplified as production scheduling was simplified. Management accounting systems also had to change and a simpler system, such as backflush accounting, could be introduced.

4.4   In 1987 *George Staubus* wrote an excellent article in *The Accounting Historians Journal* entitled 'The Dark Ages of Cost Accounting'. Its main thrust makes rather depressing reading. He made two assertions.

(a)   The concept of cost itself is unclear

(b)   **The conceptual and theoretical development of cost accounting has been at a standstill for several decades** despite considerable changes in the environment that should have warranted changes in costing systems and methods.

4.5   *Staubus* started his paper with a quote from *J. M. Clark* (1923): 'We may start with the general proposition that the terminology of costs is in a state of much confusion ..' Today, **at the beginning of the twenty-first century**, not a lot has changed; we are **scarcely further on conceptually** than at the start of the twentieth century. If we could remove the developments that improvements in IT and IS have allowed us to make, we would find that the world of cost accounting did not change a great deal during the twentieth century. Yet throughout most of the last century, until the mid-1980s, hardly a word was said expressing dissatisfaction with this sad, static state of affairs.

4.6   In 1987 *Johnson and Kaplan* asked the question **"What have management accounting practitioners been doing for the past sixty years?"** One would like to imagine that they had been so busy developing new concepts and systems that they had had no time to write them up. But there is no evidence of this. *Johnson and Kaplan* were the first writers to make the majority of management accountants aware of the stagnation and inadequacies of the profession. As a result a number of new techniques suddenly appeared, some of which have been discussed in earlier chapters including ABC, DPP and throughput accounting. However a strong body of accountants is still murmuring 'the emperor's new clothes', and none of the really basic issues have been fully addressed.

4.7   Staubus identified four issues that he felt illustrated the stagnation of cost accounting in the twentieth century. They were much discussed early in the twentieth century but were left unresolved at that time and they still remain to haunt us today. Here are the four issues he raised.

(a) **The historical/current cost issue.** This affects the issue price of materials. Should it be original cost or replacement value? If we assume that JIT systems are now employed by the majority of manufacturing organisations, and that the majority of organisations are now service businesses, this issue becomes of little consequence.

(b) **The average/variable cost issue.** This is still an important issue throughout the world. It has been much discussed in recent years because of the appearance of throughput accounting (variable costing) and ABC (average cost) which have also been used to make decisions. The use of both techniques in the same organisation may help the organisation to make sound decisions, assuming that the right technique is used at the right time. However this does not address the academic issues.

(c) **The allocation issue.** Academics remain largely opposed to any sort of allocation or absorption method yet it is widely used in practice. The widespread adoption of ABC speaks for itself, but this may be a variation on the average/variable cost argument.

(d) **The cost of capital issue.** In the UK the cost of capital is rarely included in cost accounts, and its exclusion is always assumed and never justified today. Yet at the beginning of the twentieth century there was much debate on the issue in the UK and the cost of capital was widely incorporated in profit statements. The cost of capital is used in other countries, such as Germany.

4.8 However, this is Staubus' most telling criticism.

'But what is the modern cost accountant's and cost-accounting textbook writer's **excuse for accepting the linear view of cost behaviour**? As far as I know, the curvilinear view of marginal cost, subject to various shapes, is generally accepted now. There is no justification for general acceptance of a costing method that is based on the assumption that marginal cost is materially below average cost. And if variable costing does not rest on that assumption, on what does it rest? **On the whole, the direct costing literature is now a handicap to the development of cost accounting**. A linear view of cost behaviour and great emphasis on the cost of data processing are out of date.'

4.9 Modern computer technology can cope with complicated, non-linear cost behaviour but most organisations still adhere to the linear view. Why is this? Is forecasting so inaccurate that only very crude cost behaviour patterns need to be considered? Perhaps management accountants should not worry unduly about academic issues and concentrate on providing the information required by management on the grounds that perceived need is sufficient justification?

Future developments

4.10 Following *Johnson and Kaplan's* series of articles and books in the mid-1980s a number of new techniques have appeared and the next ten years may well be a period of consolidation.

(a) The rapid improvement in IT and IS systems has allowed management accountants to develop information for specific users rather than producing broad general statements which are supposed to suit all needs.

(b) Management accounting statements cover a broader range of information and cope with a number of different time periods (target and life cycle costing).

(c) The range of data has increased. It is no longer purely internal information and some external information is included.

(d) Traditional systems were devised mainly for product costing, but now systems provide information on a range of cost objects, including customers (customer profitability analysis).

4.11 *Bjørnenak and Olsen* (1999) wrote "Traditional management accounting has primarily functioned as one integrated co-ordinated system. ...new ideas have expanded the co-ordinating role, but also exploited the roles of supporting operational and strategic processes. This development shows that management accounting has adapted to the idea that **different organisational contexts have different criteria of information relevance,** and this has changed the view of how management accounting systems are being used."

Chapter roundup

- Management accounting systems **differ throughout the world** and are influenced by **cultural and political factors**.

- In the 'West' **financial accounting has had a strong influence on the development of management accounting**, for example the absorption rates used and variance analysis.

- Most countries in 'Europe' operate a **chart of accounts**.

- Most French companies use a *tableau de bord* for day to day control purposes. Most German companies use **marginal costing**.

- Japanese companies draw up financial accounts in order to **minimise tax payments**. The government has facilitated company success. Many Japanese companies **use matrices for recording cost information**.

- There are considerable **differences in the approach required for financial and management accounting**.

- The first cost accounting systems date from around 3000 BC. Many companies used quite **sophisticated recording and costing systems** by the 18th and 19th centuries, which included standard costing, budgets, overhead absorption methods and performance measures.

- **The 20th century was dominated by developments introduced in large organisations in the USA**. ROI, flexible budgets, opportunity and relevant costs were developed in the first half of the century. The second half saw the development of a number of techniques including discounted cash flow, operations research, zero-based budgeting, JIT, target costing, ABC and throughput costing.

- Despite the developments during the 20th century many issues still remain to be resolved, and the discipline needs to move forward on both fronts: academic and practical.

Quick quiz

Identify whether the statements below are true or false

1 Companies in the UK use similar management accounting systems to those used in Germany.

2 The majority of German companies use absorption costing.

3 Cost accounting systems were first introduced early in the 20th century, with the formation of the first professional, management accounting bodies.

4 Management accounting statements that predict future costs and revenues should be produced using a conservative approach.

5 Standard costing was 'invented' in the 1920s.

6 The development of IT has allowed companies to use data in a number of different management accounting systems.

Answers to quick quiz

1　False – generally they are quite different.

2　False – the majority of companies use marginal costing.

3　False – costing systems were used in 3000 BC.

4　False – a realistic approach is needed.

5　False – it dates back to the 19th century, and possibly earlier.

6　True – without IT the work involved was too onerous.

Now try the questions below from the Exam Question Bank

Number	Level	Marks	Time
19	Introductory	n/a	n/a
20	Examination (pilot)	25	45 mins

BPP PUBLISHING

Exam question bank

1   BACKLOG   *45 mins*

You are employed as the administration manager of Weeble Ltd, a medium-sized software consulting and development house. A backlog of software development work has built up due to staff turnover and sickness and the partners have decided it must be cleared. It will require 2,000 software development staff hours to clear the backlog.

Three alternatives have been suggested.

(a) Cancel a development job which is estimated to need a further 2,500 hours work. It would produce a fee income of £47,000 if completed. There is no cancellation penalty clause in the contract. This action would release sufficient staff to clear the backlog within three months.

(b) Sub-contract 2,000 hours of development work to another firm at an estimated fee cost of £35,000.

(c) Employ four extra temporary staff for the next three months.

Set out below is some additional information.

(a) Software development staff are employed at an average salary of £25,000 pa and produce about 2,000 hours work pa each. Employment taxes and employers' pension contributions add a further 25% to salary costs.

(b) When pricing work for clients Weeble Ltd usually add 80% to estimated staff costs to cover overheads and profit.

(c) If the work were to be sub-contracted a senior consultant would need to spend about 80 hours overseeing the contract. Consultants work about 2,000 hours per year at an employment cost of £75,000 pa. Their time is usually charged to clients at £100 per hour.

(d) Temporary staff would be paid for the hours they work at £15 per hour. No pension contributions would be payable by Weeble Ltd.

(e) Employment tax is payable in respect of temporary staff at 15% of salary.

(f) Recruitment costs for the temporary staff (agency fees and interview expenses) are likely to be £750 each.

(g) Four extra personal computers would be needed at a cost of £2,000 each if temporary staff were employed. Their second-hand value after the work has been completed is expected to be £1,500 each. They would have a four-year life if kept. Alternatively computers could be leased for £750 per quarter each.

(h) Weeble Ltd are located in open plan offices on the third and fourth floors of a six-storey office block at a rental cost of £200 per square metre per annum. Each floor comprises 400 square metres. If temporary staff were employed forty square metres of extra space would be needed. This could be obtained by transferring the contents of 20 large filing cabinets to CD ROM at a total cost of £1,300. The cabinets could then be sold for £20 each. An alternative would be to rent a spare office (which has an area of fifty square metres) on the fifth floor of the same building for three months at a rental cost of £1,500 per quarter.

(i) Heating and lighting costs in the office block average £50 per square metre per annum and are not included in the rent.

(j) Weeble Ltd have sufficient spare desks and chairs in store for the temporary staff. This furniture was bought two years ago at a total cost of £3,000 and now has a second hand value of £1,500. It is partnership policy to depreciate furniture at 10% of cost per annum.

REQUIREMENTS:

(a) Advise the management which option is the most cost effective. Show your calculations. **10 Marks**

(b) For each of the 'costs' (a) to (j) above, explain why you decided to include it in or exclude it from your calculations for part (a).   **12 Marks**

(c) Describe non-cost factors which would be relevant when considering the three options.   **3 Marks**

Total Marks = 25

2   CERAMICS COMPANY (Pilot)

D runs a ceramics company that employs twenty staff. The employees work a basic 40-hour week for 48 weeks a year, and are paid on an hourly basis. The average wage per hour is £10.42. The fixed costs for the pottery total £30,000 per annum.

The company makes tableware and tiles. A set of tableware sells for £50. The costs per set are:

	£
Direct materials	10
Direct labour	10
Variable overheads	10

Tiles sell for £200 per 100 tiles and the costs per hundred are:

	£
Direct materials	20
Direct labour	50
Variable overhead	50

The normal sales mix is 600 tiles to 20 sets of tableware. In most years the company works close to normal capacity, but at present the business is operating at 60 per cent of capacity. Because of this, D has assigned two members of staff to refurbish the pottery showroom, which should take them eight weeks to complete. He has also recently agreed to redecorate and tile the changing rooms and surround of the local swimming pool. This is a charitable work and should take three of D's staff half a year to complete. However, D has since been offered two large contracts, which he bid for a few months ago.

Fish-and-chip shops contract

The first contract is from a company that owns a chain of upmarket fish-and-chip shops. The company needs tiles for five new fish-and-chip shops that it is about to open. D has heard from a reliable source that the company plans to open a further 30 new shops over the next two or three years. The tiles for the five shops are required in six months' time, and each shop will require 20,000 tiles at the normal selling price less 5 per cent. £190   100,000

Z plc contract

£42·50

The second potential contract is from a department store, Z plc, which requires 40,000 sets of pastel coloured tableware in one year's time. This may lead to further annual orders from Z plc. D has already produced designs for the product, which the company has agreed; D reckons that this took £2,500 of his time. The price agreed per set is the normal price less 15 per cent quantity discount. If he accepts the contract he will need to have the moulds made, which will cost £15,000. In order to complete this contract a considerable amount of production space is required to store and dry the moulds and to store the completed goods ready for despatch in one year's time.

D owns a warehouse adjacent to the pottery. This warehouse is leased to another business on an annual basis at a rental of £10,000 per annum. Fortunately, the lease is due for renewal this month and D could use the warehouse to complete the large contract for Z plc. He estimates that its use would cost him £3,000 in extra fixed operating costs per annum.

Staffing and capacity information

D has no difficulty in recruiting staff as required, but he feels that he could not absorb more than eight new employees in the coming year. Recruitment costs are £500 per employee. He also has little difficulty in getting staff to work six hours' overtime per week at 150 per cent of their normal rate of pay. However, they could only work at this level for half of the 48 weeks worked per annum.

If D accepted either job he could stop the two members of staff decorating the showroom and hire a contractor, which would cost £5,000. If he brought the three staff back from the work on the swimming pool he would feel obliged to make a donation of £35,000 which would pay for a contractor to finish the work. Twenty-five per cent of the pottery's output each year is made up of new one-off orders from small outlets. D feels that, if he wished to do other, more profitable, work, he could stop supplying these customers without long-term detriment to his business.

REQUIREMENTS:

(a) Produce calculations that show whether the contracts are feasible and profitable. Where appropriate, explain your reasoning, and the figures in your calculations.   **23 Marks**

(b) Recommend, with reasons, whether D should accept either or both of the contracts. Describe the longer-term implications of the actions you recommend.   **7 Marks**

Total Marks = 30

3   **DIFFERENT METHODS**   *45 mins*

A distribution and marketing organisation sells three products named A, B and C in two areas which are designated as Area 1 and Area 2. The information given below is for 20X0.

	Product A	Product B	Product C
Selling price per unit	£40	£48	£60
Purchase price per unit	£32	£36	£44

Sales, in units

	Product A	Product B	Product C
Area 1	92,000	40,000	28,000
Area 2	30,000	40,000	40,000

	Product A	Product B	Product C
Number of orders			
Area 1	40,000	20,000	10,000
Area 2	6,000	10,000	8,000
Volume in cubic metres per unit	2.0	1.5	1.0

	Variable	Fixed	Basis of apportionment
Costs	£'000	£'000	
Selling	188	376	Number of orders
Warehousing/distribution	432	648	Volume sold
Advertising	270	540	Units sold
Administration	64	256	Sales value

REQUIREMENTS:

(a) Prepare a budget for 20X0 showing the profit or loss for each area and in total, using absorption costing.   **10 Marks**

(b) Prepare a budget for Area 1 only, using marginal costing and showing relevant information for each product and the total profit or loss for that area.

8 Marks

(c) Comment on the result shown in your answer to (b) above and suggest action which management ought to take.   **7 Marks**

Total Marks = 25

4   **AB LTD**   *54 mins*

AB Ltd produces a consumable compound X, used in the preliminary stage of a technical process that it installs in customers' factories worldwide. An overseas competitor, CD, offering an alternative process which uses the same preliminary stage, has developed a new compound, Y, for that stage which is both cheaper in its ingredients and more effective than X.

At present, CD is offering Y only in his own national market, but it is expected that it will not be long before he extends its sales overseas. Both X and Y are also sold separately to users of the technical process as a replacement for the original compound that eventually loses its strength. This replacement demand amounts to 60% of total demand for X and would do so for Y. CD is selling Y at the same price as X (£64.08 per kg).

AB Ltd discovers that it would take 20 weeks to set up a production facility to manufacture Y at an incremental capital cost of £3,500 and the comparative manufacturing costs of X and Y would be:

	X	Y
	£ per kg	£ per kg
Direct materials	17.33	4.01
Direct labour	7.36	2.85
	24.69	6.86

AB Ltd normally absorbs departmental overhead at 200% of direct labour: 30% of this departmental overhead is variable directly with direct labour cost. Selling and administration overhead is absorbed at one-half of departmental overhead.

The current sales of X average 74 kgs per week and this level (whether of X or of Y if it were produced) is not expected to change over the next year. Because the direct materials for X are highly specialised, AB Ltd has always had to keep large stocks in order to obtain supplies. At present, these amount to £44,800 at cost. Its stock of finished X is £51,900 at full cost. Unfortunately, neither X nor its raw materials have any resale value whatsoever: in fact, it would cost £0.30 per kg to dispose of them.

Over the next three months AB Ltd is not normally busy and, in order to avoid laying off staff, has an arrangement with the trade union whereby it pays its factory operators at 65% of their normal rate of pay for the period whilst they do non-production work. AB Ltd assesses that it could process all its relevant direct materials into X in that period, if necessary.

There are two main options open to AB Ltd:

(a) to continue to sell X until all its stocks of X (both of direct materials and of finished stock) are exhausted, and then start sales of Y immediately afterwards;

(b) to start sales of Y as soon as possible and then to dispose of any remaining stocks of X and/or its raw materials.

REQUIREMENTS:

(a) Recommend with supporting calculations, which of the two main courses of action suggested is the more advantageous from a purely cost and financial point of view. **16 Marks**

(b) Identify three major non-financial factors that AB Ltd would need to consider in making its eventual decision as to what to do. **6 Marks**

(c) Suggest one other course of action that AB Ltd might follow, explaining what you consider to be its merits and demerits when compared with your answer at (a) above. **8 Marks**

Total Marks = 30

5 **SCIENTO PRODUCTS LIMITED** *23 mins*

Sciento Products Limited manufactures complex electronic measuring instruments for which highly skilled labour is required. Conventional standard costing has been used for some time but problems have been experienced in setting realistic standards for labour costs.

Analysis of production times has shown that there is a learning curve effect on the labour time required to manufacture each unit and it has been decided to allow for this in establishing standard times and in the subsequent variance analysis. Records have been kept of the production times for the electronometer, an extract of which follows.

Cumulative production	Cumulative time	Average time per unit
Units	Hours	Hours
1	200	200.0
2	360	180.0
4	648	162.0
8	1,166	145.8

The labour time analyses have shown that the learning curve follows the general form $y = ax^b$

where y = average labour hours per unit   x = cumulative number of units
       a = number of labour hours for first unit   b = the learning index

During period 11 the following data were recorded.

Cumulative production at start of period	528 units
Production in period	86 units

Budgeted and standard cost data for electronometers are as follows.

Budgeted production	86 units
Budgeted overheads	£150,903
Standard labour cost	£10 per hour
Standard material cost per unit	£250

REQUIREMENTS:

(a) Calculate a total standard cost for electronometers. **7 Marks**
(b) Discuss the usefulness of allowing for the learning effect in establishing labour standards. **6 Marks**

Total Marks = 13

6 PARADOX

'The paradox is that, while cost plus pricing is devoid of any theoretical justification, it is widely used in practice.'

Discuss possible justifications for its use.

7 TWO COMPANIES

A group has two companies, K Ltd, which is operating at just above 50% capacity and L Ltd, which is operating at full capacity (7,000 production hours).

L Ltd produces two products, X and Y, using the same labour force for each product. For the next year its budgeted capacity involves a commitment to the sale of 3,000 kg of Y, the remainder of its capacity being used on X. Direct costs of these two products are as follows.

	X		Y	
	£ per kg		£ per kg	
Direct materials	18		14	
Direct wages	15	(1 production hour)	10	(^{2}/3 production hour)

The company's overhead is £126,000 per annum relating to X and Y in proportion to their direct wages. At full capacity £70,000 of this overhead is variable. L Ltd prices its products with a 60% mark-up on its total costs.

For the coming year, K Ltd wishes to buy from L Ltd 2,000 kg of product X which it proposes to adapt and sell, as product Z, for £100 per kg. The direct costs of adaptation are £15 per kg. K Ltd's total fixed costs will not change, but variable overhead of £2 per kg will be incurred.

REQUIREMENTS:

As group management accountant, make the following recommendations.

(a) The range of transfer prices, if any, at which 2,000 kg of product X should be sold to K Ltd

(b) The other points that should be borne in mind when making any recommendations about transfer prices in the above circumstances

8 SINGLE PRODUCT

The following details relate to a manufacturing organisation which produces a single product whose list price is £1.20 per unit. The organisation sells to five different customers: A, B, C, D and E. The figures below relate to a particular month.

	A	B	C	D	E
Items sold to customer	25,000	100,000	750,000	350,000	50,000
Discount allowed	-	1%	5%	3%	5%
No. of sales visits	2	5	5	2	4
No. of orders	15	26	30	24	30
No. of deliveries	12	30	70	30	15
Kilometres per delivery	20	5	5	15	10
No of rush orders	-	-	2	-	1

Activities costs	£
Sales visits	2,400
Order taking	10,000
Delivery	14,400
Product handling	20,000
Rush orders	900

REQUIREMENTS:

(a) Calculate:

(i) the net gain per customer for the month, and
(ii) the net gain per unit sold for each customer.

(b) What information would you need when making a decision about whether to cease supplying a particular customer?

9   ABC

(a) It is sometimes claimed that activity based costing (ABC) simply provides a *different* picture of product costs to traditional absorption costing, rather than a more accurate picture.

Explain the concepts that underlie ABC and discuss the claim above.

(b) Some advocates of ABC claim that it provides information which can be used for decision making. Critically appraise this view.

10   RS PLC (Pilot)   *45 mins*

RS plc is a retail organisation. It has fifteen supermarkets, all of which are the same size. Goods are transported to RS plc's central warehouse by suppliers' vehicles, and are stored at the warehouse until needed at the supermarkets - at which point they are transported by RS plc's lorries.

RS plc's costs are:

	£'000
Warehouse costs, per week	
Labour costs	220
Refrigeration costs	160
Other direct product costs	340
	720
Head office costs, per week	
Labour costs	80
Other costs	76
	156
Supermarket costs, per week	
Labour costs	16
Refrigeration costs	24
Other direct product costs	28
	68

Transport costs per trip	£
Standard vehicles	3,750
Refrigerated vehicles	4,950

The company has always used retail sales revenue less bought-in price to calculate the relative profitability of the different products. However, the chief executive is not happy with this method and has asked for three products – baked beans, ice cream and South African white wine – to be costed on a direct product profit basis. The accountant has determined the following information for the supermarket chain.

	Baked beans	Ice cream	White wine
No of cases per cubic metre (m³)	28	24	42
No of items per case	80	18	12
Sales per week – items	15,000	2,000	500
Time in warehouse – weeks	1	2	4
Time in supermarket – weeks	1	2	2
Retail selling price per item	£0.32	£1.60	£3.45
Bought-in price per item	£0.24	£0.95	£2.85

Additional information:

Total volume of all goods sold per week	20,000 m³
Total volume of refrigerated goods sold per week	5,000 m³
Carrying volume of each vehicle	90 m³
Total sales revenue per week	£5m
Total sales revenue of refrigerated goods per week	£650,000

REQUIREMENTS:

(a)   Calculate the profit per item using the direct product profitability method.   **13 marks**

(b)   Discuss the differences in profitability between the company's current method and the results of your calculations in (a), and suggest ways in which profitability could be improved.   **7 marks**

(c)   Explain how the direct product profit method differs from traditional overhead absorption. **5 marks**

Total Marks = 25

11   **RESOURCES AND PROFITABILITY**   *45 mins*

(a)   'ABC systems are *resource-consumption models.* That is, they attempt to measure the cost of *using* resources, not the cost of *supplying* resources.'

Colin Drury, *Management Accounting Business Decisions*

Required

Discuss the statement above using figures, if you wish, to illustrate the points made.

14 marks

(b)

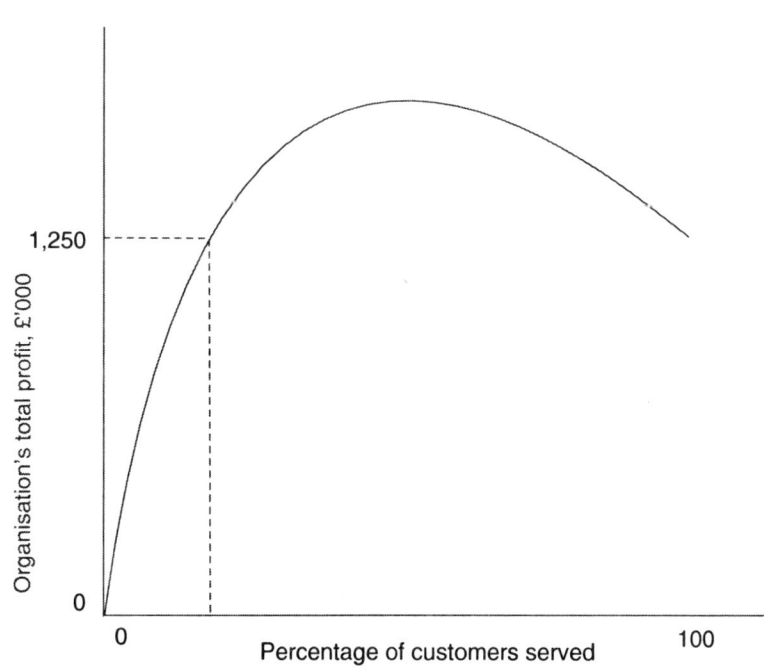

REQUIREMENTS:

As the management accountant of XY Ltd you have undertaken an analysis of the company's profitability in relation to the number of customers served. The results of your analysis are shown in the graph above. Write a report to management which:

(i)   explains the general concept that is encapsulated by the graph   **4 marks**

ii)   advises management on the actions that are open to it to improve the profitability of the organisation.   **7 marks**

Total Marks = 25

12   WAQ PLC

WAQ plc produces a single product, X, which passes through three different processes, A, B and C. The throughput per hour of the three processes is 12, 10 and 15 units of X respectively. The company works an 8-hour day, 6 days a week, 48 weeks a year. The selling price of X is £150 per unit and its material cost is £30 per unit. Conversion costs are planned to be £24,000 per week.

REQUIREMENTS:

(a)   What is the throughput accounting (TA) ratio per day?

(b)   How much could the company spend on equipment to improve the throughput of process B if it wished to recover its costs in:
    (i)   2 years
    (ii)   12 weeks?

(c)   What is the revised TA ratio if this money is spent?

13   TXL PLC

TXL plc manufactures a single product. Standard costs for materials and conversion costs are £40 and £30 per unit respectively. The company uses a backflush accounting system with two trigger points: raw materials purchased and goods transferred to finished goods store. At the beginning of March there was no opening stock of raw materials or WIP and at the end of the month there was no WIP. Other data for the month is:

No. of completed production units	15,000
No. of products sold	14,000
Raw materials purchased	£630,000
Conversion costs incurred	£470,000

REQUIREMENTS:

(a)   Prepare summary journal entries for March assuming that there were no material cost variances and without writing off under or over absorbed conversion costs.

(b)   If the company switched to a total JIT system how would you modify the accounting system? Prepare specimen journal entries using the data above and the new trigger point(s). Write off the under or over absorbed conversion costs.

14   TWO PROJECTS   *45 mins*

A company is considering which of two mutually exclusive projects it should undertake. The finance director thinks that the project with the higher NPV should be chosen whereas the managing director thinks that the one with the higher IRR should be undertaken especially as both projects have the same initial outlay and length of life. The company anticipates a cost of capital of 10% and the net after tax cash flows of the projects are as follows.

		Project X	*Project Y*
		£000	£000
Year	0	-200	-200
	1	35	218
	2	80	10
	3	90	10
	4	75	4
	5	20	3

REQUIREMENTS:

(a) Calculate the NPV and IRR of each project. **8 Marks**

(b) Recommend, with reasons, which project you would undertake (if either). **5 Marks**

(c) Explain the inconsistency in ranking of the two projects in view of the remarks of the directors. **5 Marks**

(d) Identify the cost of capital at which your recommendation in (b) would be reversed. **7 Marks**

Total Marks = 25

15 SENSITIVITY ANALYSIS *45 mins*

A company is considering investing in a new manufacturing facility with the following characteristics.

A Initial investment £350,000, scrap value nil
B Expected life ten years
C Sales volume 20,000 units a year
D Selling price £20 a unit
E Variable direct costs £15 a unit
F Fixed costs excluding depreciation £25,000 a year.

The project shows an internal rate of return (IRR) of 17%. The managing director is concerned about the viability of the investment as the return is close to the company's hurdle rate of 15%. He has requested a sensitivity analysis.

REQUIREMENTS:

(a) Recalculate the internal rate of return (IRR) assuming each of the characteristics A to F above, in isolation, varies adversely by 10%. **10 Marks**

(b) Advise the managing director of the most vulnerable area likely to prevent the project meeting the company's hurdle rate. **5 Marks**

(c) Explain what further work might be undertaken to improve the value of the sensitivity analysis undertaken in (a). **5 Marks**

(d) Reevaluate the situation if another company, already manufacturing a similar product, offered to supply the units at £18 each. This would reduce the investment required to £25,000 and the fixed costs to £10,000. **5 Marks**

Total Marks = 25

16 DINARD *36 mins*

(a) Explain the difference between real rates of return and money rates of return and outline the circumstances in which the use of each would be appropriate when appraising capital projects under inflationary conditions. **6 Marks**

(b) Dinard plc has just developed a new product to be called Rance and is now considering whether to put it into production. The following information is available.

(i) Costs incurred in the development of Rance amount to £480,000.

(ii) Production of Rance will require the purchase of new machinery at a cost of £2,400,000 payable immediately. This machinery is specific to the production of Rance and will be obsolete and valueless when that production ceases. The machinery has a production life of four years and a production capacity of 30,000 units per annum.

(iii) Production costs of Rance (at year 1 prices) are estimated as follows.

	£
Variable materials	8.00
Variable labour	12.00
Variable overheads	12.00

In addition, fixed production costs (at year 1 prices), including straight line depreciation on plant and machinery, will amount to £800,000 per annum.

(iv) The selling price of Rance will be £80.00 per unit (at year 1 prices). Demand is expected to be 25,000 units per annum for the next four years.

(v) The retail price index is expected to increase at 5% per annum for the next four years and the selling price of Rance is expected to increase at the same rate. Annual inflation rates for production costs are expected to be as follows.

	%
Variable materials	4
Variable labour	10
Variable overheads	4
Fixed costs	5

(vi) The company's cost of capital in money terms is expected to be 15%.

REQUIREMENT:

Advise the directors of Dinard plc whether it should produce Rance on the basis of the information above.   **14 marks**

Notes

Unless otherwise specified all costs and revenues should be assumed to rise at the end of each year. Ignore taxation.

Total Marks = 20

---

17   H PLC (Pilot)   *45 mins*

H plc is considering purchasing a new machine to alleviate a bottleneck in its production facilities. At present it uses an old machine which can process 200 units of product P per hour. H plc could replace it with machine AB, which is product-specific and can produce 500 units an hour. Machine AB costs £500,000. If it is installed, two members of staff will have to attend a short training course, which will cost the company a total of £5,000. Removing the old machine and preparing the area for machine AB will cost £20,000.

The company expects demand for P to be 12,000 units per week for another three years. After this, early in the fourth year, the new machine would be scrapped and sold for £50,000. The existing machine will have no scrap value. Each P earns a contribution of £1.40. The company works a 40-hour week for 48 weeks in the year. H plc normally expects a payback within two years, and its after-tax cost of capital is 10 per cent per annum. The company pays corporation tax at 30 per cent and receives writing-down allowances of 25 per cent, reducing balance. Corporation tax is payable quarterly, in the seventh and tenth months of the year in which the profit is earned, and in the first and fourth months of the following year.

REQUIREMENTS:

(a) Prepare detailed calculations that show whether machine AB should be bought, and advise the management of H plc as to whether it should proceed with the purchase.

Make the following assumptions.

(i) The company's financial year begins on the same day that the new machines would start operating, if purchased.

(ii) The company uses discounted cash-flow techniques with annual breaks only.

(iii) For taxation purposes, H plc's management will elect for short-life asset treatment for this asset.   **18 marks**

(b) The investment decision in part (a) is a closely defined manufacturing one. Explain how a marketing or an IT investment decision might differ in terms of approach and assessment.
                                                                                                            7 marks

Total Marks = 25

---

18   DIVISIONAL PERFORMANCE   *45 mins*

(a) Compare and contrast the use of residual income and return on investment in divisional performance measurement, stating the advantages and disadvantages of each.

(b) Explain what is meant by net present value and discuss its use in investment appraisal.

(c) Division Y of Chardonnay Ltd currently has capital employed of £100,000 and earns an annual profit after depreciation of £18,000. The divisional manager is considering an investment of £10,000 in an asset which will have a ten-year life with no residual value and will earn a constant annual profit after depreciation of £1,600. The cost of capital is 15%.

Calculate the following and comment on the results.

(i)	The return on divisional investment, before and after the new investment	**10 Marks**
(ii)	The divisional residual income before and after the new investment	**5 Marks**
(iii)	The net present value of the new investment	**10 Marks**

Total Marks = 25

19 HISTORY OF MANAGEMENT ACCOUNTING

Discuss how management accounting has changed in the last twenty years to cope with the rapid change in the business environment.

20 COST MANAGEMENT (Pilot)   45 mins

'Cost management is … for the automobile industry in the 1990s what quality control was in the 1970s and 80s.'   *Extract from a recent company annual report*

REQUIREMENTS:

(a) Explain the meaning of the statement above.   **4 marks**

(b) Explain the term cost management (sometimes known as cost management information). Discuss why it might be considered important in today's world.   **13 marks**

(c) Discuss how a management accountant might use investment appraisal techniques to analyse customers in order to aid cost management.   **8 marks**

Total Marks = 25

Exam answer bank

1 BACKLOG

> *Tutorial note.* Make sure you understand in this question the reasons why some costs are relevant costs, some costs are not relevant.

(a) *Option 1 (cancel job)*

	£
Cost of cancelling job	47,000

Option 2 (sub-contract)

	£
Fee	35,000
Lost revenue from senior consultant's work (80 × £100)	8,000
	43,000

Option 3 (temporary staff)

	£
Temporary staff pay (£15 × 2,000 × 4 × ¼)	30,000
Temporary staff employment tax (15% × £30,000)	4,500
Recruitment costs (£750 × 4)	3,000
Computers, lower of:	
Purchase cost = (4 × £(2,000 – 1,500)) = £2,000	
Lease cost = 4 × £750 = £3,000	2,000
Office space (and heat and light), lower of	
*Transfer to CD ROM = (£(1,300 – (20 × £20) + (40 × £50))) = £2,900	
Spare office = £1,500 + (£50 × 50) = £4,000	2,900
	42,400

*Assume space made free by removal of filing cabinets requires heating and lighting.

Option 3 is the most cost effective.

(b) (i) *Exclude (a).* The costs associated with the employment of software development staff will be incurred regardless of the option chosen and hence they are not relevant to the decision.

(ii) *Exclude (b).* Since the employment costs will be paid regardless of whether or not the job is cancelled, the information about the margin is irrelevant. It is the total fee income which is affected by the decision.

(iii) *Include (c).* If the consultant has to oversee the contract he will be unable to work for other clients and hence the revenue from such work will be lost. The employment costs will be incurred regardless of the decision taken and so are not relevant.

(iv) *Include (d).* Temporary staff will only be paid if the decision is taken to employ them.

(v) *Include (e).* Employment tax is only payable if the decision is taken to employ the temporary staff.

(vi) *Include (f).* Recruitment costs will only be incurred if the temporary staff are employed.

(vii) *Include (g).* The costs associated with each alternative are relevant since they will only be incurred if temporary staff are employed. The following assumptions are made.

    (1) The organisation will sell the computers after the work has been completed so as to recoup some of the cash outlay and hence the information about their life is not relevant.

    (2) The organisation will choose the cheapest of the two alternatives.

(viii) *Include (h).* The costs associated with both alternatives are relevant and it is assumed that the company would choose the cheapest alternative. Either the cost associated with the transfer to CD ROM or the rental cost of the spare office would only be incurred if temporary staff were employed.

(ix) *Include (i).* If extra space is needed because of taking on the temporary staff then the heating and lighting costs will be incurred.

(x) *Exclude (j).* The purchase price of the furniture is a sunk cost. The second-hand value has not been included as an opportunity cost since it is assumed that the furniture is not being

sold if it is not required. Depreciation is not a cash flow and hence is never relevant in a decision-making situation.

(c) Non-cost factors relevant when considering the three options are as follows.

(i) Cancelling the job may have commercial implications which could affect the long-term profitability of the organisation. Potential customers may be loath to deal with Weeble, fearing that other jobs may be cancelled. Alternatively customers might demand that high cancellation penalty clauses be inserted into future contracts.

(ii) The reliability of any firm subcontracted to do the work should be checked. Weeble will, of course, lose a certain degree of control over the work should it be sub-contracted.

(iii) Weeble would need to ensure that the temporary staff had the necessary skills and expertise to perform the development work.

(iv) The effect on the organisation's software development staff of the option chosen should be considered.

2 CERAMICS COMPANY

a) Contract profitability and feasibility

Both contracts are feasible within the 57,792 hours available to D (see workings 1 and 2), and both contracts are profitable (see working 3 and below).

The fish and chip shop contract offers the higher contribution per hour of scarce resource for the two projects (£14.58 see working 3) and would be accepted first.

The staffing of this contract would be as follows.

	hours
Time required over six months	4,800
Current time available (18 x 40 x 24)	17,280
less time on current production (23,040 ÷ 2)	11,520
	5,760 hours

Thus the fish and chip contract can be accepted in the first six months of the year and could be carried out using the capacity currently available.

The contract from Z plc would require extra staff. The additional costs incurred by doing this would be as follows.

	£	
Contractor to finish showroom	5,000	
Recruiting eight new staff (£500 each)		4,000
Overtime premium –		
28 employees x 24 weeks x 6 hours x (10.42 x 0.5), say		21,000
Donation for pool		35,000
		65,000

The contribution from this contract would be as follows.

	£
Profit after additional fixed costs etc. (working 3)	472,000
less staff costs in excess of standard £10.42 per hour	(65,000)
contribution forgone from sales of standard product (w5)	154,852)
	252,148

Contribution per hour (÷ 38,400)	£6.57

It is assumed that there is no impact on the capacity of tiles produced from D's decision to tile or contract-out the tiling of pool and that the tiles required are not being supplied out of current production.

b) Recommendation

D should accept the offer to supply the fish and chip contract. It generates an additional contribution of £70,000, can be absorbed within existing capacity and offers the prospect of six similar orders over the next two to three years.

Whether or not D accepts the department store order will be a matter of personal choice. The order will generate an additional £252,148 profit in the current year.

To earn this additional profit D must consider the following.

- The size of his business would double in the period.

- He may have to lay off the eight staff recruited depending on whether future orders were secured.

- He would have to find a tenant for his warehouse at the end of this period.

- He may well have to borrow, with consequent borrowing costs, to finance the store's stock for a year.

- There is a risk that the store may default on buying all or some of this stock.

- In addition to having to stop supplying the 25% of new, one-off orders D feels he can do without, he would also lose a further (8,448 − (.25 x 23,040)) 2,688 hours of production to ongoing customers. This would reduce contribution from these customers by (2,688 x £18.33) £49,271 in future periods.

Workings

1. *Labour time per unit*

	Tableware	Tiles
Direct labour cost	£10 per set	£50 per 100 tiles
÷ labour cost per hour	£10.42	£10.42
Labour time per unit	0.96hrs	4.8 hrs

2. *Labour time required/used*

Fish and chip shop:	5 shops x 20,000 tiles	= 100,000 tiles
	÷ 100 per batch	= 1,000 batches of 100 tiles
	x 4.8 hours per batch	= 4,800 hours

Z plc:	40,000 sets x 0.96hrs	= 38,400 hours
Hours required for new projects		43,200 hours

			Hours
Maximum hours available:			
per employee normal time		40 x 48	1,920
overtime		6 x 24	144
			2,064
x maximum number of employees			x 28
			57,792 hours
Hours available for normal production			14,592 hours

Current hours:
  maximum capacity at normal time 20 x 1,920 = 38,400
  currently operating at 60% capacity   x 0.6
                                                          23,040
Shortfall in hours required for normal production   8,448 hours

Both projects are feasible in terms of available labour time. However, the hours available for normal production would be 8,448 hours lower than the current level.

3. *Contract profitability (ignoring overtime etc.)*

			£ per batch
Fish and chip shop:	selling price	(£200 x 0.95)	190
	variable costs		120
	contribution		70
number of sets			1,000
	total contribution		£70,000
Contribution per hour	(÷ 4,800)		£14.58

		£ per set
Z plc:	selling price (£50 x 0.85)	42.50
	variable costs	30.00
	contribution	12.50
	number of sets	x 40,000
	total contribution	£500,000
	less: rent forgone	(10,000)
	additional fixed costs	(3,000)
	moulds	(15,000)
	total contribution	£472,000

Contribution per hour	(÷ 38,400)	£12.29

Both contracts are profitable.

4. Contribution per hour at present

	Mix	Contribution £	Time	Contribution hours	£ per hour
Tableware	20 sets	400	19.2	20.83	
Tiles	6 batches	480	28.8	16.67	
		880	48.0	18.33	

5. Contribution forgone from sales of standard product

Average contribution per hour (W 4)

	£18.33
x number of hours lost (W 2)	x 8,448
	154,852

3   DIFFERENT METHODS

> *Tutorial note.* The marginal costing information demonstrates all three products are making a positive contribution in area 1; this is not apparent from the absorption costing statement.

(a) BUDGET FOR 20X0 - ABSORPTION COSTING

	Area 1				Area 2				Total
	A	B	C	Total	A	B	C	Total	Total
	£'000	£'000	£'000	£'000	£'000	£'000	£'000	£'000	£'000
Sales revenue	3,680	1,920	1,680	7,280	1,200	1,920	2,400	5,520	12,800
Purchase cost	2,944	1,440	1,232	5,616	960	1,440	1,760	4,160	9,776
Gross profit	736	480	448	1,664	240	480	640	1,360	3,024
Overhead costs (i)									
Selling costs	240	120	60	420	36	60	48	144	564
Wareh/distn costs (ii)	460	150	70	680	150	150	100	400	1,080
Advertising	276	120	84	480	90	120	120	330	810
Administration	92	48	42	182	30	48	60	138	320
Profit/(loss)	(332)	42	192	(98)	(66)	102	312	348	250

Notes

(i)   Absorption costing does not distinguish between fixed and variable costs, therefore the total costs are apportioned using the bases given.

(ii)   Calculation of volume sold, to use as basis of apportionment:

	Area 1			Area 2			Total
	A	B	C	A	B	C	
Sales units ('000)	92	40	28	30	40	40	
× volume in m³ per unit	× 2.0	× 1.5	× 1.0	× 2.0	× 1.5	× 1.0	
Volume sold	184	60	28	60	60	40	432

(b) A marginal costing statement does not apportion fixed costs to products, but treats them instead as an overall period cost.

BUDGET FOR 20X0 - MARGINAL COSTING

	A	*B*	*C*	*Total*
	Area 1			
	£'000	£'000	£'000	£'000
Sales revenue	3,680.0	1,920.0	1,680.0	7,280.0
Purchase cost	2,944.0	1,440.0	1,232.0	5,616.0
Gross contribution	736.0	480.0	448.0	1,664.0
Variable overhead costs				
Selling costs (iii)	80.0	40.0	20.0	140.0
Wareh/distrn costs (iv)	184.0	60.0	28.0	272.0
Advertising (v)	92.0	40.0	28.0	160.0
Administration (vi)	18.4	9.6	8.4	36.4
Net contribution	361.6	330.4	363.6	1,055.6
Fixed costs				1,153.6
Loss				(98.0)

Notes			*Total cost apportioned to area 1 (from a)*	*Variable cost proportion*	*Variable cost apportioned*
(iii)	Selling costs:	A	240		80.0
		B	120	$\times \dfrac{188}{376 + 188}$	40.0
		C	60		20.0
(iv)	Warehousing costs:	A	460		184.0
		B	150	$\times \dfrac{432}{432 + 648}$	60.0
		C	70		28.0
(v)	Advertising:	A	276		92.0
		B	120	$\times \dfrac{270}{270 + 540}$	40.0
		C	84		28.0
(vi)	Administration:	A	92		18.4
		B	48	$\times \dfrac{64}{64 + 256}$	9.6
		C	42		8.4

(c)   The result shown in the answer to (b) above indicates that although area 1 makes an overall loss, it does earn a contribution towards the apportioned fixed costs. If it can be assumed that fixed costs would be incurred even if area 1 was discontinued, then management should continue to operate in area 1.

Management should concentrate on improving the contribution earned in area 1, which will involve an investigation of the individual product contributions.

	A	*B*	*C*
Gross contribution to sales %	20.0	25.0	26.7
Net contribution to sales %	9.8	17.2	21.6

Product A's profitability in terms of gross contribution is lower than B and C, and the difference in the net contribution percentages is even more marked.

Management actions which could be taken are as follows.

(i)   Sell proportionately more of products B and C, as long as sales are not inter-related.

(ii)   Raise the price of A, as long as this does not result in a significant drop in sales.

(iii) Seek a cheaper supplier for A, or perhaps negotiate a discount with the current supplier.

(iv)   Exercise tighter control over the variable overhead costs associated with product A.

4   AB LTD

> *Tutorial note.* This question has four ingredients of a good and testing problem on decision making.
>
> (a)   It tests your ability to grasp the nature of a decision problem, and think about the assumptions you may have to make.
>
> (b)   It tests your knowledge of relevant costs.
>
> (c)   It includes a consideration of non-financial factors.
>
> (d)   Part (c) of the question introduces the very practical issue of searching for alternative opportunities. Have all the possible courses of action been identified and considered?

(a)   It is assumed that stock in hand of finished X, valued at £51,900 at full cost, is valued at the full cost of production and not at the full cost of sale. This would be in keeping with SSAP 9, although the wording of the question is ambiguous on this point.

The full cost of production per kg of X is:

	£
Direct materials	17.33
Direct labour	7.36
Production overhead (200% of labour)	14.72
	39.41

The quantity of stock-in-hand is therefore £51,900/£39.41 = 1,317 kg

At a weekly sales volume of 74 kg, this represents 1,317/74 = about 18 weeks of sales

It will take 20 weeks to set up the production facility for Y, and so stock in hand of finished X can be sold before any Y can be produced. This finished stock is therefore irrelevant to the decision under review; it will be sold whatever decision is taken.

The problem therefore centres on the stock in hand of direct materials. Assuming that there is no loss or wastage in manufacture and so 1 kg of direct material is needed to produce 1 kg of X then stock in hand is £44,800/£17.33 = 2,585 kg.

This would be converted into 2,585 kg of X, which would represent sales volume for 2,585/74 = 35 weeks.

If AB Ltd sells its existing stocks of finished X (in 18 weeks) there are two options.

(i)   To produce enough X from raw materials for 2 more weeks, until production of Y can start, and then dispose of all other quantities of direct material - ie 33 weeks' supply.

(ii)   To produce enough X from raw materials to use up the existing stock of raw materials, and so delay the introduction of Y by 33 weeks.

The relevant costs of these two options must be considered.

(i)   *Direct materials.* The relevant cost of existing stocks of raw materials is £(0.30). In other words the 'cost' is a benefit. By using the direct materials to make more X, the company would save £0.30 per kg used.

(ii)   *Direct labour.* It is assumed that if labour is switched to production work from non-production work in the next three months, they must be paid at the full rate of pay, and not at 65% of normal rate. The *incremental* cost of labour would be 35% of the normal rate (35% of £7.36 = £2.58 per kg produced).

Relevant cost of production of X

	£
Direct materials	(0.30)
Direct labour	2.58
Variable overhead (30% of full overhead cost of £14.72)	4.42
Cost per kg of X	6.70

Relevant cost per kg of Y

	£
Direct materials	4.01

Direct labour	2.85
Variable overhead (30% of 200% of £2.85)	1.71
	8.57

(*Note*. Y cannot be made for 20 weeks, and so the company cannot make use of spare labour capacity to produce any units of Y.)

It is cheaper to use up the direct material stocks and make X (£6.70 per kg) than to introduce Y as soon as possible, because there would be a saving of (£8.57 - £6.70) = £1.87 per kg made.

AB Ltd must sell X for at least 20 weeks until Y could be produced anyway, but the introduction of Y could be delayed by a further 33 weeks until all stocks of direct material for X are used up. The saving in total would be about £1.87 per kg x 74 kg per week x 33 weeks = £4,567.

(*Note*. The £3,500 capital cost of Y will be incurred whatever course of action is taken, although with the recommended alternative the spending could be deferred by 33 weeks. Selling and administration overhead has been assumed to be a fixed cost and so is irrelevant to the decision.)

(b)   There are several non-financial factors that must be considered in reaching the decision. Three major items to consider are the workforce, customers' interests and competition in the market from CD.

(i)   *The workforce*. If the recommended course of action is undertaken, the workforce will produce enough units of X in the next 13 weeks to satisfy sales demand over the next year, (with 18 weeks' supply of existing finished goods stocks and a further 35 weeks' supply obtainable from direct materials stocks). When production of Y begins, the direct labour content of production will fall to £2.85 per kg - less than 40% of the current effort per kg produced - but sales demand will not rise. The changeover will therefore mean a big drop in labour requirements in production. Redundancies seem inevitable, and might be costly. By switching to producing Y as soon as possible, the redundancies might be less immediate, and could be justified more easily to employees and their union representatives than a decision to produce enough X in the next 3 months to eliminate further production needs for about 9 months.

(ii)   *Customers' interests*. Product Y is a superior and 'more effective' compound than X. It would be in customers' interests to provide them with this improved product as soon as possible, instead of delaying its introduction until existing stocks of direct materials for X have been used up.

(iii)   *Competition*. CD is expected to start selling Y overseas, and quite possibly in direct competition with AB Ltd. CD has the advantage of having developed Y itself, and appears to use it in the preliminary stage of an alternative technical process. The competitive threat to AB Ltd is two-fold:

(1)   CD might take away some of the replacement demand for Y from AB Ltd so that AB Ltd's sales of X or Y would fall.

(2)   CD might compete with AB Ltd to install its total technical process into customers' factories, and so the competition would be wider than the market for compound Y.

(c)   An alternative course of action would be:

(i)   to produce enough units of X in the next 13 weeks to use up existing stocks of direct materials; but

(ii)   to start sales of Y as soon as possible, and to offer customers the choice between X and Y. Since X is an inferior compound, it would have to be sold at a lower price than Y.

The merits of this course of action are that:

(i)   the work force would be usefully employed for the next 13 weeks and then production of Y would begin at once. Although redundancies would still seem inevitable, the company would be creating as much work as it could for its employees;

(ii)   AB's customers would be made aware of the superiority of Y over X in terms of price, and of AB's commitment to the new compound. AB's marketing approach would be both 'honest' and would also give customers an attractive choice of buying the superior Y or, for a time, an inferior X but at a lower price. This might well enhance AB's marketing success.

The demerits of this course of action are that:

(i)   it is unlikely to be a profit-maximising option, because selling X at a discount price would reduce profitability;

(ii)   customers who get a discount on X might demand similar discounts on Y;

(iii)   some customers might query the technical differences between X and Y, and question why AB Ltd has been selling X at such a high price in the past - this might lead to some customer relations difficulties;

(iv)   AB Ltd must decide when to reduce the price of X, given that Y cannot be made for 20 weeks. The timing of the price reduction might create some difficulties with customers who buy X just before the price is reduced.

(*Tutorial note*. This alternative course of action seems the most obvious one to suggest, but you might think otherwise, and a sensible alternative would be equally acceptable as a solution.)

5   SCIENTO PRODUCTS LIMITED

Workings for solution

A 90% learning curve applies because the cumulative average time per unit is 90% of what it was previously each time that cumulative total output doubles.

$$y = ax^b, \text{ where } b = \text{log of the learning rate (as a proportion)/log of 2}$$

With a 90% learning curve, $b = \log 0.9/\log 2 = -0.152$

(1)   When x   =   528,

the average
labour hours per unit   = $ax^{-0.152}$

                         = $(200)(528)^{-0.152}$

                         =   77.124

(2)   When x   =   (528 + 86) = 614,

the average
labour hours per unit   = $ax^{-0.152}$

                         = $(200)(614)^{-0.152}$

                         =   75.375

Total output	Average time	Total time per unit
Units	Hours	Hours
614	75.375	46,280
528	77.124	40,721
86		5,559

The average time per unit for the 86 units produced in the period should be 5,559/86 = 64.64 hours, say 65 hours per unit.

(*Tutorial note*. It would be tempting perhaps to take the average time as (77.124 + 75.375)/2 = 76.25 hours per unit, but this would be wrong, since this average would include the time taken for the first unit (200 hours) and the 2nd, 3rd, 4th etc units, whereas we should really be wanting a 'standard' time for the units currently being produced. Our average of 65 hours per unit is the average time needed for the 528th to the 614th units produced, which is much less than 76.25 hours per unit.)

Suggested solution

(a)   The standard overhead rate per hour = £150,903/(86 × 65 hrs) = £27

	Standard cost per electronometer
	£
Material cost	250
Labour cost (65 hours × £10 per hour)	650
Overheads (65 hours × £27 per hour)	1,755
Standard cost per unit	2,655

(b)   *Usefulness*

(i)   Where there is a learning effect, it would be inaccurate and unrealistic to budget for labour times and labour costs without taking this effect into account.

(ii)   It is particularly important where the learning effect applies to labour which makes up a large proportion of total costs of production and sales.

(iii) Accurate estimates of labour times are needed for efficient capacity scheduling and competitive pricing, if prices are set on a cost plus basis.

Limitations

(i) An accurate estimate of standard labour times depends on reliable estimates of:

(1) the learning rate; and
(2) budgeted output in the period.

There will almost certainly be some margin of error in the estimated times.

(ii) The learning effect does not apply in all situations. When a product is long-established, the learning effect will have worn off, and standard times per unit will be constant. The learning effect will not be significant in capital intensive work either.

6 PARADOX

Full cost pricing has frequently been condemned in accounting and management text books for its lack of theoretical justification. The major criticism is that it fails to recognise the interaction of the forces of supply and demand. Since demand will be determined by price there will be a profit maximising combination of price and demand. A cost plus based approach to pricing will be most unlikely, except by coincidence, to arrive at the profit maximising price.

In order to be able to establish the profit maximising price, it is necessary for the firm to determine its demand and cost functions. In practical terms, this will never be an easy task and, because of the expense and uncertainties involved, many multi-product firms would not consider the exercise to be justified. Instead they may resign themselves to earning a reasonable profit rather than aiming to achieve the maximum profit.

Despite the criticisms of full cost pricing, it does have a number of points in its favour.

(a) It is simple to apply and its use can be delegated to relatively junior staff. This is particularly important for firms which sell a large range of low cost items where the expense of economic pricing may not be justified.

(b) It may be considered equitable that the price at which a product is sold should be linked to the cost of its production.

(c) Because of (b) full cost pricing is often required when tendering for public sector contracts.

(d) For some firms there may be no readily identifiable market for the product (for example for jobbing engineers). In such cases it will be difficult to determine a suitable starting point for pricing other than full cost.

(e) The criticism that the addition to cost of a standard mark-up is arbitrary and takes no account of market conditions is sometimes countered by firms who argue that their experience of the market over a considerable period of time enables them to know what level of mark-up is likely to be acceptable to customers.

Although full cost pricing is widely used in practice, there is little evidence to suggest that, except in special circumstances, it is used in isolation. Commonly, the full cost price is used as a starting point which may be modified upwards or downwards depending on the judgement of the company's sales staff. Whilst this process may be somewhat subjective the resulting price is often not far from that at which profits would be maximised.

7 TWO COMPANIES

(a) The first thing to do is to calculate the unit costs and selling price of product X. We are told that overheads are apportioned to X and Y in proportion to direct wages. Since hourly rates for labour are the same for both products, the same results will be obtained by apportioning the overheads according to labour hours.

Product X

	£ per kg
Direct materials	18.00
Direct wages	15.00
Variable overhead ((£70,000/7,000 hours) × 1 hr)	10.00
	43.00
Fixed overhead ((£56,000/7,000 hours) × 1 hr)	8.00
	51.00
Profit mark up 60%	30.60
Selling price	81.60

If product X is used by K Ltd in manufacturing product Z, the opportunity cost to the company is the sales revenue forgone, £81.60 per kg.

Relevant cost per kg of Z = £81.60 + £15 adaptation + £2 variable overhead = £98.60

Contribution per kg of Z = £100 – £98.60 = £1.40 per kg

Product Z earns a positive contribution and therefore 2,000 kg of product X should be sold to K Ltd.

We can now consider the transfer price.

£81.60 would be the arm's length price at which a transfer could be made, and this price would make K Ltd aware of the full opportunity cost of using X to make product Z.

However, K Ltd may argue that certain variable costs may be saved with internal transfers, for instance packaging, credit control and transport costs. If these are, say, £3 per kg, then the transfer price could be reduced by £3 + 60% = £4.80, to say £(81.60 – 4.80) = £76.80.

K Ltd is also likely to be unhappy that L Ltd is taking a much larger profit mark up, 60% compared with £1.40/£17 × 100% = 8.2% mark up on K Ltd's costs.

However, it is unlikely that K Ltd can justify a substantial reduction in the transfer price, because of the opportunity costs involved.

The suggested range of transfer prices is therefore £76.80 to £81.60 per kg.

(b) Other points which should be borne in mind when making any recommendations about transfer prices in these circumstances are as follows.

(i) What are the personal goals and aspirations of the individual managers, and the consequent motivational impact of any transfer price?

(ii) Are there any other uses for L Ltd's and K Ltd's facilities?

(iii) What will be the short-term and long-term effect on L Ltd's sales, if 2,000 kg of product X are withdrawn from the external market?

(iv) What is the likely effect of the new product on the morale of K Ltd's staff, who must be aware of the current under-utilisation of capacity?

(v) What are the long-term prospects for product Z?

(vi) Can the constraint on production hours in L Ltd be removed without any significant effect on unit costs?

(vii) The forecast profit margin on Product Z is fairly small. It may therefore be risky to rely on this forecast for a new product.

8 SINGLE PRODUCT

(a) (i)

	A £	B £	C £	D £	E £
Sales revenue	30,000	120,000	900,000	420,000	60,000
Less: discount	-	1,200	45,000	12,600	3,000
	30,000	118,800	855,000	407,400	57,000
Costs					
Sales visits (£2,400/18x12)	267	667	667	266	533
Order taking	1,200	2,080	2,400	1,920	2,400
Delivery (no x km)	2,580	1,612	3,760	4,836	1,612
Product handling (units)	392	1,569	11,765	5,490	784
Rush orders	-	-	600	-	300
	4,439	5,928	19,192	12,512	5,629
Net gain per customer	25,561	112,872	835,808	394,888	51,371
(ii)					
Net gain per product	1.022	1.129	1.114	1.128	1.027

(b)
- The profitability or otherwise of the customer
- How this profitability compares with the profitability of other customers
- Whether the company is operating at full capacity
- Whether there are other potential customers to supply
- The amount of business transacted with the customer
- Whether the customer is new and therefore not so profitable because of unfamiliarity, etc.

9 ABC

(i) ABC attempts to relate all costs with the possible exception of facility sustaining costs, to cost objects such as products, services or customers. It does this by collecting costs/resources and relating them to either primary or support activities via resource cost drivers. Support activity costs are then spread across primary activities. Finally the cost of the primary activities are related to cost units using activity cost drivers.

It is likely that ABC will provide a different picture of product costs than that produced using traditional absorption costing. This is because different assumptions are made because the costs are spread across the activities, etc. As both methods make assumptions about the behaviour and cause of costs, it is impossible to say categorically that ABC results are more accurate than those produced using traditional absorption costing.

Nevertheless there are usually more activities than cost centres and this should make the process more accurate. Furthermore it is easier to justify the selection of cost driver rates with ABC than the absorption rates used with traditional absorption costing. ABC also allows costs to be accumulated per batch or per number of products made, as well as per unit.

These factors all suggest that in most cases ABC will produce a more accurate answer.

(ii) Some commentators argue that only marginal costing provides suitable information for decision making. This is untrue. Marginal costing provides a crude method of differentiating between different types of cost behaviour by splitting costs into their variable and fixed elements. Marginal costing can only be used for short-term decisions and usually even these have longer-term implications which ought to be considered.

ABC spreads costs across products or other cost units according to a number of different bases. The analysis may show that one activity which is carried out for one or two products is expensive. If costs have been apportioned using the traditional method prior to this the cost of this activity is likely to have been spread across all products, thus hiding the fact that the products using this activity may be loss making. If these costs are not completely variable costs but are, for example, batch costs marginal costing would not have related them to the products at all. Therefore ABC can be used to make decisions about pricing, discontinuing products, etc.

10 RS PLC

(a) *Initial costings* £ per cubic metre

Warehouse costs per week:

refrigeration	£160,000/5,000	32.00 per week
other	£560,000/20,000	28.00 per week

Supermarket costs per week:

refrigeration	15 x £24,000/5,000	72.00 per week
other	15 x £44,000/20,000	33.00 per week

Transport costs per trip:

refrigerated	£4,950/90 cubic metres	55.00 per week
standard	£3,750/90 cubic metres	41.67 per week

Direct product profit (DPP)

		Baked beans		Ice cream		White wine	
		£ per item	£ per item	£ per item	£ per item	£ per item	£ per iter
Sales revenue			0.320		1.600		3.4!
Direct cost			0.240		0.950		2.8!
Gross profit			0.080		0.650		0.6(
Warehouse costs							
refrigeration	£32÷24÷18 x 2 weeks			0.148			
other	£28÷28÷80 x 1 week	0.012					
	£28÷24÷18 x 2 weeks			0.130			
	£28÷42÷12 x 4 weeks					0.222	
Supermarket costs							
refrigeration	£72÷24÷18 x 2 weeks			0.333			
other	£33÷28÷80 x 1 week	0.015					
	£33÷24÷18 x 2 weeks			0.153			
	£33÷42÷12 x 2 weeks					0.131	
Transport	£41.67÷28÷80	0.019					
	£55÷24÷18			0.127			
	£41.67÷42÷12					0.083	
			0.046		0.891		0.4:
Direct product profit			0.034		(0.241)		0.1●
% of sales			10.6%		(15.1%)		4.8●

(b)

		Baked beans	Ice cream	White wine
Traditional method profit:	£ per item	0.08	0.65	0.60
	% of sales	25%	40.6%	17.4%

Using DPP the ranking of profits is as follows

1. Baked beans
2. White wine
3. Ice cream – loss-making

Using the traditional method the ranking was:

1. Ice cream
2. Baked beans
3. White wine

The main causes of the differences in profits between the two methods

(i) The traditional method focused on the gross margin only and did not apportion overhead costs

(ii) With DPP ice cream is charged a higher proportion of overhead to reflect the fact that it uses the high cost activities of refrigerated transport and storage. The beans and the wine absorb only the costs of the (lower cost) resources that they use.

Ways in which profitability could be improved

(i) *Refrigerated transport* . At £4,950 per trip this is a high cost activity.

- Care must be taken to ensure all journeys using refrigerated transport carry full loads.

- Suppliers of goods requiring refrigeration should be contacted to determine whether they would be able to deliver direct to the store, thus eliminating this cost for RS.

(ii) *Adjust selling prices.* A full DPP analysis should be carried out and adjustments made to selling prices wherever possible to reflect any costs which are found not to be covered.

(iii) *Adjust the product range.* Where prices cannot be increased sufficiently and where the product does not need to be stocked in order to attract customers, consideration might be given to discontinuing that product and replacing it with a line with a higher DPP.

(c) *Ways in which DPP differs from traditional overhead absorption*

(i) Traditional absorption costing would utilise an overhead rate by department rather than by activity. Products that generate a high level of overhead spending would not be penalised as the spending would be averaged out over all products which use a department's facilities regardless of the level of cost generated by that use.

(ii) Traditional overhead absorption may have attempted to include a share of the head office costs whereas DPP would ignore this because the costs are not caused by the individual product units.

(iii) DPP is likely to provide better information for planning and control. High cost activities will be recognised and controlled more tightly. The stocking of products which utilise only the low cost activities may be encouraged. Selling prices should more accurately reflect the actual costs generated.

11 RESOURCES AND PROFITABILITY

(a) To a certain extent Drury is correct when he states that ABC systems are resource-consumption models.

When ABC systems were first discussed companies were using other systems, usually absorption-based, for the purposes of stock valuation. ABC analysis and supporting calculations would be carried out using actual data to see what the 'actual' costs of products were as a way of improving decision making and operational control.

In this retrospective context ABC starts with the processes of allocating costs to cost pools and determining an appropriate cost driver. For example £250,000 may have been spent on labour and materials for the packing department which processed 25,000 customer orders. This results in a cost of £10 per order to trace back to products, where 'number of orders' is the identified cost driver.

Clearly, in this context, ABC is looking at the cost of using resources within the packing department.

Increasingly, however, companies are using ABC as their main costing system but as part of a broader system of Activity Based Cost Management (ABCM). Here an Activity Based Budget (ABB) will be prepared, using budgeted costs and levels of activity, and compared to the ABC figures over the period for the purposes of exercising control.

It is likely that when the ABB is being prepared it will start with expected sales volumes and from there consider what activities will be required in order to generate the required volume of product. Thus the example above would shift emphasis from 'we spent £250,000 in packing last year' to 'how much resource should we supply the packing department with so as to have them pack the expected volume?' If the ABB is accurate then the ABB figure for packing will be the same as the figures obtained through ABC.

Hopefully companies that are using ABC are using it in the broader context of ABCM so as to be able to obtain a broader range of benefits. Although ABC in isolation does focus on resource consumption, ABCM will consider both the consumption and the supply of resources.

(b)

To: Management of XY Ltd
From: Management Accountant
Date: 20/05/X0

Title: XY's profitability in relation to the number of our customers served

(i) The graph illustrates what is often referred to as the 80:20 rule, that is that 80% of our profits are generated by a core 20% of our customer base.

The same principle (known as Pareto analysis) can be applied in other spheres, for example in Information Systems 20% of systems design effort may provide systems meeting 80% of business requirements, with 80% of the effort being expended to meet the final 20% of requirements.

In the case of profitability in relation to the customer base those 20% of customers who buy our standard product, pay invoices in full and on time and in all other respects conform to our procedures will be the ones who generate 80% of our profits. The other 80% of our customers will generate further costs through their non-compliance with our processes.

(ii) To build upon the principles of the 80:20 rule there are a number of steps which can be taken.

(1) *Conduct a survey of Customer Profitability*. It may be possible to identify specific customers who, as a result of particular requirements they have regarding the product they buy or special ordering or payment procedures they demand, are not being fully charged for the costs which they generate.

If this is the case a new selling price should be established which does cover the additional costs they generate and if they are not willing to pay this higher price it may be necessary to consider discontinuing supply. Although this may reduce turnover it will increase profits because dealings with these customers are likely to be generating losses.

(2) *Review internal processes*. It may be possible to align these more closely to those of our customers, thus increasing our overall profit.

The 20% most profitable customers need to be recognised and steps taken to ensure that they are retained and if possible sales to them are increased. Marketing need to ensure that these customers' needs are continually being identified and met. Investigations should be conducted to see whether it is possible to increase sales to these customers, for example by encouraging them to use XY Ltd as their sole supplier.

12   WAQ PLC

(a)

	Process A	Process B	Process C
Throughput per hour (units)	12	10	15
Throughput per day (units)	96	80	120
Throughput contribution per unit		£120	

$$\text{Throughput accounting ratio} = \frac{£120 \times 80 \text{ units}}{£24,000/6}$$

$$= 2.4$$

(b) (i) Gain if bottleneck at process B is eliminated = 96 – 80 units = 16 units per day.
Gain over two years = 16 units x 6 days x 48 weeks x 2 x £120 = £1,105,920
Therefore £1.1 million could be spent if the cost was to be recovered over two years.

(ii) Gain over 12 weeks = 16 units x 6 days x 12 weeks x £120 = £138,240
Therefore £1.1M could be spent if the cost was to be recovered over 12 weeks.

(c)   TA ratio = $\frac{96\ units \times £120}{4,000}$ = $\frac{11,520}{4,000}$ = 2.88

13   TXL PLC

(a)

	Debit £	Credit £
Raw materials	630,000	
Creditors control		630,000
Being the purchase of direct materials		
Conversion cost control	470,000	
Creditors, etc		470,000
Being the conversion costs incurred		
Finished goods	1,050,000	
Raw materials		600,000
Conversion costs absorbed		450,000
Being the standard cost of completed goods		
Cost of goods sold	980,000	
Finished goods		980,000
Being the standard cost of goods sold		

(b)   There would be no raw material stock therefore there would be only one trigger point which would be either transfer to finished goods or sale of goods. The following entries based on the sale of goods.

	Debit £	Credit £
Conversion cost control	470,000	
Creditors, etc a/c		470,000
Being the conversion costs incurred		
Cost of goods sold	980,000	
Raw materials		560,000
Conversion cost absorbed		420,000
Being the standard cost of goods sold		
Conversion cost control		470,000
Conversion cost absorbed	420,000	
Cost of goods sold	50,000	
Being the under absorption of conversion costs		

14   TWO PROJECTS

(a)   *Project X*

Year	Cash flow £'000	Disc factor 10%	PV £	Disc factor 20%	PV £
0	(200)	1.000	(200,000)	1.000	(200,000)
1	35	0.909	31,815	0.833	29,155
2	80	0.826	66,080	0.694	55,520
3	90	0.751	67,590	0.579	52,110
4	75	0.683	51,225	0.482	36,150
5	20	0.621	12,420	0.402	8,040
			29,130		(19,025)

IRR = 10% + [(29,130/(19,025 + 29,130)) × 10]% = 16.05%

NPV at 10% = £29,130

Project Y

Year	Cash flow	Disc factor	PV	Disc factor	PV
	£'000	10%	£	20%	£
0	(200)	1.000	(200,000)	1.000	(200,000)
1	218	0.909	198,162	0.833	181,594
2	10	0.826	8,260	0.694	6,940
3	10	0.751	7,510	0.579	5,790
4	4	0.683	2,732	0.482	1,928
5	3	0.621	1,863	0.402	1,206
			18,527		(2,542)

IRR = 10% + [(18,527/(18,527 + 2,542)) × 10]% = 18.8%

NPV at 10% = £18,527

(b) Both projects are acceptable because they generate a positive net present value at the company's cost of capital.

The company should undertake project X, because it has the highest forecast net present value. Although the internal rate of return for Y is greater, the NPV is generally accepted to be the better performance measure for maximising company wealth.

(c) The inconsistency in the ranking of the two projects - ie the conflicting results obtained with IRR and NPV - has arisen because of the difference in timing of the cash flows of the two projects. Project X cash flows occur mainly in the middle three years, whereas project Y generates most of its forecast cash flows in the first year, resulting in a higher IRR.

(d)

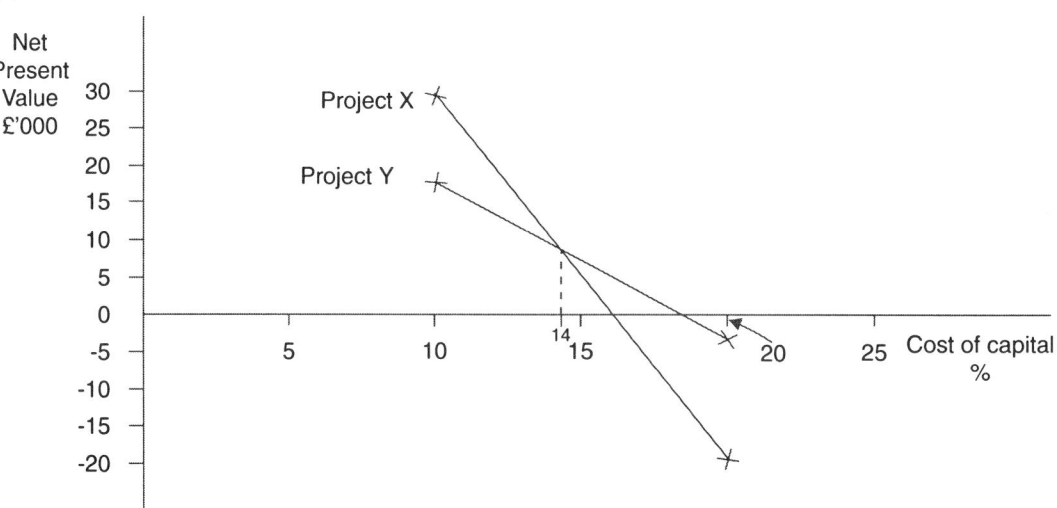

The recommendation in (b) would be reversed if the cost of capital was 14% or more.

15   SENSITIVITY ANALYSIS

(a)   Original forecast

	£'000
Sales revenue 20,000 × £20	400
Less variable costs 20,000 × £15	300
Contribution	100
Less cash fixed costs	25
Annual cash inflow	75

£'000	A	B	C	D	E	F
(i) Investment	385	350	350	350	350	350
(ii) Annual cash flow	75	75	65(W1)	35(W2)	45(W3)	72.5(W4)

(i) ÷ (ii)						
= DCF index	5.133	4.667	5.385	10.000	7.778	4.828
From cumula-tive tables,						
IRR = approx	14.5%	15.5%	13.0%	0.0%	5.0%	16.0%

These returns are found for A and C to F by looking along the ten-year line of cumulative PV factors for the value nearest to the calculated DCF index. For B, the factor is found by looking along the nine-year line.

Workings

1   10% reduction in sales volume = 10% × £100,000 contribution = £10,000 reduction in cash flow

2   10% reduction in selling price = 10% × £400,000 sales = £40,000 reduction in cash flow

3   10% increase in variable cost = 10% × £300,000 cost = £30,000 reduction in cash flow

4   10% increase in fixed cost = 10% × £25,000 cost = £2,500 reduction in cash flow

(b)   The first step is to list the recalculated IRR's in ascending order.

Characteristic altered by 10%	*Resulting IRR*
	%
D: selling price	0.0
E: variable cost	5.0
C: sales volume	13.0
A: initial investment	14.5
B: expected life	15.5
F: fixed cost	16.0

This ranking shows that the selling price is the most vulnerable area likely to prevent the project meeting the company's hurdle rate. A 10% reduction in selling price would cause a dramatic drop in IRR.

(c)   Further work which might be undertaken to improve the value of the sensitivity analysis is as follows.

(i)   We could assess the probabilities of changes in each of the characteristics, and use these probabilities to calculate an expected value for the project.

(ii)   We could use a computer simulation model to assess the likelihood of not meeting the company's hurdle rate.

(iii)   We could assess the effect of other magnitudes of changes, not only 10%.

(iv)   We could assess the effect of combinations of simultaneous changes in characteristics.

(v)   We could assess the effect of favourable changes in characteristics.

(d)   Revised contribution per unit = £(20 – 18) = £2

	£
Total contribution: £2 × 20,000	40,000
Less fixed cost	10,000
Cash inflow	30,000
Investment	£25,000

The investment would be repaid in the first year, therefore this is almost certain to be a successful project.

From a purely financial viewpoint, the company should accept the offer. However, consideration should be given to non-financial factors such as the quality and reliability of supply.

16   DINARD

(a)   The real rate of return is the rate of return which an investment would show in the absence of inflation. For example, if a company invests £100, inflation is 0%, and the investment at the end of the year is worth £110, then the real rate of return is 10%.

In reality however, there is likely to be an element of inflation in the returns due to the change in the purchasing power of money over the period. In the example above, if inflation was running at 5%, then to show a real rate of return of 10%, the investment would need to be worth £115.50 at the end of the year. In this case the money rate of return is 15.5% which is made up of the real return of 10% and inflation at 5%.

The relationship between the nominal ('money') rate of return and the real rate of return can be expressed as follows:

$$(1 + \text{nominal rate}) = (1 + \text{real rate}) \times (1 + \text{inflation rate})$$

The rate to be used in discounting cash flows for capital project appraisal will depend on the way in which the expected cash flows are calculated. If the cash flows are expressed in terms of the actual number of pounds that will be received or paid on the various future dates, then the nominal rate must be used. If however they are expressed in terms of the value of the pound at year 0, then the real rate must be used.

(b) *Workings*

	Year 1	Year 2	Year 3	Year 4
Sales volume	25,000	25,000	25,000	25,000
Unit price (£)	80	84	88	93
Variable material cost (£)	8.00	8.32	8.65	9.00
Variable labour cost (£)	12.00	13.20	14.52	15.97
Variable overhead (£)	12.00	12.48	12.98	13.50

Notes

(i) Development costs of £480,000 are sunk costs and will be excluded from the calculations.

(ii) Depreciation does not involve any movement of cash and will be excluded from the fixed overheads (£600,000 in year 1).

(iii) All figures have been adjusted for the appropriate rate of inflation. The investment will therefore be evaluated using the cost of capital expressed as a nominal rate of 15%.

Evaluation of investment
(All figures £'000)

	Year 0	Year 1	Year 2	Year 3	Year 4
Capital outlay	(2,400)				
Sales		2,000	2,100	2,205	2,315
Direct costs					
Materials		(200)	(208)	(216)	(225)
Labour		(300)	(330)	(363)	(399)
Overhead		(300)	(312)	(324)	(337)
Fixed overheads		(200)	(210)	(221)	(232)
Gross cash flow	(2,400)	1,000	1,040	1,081	1,122
Discount at 15%	1.000	0.870	0.756	0.658	0.572
Present value	(2,400)	870	786	711	642
Cumulative PV	(2,400)	(1,530)	(744)	(33)	608

The investment yields a net present value at the end of four years of £608,000. Production of the Rance should be undertaken.

17   H PLC

(a) *Initial workings*

1. *Capital allowances*

	£	Tax @30% £	Year 1 £	Year 2 £	Year 3 £	Year 4 £	Year 5 £
Machine cost	520,000						
WDA year 1, 25%	130,000	39,000	19,500	19,500			
	390,000						
WDA year 2, 25%	97,500	29,250		14,625	14,625		
	292,500						
WDA year 3, 25%	73,125	21,938			10,969	10,969	
	219,375						
Sale for scrap, year 4	50,000						
Balancing allowance	169,375	50,813				25,406	25,406
Tax payable on contribution (working 2)			(40,320)	(80,640)	(80,640)	(40,320)	
Tax relief on training costs (£5,000 x 30% x 0.5)			750	750			
Total tax recoverable/(payable)			(20,070)	(45,765)	(55,046)	(3,945)	25,406

2. *Incremental contribution*

Demand per week	12000 units
Demand per hour (1,2000/40)	300 units
Current capacity per hour	200 units
Incremental units per hour	100 units
x contribution per unit	x £1.40
x 40 hours x 48 weeks	x 1,920
Contribution per annum	£ 268,800
Tax @ 30%	80,640

Cash flows from profit

Year	Acquisition/ disposal £	Contribution £	Tax £	Total cash flow £	Discount factor	Present value £
0	(525,000)			(525,000)	1.000	(525,000)
1		268,800	(20,070)	248,730	0.909	226,096
2		268,800	(45,765)	223,035	0.826	184,227
3		268,800	(55,046)	213,754	0.751	160,529
4	50,000		(3,945)	46,055	0.683	31,456
5			25,406	25,406	0.621	15,777
Net present value						93,085

Payback period Year	Cash flow £	Cumulative cash flow £
0	(525,000)	(525,000)
1	248,730	(276,270)
2	223,035	(53,235)

Payback period   = 2 years + (£53,235/£213,754)

= 2.25 years, or approximately 2 years 3 months

The net present value (NPV) of the project is positive at £93,085 and on that basis it is recommended that the project should go ahead after consideration is given to the following.

(i) The company expects a payback within two years. In this instance payback is only reached after approximately 2 years and 3 months but this should be over-ridden by the positive NPV.

(ii) The £50,000 recoverable value should be reconsidered in light of the fact that the current machine would be scrapped at a cost of £20,000.

(iii) Consideration should be given to alternatives such as working overtime on the old machine as a way of alleviating the bottleneck, thus eliminating the need for this investment.

(iv) It is noted that the new machine would be operating at 60% capacity. Is there an alternative machine with a capacity matched to our needs of 300 units per hour at a correspondingly lower price? Alternatively, are there actions we could take which would stimulate demand to be closer to our potential 500 unit capacity (assuming there would be no other bottlenecks) which would make this a more attractive investment?

(b) There are a number of reasons why investment decision-making will be different when the investment involves a marketing or IT project rather than tangible manufacturing equipment.

(i) Although most projects will have specific outflows of cash in the investing period, neither IT nor marketing will necessarily give rise to the same sorts of identifiable and easily measurable cash flows as manufacturing equipment. In the case of marketing it may be possible to forecast an expected value of additional revenues as an estimate of future cash inflows, but for IT projects there may not be any easily attributable cash inflow.

(ii) The estimation of the expected future life of an IT investment is made difficult by the rapid rate of technological change in this area, and estimating the time that a marketing campaign's impact may be felt is even more problematic.

(iii) In terms of approach it is often recommended that NPV is used as a way of assessing IT investments. A high discount factor should be used to reflect the fact that any identified cash inflows are subject to a high risk of obsolescence.

(iv) It is possible that a negative net present value will be generated from an IT project. The investment decision will be based on management's assessment of whether the negative present value is a price worth paying for the intangible benefits of the system (increased user-friendliness, faster processing etc.)

(v) For marketing investments the decision-making approach will depend on the value of marketing spend.

- For small marketing campaigns it should be adequate merely to consider whether there are sufficient profits available to absorb the cost of the campaign and still leave an acceptable level of reported profit.

- For larger proposed expenditure an expected value of revenue increases should be calculated and compared to the campaign cost. The length of the campaign and its expected impact will often be so short that no discount factor will need to be applied to calculate the net present value of the campaign.

18 DIVISIONAL PERFORMANCE

(a) The *residual income* (RI) for a division is calculated by deducting from the divisional profit an imputed interest charge, based on the investment in the division.

The *return on investment* (ROI) is the divisional profit expressed as a percentage of the investment in the division.

Both methods use the same basic figure for profit and investment, but residual income produces an absolute measure whereas the return on investment is expressed as a percentage.

Both methods suffer from disadvantages in measuring the profit and the investment in a division which include the following.

(i) Assets must be valued consistently at historic cost or at replacement cost. Neither valuation basis is ideal.

(ii) Divisions might use different bases to value stock and to calculate depreciation.

(iii) Any charges made for the use of head office services or allocations of head office assets to divisions are likely to be arbitrary.

In addition, return on investment suffers from the following disadvantages.

(i)   Rigid adherence to the need to maintain ROI in the short term can discourage managers from investing in new assets, since average divisional ROI tends to fall in the early stages of a new investment. Residual income can overcome this problem by highlighting projects which return more than the cost of capital.

(ii)   It can be difficult to compare the percentage ROI results of divisions if their activities are very different: residual income can overcome this problem through the use of different interest rates for different divisions.

(b)   The net present value of a project is the total of the forecast cash flows, each year's net cash flow being discounted at the cost of capital. The analysis takes account of the time value of money by giving greater weight to earlier cash flows than to later cash flows. If the resulting net present value of a project is positive then it is acceptable in financial terms, perhaps subject to other non-financial criteria.

(c)   (i)   *Return on divisional investment (ROI)*

	Before investment	After investment
Divisional profit	£18,000	£19,600
Divisional investment	£100,000	£110,000
Divisional ROI	18.0%	17.8%

The ROI will fall in the short term if the new investment is undertaken. This is a problem which often arises with ROI, as noted in part (a) of this solution.

(ii)   *Divisional residual income*

	Before investment	After investment
	£	£
Divisional profit	18,000	19,600
Less imputed interest: £100,000 × 15%	15,000	
£110,000 × 15%		16,500
Residual income	3,000	3,100

The residual income will increase if the new investment is undertaken. The use of residual income has highlighted the fact that the new project returns more than the cost of capital (16% compared with 15%).

(iii)

	£
Incremental annual profit after depreciation	1,600
Add back depreciation (£10,000 ÷ 10)	1,000
Annual cash inflow from investment	2,600
× 10 year annuity factor at 15%	× 5.019
Present value of future cash flows	13,049
Less initial investment cost	10,000
Net present value	3,049

In purely financial terms, the project is acceptable because it has a positive net present value.

19   HISTORY OF MANAGEMENT ACCOUNTING

The following changes have taken place in the business environment in the last 20 years

- More international/global competition
- Business strategies to meet customers' requirements are now often considered the most important
- IT has advanced at a considerable pace.

Monitoring of competitors has become much more difficult. In the past competitors were grouped together but now they can be on the opposite sides of the world. Monitoring is very important. Management accounting has changed from encompassing purely internal information to include external information about the environment and competition.

Management accounting must aid the achievement of the chosen strategy. If the strategy is to improve quality, quality must be measured and reported. If it is to meet customer needs as quickly as possible,

management accounting systems need to provide very quick, possibly real-time, feedback. Twenty years ago monthly reporting of variances was the main management accounting tool.

IT helped in meeting the needs outlined in the previous paragraph. It has also allowed specific reports to be produced for specific members of staff and has allowed a variety of different cost objects to be catered for. The trend has been for shorter, more focused documents.

Techniques such as target costing and life cycle costing have been introduced to encourage forward thinking and continuous cost control, and to provide a different perspective on the activities of the business.

20   **COST MANAGEMENT**

(a) In the 1970s, largely as a result of low-cost high-quality imports from Japan, car manufacturers had to take urgent action to improve the quality of their product. Makers with a reputation for low quality such as Triumph, Austin-Morris, Lancia and Alfa Romeo either went out of business or were consolidated into other groups. One manifestation of the importance of quality was the marketing ploy of Austin-Morris re-branding itself, ultimately as Rover, in an attempt to create an image of quality.

In the 1990s those manufacturers who survived had successfully addressed the issue of quality and were selling cars with a level of quality acceptable to and suitable for their customer base. With quality no longer providing a competitive advantage, competition increasingly was based on cost. This combined with the fact that in the late twentieth and early 21st century over-capacity in the car industry was estimated to run at approximately 35%.

Cost management therefore has become vital for survival to:
*   compete successfully on the critical issue of cost
*   reduce prices and stimulate demand in order to reduce over-capacity
*   remove the costs of over-capacity.

(b) Cost management is defined in CIMA's *Official Terminology* as 'The application of management accounting concepts, methods of data collection, analysis and presentation, in order to provide the information required to enable costs to be planned, monitored and controlled'.

Management accounting has long been associated with providing information to assist management to monitor and control costs, most often through budgets and regular variance analysis.

Cost management is an extension of this. It will look much more proactively at costs, considering whether the costs are avoidable or unavoidable and if they are unavoidable, trying to engineer and negotiate those costs down to as low a level as possible.

If, as suggested in part a) above, cost has become one of the critical success factors for ongoing competition then there must be a corresponding increase in the importance of cost management.

One of the indicators that this is so is the increasing use of cost-focused management accounting techniques such as target costing.

Target costing is a process which focuses on ensuring that new products are designed with reference to their expected selling price Having set this expected selling price, target costing ensures that the product can be manufactured for a cost that will allow it to be sold at a profit.

There are many who would say cost management is nothing new. It can be argued that techniques such as target costing are not new techniques. For example target costing uses the same principles as ABC.

Although there is some truth in this argument it does seem that organisations are obtaining considerable benefits from applying established techniques such as target costing in their current context.

Whether cost management is something genuinely new or something which has been around for decades is, to an extent, irrelevant. With low inflation (prevalent in most of the major economies) making it difficult to hide price increases, and with downward pressure on selling prices coming from new technology and competition, cost management is vital for success in today's competitive climate.

(c) Most investment appraisal techniques will consider cash flows over a period of time. To use investment appraisal techniques for specific customers there will therefore have to be an ongoing relationship between the company and the customer.

Examples of industries where this is the case

- Financial services where, for example, the customer will be making mortgage repayments over, say, a 25 year period
- Tobacco (and other addictive substances) where the costs of converting someone into being a smoker can be recouped over the lifetime of that customer
- Photocopier manufacturers who try to encourage customers to lease machines on a long-term (often five year) contract.

In the financial services industry, investment appraisal techniques could be used for cost management by calculating the relatively high initial administrative costs of providing a mortgage advance to a customer. This information could be used to build in margins which would provide a payback within a reasonable period, say five years.

In the tobacco industry investment appraisal could be used as part of managing the costs of advertising campaigns. The design and media buying costs of each campaign should be compared to the present value of future revenues from the number of customers the campaign is expected to convert.

The photocopier sector might use investment appraisal techniques in order to set contract prices. They need to consider both the costs of supplying the product initially and the present value of the future costs of maintenance over the contract life.

Appendix
Mathematical tables

LOGARITHMS

	0	1	2	3	4	5	6	7	8	9	1	2	3	4	5	6	7	8	9
10	0000	0043	0086	0128	0170	0212	0253	0294	0334	0374	4	9	13	17	21	26	30	34	38
											4	8	12	16	20	24	28	32	37
11	0414	0453	0492	0531	0569	0607	0645	0682	0719	0755	4	8	12	15	19	23	27	31	35
											4	7	11	15	19	22	26	30	33
12	0792	0828	0864	0899	0934	0969	1004	1038	1072	1106	3	7	11	14	18	21	25	28	32
											3	7	10	14	17	20	24	27	31
13	1139	1173	1206	1239	1271	1303	1335	1367	1399	1430	3	7	10	13	16	20	23	26	30
											3	7	10	12	16	19	22	25	29
14	1461	1492	1523	1553	1584	1614	1644	1673	1703	1732	3	6	9	12	15	18	21	24	28
											3	6	9	12	15	17	20	23	26
15	1761	1790	1818	1847	1875	1903	1931	1959	1987	2014	3	6	9	11	14	17	20	23	26
											3	5	8	11	14	16	19	22	25
16	2041	2068	2095	2122	2148	2175	2201	2227	2253	2279	3	5	8	11	14	16	19	22	24
											3	5	8	10	13	15	18	21	23
17	2304	2330	2355	2380	2405	2430	2455	2480	2504	2529	3	5	8	10	13	15	18	20	23
											2	5	7	10	12	15	17	19	22
18	2553	2577	2601	2625	2648	2672	2695	2718	2742	2765	2	5	7	9	12	14	16	19	21
											2	5	7	9	11	14	16	18	21
19	2788	2810	2833	2856	2878	2900	2923	2945	2967	2989	2	4	7	9	11	13	16	18	20
											2	4	6	8	11	13	15	17	19
20	3010	3032	3054	3075	3096	3118	3139	3160	3181	3201	2	4	6	8	11	13	15	17	19
21	3222	3243	3263	3284	3304	3324	3345	3365	3385	3404	2	4	6	8	10	12	14	16	18
22	3424	3444	3464	3483	3502	3522	3541	3560	3579	3598	2	4	6	8	10	12	14	15	17
23	3617	3636	3655	3674	3692	3711	3729	3747	3766	3784	2	4	6	7	9	11	13	15	17
24	3802	3820	3838	3856	3874	3892	3909	3927	3945	3962	2	4	5	7	9	11	12	14	16
25	3979	3997	4014	4031	4048	4065	4082	4099	4116	4133	2	3	5	7	9	10	12	14	15
26	4150	4166	4183	4200	4216	4232	4249	4265	4281	4298	2	3	5	7	8	10	11	13	15
27	4314	4330	4346	4362	4378	4393	4409	4425	4440	4456	2	3	5	6	8	9	11	13	14
28	4472	4487	4502	4518	4533	4548	4564	4579	4594	4609	2	3	5	6	8	9	11	12	14
29	4624	4639	4654	4669	4683	4698	4713	4728	4742	4757	1	3	4	6	7	9	10	12	13
30	4771	4786	4800	4814	4829	4843	4857	4871	4886	4900	1	3	4	6	7	9	10	11	13
31	4914	4928	4942	4955	4969	4983	4997	5011	5024	5038	1	3	4	6	7	8	10	11	12
32	5051	5065	5079	5092	5105	5119	5132	5145	5159	5172	1	3	4	5	7	8	9	11	12
33	5185	5198	5211	5224	5237	5250	5263	5276	5289	5302	1	3	4	5	6	8	9	10	12
34	5315	5328	5340	5353	5366	5378	5391	5403	5416	5428	1	3	4	5	6	8	9	10	11
35	5441	5453	5465	5478	5490	5502	5514	5527	5539	5551	1	2	4	5	6	7	9	10	11
36	5563	5575	5587	5599	5611	5623	5635	5647	5658	5670	1	2	4	5	6	7	8	10	11
37	5682	5694	5705	5717	5729	5740	5752	5763	5775	5786	1	2	3	5	6	7	8	9	10
38	5798	5809	5821	5832	5843	5855	5866	5877	5888	5899	1	2	3	5	6	7	8	9	10
39	5911	5922	5933	5944	5955	5966	5977	5988	5999	6010	1	2	3	4	5	7	8	9	10
40	6021	6031	6042	6053	6064	6075	6085	6096	6107	6117	1	2	3	4	5	6	8	9	10
41	0120	0130	6140	6160	6170	6180	6191	6201	6212	6222	1	2	3	4	5	6	7	8	9
42	6232	6243	6253	6263	6274	6284	6294	6304	6314	6325	1	2	3	4	5	6	7	8	9
43	6335	6345	6355	6365	6375	6385	6395	6405	6415	6425	1	2	3	4	5	6	7	8	9
44	6435	6444	6454	6464	6474	6484	6493	6503	6513	6522	1	2	3	4	5	6	7	8	9
45	6532	6542	6551	6561	6571	6580	6590	6599	6609	6618	1	2	3	4	5	6	7	8	9
46	6628	6637	6646	6656	6665	6675	6684	6693	6702	6712	1	2	3	4	5	6	7	7	8
47	6721	6730	6739	6749	6758	6767	6776	6785	6794	6803	1	2	3	4	5	5	6	7	8
48	6812	6821	6830	6839	6848	6857	6866	6875	6884	6893	1	2	3	4	4	5	6	7	8
49	6902	6911	6920	6928	6937	6946	6955	6964	6972	6981	1	2	3	4	4	5	6	7	8

BPP PUBLISHING

LOGARITHMS

	0	1	2	3	4	5	6	7	8	9	1	2	3	4	5	6	7	8	9
50	6990	6998	7007	7016	7024	7033	7042	7050	7059	7067	1	2	3	3	4	5	6	7	8
51	7076	7084	7093	7101	7110	7118	7126	7135	7143	7152	1	2	3	3	4	5	6	7	8
52	7160	7168	7177	7185	7193	7202	7210	7218	7226	7235	1	2	2	3	4	5	6	7	7
53	7243	7251	7259	7267	7275	7284	7292	7300	7308	7316	1	2	2	3	4	5	6	6	7
54	7324	7332	7340	7348	7356	7364	7372	7380	7388	7396	1	2	2	3	4	5	6	6	7
55	7404	7412	7419	7427	7435	7443	7451	7459	7466	7474	1	2	2	3	4	5	5	6	7
56	7482	7490	7497	7505	7513	7520	7528	7536	7543	7551	1	2	2	3	4	5	5	6	7
57	7559	7566	7574	7582	7589	7597	7604	7612	7619	7627	1	2	2	3	4	5	5	6	7
58	7634	7642	7649	7657	7664	7672	7679	7686	7694	7701	1	1	2	3	4	4	5	6	7
59	7709	7716	7723	7731	7738	7745	7752	7760	7767	7774	1	1	2	3	4	4	5	6	7
60	7782	7789	7796	7803	7810	7818	7825	7832	7839	7846	1	1	2	3	4	4	5	6	6
61	7853	7860	7868	7875	7882	7889	7896	7903	7910	7917	1	1	2	3	4	4	5	6	6
62	7924	7931	7938	7945	7952	7959	7966	7973	7980	7987	1	1	2	3	3	4	5	6	6
63	7993	8000	8007	8014	8021	8028	8035	8041	8048	8055	1	1	2	3	3	4	5	5	6
64	8062	8069	8075	8082	8089	8096	8102	8109	8116	8122	1	1	2	3	3	4	5	5	6
65	8129	8136	8142	8149	8156	8162	8169	8176	8182	8189	1	1	2	3	3	4	5	5	6
66	8195	8202	8209	8215	8222	8228	8235	8241	8248	8254	1	1	2	3	3	4	5	5	6
67	8261	8267	8274	8280	8287	8293	8299	8306	8312	8319	1	1	2	3	3	4	5	5	6
68	8325	8331	8338	8344	8351	8357	8363	8370	8376	8382	1	1	2	3	3	4	4	5	6
69	8388	8395	8401	8407	8414	8420	8426	8432	8439	8445	1	1	2	2	3	4	4	5	6
70	8451	8457	8463	8470	8476	8482	8488	8494	8500	8506	1	1	2	2	3	4	4	5	6
71	8513	8519	8525	8531	8537	8543	8549	8555	8561	8567	1	1	2	2	3	4	4	5	5
72	8573	8579	8585	8591	8597	8603	8609	8615	8621	8627	1	1	2	2	3	4	4	5	5
73	8633	8639	8645	8651	8657	8663	8669	8675	8681	8686	1	1	2	2	3	4	4	5	5
74	8692	8698	8704	8710	8716	8722	8727	8733	8739	8745	1	1	2	2	3	4	4	5	5
75	8751	8756	8762	8768	8774	8779	8785	8791	8797	8802	1	1	2	2	3	3	4	5	5
76	8808	8814	8820	8825	8831	8837	8842	8848	8854	8859	1	1	2	2	3	3	4	5	5
77	8865	8871	8876	8882	8887	8893	8899	8904	8910	8915	1	1	2	2	3	3	4	4	5
78	8921	8927	8932	8938	8943	8949	8954	8960	8965	8971	1	1	2	2	3	3	4	4	5
79	8976	8982	8987	8993	8998	9004	9009	9015	9020	9025	1	1	2	2	3	3	4	4	5
80	9031	9036	9042	9047	9053	9058	9063	9069	9074	9079	1	1	2	2	3	3	4	4	5
81	9085	9090	9096	9101	9106	9112	9117	9122	9128	9133	1	1	2	2	3	3	4	4	5
82	9138	9143	9149	9154	9159	9165	9170	9175	9180	9186	1	1	2	2	3	3	4	4	5
83	9191	9196	9201	9206	9212	9217	9222	9227	9232	9238	1	1	2	2	3	3	4	4	5
84	9243	9248	9253	9258	9263	9269	9274	9279	9284	9289	1	1	2	2	3	3	4	4	5
85	9294	9299	9304	9309	9315	9320	9325	9330	9335	9340	1	1	2	2	3	3	4	4	5
86	9345	9350	9355	9360	9365	9370	9375	9380	9385	9390	1	1	2	2	3	3	4	4	5
87	9395	9400	9405	9410	9415	9420	9425	9430	9435	9440	0	1	1	2	2	3	3	4	4
88	9445	9450	9455	9460	9465	9469	9474	9479	9484	9489	0	1	1	2	2	3	3	4	4
89	9494	9499	9504	9509	9513	9518	9523	9528	9533	9538	0	1	1	2	2	3	3	4	4
90	9542	9547	9552	9557	9562	9566	9571	9576	9581	9586	0	1	1	2	2	3	3	4	4
91	9590	9595	9600	9605	9609	9614	9619	9624	9628	9633	0	1	1	2	2	3	3	4	4
92	9638	9643	9647	9652	9657	9661	9666	9671	9675	9680	0	1	1	2	2	3	3	4	4
93	9685	9689	9694	9699	9703	9708	9713	9717	9722	9727	0	1	1	2	2	3	3	4	4
94	9731	9736	9741	9745	9750	9754	9759	9763	9768	9773	0	1	1	2	2	3	3	4	4
95	9777	9782	9786	9791	9795	9800	9805	9809	9814	9818	0	1	1	2	2	3	3	4	4
96	9823	9827	9832	9836	9841	9845	9850	9854	9859	9863	0	1	1	2	2	3	3	4	4
97	9868	9872	9877	9881	9886	9890	9894	9899	9903	9908	0	1	1	2	2	3	3	4	4
98	9912	9917	9921	9926	9930	9934	9939	9943	9948	9952	0	1	1	2	2	3	3	4	4
99	9956	9961	9965	9969	9974	9978	9983	9987	9991	9996	0	1	1	2	2	3	3	3	4

PRESENT VALUE TABLE

Present value of £1 ie $(1+r)^{-n}$ where r = interest rate, n = number of periods until payment or receipt.

Periods					Interest rates (r)					
(n)	1%	2%	3%	4%	5%	6%	7%	8%	9%	10%
1	0.990	0.980	0.971	0.962	0.952	0.943	0.935	0.926	0.917	0.909
2	0.980	0.961	0.943	0.925	0.907	0.890	0.873	0.857	0.842	0.826
3	0.971	0.942	0.915	0.889	0.864	0.840	0.816	0.794	0.772	0.751
4	0.961	0.924	0.888	0.855	0.823	0.792	0.763	0.735	0.708	0.683
5	0.951	0.906	0.863	0.822	0.784	0.747	0.713	0.681	0.650	0.621
6	0.942	0.888	0.837	0.790	0.746	0.705	0.666	0.630	0.596	0.564
7	0.933	0.871	0.813	0.760	0.711	0.665	0.623	0.583	0.547	0.513
8	0.923	0.853	0.789	0.731	0.677	0.627	0.582	0.540	0.502	0.467
9	0.914	0.837	0.766	0.703	0.645	0.592	0.544	0.500	0.460	0.424
10	0.905	0.820	0.744	0.676	0.614	0.558	0.508	0.463	0.422	0.386
11	0.896	0.804	0.722	0.650	0.585	0.527	0.475	0.429	0.388	0.350
12	0.887	0.788	0.701	0.625	0.557	0.497	0.444	0.397	0.356	0.319
13	0.879	0.773	0.681	0.601	0.530	0.469	0.415	0.368	0.326	0.290
14	0.870	0.758	0.661	0.577	0.505	0.442	0.388	0.340	0.299	0.263
15	0.861	0.743	0.642	0.555	0.481	0.417	0.362	0.315	0.275	0.239
16	0.853	0.728	0.623	0.534	0.458	0.394	0.339	0.292	0.252	0.218
17	0.844	0.714	0.605	0.513	0.436	0.371	0.317	0.270	0.231	0.198
18	0.836	0.700	0.587	0.494	0.416	0.350	0.296	0.250	0.212	0.180
19	0.828	0.686	0.570	0.475	0.396	0.331	0.277	0.232	0.194	0.164
20	0.820	0.673	0.554	0.456	0.377	0.312	0.258	0.215	0.178	0.149

Periods					Interest rates (r)					
(n)	11%	12%	13%	14%	15%	16%	17%	18%	19%	20%
1	0.901	0.893	0.885	0.877	0.870	0.862	0.855	0.847	0.840	0.833
2	0.812	0.797	0.783	0.769	0.756	0.743	0.731	0.718	0.706	0.694
3	0.731	0.712	0.693	0.675	0.658	0.641	0.624	0.609	0.593	0.579
4	0.659	0.636	0.613	0.592	0.572	0.552	0.534	0.516	0.499	0.482
5	0.593	0.567	0.543	0.519	0.497	0.476	0.456	0.437	0.419	0.402
6	0.535	0.507	0.480	0.456	0.432	0.410	0.390	0.370	0.352	0.335
7	0.482	0.452	0.425	0.400	0.376	0.354	0.333	0.314	0.296	0.279
8	0.434	0.404	0.376	0.351	0.327	0.305	0.285	0.266	0.249	0.233
9	0.391	0.361	0.333	0.308	0.284	0.263	0.243	0.225	0.209	0.194
10	0.352	0.322	0.295	0.270	0.247	0.227	0.208	0.191	0.176	0.162
11	0.317	0.287	0.261	0.237	0.215	0.195	0.178	0.162	0.148	0.135
12	0.286	0.257	0.231	0.208	0.187	0.168	0.152	0.137	0.124	0.112
13	0.258	0.229	0.204	0.182	0.163	0.145	0.130	0.116	0.104	0.093
14	0.232	0.205	0.181	0.160	0.141	0.125	0.111	0.099	0.088	0.078
15	0.209	0.183	0.160	0.140	0.123	0.108	0.095	0.084	0.074	0.065
16	0.188	0.163	0.141	0.125	0.107	0.093	0.081	0.071	0.062	0.054
17	0.170	0.146	0.125	0.108	0.093	0.080	0.069	0.060	0.052	0.045
18	0.153	0.130	0.111	0.095	0.081	0.069	0.059	0.051	0.044	0.038
19	0.138	0.116	0.098	0.083	0.070	0.060	0.051	0.043	0.037	0.031
20	0.124	0.104	0.087	0.073	0.061	0.051	0.041	0.037	0.031	0.026

CUMULATIVE PRESENT VALUE TABLE

This table shows the present value of £1 per annum, receivable or payable at the end of each year for *n* years $\dfrac{1-(1+r)^{-n}}{r}$.

Periods (n)	Interest rates (r)									
	1%	**2%**	**3%**	**4%**	**5%**	**6%**	**7%**	**8%**	**9%**	**10%**
1	0.990	0.980	0.971	0.962	0.952	0.943	0.935	0.926	0.917	0.909
2	1.970	1.942	1.913	1.886	1.859	1.833	1.808	1.783	1.759	1.736
3	2.941	2.884	2.829	2.775	2.723	2.673	2.624	2.577	2.531	2.487
4	3.902	3.808	3.717	3.630	3.546	3.465	3.387	3.312	3.240	3.170
5	4.853	4.713	4.580	4.452	4.329	4.212	4.100	3.993	3.890	3.791
6	5.795	5.601	5.417	5.242	5.076	4.917	4.767	4.623	4.486	4.355
7	6.728	6.472	6.230	6.002	5.786	5.582	5.389	5.206	5.033	4.868
8	7.652	7.325	7.020	6.733	6.463	6.210	5.971	5.747	5.535	5.335
9	8.566	8.162	7.786	7.435	7.108	6.802	6.515	6.247	5.995	5.759
10	9.471	8.983	8.530	8.111	7.722	7.360	7.024	6.710	6.418	6.145
11	10.368	9.787	9.253	8.760	8.306	7.887	7.499	7.139	6.805	6.495
12	11.255	10.575	9.954	9.385	8.863	8.384	7.943	7.536	7.161	6.814
13	12.134	11.348	10.635	9.986	9.394	8.853	8.358	7.904	7.487	7.103
14	13.004	12.106	11.296	10.563	9.899	9.295	8.745	8.244	7.786	7.367
15	13.865	12.849	11.938	11.118	10.380	9.712	9.108	8.559	8.061	7.606
16	14.718	13.578	12.561	11.652	10.838	10.106	9.447	8.851	8.313	7.824
17	15.562	14.292	13.166	12.166	11.274	10.477	9.763	9.122	8.544	8.022
18	16.398	14.992	13.754	12.659	11.690	10.828	10.059	9.372	8.756	8.201
19	17.226	15.679	14.324	13.134	12.085	11.158	10.336	9.604	8.950	8.365
20	18.046	16.351	14.878	13.590	12.462	11.470	10.594	9.818	9.129	8.514

Periods (n)	Interest rates (r)									
	11%	**12%**	**13%**	**14%**	**15%**	**16%**	**17%**	**18%**	**19%**	**20%**
1	0.901	0.893	0.885	0.877	0.870	0.862	0.855	0.847	0.840	0.833
2	1.713	1.690	1.668	1.647	1.626	1.605	1.585	1.566	1.547	1.528
3	2.444	2.402	2.361	2.322	2.283	2.246	2.210	2.174	2.140	2.106
4	3.102	3.037	2.974	2.914	2.855	2.798	2.743	2.690	2.639	2.589
5	3.696	3.605	3.517	3.433	3.352	3.274	3.199	3.127	3.058	2.991
6	4.231	4.111	3.998	3.889	3.784	3.685	3.589	3.498	3.410	3.326
7	4.712	4.564	4.423	4.288	4.160	4.039	3.922	3.812	3.706	3.605
8	5.146	4.968	4.799	4.639	4.487	4.344	4.207	4.078	3.954	3.837
9	5.537	5.328	5.132	4.946	4.772	4.607	4.451	4.303	4.163	4.031
10	5.889	5.650	5.426	5.216	5.019	4.833	4.659	4.494	4.339	4.192
11	6.207	5.938	5.687	5.453	5.234	5.029	4.836	4.656	4.486	4.327
12	6.492	6.194	5.918	5.660	5.421	5.197	4.988	4.793	4.611	4.439
13	6.750	6.424	6.122	5.842	5.583	5.342	5.118	4.910	4.715	4.533
14	6.982	6.628	6.302	6.002	5.724	5.468	5.229	5.008	4.802	4.611
15	7.191	6.811	6.462	6.142	5.847	5.575	5.324	5.092	4.876	4.675
16	7.379	6.974	6.604	6.265	5.954	5.668	5.405	5.162	4.938	4.730
17	7.549	7.120	6.729	6.373	6.047	5.749	5.475	5.222	4.990	4.775
18	7.702	7.250	6.840	6.467	6.128	5.818	5.534	5.273	5.033	4.812
19	7.839	7.366	6.938	6.550	6.198	5.877	5.584	5.316	5.070	4.843
20	7.963	7.469	7.025	6.623	6.259	5.929	5.628	5.353	5.101	4.870

Time series

Additive model: Series = Trend + Seasonal + Random

Multiplicative model: Series = Trend * Seasonal * Random

Regression analysis

The linear regression equation of Y on X is given by:

$$Y = a + bX \text{ or}$$

$$Y - \overline{Y} = b(X - \overline{X}), \text{ where}$$

$$b = \frac{\text{Covariance (XY)}}{\text{Variance (X)}} = \frac{n\sum XY - (\sum X)(\sum Y)}{n\sum X^2 - (\sum X)^2}$$

and $a = \overline{Y} - b\overline{X}$,

or solve

$$\sum Y = na + b\sum X$$

$$\sum XY = a\sum X + b\sum X^2$$

Exponential $Y = ab^x$

Geometric $Y = aX^b$

Learning curve/Learning index

1   Learning curve $= Yx = ax^b$

2   Learning index $= Yx = ax^b$ where Yx = cumulative average time to produce a cumulative number of units; a = time to produce the first unit; x = cumulative number of units, and b = index of learning.

(The index of learning is the log of the learning curve divided by the log of 2.)

BPP PUBLISHING

List of key terms and index

BPP PUBLISHING

See overleaf for information on other
BPP products and how to order

CIMA Order

To BPP Publishing Ltd, Aldine Place, London W12 8AW
Tel: 020 8740 2211. Fax: 020 8740 1184
www.bpp.com

Mr/Mrs/Ms (Full name)

Daytime delivery address

Postcode

Daytime Tel   E-mail

Date of exam (month/year)

	7/00 Texts	1/01 Kits	1/01 Passcards	9/00 Tapes	7/00 Videos	MCQ cards**
FOUNDATION *						
1 Financial Accounting Fundamentals	£19.95	£10.95	£6.95	£12.95	£25.00	£4.50
2 Management Accounting Fundamentals	£19.95	£10.95	£6.95	£12.95	£25.00	£4.50
3A Economics for Business	£19.95	£10.95	£6.95	£12.95	£25.00	£4.50
3B Business Law	£19.95	£10.95	£6.95	£12.95	£25.00	£4.50
3C Business Mathematics	£19.95	£10.95	£6.95	£12.95	£25.00	£4.50
INTERMEDIATE *						
4 Finance	£19.95	£10.95	£6.95	£12.95	£25.00	£4.50
5 Business Tax (FA 2000)	£19.95	(9/00)£10.95	£6.95	£12.95	£25.00	£3.50
6 Financial Accounting	£19.95	£10.95	£6.95	£12.95	£25.00	
6I Financial Accounting International	£19.95	£10.95				
7 Financial Reporting	£19.95	£10.95	£6.95	£12.95	£25.00	
7I Financial Reporting International	£19.95	£10.95				
8 Management Accounting - Performance Mgmt	£19.95	£10.95	£6.95	£12.95	£25.00	£3.50
9 Management Accounting - Decision Making	£19.95	£10.95	£6.95	£12.95	£25.00	£3.50
10 Systems and Project Management	£19.95	£10.95	£6.95	£12.95	£25.00	
11 Organisational Management	£19.95	£10.95	£6.95	£12.95	£25.00	
FINAL						
12 Management Accounting - Business Strategy	£20.95	£10.95	£6.95	£12.95	£25.00	
13 Management Accounting - Financial Strategy	£20.95	£10.95	£6.95	£12.95	£25.00	
14 Management Accounting - Information Strategy	£20.95	£10.95	£5.95	£12.95	£25.00	
15 Case Study	£15.95 (1)	£15.95 (2)		£15.95 (12/00)	£15.95 (12/00)	

(1) Workbook   (2) Case Question Book

* There will also be a selection of Master CDs available in 2001
** (FREE WITH TEXT)

POSTAGE & PACKING

Study Texts

	First	Each extra
UK	£3.00	£2.00
Europe*	£5.00	£4.00
Rest of world	£20.00	£10.00 £

Kits/Passcards/Success Tapes

	First	Each extra
UK	£2.00	£1.00
Europe***	£2.50	£1.00
Rest of world	£15.00	£8.00 £

Master CDs(2001)/Breakthrough Videos

	First	Each extra
UK	£2.00	£2.00
Europe***	£2.00	£2.00
Rest of world	£20.00	£10.00 £
MCQ cards	£1.00	£1.00 £

Grand Total (Cheques to *BPP Publishing*) I enclose a cheque for (incl. Postage) £

Or charge to Access/Visa/Switch

Card Number

Expiry date   Start Date

Issue Number (Switch Only)

Signature

We aim to deliver to all UK addresses inside 5 working days. Orders to all EU addresses should be delivered within 6 working days. All other orders to overseas addresses should be delivered within 8 working days.

*** Europe includes the Republic of Ireland and the Channel Islands.

REVIEW FORM & FREE PRIZE DRAW

All original review forms from the entire BPP range, completed with genuine comments, will be entered into one of two draws on 31 January 2001 and 31 July 2001. The names on the first four forms picked out on each occasion will be sent a cheque for £50.

Name: _____ **Address:** _____

_____

_____

How have you used this Text?
(Tick one box only)

☐ Self study (book only)

☐ On a course: college (please state)_____

_____

☐ With 'correspondence' package

☐ Other _____

Why did you decide to purchase this Text?
(Tick one box only)

☐ Have used BPP Texts in the past

☐ Recommendation by friend/colleague

☐ Recommendation by a lecturer at college

☐ Saw advertising

☐ Other _____

During the past six months do you recall seeing/receiving any of the following?
(Tick as many boxes as are relevant)

☐ Our advertisement in CIMA *Student*

☐ Our advertisement in *Management Accounting*

☐ Our advertisement in *Pass*

☐ Our brochure with a letter through the post

☐ Our website www.bpp.com

Which (if any) aspects of our advertising do you find useful?
(Tick as many boxes as are relevant)

☐ Prices and publication dates of new editions

☐ Information on product content

☐ Facility to order books off-the-page

☐ None of the above

[For foundation only] How did you/will you take the exam for this paper (Tick one box only)

Written exam ☐   Computer based assessment ☐

Your ratings, comments and suggestions would be appreciated on the following areas

	Very useful	Useful	Not useful
Introductory section (Key study steps, personal study)	☐	☐	☐
Chapter introductions	☐	☐	☐
Key terms	☐	☐	☐
Quality of explanations	☐	☐	☐
Case examples and other examples	☐	☐	☐
Questions and answers in each chapter	☐	☐	☐
Chapter roundups	☐	☐	☐
Quick quizzes	☐	☐	☐
Exam focus points	☐	☐	☐
Question bank	☐	☐	☐
Answer bank	☐	☐	☐
List of key terms and index	☐	☐	☐
Icons	☐	☐	☐
Mind maps	☐	☐	☐

	Excellent	Good	Adequate	Poor
Overall opinion of this Study Text	☐	☐	☐	☐

Do you intend to continue using BPP products?   ☐ Yes   ☐ No

Please note any further comments and suggestions/errors on the reverse of this page. The BPP author of this edition can be e-mailed at: alisonmchugh@bpp.com

Please return this form to: Alison McHugh, CIMA Range Manager, BPP Publishing Ltd, FREEPOST, London, W12 8BR

REVIEW FORM & FREE PRIZE DRAW (continued)

Please note any further comments and suggestions/errors below.

FREE PRIZE DRAW RULES

1   Closing date for 31 January 2001 draw is 31 December 2000. Closing date for 31 July 2001 draw is 30 June 2001.

2   Restricted to entries with UK and Eire addresses only. BPP employees, their families and business associates are excluded.

3   No purchase necessary. Entry forms are available upon request from BPP Publishing. No more than one entry per title, per person. Draw restricted to persons aged 16 and over.

4   Winners will be notified by post and receive their cheques not later than 6 weeks after the relevant draw date. Lists of winners will be published in BPP's *focus* newsletter following the relevant draw.

5   The decision of the promoter in all matters is final and binding. No correspondence will be entered into.